Takings

Takings

PRIVATE PROPERTY AND THE
POWER OF EMINENT DOMAIN

Richard A. Epstein

HARVARD UNIVERSITY PRESS
Cambridge, Massachusetts, and
London, England

Library of Congress Cataloging in Publication Data

Epstein, Richard Allen, 1943–
    Takings: private property and the power of eminent
domain.

    Includes index.
    1. Eminent domain—United States.   2. Right of
property—United States.   I. Title.
KF5599.E67   1985   343.73'0252   85-5884
                        347.30352
ISBN 0-674-86728-9 (lib. bdg : alk. paper) (cloth)
ISBN 0-674-86729-7 (paper)

*To my mother and
the memory of my father*

Preface

From the time I first entered teaching in 1968, my main interest has been in the common law, its historical growth, and its logical structure. I am an outsider to constitutional law. Nevertheless, this book challenges the central assumptions of modern constitutional law governing property rights and economic liberties. This enterprise is a risky one. It is worth explaining why I have undertaken it.

In thinking about the common law—about property, contracts, and torts—the obvious question is, do they exhibit any abiding intellectual unity? I believe they do. Property law governs acquisition of the rights persons have in external things and even in themselves. Torts governs protection of the things reduced to private ownership. Contracts governs transfer of the rights so acquired and protected. This trinity—acquisition, protection, and transfer—exhausts the range of legal relationships between persons. It is just this universality that lends coherence and power to the legal achievements of the classical common law.

Originally I considered these relationships strictly a matter of private law. Public law, and certainly political theory, had no place in my thinking about the organization of the common law system. But working in these areas has convinced me that the separation between public and private law breaks down, in both theory and practice.

Start with property. The general rule of acquisition is a rule of first possession. At first glance it seems that only one person and one thing are at issue, surely a private transaction. But a moment's reflection shows that this perception is false. The rule of first possession is said to give the first possessor rights against the rest of the world. Although the transaction looks private, a statement of its legal consequences reveals the social conception of ownership at its roots.

Similarly in torts, a theory of causation might start with a simple case of A hitting B. No transaction could look more private. But we see this as a two-party relationship only after deciding that B has the right of action for damage to his person. Why B instead of someone else? What is the source of duty that requires all persons to refrain from hitting B or taking his things? Beneath the law of tort, therefore, lies a theory of property rights, again good against the world. Tort law also presupposes a social conception of ownership.

Finally, with contracts, C's promise to D seems like a private transaction between two persons. Yet if one asks why C and D are entitled to enter into a contract with each other, the answer presupposes that the rest of the world has a duty not to interfere with the formation of their agreement. Thus are born the torts of defamation and interference with prospective advantage. C's right to enter into a contract with D cannot be acquired by a contract between themselves. It must be part of the original bundle of property rights good against the rest of the world. Again, collective recognition of the entitlement lies at the root of the common law.

These common law rules of property, tort, and contract represent more than social abstractions. While they are the basis of our legal culture, they are not self-executing. There is the further question of the costs of enforcing them. In examining doctrines of property, contract, and tort it is convenient to begin by assuming that the costs of bargaining and the costs of legal enforcement are zero or close to it. Given this strong premise, we tend to organize legal doctrine around a principle of individual autonomy and to extol the virtues of individualized justice on a case-by-case basis. Both these elements were prominent in the legal thinking of the nineteenth century, which was dominated by two-person lawsuits, with their relatively low transaction costs. Everywhere the emphasis was on individual self-determination and consent, upon social recognition of the perimeter of rights surrounding each individual.

Yet some cracks in the system were evident even in the early common law cases. Transaction costs are not always so low as to give the pursuit of individual justice free rein. Autonomy is indispensable to the social order, but in emergencies physicians must be given some leeway to treat unconscious patients. Similarly, where a person takes or uses the property of another in order to preserve his own life, a forced exchange is allowed against the will of a property owner: the drowning man may tie his boat to a stranger's dock, but he can be made to compensate for the damage he inflicts. And the law of nuisance abounds in many forced exchanges that are allowed because of the difficulties of working out mutually advantageous bargains among large numbers of interested parties. More generally, where the costs of transacting exceed the gains yielded, voluntary transactions will not take place, even if everyone would be better off if they did. What is true of relations among neighboring landowners seems to be true of relations in a larger social order.

The study of the private law then depends upon a detailed analysis of the uses and limits of the autonomy principle. Nonetheless, the very questions one asks about the common law can also be asked about state action that infringes on individual autonomy. The law of eminent domain illustrates par excellence the social limitations upon the private rights of ownership. The matter is evident from the text of the takings clause of the Constitution, which says, "Nor shall private property be taken for public use, without just compensation." No matter where one looks in the catalogue of common law wrongs, one finds the theme of taking another's private property, a theme now captured in the eminent domain clause. The scope of the clause is as broad as the manifold types of takings that human ingenuity can devise. Yet in every case the takings clause recognizes that the claims of individual autonomy must be tempered by the frictions that pervade everyday life. It authorizes at the constitutional level the forced exchanges found in the laws of necessity and nuisance. Autonomy must be protected by supplying an equivalent for what is lost, but it is not protected absolutely.

There is no internal limitation on the scope of the takings clause. As we move from simple to complex cases, we move down the continuum from private to public law. There is no clean break on that continuum between disputes with two parties and those with two hundred million. Private law and public law no longer fall into separate domains. The modern view is that private law gets submerged in the rush to public law. My position is exactly the reverse: to make sense of the system, we must "go public" with private law. The rules of public law make sense only if they can be "reduced" to propositions that are understandable in private-law terms. Statements about groups of individuals must be translated into statements about individuals. Two-party transactions are the atoms from which the complex structure of the state is constructed.

Or so I thought. The case law, however, tells a very different story. The law of the Constitution is the law of the Supreme Court. Even a cursory examination of its decisions shows a radical disjunction between the private and the public faces of the law. In instance after instance the Court has held state controls to be compatible with the rights of private property. The state can now rise above the rights of the persons whom it represents; it is allowed to assert novel rights that it cannot derive from the persons whom it benefits. Private property once may have been conceived as a barrier to government power, but today that barrier is easily overcome, almost for the asking. The Court's decisions rightly speak of partial takings, of causation, of the police power, of assumption of risk, of disproportionate impact. Each of these great themes has its common law parallel, and each is an indispensable element of a comprehensive theory of eminent domain. Yet while the notes are the same, the melody is not, because the Supreme Court has combined these legal conceptions in ways unrecognizable to students of the private law. Under the present law the institution of private property places scant limitation upon the size and direction of the government activities that are characteristic of the modern welfare state.

This book is about the conflict between the original constitutional design and the expansion of state power. At a general level it argues that the system of limited government and private property is not elastic enough to accommodate the massive reforms of the New Deal or those reforms that preceded or followed it. I argue that the eminent domain clause and parallel clauses in the Constitution render constitutionally infirm or suspect many of the heralded reforms and institutions of the twentieth century: zoning, rent control, workers' compensation laws, transfer payments, progressive taxation. Where these governmental innovations do survive in principle, it is often in a truncated and limited form.

My original intention was to write a short article showing the obvious tension between private and public law, between the original constitutional structure and its current design. I thought I could confine my attention to the decided cases. But the demands of theory were so severe that the inquiry expanded. Settling one problem only posed another: if all taxes, regulations, and changes in the common law rules of property, tort, and contract are takings, then how can the government function at all? Under the prodding of countless criticisms and counterexamples, the original article grew by degrees into this book. I do not pretend to have exhausted the subject, but I do hope I have outlined the central features of my own system of analysis.

This book has been in the works for close to eight years, and I have departed from my original design more than once on points both large and small. I began work on the text as a fellow at the Center for Advanced Studies in the Behavioral Sciences during the winter of 1978. In following years I presented portions of the book in lectures or seminars at Brigham Young University, the Claremont Colleges, Northwestern Law School, the University of San Diego Law School, Wabash College, and the Yale Law School. My work has been supported by the Law and Economics Program of the University of Chicago and, in the fall of 1983, by a generous grant from the Institute of Educational Affairs.

I have benefited enormously from the comments of many friends and colleagues. Larry Alexander, Douglas Baird, David Currie, Frank Easterbrook, Lance Liebman, Frank Michelman, Geoffrey Miller, Daniel Rubinfeld, Carol Rose, Geoffrey Stone, and Cass Sunstein all gave extended and spirited criticisms of early drafts, to which I have tried to respond. I have also benefited from conversations with Bruce Ackerman, Randy Barnett, Gary Becker, Mary Becker, Walter Blum, James Capua, Gerhard Casper, Robert Cooter, Robert Ellickson, Donald Elliott, Dennis Hutchinson, John Langbein, Richard Posner, Joseph Sax, and Alan Schwartz. Several generations of students at the University of Chicago have provided diligent research assistance: Alan van Dyke, whose work was supported by a grant from the Illinois Bar Association, spent endless hours on earlier drafts of the book, and Russell Cox did the same for the final rounds of rewriting. I am also grateful for the able assistance of Sharon Epstein, Ross Green, Matthew Hamel, Janet Hedrick, Mark Holmes, Melissa Nachman, and Judy Rose. Susan Carol Weiss retyped the endless revisions of the earlier draft. Peg Anderson of Harvard University Press rounded the final manuscript into shape with an astute eye and a clear touch. Finally, a special note of thanks to Michael Aronson of Harvard University Press, who shepherded the book through to publication.

Contents

PART I

Philosophical Preliminaries

1   A Tale of Two Pies

This book is an extended essay about the proper relationship between the individual and the state. The specific vehicle for examining this question is the eminent domain (or takings) clause of the Constitution, which provides: "nor shall private property be taken for public use, without just compensation." In the course of this study, I subject other constitutional provisions to examination as well. The problem to which the eminent domain clause is directed is that of political obligation and organization. What are the reasons for the formation of the state? What can the state demand of the individual citizens whom it both governs and represents? The simplest way to present the problem is to draw two pies: see the figure on the next page.

The first of these pies represents the situation in a world without effective government control. Each individual is endowed (according to the natural rights tradition) with certain individual rights. Yet the value of these rights in a state of nature is low because some individuals continually try to take that which by right belongs to others. Uncertainty and insecurity make it difficult to plan, which prevents individuals from effectively utilizing their talents and external goods. The question of governance is how the natural rights over labor and property can be preserved in form and enhanced in value by the exercise of political power, defined by Locke "to be a right of making laws with penalties of death, and consequently all less penalties, for regulating and preserving of property, and of employing the force of the community in the execution of such laws, and in defence of the

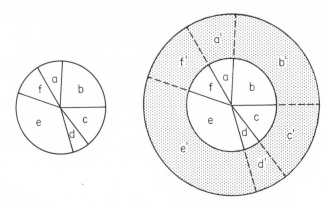

common wealth from foreign injury, and all this only for the public good."[1]

The larger pie indicates the gains that are possible from political organization. The outer ring represents the total social gains, while the dotted lines indicate the proportion of the gain received by each individual member. The implicit normative limit upon the use of political power is that it should preserve the relative entitlements among the members of the group, both in the formation of the social order and in its ongoing operation. All government action must be justified as moving a society from the smaller to the larger pie.

These two pies allow us to isolate all the elements that surround both the origins of the state and the operation of the takings clause. The boundaries of the slices in the first pie are the limits of the private rights to be protected by the state: they identify the private property that cannot be taken without just compensation. To achieve this end a police power must be vested in the sovereign to prevent the private violation of the boundaries so defined. We now have the inherent power of all government, but it must be limited in the ends that will be served and in the means chosen to serve them. The formation and operation of the state, moreover, requires transfering resources from private to public hands. Private property must be converted to public use. Yet the power in the state to take for public use arises because the state will not obtain the resources needed to operate by voluntary donation or exchanges. If these sources of revenue and power were sufficient, then the state would raise no problem that a system of ordinary markets could not solve. But these exchanges do not occur voluntarily and must therefore be coerced. It

1. John Locke, *Of Civil Government,* ch. 1, ¶3 (1690).

becomes critical to regulate the terms on which the exchanges take place. The requirement of just compensation assures that the state will give to each person a fair equivalent to what has been taken; that is, area *a* in the second pie equals area *a* in the first, and so forth. Finally, the public use requirement conditions the use of the coercive power by demanding that any surplus generated by the action, here the outer ring, is divided among individuals in accordance with the size of their original contributions. Each gain from public action therefore is uniquely assigned to some individual, so that none is left to the state, transcending its citizens.

In essence the entire system of governance presupposes that in a state of nature there are two, and only two, failures of the system of private rights. The first is the inability to control private aggression, to which the police power is the proper response. The second is that voluntary transactions cannot generate the centralized power needed to combat private aggression. There are transaction costs, holdout, and free-rider problems that are almost insuperable when the conduct of a large number of individuals must be organized. To this problem, the proper response is the power to force exchanges upon payment for public use. The eminent domain solution shows how a government can be organized to overcome the twin problems of aggression and provision of public goods. As these two problems are the only ones that call forth the state, so they define the limits to which the state may direct its monopoly of force. The theory that justifies the formation of the state also demarcates the proper ends it serves.

The simple structure of the two pies presupposes that we have a very clear sense of what counts as individual rights and of why government is called upon to protect them. Thus the political tradition in which I operate, and to which the takings clause itself is bound, rests upon a theory of "natural rights." That theory does not presuppose the divine origin of personal rights and is consistent, I believe, with both libertarian and utilitarian justifications of individual rights, which, properly understood, tend to converge in most important cases. Whatever their differences, at the core all theories of natural rights reject the idea that private property and personal liberty are solely creations of the state, which itself is only other people given extraordinary powers. Quite the opposite, a natural rights theory asserts that the end of the state is to protect liberty and property, as these conceptions are understood independent of and prior to the formation of the state. No rights are justified in a normative way simply because the state chooses to protect them, as a matter of grace. To use a common example of personal liberty: the state should prohibit murder because it is wrong; murder is not wrong because the state prohibits it. The same applies to property: trespass is not wrong because the state prohibits it; it is wrong because individuals own private property. At each critical juncture, therefore, independent rules, typically the rules of acquisition, protection, and disposition, specify how property is acquired and what rights its acquisition entails. None of these rules rests entitlements on the state, which only enforces the rights and obligations generated by theories of private entitlement.

2 Hobbesian Man, Lockean World

It may seem odd to find in Hobbes, the defender of absolute sovereign power, one of the fathers of our constitutional system.[1] Yet Hobbes gave us the account of human nature on which a system of limited government rests. His account leaves no illusions about the perfectability of mankind but repeatedly emphasizes the selfish behavior of selfish individuals in a world without any external authority to restrain their appetites, passions, and ambitions. In this world the only "right" is that of self-preservation, so each individual either engages in actions of aggression against his neighbor or is forced to act in self-defense. Lives in this condition are "solitary, poore, nasty, brutish and short."[2] The state of nature is a state of war, "of every man, against every man."[3] Without organized government, the uncertainty and instability of the human condition prevent the development of individual personality, the growth of art and culture, and the acquisition of learning and knowledge.

Against this backdrop, Hobbes framed the central question of political theory as follows: how can one escape the omnipresent peril of a state of nature and obtain in exchange a fair measure of personal security and social order? The Hobbesian solution is both simple and dramatic. The price for order is the surrender of liberty and property to an absolute sovereign. Human greed and self-interest make total subjection prefera-

1. The connection is noted in Walter Berns "Judicial Review and the Rights and Laws of Nature," *1982 Sup. Ct. Rev.* 49, 62–63.
2. Thomas Hobbes, *Leviathan,* ch. 13 (1651).
3. Id.

ble to original liberty, so all right-minded persons must surrender to the sovereign. No intermediate position—no theory of limited government—could endure the pressures against it. The control of power must be lodged in a single person, and no individual can set their own private judgments of right and wrong in opposition to the sovereign's commands.[4]

Our Constitution rejects this crude Hobbesian conception. But it contains two elements central to the understanding of the relationship between private property and our own system of governance. The first is Hobbes's account of the perils of unbridled self-interest, which can turn neighbor against neighbor and against the common good. The second is his implicit appeal to an idea of a comprehensive (if hypothetical) contract—"covenant" is Hobbes's preferred term—whereby all persons surrender liberty and property in exchange for security. Hobbes's contract is simple, it has the attractive feature of leaving all parties to the contract better off under sovereign rule than they were without it in the state of nature. The Hobbesian argument thus contains an implicit utilitarian justification for the formation of the state, which in turn can be cast in familiar Pareto form: everyone is made better off and no one is made worse off by the move from the state of nature to civil society.

The difficulties with Hobbes's arrangement, however, are manifest. Although the individuals who are made to participate in this scheme are somewhat better off than they were before, the sovereign is the great winner. Weber's celebrated account of the sovereign, implicit first in Hobbes's and then in Locke's, locates the source of the dilemma. The sovereign "claims the *monopoly of legitimate use of physical force* within a given territory."[5] This legal monopolist will act like any other monopolist whose conduct is left unconstrained. His laws and rules will expropriate most of the benefits of political union by allowing each individual member only the minimum inducement to remain quiescent. If the sum of private happiness in the state of nature is 100, and in organized society 150, the sovereign will be able to keep for himself most, but not quite all, of the 50 units of gain. He may be constrained because he does not know the reservation price of individual citizens and because he fears revolution. But the only limitations upon expropriating the surplus

4. Well emphasized in Berns, supra note 1, at 62.
5. See Max Weber, "Politics as a Vocation," in *From Max Weber: Essays in Sociology* 78 (H. H. Gerth & C. Wright Mills ed., trans., Galaxy ed. 1958). Weber speaks of his definition as applying to a "human community," which does not fit well with Hobbes's absolute conception.

are prudential, not moral. The question of political order is answered; the question of the just distribution of deserts is ignored.

The growth of modern constitutional theory is best understood as a response to Hobbes. His formulation of the question was left unchallenged in the rejection of his solution to it. As we move to Locke, two elements in the Hobbesian account control the subsequent discourse. First, Hobbes's account of individual self-interest and greed underscored the need to answer the question of order. To be sure, Locke claimed that individuals in a state of nature lived in peace and harmony with each other, governed by the powers of "reason."[6] But this happy view of normal times did not conceal from Locke the simple truth that without government, individuals could be in a state of war with each other, where force was necessary to resist force.[7] It was this danger of aggression, and the uncertain worth of the right of self-defense, that drove responsible individuals from a state of nature into a civil society, where the centralized control of power made it possible to resolve private disputes, once and for all, in an impartial forum, free of personal bias and animosity.[8] It was the bad apples in the barrel that forced the move from nature to civil society or, as Locke put it: "And were it not for the corruption and viciousness of degenerate men there would be no need of any other, no necessity that men should separate from this great and natural community, and associate into lesser combinations."[9] Locke thus disputed Hobbes's view that all men are driven by base instincts. Still, the legacy of Hobbes remained in the recognition that sufficient numbers of men can so behave as to make civil society imperative for the protection of the remainder.

The second element that survives from Hobbes was the use of contractarian logic to account for the move from a state of nature into civil society. Locke did not challenge the *form* of Hobbes's argument but only sought the *terms* of the contract whereby individuals assumed sovereign power. The Hobbesian solution was in essence a compact among all individuals to renounce force against each other save in cases of immediate self-defense.[10] In contrast, Locke searched for the *tertium quid,* that is, for

6. John Locke, *Of Civil Government,* ¶19 (1690).

7. Id. at ¶21.

8. Id. at ¶125. "*Secondly,* In the state of nature there wants a known and indifferent judge, with authority to determine all differences according to the established law."

9. Id. at ¶128. The context makes clear that the lesser associations are individual civil societies.

10. Thus Hobbes's second law: "*[t]hat a man be willing, when others are so too, as far-forth, as for Peace, and defence of himself he shall think it necessary, to lay down*

a set of institutional arrangements that would allow individuals to escape the uncertainty and risks of social disorder without having to surrender to the sovereign the full complement of individual rights. Stated in more modern terms, Locke sought to create a sovereign that could maintain good order without extracting monopoly rents from the exclusive legitimate use of force. Accordingly, his theory of civil government had to explain how government could be formed while leaving the surplus gain from union in the hands of the citizens so governed rather than the sovereign. To revert to the simple example above, if the sum of all happiness in the state of nature is 100, and that in civil society is 150, the task of governance is to ensure that all of the surplus, save that necessary to govern the state, is retained by the individual members of the union. While it is easy to design institutional arrangements that grant the sovereign absolute power, this intermediate position is a good deal harder to achieve. How did he do this?

First, Locke was emphatic in his emphasis that individual natural rights, including rights to obtain and hold property, are not derived from the sovereign but are the common gift of mankind.[11] The Lockean labor theory of value is itself problematic because it starts with the assumption, derived from Biblical sources, "that God . . . 'has given the earth to the children of men,' given it to mankind in common." This assertion of the original position created no little difficulty for Locke, because he was then hard pressed to explain how any individual can, without the consent of others, reduce common property to the private ownership in which he so believed. His answer was to rely upon a simple method of individual acquisition; individuals are allowed to keep that which they first reduce to their own possession. Locke's rule has close affinities to the general common law rule (well established in Locke's time), which denies that external things are held in common by mankind and awards ownership of any *unowned* thing to its first possessor.

To Locke, the first-possession rule works for two separate reasons. First, talent and labor are not owned in common but by each person individually: "Though the earth and all inferior creatures be common to

---

this right to all things; and be contented with so much liberty against other men, as he would allow other men against himself." Hobbes, supra note 2, at ch. 14. Berns rightly describes this passage as follows: "Except that no man can give up the right to resist them 'that assault by force or take away his life,' the laws of nature require men mutually to lay down their natural rights by entering into a covenant one with another." Berns, supra note 1, at 59.

11. Locke, supra note 6, at ch. 5.

all men, yet every man has a property in his own person; this nobody has any right to but himself. The labour of his body and the work of his hands we may say are properly his."[12] Second, when labor is mixed with property, 99 percent of their combined value is attributable to labor.[13] It is as though the common contribution can be ignored, on something close to *de minimis* grounds.

Nonetheless, the Lockean view does lead to certain limitations upon property by virtue of its common ownership. Locke noted that labor can acquire external things, "at least where there is enough, and as good left in common for others."[14] Elsewhere he noted that property must be acquired for beneficial use and not for mere waste. Locke did not think that these conditions prevented all acquisition of private property. But he did consider it a breach of duty for one person to take everything from the common pool, to the necessary exclusion of others. Yet in placing this inexact restriction upon individual rights of acquisition, Locke ignored the gains that property rights in things generate for nonowners. When property rights become well defined, nonowners (who still own their labor) receive enhanced opportunities to gain from exchange. What is lost to late-comers from the world of acquisition is provided for in the world of trade and commerce for the betterment of those who did not acquire anything from the original commons.

The proper position would have been reached if Locke had dispensed with the idea of divine justification for private property and had adopted the traditional common law view of the original position. That is, each individual owns his own labor; no one owned the external things of the world until the first possessor acquired them. Without the original common ownership, the first-possession rule is used only to subject unowned things to ownership. It does not have to simultaneously oust common ownership and create individual ownership.[15] But the weaknesses in Locke's account of the acquisition of property are not critical to its political significance. At most they show that Locke did not justify private property as securely as he might have. Nonetheless he believed that his arguments had achieved his central mission of justifying the institution of private property through the labor theory of value. Indeed, if we correct his account of the original position to remove all traces of original ownership in common, then the soundness of his position is true,

12. Id. at ¶27.
13. Id at ¶27; ¶40.
14. Id. at ¶27.
15. See, for more detailed comments, Richard A. Epstein, "Possession as the Root of Title," 13 *Ga. L. Rev.* 1221 (1979).

a fortiori. For questions of political theory, Locke's error does not bind the next generation. And for questions of constitutional theory, the critical point is that he, and those who followed him, thought he did justify private property. It is quite beside the point that there were errors in his argument that a more careful rendition of his position can avoid.

The second point in Locke's argument is that the organization of the state does not require the surrender of all natural rights to the sovereign. The sovereign no longer controls the surplus. Instead Locke proposed a system of governance that leaves the net benefits of government with the people at large. The key elements are his theory of representative government and his prohibition against the taking of private property by the "supreme power" of the state.

Locke wrote of the legislature as follows:

> *First,* It is not nor can possibly be absolutely arbitrary over the lives and fortunes of the people. For it being but the joint power of every member of society given up to that person, or assembly, which is legislator, it can be no more than those persons had in a state of nature before they entered into society, and gave it up to the community. For nobody can transfer to another more power than he has in himself; and nobody has an absolute arbitrary power over himself, or over any other to destroy his own life, or to take away the life or property of another.[16]

This position forms one of the pillars of the subsequent analysis in this book. As a first approximation, the rights of government are derived only from the individuals whom it represents in any given transaction. *Nemo dat quod non habet*—no one can convey what he does not own—is the analogous maxim of the common law. By Locke's view the state itself does not furnish new or independent rights, qua sovereign, against the persons subject to its control. There is no divine right of kings which suspends the ordinary rules of right and obligation between individuals in the state of nature. The sovereign has no absolute power to generate rights. The state can acquire nothing by simple declaration of its will but must justify its claims in terms of the rights of the individuals whom it protects: "a State, by *ipse dixit,* may not transform private property into public property without compensation . . ."[17] The private rights of

16. Locke, supra note 6, at ¶135.
17. Webb's Fabulous Pharmacies, Inc. v. Beckwith, 449 U.S. 155, 164 (1980). The sentence continues, "even for the limited duration of the deposit in court." The case itself concerned a Florida statute which decreed that all interest earned in moneys placed with the state as a stakeholder in an interpleader suit were public property and hence belonged to the state. The pas-

individual relationships are thereby preserved as much as possible even after the formation of civil society, modified only to secure the internal and external peace for which the political power is necessary. The sovereign is demystified; at every stage he is required to justify his own assertion of power. Every transaction between the state and the individual can thus be understood as a transaction between private individuals, some of whom have the mantle of sovereignty while others do not.

A private analogy to the state's position clarifies the basic relation. The law of corporations is often called upon in analyzing transactions between the corporation and its individual shareholders, (for example, a corporate buy-back of shares), just as it is called upon in analyzing transactions between shareholders on their own account. The critical insight is that any transaction between the corporation and its shareholders must be disaggregated into a set of transactions between shareholders. No independent rights and duties attach to the corporate form. Of natural necessity, individuals bear rights and duties. Those in control of the corporation, like those in control of the government, can justify their actions only with reference to the rights they have acquired from the shareholders they represent. Groups, whether shareholders or citizens, are of course important within the theory, but at all points the rights of groups depend upon the rights of their members. No group has a right which is more than the summation of its parts.

Locke's second central contribution concerns the critical role of private property in the overall scheme of governance. Private property represents the sum of the goods that the individual gets to keep outside of the control of the state. By setting certain elements of value outside of public control, Locke provided an implicit answer to Hobbes's challenges by outlining a rule whereby the sovereign rule no longer generates monopoly profits. The state gets what it needs to rule—its costs—and nothing more:

---

sage quoted was used to refute that proposition. The statute also allowed the state to recover fees equal to its costs of running the interpleader action. Note the implicit assumptions of the case. The takings clause applies to partial takings; that simple declaration does not avail against the clause. The state fees cover only its costs and do not reach the benefits that interpleader gives the private parties. In principle all these arguments could apply to every other form of government regulation, from control over public waters to zoning regulation. See Chapters 15 and 17, respectively. But the court's mode of argument suppresses logical deductions from general premises, so *Webb's Fabulous Pharmacies* governs a tiny corner of the law instead of outlining major constitutional structures.

> The supreme power cannot take away from any man any part of his property without his own consent. For the preservation of property being the end of government, and that for which men enter into society, it necessarily supposes and requires that the people should have property, without which they must be supposed to lose that by entering into society, which was the end for which they entered into it, too gross an absurdity for any man to own.[18]

Here, however, an important ambiguity emerges in Locke's account of government, specifically in his treatment of consent. The formation of the state cannot be accounted for by actual consent, as there are too many parties for any such contract ever to occur in fact. In modern terms, a set of pervasive market failures prevents the state's emergence by a set of actual contracts among natural persons. Locke himself was well aware of this obvious difficulty, which he sought to circumvent by appealing to the idea of tacit consent: "that every man that hath any possession or enjoyment of any part of the dominions of any government doth thereby give his tacit consent, and is as far forth obliged to obedience to the laws of that government during such enjoyment as any one under it."[19]

Locke's observation is in powerful tension with the theory of representative government set out above. If tacit consent is not real consent, then the theory of representational government cannot live up to its own billing because the state must exercise power that it does not derive explicitly from the consent of the governed. Yet Locke never explained how any theory of limited government can escape reliance upon express consent. His account of tacit consent is defective because it rests upon a linguistic switch from the idea of consent (which may be implied in fact, as from a course of conduct) to the idea of being bound because one receives in return the benefit of state protection. But the idea of return benefit means that tacit consent speaks less to a theory of contract and more to a theory of restitution for benefits conferred or, as lawyers say, of quasi-contract, which points out both the links to and the distance from ordinary contractual ideals. Nonetheless, Locke's view must place some limit on the sovereign's right to justify any exaction it imposes on the ground of tacit consent. Without that limitation, tacit consent becomes the thin edge of the wedge that grants legislators the lion's

18. Locke, supra note 6, at ¶138.
19. Id. at ¶119.

share of the surplus that Lockean institutions wish to keep out of their hands.[20]

To make the Lockean conception viable, it is necessary to abandon the idea of tacit consent as a source of contractual obligation. In its place belongs an explicit and rigorous theory of forced exchanges between the sovereign and the individual that can account both for the monopoly of force and for the preservation of liberty and property. The bulwark of the individual is no longer the absolute protection of his property. Now it is that whenever any portion of it is taken from him, he must receive from the state (that is, from the persons who take it) some equivalent or greater benefit as part of the same transaction. The categorical command that property shall not be taken without tacit consent must therefore be rewritten to provide that property may be taken upon provision of just compensation. Locke's move from the state of nature to civil society now incorporates two elements of the eminent domain equation. What individuals must give up is their right to use force; what they are given in exchange is a superior form of public protection. There is no contract as such, only a network of forced exchanges designed to leave everyone better off than before.

The public-use language of the takings clause is also consistent with Locke's general conception. Locke defined political power as power that is to be exercised only for the public good,[21] an expression he did not formally analyze in his writing. Nonetheless his articulation of the public good issue was part of his effort to ensure that the surplus created by the formation of a political union did not inure solely (or even largely) to the benefit of the discrete individuals vested with sovereign power. The contrast between takings for private and for public use implicit in the constitutional structure will be shown to have just that internal structure: to guarantee a proportionate distribution of the gain among all of the parties from whom the government takes private property.[22]

The police-power limitation upon the eminent domain clause also fits

---

20. The fear is not just a hypothetical one. All extensions of the power of taxation have rested upon the idea that the simple benefit of living in civilized society is sufficient quid pro quo for whatever tax the government wishes to impose. See the discussion of Carmichael v. Southern Coal & Coke Co., 301 U.S. 495 (1937), in Chapter 19.

21. Locke, supra note 6, ¶3.

22. See Chapter 12.

well into the Lockean scheme. The central purpose of government is to maintain peace and order within the territory, so the prohibition against taking private property could not be read to prevent the government from discharging the very mission that justifies its existence. If private parties have the right of self-defense, then the government must have like powers if it is to compensate private persons for their loss of natural rights. The ends of the power and the means that might be used to achieve it accordingly have to be fitted into the basic scheme, and the elaborate nineteenth-century accounts of the police power show how a coherent conception of sovereign power is critical to the overall structure of government.[23]

The Lockean system was dominant at the time when the Constitution was adopted. His theory of the state was adopted in Blackstone's *Commentaries,* and the protection of property against its enemies was a central and recurrent feature of the political thought of the day.[24] Although protection of private property was a central objective of the original constitutional scheme, the Constitution was not one eminent domain clause writ large. Indeed the most casual inspection reveals that explicit protection of individual rights played only a small part in the original design, of which the eminent domain clause proper was not a part. The basic constitutional plan seeks to limit government by indirection. The first provisions define the separate branches of government; Congress is taken up in Article I, the executive in Article II, and the judiciary in Article III. Thereafter it defines the mode of selection and the power of the officials entrusted with various powers. At every turn the constitutional concern is with preventing the concentration of power in a few hands. The complex provisions on selecting public officials are designed

23. See, e.g., Thomas M. Cooley, *A Treatise on the Constitutional Limitations Which Rest upon the Legislative Power of the States of the American Union* (1868); Ernst Freund, *The Police Power, Public Policy and Constitutional Rights* (1904); Christopher G. Tiedeman, *A Treatise on the Limitations of Police Power in the United States* (1886). One measure of the historical importance of the subject is that the precise question before the court in *Lochner* was not whether liberty of contract was protected under the due process clause—it was assumed that it was—but whether the limitation of contract so imposed was justified under the police power. Holmes's famous remark, "The fourteenth Amendment does not enact Mr. Herbert Spencer's Social Statics," may well have been directed to Tiedeman, who quite clearly thought that it did. See, e.g., Tiedeman at 67, 329.

24. Charles Beard, *Judicial Review and the American Constitution* (1913); Jennifer Nedelsky, "American Constitutionalism and the Paradox of Private Property" (manuscript 1982); Nedelsky, Book Review, 96 *Harv. L. Rev.* 340 (1982).

to control the risks of popular sovereignty by making sure that the electorate cannot speak at once and with one voice. Senators are chosen for six years by the state legislatures.[25] Members of the House of Representatives are more numerous and are selected every two years. The president serves for four years and is indirectly elected by the Electoral College, an institution created just for this purpose.

Similarly, the jurisdictional limitation on federal power is a further effort to limit the power of the sovereign by ruling certain areas out of bounds to collective governance. Federal powers are not plenary but enumerated, and confined largely to matters of Lockean public good: the army, the navy, the post office, and, most open-ended, commerce. The system of checks and balances, or separation of powers, then makes it more difficult to exercise the powers granted to government. This idea was hinted at by Locke, who found reason to separate legislature from executive,[26] but it received its most famous and influential articulation in Montesquieu's *The Spirit of Laws,* which coined the phrase "separation of powers" and justified the doctrine.[27] By setting strength against strength, the system helped to guarantee the liberties of the individual. So long as the temptation to abuse power exists, power must be divided in order to be checked. The Constitution then elaborates specific means to achieve that end. The president may veto legislation, subject to Congressional override; the judiciary is independent, subject to presidential nomination and Senate confirmation. Congress has the power to declare war, but the president is commander-in-chief, subject to the power of the purse in the Congress.

Thus far the Constitution does not speak a word of individual substantive protections. Within the original framework the rich array of procedural and jurisdictional protections was expected to serve some substantive end. And that end was, of course, the protection of private property, of "lives, liberties, and estates" that Locke considered the purpose of government. The procedural safeguards worked to guarantee by indirection that the government would not pass laws that encroached upon the property rights that government was designed to protect. "The Constitution," Hamilton wrote, "is itself, in every rational sense, and to every useful purpose, A BILL OF RIGHTS."[28]

25. See Berns, supra note 1, at 81–82.
26. Locke, supra note 6, at ¶143–144.
27. Montesquieu, *The Spirit of the Laws,* Book 11 (1748).
28. *The Federalist* no. 84, at 515 (A. Hamilton, Mentor ed. 1961); referred to by Berns, supra note 1, at 66. Note too that the Constitution does have provisions that limit the power of state governments, see art. I. cl. 10, which

With this background it is now possible to see how the Bill of Rights fits into the original constitutional scheme. The Bill identifies the ends of government, the rights that the system of limited jurisdiction, indirect voting, and separation of powers is designed to protect. Here the brute fact of federalism complicates the application of political theory, for the Bill of Rights functioned originally as a limitation upon the federal government and not upon the power of the states, a point which was explicitly and correctly held by Justice Marshall for a unanimous court in *Barron v. Baltimore.*[29] Limitations upon the powers of the state have been answered in practice by incorporating specific protections for individuals against the state as well, including the eminent domain clause.[30] Since this book is a mix of political and constitutional theory, I shall follow the present law and treat the clause as though it applies both to state and federal action, which is consistent with the basic Lockean design, as is reflected by the inclusion of some version of the eminent domain clause in all state constitutions.

---

are substantive in nature precisely because the federal constitution cannot define (save for the broad guarantee of a "republican government") the allocation of power within the state.

29. 32 U.S. (7 Pet.) 243 (1833).

30. Chicago, Burlington & Quincy R.R. v. Chicago, 166 U.S. 226 (1896).

The Integrity of Constitutional Text

The Burdens of Constitutional Interpretation

The political speculations of Hobbes and Locke bore fruit in our own Constitution with its elaborate network of procedural and substantive provisions. The formation of government in accordance with a particular outlook, however, marks only the first stage in the long journey to sound governance. The second stage is to preserve the political arrangements that the Constitution ordains. In this country the preservation of institutional arrangements rests in large measure upon the theory of separation of powers in ways that neither Locke nor Montesquieu quite foresaw. The institution of judicial review divides the power to make laws between legislatures and the courts in accordance with a simple but powerful plan. The legislature alone has the power to initiate legislation, but the court, even though it cannot legislate, can strike down that legislation. The eminent domain clause in particular commands courts to strike down legislation where property is taken but just compensation is not paid.

The institution of judicial review in turn places enormous demands upon the rules of constitutional interpretation. Judges, who serve on good behavior, which typically means for life, can nullify the decision of elected officials, even though they themselves are not elected. If the power of the judges is to be legitimated, they cannot be just another political organ of government. As they cannot appeal to popular will, they must be able to provide authoritative interpretations of the constitutional text that are not simply manifestations of their own private beliefs about what legislation should accomplish. In order for judges to make principled interpretations, the language of the Constitution must be clear and precise enough to bind even those who disagree with what it says, for the mission of constitutional government must soon founder if judges can decide cases as freely with the Constitution in place as without it.

The power of language to bind the judicial will is tested in the limit by many of the central provisions of the Constitution. The eminent domain clause contains a set of terms that are not defined in the Constitution itself: private property, taken, just compensation, and public use. The contracts, due process, equal protection, establishment, and freedom of speech clauses all contain the most common and difficult terms in our legal lexicon, linked together in sentences of great power but of equally great abstraction. The community of understanding that lends meaning to the Constitution comes of necessity from outside the text, in the way these words are used in ordinary discourse by persons who are educated in the normal social and cultural discourse of their own time.

Vagueness in Perspective

It is often said that this standard of ordinary language is simply too vague to permit any consensus to be reached on the meaning of difficult texts. Thomas Grey has argued forcefully that in ordinary discourse the term "private property" has no uniform meaning.[1] Grey notes that in some instances property refers to real estate; in other contexts it refers to rights good against the world (as opposed to rights against particular persons under contract). Property can refer to a remedy of restoration or injunction, as opposed to damages. Still other accounts of property are result-oriented. It can be regarded as a means to promote allocative efficiency or to protect individual security and independence. And, most instructively, Grey notes that property can refer to the (different) set of rights protected against government takeover under the eminent domain clause. Having set out the possible permutations of the term, he concludes that it is of not much value at all.

> The conclusion of all this is that discourse about property has fragmented into a set of discontinuous usages. The more fruitful and useful of these usages are those stipulated by theorists; but these de-

1. Thomas Grey, "The Disintegration of Property," in *Property* (J. Roland Pennock and John W. Chapman eds., NOMOS monograph no. 22, 1980).

part drastically from each other and from common speech. Conversely, meanings of "property" in the law that cling to their origin in the thing-ownership conception are integrated least successfully into the general doctrinal framework of law, legal theory, and economics. It seems fair to conclude from a glance at the range of current usages that the specialists who design and manipulate legal structures of the advanced capitalist economies could easily do without using the term "property" at all.[2]

Try it. The great vice in Grey's argument is that it fosters an unwarranted intellectual skepticism, if not despair. He rejects a term that has well-nigh universal usage in the English language because of some inevitable tensions in its meaning, but he suggests nothing of consequence to take its place. Eliminate the sense of the term "private property," and it becomes easy to knock out the constitutional pillars that support the institution, thereby expanding both the size and discretionary power of government.

There is, however, no reason to give up on language at the first sign of difficulty. A far superior approach to the problem is set out by Hanna Pitkin in her excellent study, *The Concept of Representation.*[3] One key passage deserves to be quoted at some length because it well captures the proper attitude toward interpretative efforts.

The confused state of representation theory does not seem to me a cause for despair; nor do I think we should abandon the concept, that it lacks fixed meaning, is vague, or differs in regard from our other concepts. It *is* "used in various senses in different connections," but it does not follow that the word can be (correctly) used in various senses in any given connection; in a particular context, the appropriate use of the word may be obligatory. "A varied usage is not the same thing as a vague usage"; quite the opposite: "the need for making distinctions is exactly contrary to the vagueness which results from failure to distinguish." In that case, however, the problem is not to state the correct meaning of the word, but to specify all the varieties of its application to various contexts.

Thus my first working assumption has been that representation does have an identifiable meaning, applied in different but controlled and discoverable ways in different contexts. It is not vague and shifting, but a single, highly complex concept that has not

2. Id. at 163.
3. Hanna Fenichel Pitkin, *The Concept of Representation* (1967).

changed much in its basic meaning since the seventeenth century. There is, indeed, no great difficulty about formulating a one-sentence definition of this basic meaning, broad enough to cover all its applications in various contexts. Several commentators have done so, and in that sense one correct definition can be singled out: representation means, as the word's etymological origins suggest, a *representation,* a making present again. Except in its earliest use, however, this has always meant more than a literal bringing into presence, as one might bring a book into a room. Rather, representation, taken generally, means the making present *in some sense* of something which is nevertheless *not* present literally or in fact.[4]

The same conceptual approach can be taken with the term "private property," which so troubles Grey. Its basic sense can be well captured, notwithstanding the network of meanings that surrounds its use. Consider Blackstone's definition in his *Commentaries:* "There is nothing which so generally strikes the imagination, and engages the affections of mankind, as the right of property; or that sole and despotic dominion which one man claims and exercises over the external things of the world, in total exclusion of the right of any other individual in the universe."[5] Elsewhere Blackstone elaborated upon the rights implicit in the ownership of property. "The third absolute right, inherent in every Englishman, is that of property, which consists in the free use, enjoyment, and disposal of all his acquisitions, without any control or diminution, save only by the laws of the land."[6]

Blackstone sought to understand what ordinary words mean, and the definition he offered holds open the possibility of future elaboration. Moreover, his definition is powerful enough to overcome all of Grey's counterarguments in exactly the way that Pitkin indicates. Thus it is no rebuke to the Blackstone definition that real estate is one of the most important forms of private property, that property can be set in opposi-

4. Id at 8–9, citing in part Harvey Pinney, "Government—by Whose Consent?" 13 *Social Science* 298 (1938).

5. W. Blackstone, *Commentaries* 2 (1765). (In all citations to Blackstone, page numbers given refer to the original edition.)

6. Id. at 2. Some question could be raised about Blackstone's meaning, given the last clause, on the "law of the land." But its meaning seems to have been only that regular procedures had to be used to deprive an individual of property, that extraordinary ad hoc procedures could not substitute for adjudication. It makes little sense to read the passage as saying that property was held at the grace of the legislature, even in a system that holds open just that possibility because of the growth of parliamentary supremacy, a development not completed in Blackstone's day.

tion to contract, or that violations of property rights sometimes result in an award of damages and sometimes in an injunction. Indeed, each of these areas can be studied in great detail, as is done throughout this book.

Nor do the multiple purposes that private property serves prevent us from understanding the meaning of the phrase. Private property could serve the ends of allocative efficiency and of personal security and independence. It is likely that it serves both and that these turn out to be highly interdependent. Similarly Blackstone's definition does not preclude but in fact facilitates the social and economic forms of ownership of the advanced capitalistic state. The condominium and the corporation are created by the repeated use of the rights of disposition that are inherent in private property—rights that are transferred and not lost by their exercise. The protean ways in which vested entitlements can be recombined show the flexibility, not the unintelligibility, of the institution of private property.

Most important for this inquiry, Blackstone's account of private property explains what the term means in the eminent domain clause. A constitution that wishes to protect private property must take the meaning of private property from ordinary usage. Grey does not offer any definition of the term that can begin to rival Blackstone's in completeness, universality, and relevance. Grey wishes to rid the English language of a central term, but he provides nothing in its place for constitutional discourse. Following this wonderful prescription would lead to the ruination of constitutional protections of freedom of speech, press, religion, and association. These words are difficult to understand as well, especially when social decisions hinge on them.

It follows that in constitutional inquiry the question of vagueness must, as Pitkin notes, be kept in proper perspective. To be sure, there are difficult cases in the application of any concept, especially one as pervasive as private property. Occasionally it is close to impossible to determine whether A or B is the owner of land: A's occupation is prior to B's, but B has fenced first. A's deed may be first in time, but B's deed may be first recorded. Yet the greater danger is an acute attack of lawyers' disease. Marginal cases are the stuff of litigation; they are not the stuff of basic human arrangements. For private property, as for other concepts, the vast range of cases outside litigation is well understood in terms of the basic legal conceptions.[7] The long volumes written on what it

7. For an elaboration of this theme, see Richard A. Epstein, "The Social Consequences of Common Law Rules", 95 *Harv. L. Rev.* 1717 (1982).

means to possess land or chattels reveal the ambiguities in the word "possession," on which legal rights so often turn: may a bailee or a servant claim possession? How is possession lost by abandonment? Does an heir have constructive possession?[8] Yet through all the doctrinal murkiness, the settled legal rules make perfectly clear, more than 99.9 percent of the time, who, if anyone, possesses and owns anything. Vagueness and ambiguity are not fatal to the health of a legal system, any more than infection is necessarily fatal to the human body. In some cases vagueness and ambiguity can kill, but in most cases they do not. Lawyers can speak with precision about legal problems even though language is vague and messy at the edges. To quote an old English maxim, just because there is twilight, it does not mean there is neither day nor night.

A Changing Constitution?

The rise of linguistic skepticism also lends currency to the idea that constitutional provisions necessarily change in meaning over time, so that each new generation must interpret them afresh for itself.[9] But the idea that constitutions must evolve to meet changing circumstances is an invitation to destroy the rule of law. If the next generation can do what it wants, why bother with a constitution to begin with, when it is only an invitation for perpetual revision?

It is plausible to make constitutional interpretation time-bound only by confusing two distinct senses of linguistic meaning. The first sense is directed to the question, what is the semantic meaning of any proposition? The second, once we know what a proposition means, is, does it have significance for, or resonate with, the desires of any individual group? On the first question, some asserted definitions are just wrong; stable and unique meanings are possible in principle and usually obtainable in fact. On the question of social acceptability, enormous differences in temperament and mood can emerge within and between generations. A principled Marxist favors the abolition of private property because it allows the rich to exploit the poor. A democratic socialist retains private ownership of production, subject to redistributive taxes. Finally a Lockean, like myself, believes that the system of private property functions well on matters of both production and distribution and accordingly confines taxation to the common defense and other eco-

8. See, e.g., Oliver Wendell Holmes, Jr., *The Common Law* ch. 6 (1881); F. Pollock and R. Wright, *Possession in the Common Law* (1888).
9. See, e.g., Bruce A. Ackerman, *Rediscovering the Constitution* (1984).

nomic public goods. The differences in outlook among these three positions are profound and important. Yet the term "private property" carries the same meaning for the Marxist who wants to abolish it, for the social democrat who wants to limit it, and the Lockean who wants to protect it. The Marxist has good reason to keep the takings clause out of his constitution.

To all this one may respond that social organizations must be dynamic and change over time. But it does not follow that legal institutions must change in fundamental ways simply because there are changes in taste or in technology.[10] A system of private rights, for example, only specifies how property is acquired and what means are used to transfer it from one person to another. It does not specify what things must be acquired, when they must be transferred, or what price is to be paid. In most instances external changes can be accounted for by changes in the relative prices of the things exchanged in voluntary transactions. There is rarely a reason to redo the institutional structure in which exchanges take place. A similar analysis applies in the public sector. The demands upon government may be greater in time of war, but these are best handled by an increase in overall tax rates, not by resorting to the confiscation proscribed by the eminent domain clause. The glorification of institutional uncertainty only increases the demands upon collective decision making without improving its quality. Stable institutions can eliminate one dimension of uncertainty, with the result that private and public energies alike can be directed toward creating institutions to minimize the costs associated with the irreducible uncertainty present in the world generally.

Constitutional Values

The fact that words have regular, disciplined meanings also calls into question an approach to interpretation that finds the meanings of legal propositions in the ends they are said to serve. A common form of argument runs as follows: because the First Amendment is intended to foster open and robust political debate, a public official or public figure who brings a defamation action must establish actual malice by the critic.[11] To understand the meaning of the First Amendment it becomes necessary to understand the ends or social values that it is intended to serve.

10. I have elaborated on this point in Richard A. Epstein, "The Static Conception of the Common Law," 9 *J. Legal Stud.* 253 (1980).
11. See, e.g., New York Times Co. v. Sullivan, 376 U.S. 254 (1976).

But the great question is, who picks the values? Do the values picked serve social or private ends? Nor does the pursuit of values allow one to escape the task of finding semantic meaning. Propositions about constitutional ends are also expressed in words, often very slippery ones. The premises about value will in turn need as much explication as the constitutional text they are designed to illuminate; only now there are no additional values to turn to. But it is possible to escape the dilemma. With defamation, the question is what does *freedom* of speech mean. The freedom to talk does not mean the right to say anything one pleases, any more than the freedom of motion means the right to go anywhere one pleases. The normal rules of defamation define the limits of freedom of speech in the way the laws of trespass define the limits of the freedom of motion. Defamation cannot obtain absolute protection because freedom does not countenance wrongs by words any more than it countenances wrongs by deeds: defamation is a wrong precisely because it entails false statements about third parties, to their detriment.[12]

The same principles apply to the eminent domain clause. If private property is considered essential for the protection of autonomy or for the maximization of wealth, as Grey suggests, then someone must give an account of the meaning of these terms. If all terms can be understood only with reference to their purposes, then explication quickly turns into an infinite regress. Little can be gained from the search. The task of meaning must be faced sooner or later, and it seems better to face it sooner. There may be a debate over whether the framers introduced the eminent domain clause to protect markets or autonomy or both. But in the end, greater progress will be made by assuming that the clause is designed to do what it says, to ensure that private property is not taken for public use without just compensation.

Historical Sources

The account just given places enormous stress upon the internal intellectual integrity of the constitutional provision and does not take into account the actual historical intention of any of the parties who drafted or signed the document. One simple justification for this emphasis is that looking to those historical particulars is likely to generate more confusion than it eliminates. Constitutional documents are drafted by some persons and ratified by others. Many make speeches about the sig-

12. See Chapter 7 for a discussion of what defamation is covered by the takings clause.

nificance or function of a clause in order to ensure its passage. They may think that the provision has very broad scope, but to deflect the opposition they announce publicly that its scope is narrow. The same process works in reverse with the statements of those opposed to the legislation. Thus every bit of external evidence uses language, which must be explicated and understood before it can be pressed into service to explain particular constitutional provisions. The use of extensive secondary materials therefore adds more raw data, but may well increase confusion rather than understanding. The point is not one of necessary truth but one of basic probabilities. Where the number of parties is large and the divergence of views great, the best evidence of textual intention is the language of the text itself.

In part these difficulties can be avoided if one looks to the writings of standard writers of the time. As I have indicated, that approach is strictly required in order to find out what the ordinary word means. The question is whether that technique can be pressed into the service of some cause apart from textual explication, such as identifying the types of mischief that the provision is designed to forestall. One recurrent problem is that a constitutional provision may have been inspired by certain narrow examples that do not exhaust its meaning. The provisions on freedom of speech may have been motivated by outrage at government censorship of newspapers, but the language of the clause is far broader than the instance that gave rise to it. The language speaks of "freedom of speech," and the modern cases that take this guarantee seriously try to give an account of individual freedom in the area of speech. The establishment clause surely imposes a restriction upon the designation of an official church, but it also reaches the "partial" establishments created by special assistance or support to particular, or perhaps all, religious groups.

The eminent domain clause raises the same issues. The dominant motivation for the clause may have been the taking of food and supplies during time of war for the support of government troops. Yet this case is only an illustration of the abuse to be avoided. The language itself is far broader. There is some question abut how broadly the language should be read. In his careful account of the historical background of the eminent domain clause, Joseph Sax observed that Grotius believed that extensive wage and price controls did not offend the eminent domain principle.[13] But there is no reason to believe that Grotius's view of the

---

13. Joseph L. Sax, "Takings and the Police Power," 74 *Yale L.J.* 36 (1964).

subject matter was shared by others who faced the question, including those who drafted or ratified the amendment. Inferences from a single writer to constitutional text are at best troublesome.

Yet suppose that the common view of the time was that the taking of property excluded all regulation of wages and prices whatsoever. Why should the fact be decisive? The enacted provisions did not state that these laws were to be within the absolute power of the legislature. It said that takings of private property must not be allowed unless compensated and then only for public use. The dominant loyalty is to the text as written and not to the framers' views of the consequences it entailed. When the First (or even the Fourteenth) Amendment was adopted, doubtless there was little sense that the common law rules of defamation were subject to constitutional revision. Yet, in the end, if the demands of freedom of speech render imperative some limitation upon private defamation suits, then the unwritten expectations of the framers (of either the Bill of Rights or the Fourteenth Amendment) must yield to the internal written logic of the text.

The same arguments apply in takings cases. There is, to be sure, a clear sense in which comprehensive wage and price controls differ from both selective controls on designated commodities, on the one hand, and from the takings of individual land for a post office, on the other. Any adequate theory must explain what those differences are and how they tie into the general theory. But it need not be assumed that these differences are categorical in nature, so that the confiscation of land is covered by the clause while price controls, general or special, fall wholly outside of its scope. The best way to answer the question is to take a detailed look at the challenged practices to see how they tie into the eminent domain clause, treated as a self-contained intellectual proposition. Nor is this necessarily a rejection of the framers' intention. They may have meant to endorse both the takings clause and wages and price controls without knowing the implicit tension between them. If they cannot have both, then their explicit choice takes precedence over their silent one. Suppose the framers believed both A and X, when A entails not-X. If A is the constitutional text, then X is not allowed.

Categorical reliance upon historical intention must also confront the problem of novel institutions in changed social circumstances. The full range of legislative programs was wholly unknown to the framers, who were never exposed to the mysteries of rent control, workers' compensation, the pooling of oil and gas interests, or the intricacies of zoning. Any effort to make some specific historical intention the litmus test for the constitutionality of such programs drives us toward one of two unacceptable extremes. Novel institutions are either always valid or always invalid. Yet one reason to use very general language in the takings clause is to avoid just these categorical judgments, thereby allowing principled adjudication to pass upon institutions not yet known to the framers. The quest for some specific historical intention is thus wholly misplaced; the form of words chosen for the Bill of Rights indicates that the framers were as aware of the problem of legislative innovation as we are. They knew that they could not know the future and drafted accordingly.

There is then a certain proper attitude of ambivalence toward historical sources. They are exceedingly helpful in allowing us to understand the standard meanings of ordinary language as embodied in constitutional text, but they are a very imperfect tool for isolating the collective purposes and hidden agendas that secured its passage. They are of even less value in evaluating particular institutional arrangements that must be scrutinized under the clause. Generalizations about the prospective use of these sources are hard to come by, but their limited value seems especially well established with the eminent domain clause. Historical arguments have played virtually no role in the actual interpretation of the clause. To my knowledge the Supreme Court has never resorted to historical sources to explain the relationship between the eminent domain clause and particular government action.

Nor is that surprising. It is very clear that the founders shared Locke's and Blackstone's affection for private property, which is why they inserted the eminent domain provision in the Bill of Rights. Nonetheless, most of the discussion about the Bill of Rights was directed not to its substantive commands but to the procedural question of whether so fundamental a shift in constitutional design should be undertaken before the original Constitution had a chance to prove itself in operation.[14] The justifications given for the constitutional provisions were general in terms, as was fitting under the circumstances. The question of what the specific clauses meant and how they applied in particular situations was left to future generations. Indeed, insisting upon a bill of particulars could have prevented the passage of the Bill of Rights in its entirety.

Judicial Restraint and Judicial Activism

What presumption, if any, should be brought to any statute challenged under the eminent domain clause? Here the choice has been described as one between judicial activism and judicial restraint, depending upon the

14. See 1 *Annals of Congress* 440–468, 730–792 (J. Gales ed. 1789).

way in which the presumption is set. In principle, any initial presumption operates as a default provision, one that governs whenever textual and historical arguments do not give firm (conclusive?) direction one way or the other. The traditional argument in favor of judicial restraint is that choices over economic matters are best left to representatives of the people, chosen by democratic procedures.[15] The argument for judicial activism rests upon the perception that flaws in the democratic process lead to the deprivation of individual rights, including those of property.[16] The emphasis upon democracy tends to lead to a "rational basis" test that offers so little scrutiny that most legislation passes constitutional muster as a matter of course. Emphasis upon the imperfections of government leads to strict scrutiny and more extensive judicial action.

There is no way one side to this debate can vanquish the other in the abstract. The Constitution contains provisions designed to ensure that some decisions will be made by elected representatives. It also contains provisions designed to limit the powers of these same elected representatives. The traditional debate is often cast in the wrong terms by assuming that either activism or restraint gives a decent first approximation of the proper results. The Constitution clearly does not endorse any version of popular democracy, yet by the same token it does not assume that legislatures have no task to perform.

We can never do without presumptions, but it may be possible to limit their scope. Presumptions are needed only in the absence of more specific knowledge, and that is what we should seek to acquire. The rules that govern analysis should emerge from the interpretation of the text, rather than be imposed upon it. As analysis of the underlying text becomes more precise, the presumption recedes in importance, as there is less need to resort to the default provisions. Cases are decided more on the basis of theory and less upon the initial stylized conceptions of judicial role. The debate between judicial activism and restraint takes a far smaller role and is confined in the end, I believe, to cases in which there is genuine doubt about how difficult institutional arrangements square with well-established and well-formed constitutional rules.

In what follows I shall advocate a level of judicial intervention far greater than we now have, and indeed far greater than we ever have

15. See Robert H. Bork, "Neutral Principles and Some First Amendment Problems," 47 *Indiana L.J.* 1 (1971); Robert H. Bork, "The Impossibility of Finding Welfare Rights in the Constitution," 1979 *Wash. U.L.Q.* 695.

16. See, e.g., John Hart Ely, *Democracy and Distrust: A Theory of Judicial Review* (1980), for the most comprehensive statement of this process-oriented position.

had. But at no point does the argument depend upon a belief in judicial activism in cases of economic liberties. Instead I believe that the courses indicated are necessary implications derived from the constitutional text and the underlying theory of the state that it embodies.

The Agenda

How then is this theory constructed? As noted earlier, the Constitution draws on the basic theory developed by Locke. In that theory the government was conceived in the first instance as deriving all of its rights and powers from the individuals whom it governs. Accordingly, all arrangements between the state and private individuals are broken down into a network of relationships among different individuals. That approach is critical for understanding two key aspects of the eminent domain equation: First, what does it mean to take private property? And second, what possible justifications can be invoked when private property is taken? Nonetheless, the state is more than the sum of the parts, because those invested with official power are allowed to initiate forced exchanges for public use. The third and fourth questions therefore confront the regulation of forced exchanges through the public use and just compensation provisions.

In large measure the agenda can be reduced to four questions:

1. Is there a taking of private property?
2. Is there any justification for taking that private property?
3. Is the taking for a public use?
4. Is there any compensation for the property so taken?

These questions are taken up in sequence and in combination in the rest of the book.

PART II

Takings Prima Facie

4   Takings and Torts

The prohibition against the taking of private property has ancient and powerful roots in all legal systems. The early common law, for example, treated the carrying away (asportation) of chattels and the dispossession of land as paradigmatic takings of private property.[1] Cases of this sort typically must satisfy four stringent conditions that make redress straightforward. First, the property in question is equally valuable to the defendant and the plaintiff. Second, the taking by the defendant is both conscious and deliberate. Third, the taking is accomplished by the simple direct act of the defendant, without any assistance or intervention by third parties or natural events. Fourth, the taking is of the entire thing, not its part.

When all four of these conditions are conjoined, it is undeniable that private property has been taken. The limits of the takings principle are explored only when one asks whether the proposition, that the defendant has taken the plaintiff's property, remains true when any or all of these four conditions are relaxed. Suppose, for example, the defendant values the thing more than the plaintiff or the reverse. Or assume that the defendant does not retain the property but destroys it or sells it to a third party. Suppose that the taking or destruction of the thing is not deliberate but is merely negligent, or even wholly accidental. Suppose finally that the thing is not taken in its entirety, but only in part.

The central thesis of this chapter can now be stated: none of these

1. See, on trespass to chattels, James Barr Ames, *Lectures on Legal History* 56–63 (1913). On the history of the real actions, see A. W. B. Simpson, *An Introduction to the History of the Land Law* 24–44 (1961).

variations treated alone nor all of them in combination falsify the proposition that A has taken private property from B. None of them treated alone nor all of them in combination deprive a private plaintiff of a cause of action against a private defendant.[2] Relaxation of any of the conditions may influence the choice between theories of tort and of restitution; it may require resort to principles of strict liability; it may test the outer limits of causal theory; or it may alter the proper measure of damages. But none of these choices undercuts the basic proposition that the plaintiff is still, prima facie, entitled to some recovery against the defendant for property that has been taken.

The analysis of the private situation has necessary consequences for the public law. On Lockean principles the government stands no better than the citizens it represents on whether property has been taken, so a simple test determines, not the ultimate liability of the government, but whether its actions are brought within the purview of the eminent domain clause. *Would the government action be treated as a taking of private property if it had been performed by some private party?* If so, there is a taking of private property, and we must examine further to determine whether compensation must be paid. If not, there is no taking of private property, and the government has necessarily rebutted the eminent domain challenge. The first order of business, therefore, is to examine the permissible permutations of the proposition, "A has taken the private property of B."

Benefit and Loss

Suppose that A takes property from B which he then consumes or sells to C. As it is no longer possible to restore the specific property, a court must select the measure of damages payable by A to B. Where the original taking is deliberate, the plaintiff, by virtue of the "waiver of tort rules," normally has an *election* against a private defendant between tort and restitution.[3] Where the loss to the plaintiff exceeds the gain to the defendant, the plaintiff recovers the full extent of his loss under a tort theory. Where the gain to the defendant exceeds the loss to the plaintiff, the

2. See below for discussion.

3. By waiver of tort, the plaintiff may abandon the tort measure of harm to self and sue on the restitution measure of benefit to the defendant. See generally, Arthur L. Corbin, "Waiver of Tort and Suit in Assumpsit," 19 *Yale L.J.* 221 (1910). For application, see Edwards v. Lee's Administrator, 265 Ky. 418, 96 S.W. 2d 1028 (1936).

plaintiff captures that gain under a restitution theory, sometimes without any allowance for the defendant's own costs.[4] This remedial choice is presented where the benefit and loss are of roughly the same magnitude or where they are widely different. Yet the entire debate is intelligible only because it presupposes that the original wrong for which relief is required is the taking of private property. That simple proposition, and no more, is all that need be established to show that the eminent domain clause is fairly implicated, no matter what the remedial mix. The remedial choice between restitution and tort measures of damages becomes critical in evaluating both the public use and the just compensation components of the eminent domain clause, which I will discuss in their proper sequence.

Destruction of Private Property

The methods thus far developed provide the framework for analyzing cases in which the government has destroyed rather than taken private property. Here, of course, it is possible to make textual arguments that the verb "taken" should be read in opposition to the verbs "damaged or destroyed" on the grounds that a taking requires the government to assert, at least implicitly, a possessory interest in the property. This point could then be reinforced by noting that many state constitutions explicitly use the phrase "property, taken or damaged," in obvious opposition to the federal language.[5]

Such a narrow reading of the eminent domain clause should be rejected. The argument proceeds by increments. The government, like any private party, is under an obligation to compensate if it takes and incorporates the property of another into its own property, as when it renovates a courthouse with timber taken from A's land. The state obligation remains when the government takes things from private parties, uses them to improve public property, and then discards them upon completion of its work. That is what happens if the state takes A's timber for scaffolding, then throws it away when the courthouse renovations are complete. What difference should it make, therefore, if the formal trans-

---

4. See, e.g., Maye v. Tappan, 23 Cal. 306 (1863). The classical formulation denies the defendant an offset for costs where his violation of the plaintiff's rights is deliberate, but not where there is a mistake on the question of title.

5. See William B. Stoebuck, "Nontrespassory Takings" in *Eminent Domain* 5 (1977), for a collection of the numerous state constitutions that contain the word "damaged" or some equivalent thereof.

fer of the thing is simply omitted when the government goes about its business, as happens if the government burns A's timber while renovating the courthouse?

Within the private law, the only difference between taking and destroying is that a claim for conversion becomes a claim for wrongful destruction. The destruction makes it very difficult to calculate the benefit obtained by the defendant, so the tort measure—harm to the plaintiff—becomes by default the sole basis for recovery. But the resemblances between the conversion of property and its destruction are powerful. Conversion involves the use of force to remove a thing from the possession of its owner. Destruction involves the use of force to work physical changes in things that remain in the possession of the owner. Taking and destroying are close substitutes for each other and each forms an essential part of the law of tort. Just as tort liability goes beyond conversion, so too does prima facie liability of the state under the eminent domain clause. Surely no one would argue that the state does not take private property when it blows up a building, or that thereafter it can condemn the land without paying for the building it has destroyed. If the direct route of government takeover is blocked by the compensation requirement, the eminent domain clause can only limit government excesses by blocking the indirect route of property destruction. The eminent domain clause must apply whether the government takes or destroys private property.

The power of this argument was recognized in the early Supreme Court case *Pumpelly v. Green Bay Co.*, which is decisive in principle because of the normative force of its arguments.[6] There the plaintiff sought compensation from the defendant, a private company acting under government authority, for damages occasioned when the plaintiff's land was flooded by waters backed up by a dam the defendant had constructed. The defendant argued that compensation was not required because the plaintiff had remained in possession of his land even after the flooding. That contention received a quick and pointed rely:

> The argument of the defendant is that there is no *taking* of the land within the meaning of the constitutional provision, and that the damage is a consequential result of such use of a navigable stream as the government had a right to for the improvement of its navigation.
>
> It would be a very curious and unsatisfactory result, if in con-

6. 80 U.S. (13 Wall.) 166 (1871).

struing a provision of constitutional law, always understood to have been adopted for protection and security to the rights of the individual as against the government, and which has received the commendation of jurists, statesmen, and commentators as placing the just principles of the common law on that subject beyond the power of ordinary legislation to change or control them, it shall be held that if the government refrains from the absolute conversion of real property to the uses of the public it can destroy its value entirely, can inflict irreparable and permanent injury to any extent, can, in effect, subject it to total destruction without making any compensation, because, in the narrowest sense of the word, it is not *taken* for the public use. Such a construction would pervert the constitutional provision into a restriction upon the rights of the citizen, as those rights stood at the common law, instead of the government, and make it an authority for invasion of private right under the pretext of the public good, which had no warrant in the laws or practices of our ancestors.[7]

The Basis of Liability

THE DOMINANCE OF STRICT LIABILITY

Under the private law the appropriate basis of liability must be determined for both conversion and destruction of property. Again, the conversion cases establish the baseline of analysis. In the private context, the defendant must restore what he has deliberately taken. The result can hardly be different, if he has taken it by accident or mistake, even if he exercised all possible care to ascertain ownership.[8] The defendant still has the thing, and he may not profit through his own error. Negligence is neither here nor there; the obligation to return the property is strict, for only then can the imbalance created by the original wrong be corrected. Likewise with injunctions, the rights of the plaintiff are not limited to cases where the defendant acts with malice or negligence. So long as the threat to the plaintiff's property exists, it can be repelled. If strict liability affords the proper basis for injunctions against a threatened taking of property, then it governs when the lesser remedy, damages, is sought when harm no longer can be prevented.[9]

Given the parity between taking and destruction of property, the so-

7. Id at 177, 178.
8. See, e.g., Maye v. Tappan, 23 Cal. 306 (1863).
9. For the private analogies, see Richard A. Epstein, "Causation and Corrective Justice: A Reply to Two Critics," 8 *J. Legal Stud.* 477, 500–501 (1979).

lution to the tort question easily follows: strict liability rules must govern both. The clause itself confirms this view because it refers to property taken, not property taken negligently or deliberately. Moreover, although most government takings cases involve the infliction of deliberate losses upon private individuals, in the few cases that do not, strict liability principles are still proper, for example, in nuisance situations where the government's safety precautions "were of the latest approved design and its use thereof was in the generally recognized and approved manner."[10]

The central insight is not that strict liability is required, because it is in fact followed under state law in most stranger cases. It would be decisive even if the common law were otherwise, because the strict liability rule is in perfect congruence with the logic and structure of the eminent domain clause. The major point separating negligence from strict liability concerns the treatment of the expected benefits derived from the defendant's course of conduct. A negligence rule—at least any patterned on the famous Hand formula of *United States v. Carroll Towing Co.*[11]— states that harm to person or property otherwise tortious shall be excused if the benefits of not preventing harm are greater than the expected costs of the harm itself. In essence, therefore, the formula allows a defendant to trade the benefits that he (or society at large) receives from his own conduct against the costs inflicted upon the plaintiff.

The objection to this general negligence rule is that it refuses to recognize the moral necessity that the defendant—even if his conduct should not *ex ante* be enjoined—at the very least should be required prima facie to pay for the harm his conduct has caused to the person or property of others. The moral case behind strict liability is that the distribution of gains and losses matters as much as the total size of the social pie. That point can be put as follows: where expected costs exceed benefits, the negligent party must make full compensation. Where benefits exceed costs, then, by analogy to restitution arguments, the benefited defendant should make good the losses caused by taking or destroying the property. The harms inflicted upon another should be regarded, to the extent that payment of compensation can do this, as self-inflicted, just as if the de-

10. St. Louis-San Francisco Ry. Co. v. Matthews, 49 P.2d 752 at 753 (1935).

11. 159 F.2d 169 (2d Cir. 1947). For an elaboration of the formula, see Richard A. Posner, "A Theory of Negligence," 1 *J. Legal Stud.* 29 (1972). For criticism, see Richard A. Epstein, "A Theory of Strict Liability," 2 *J. Legal Stud.* 151, 152–160; Richard A. Epstein, *Modern Products Liability Law* ch. 4 (1980).

fendant had destroyed his own property. The private law point was forcefully made by Holmes: "One who diminishes the value of property by intentional damage knows it belongs to somebody. If he thinks it belongs to himself, he expects whatever harm he may do to come out of his own pocket. It would be odd if he were to get rid of the burden by discovering that it belonged to his neighbor."[12] This version of the strict liability argument has its precise parallel in eminent domain law, where the public, rather than a private defendant, must respond to the demand for compensation. The issue of whether compensation should be tendered is viewed separately from the issue of whether certain forms of primary conduct are allowed to go forward, where the benefits of the tort defendant furnish, if anything, an additional reason to compensate the plaintiff for losses sustained.[13]

FEDERAL TORT CLAIMS ACT

The relationship between private and public law is lost in the unfortunate Supreme Court decision in *Laird v. Nelms*.[14] The plaintiff's farmhouse was flattened by a sonic boom caused by government aircraft, for which damages were sought under the Federal Tort Claims Act (FTCA), which makes the government liable (subject to certain immaterial exceptions) for all property damage "caused by the negligent or wrongful act or omission of any employee of the Government . . . under circumstances where the United States, if a private person, would be liable to the claimant in accordance with the law of the place where the act or omission occurred."[15] In essence, the statute gives a legislative expression to the constitutional idea by presumptively holding the government liable for its torts on the principles applicable to private defendants.

Notwithstanding the apparent parity between the government and private defendants announced in the statute, the Supreme Court held that this case fell through the crack because the plaintiff could not show "the negligent or wrongful act or omission." No government agent was negligent, and the damages themselves were held "too indirect" to con-

---

12. O. W. Holmes, Jr., *The Common Law* 97 (1881).

13. The implicit connection between tort doctrine and the principle of just compensation is well understood in the common law cases, especially in those opinions that adopt a strict liability view of the law. See, e.g., Bamford v. Turnley, 3 B. & S. 62, 22 Eng. Rep. 27 (1862); Vincent v. Lake Erie Transportation Co., 109 Minn. 456, 124 N.W. 221 (1910).

14. 406 U.S. 797 (1972).

15. 28 U.S.C. §§ 1346(b) and 2674 (1982).

stitute a "wrongful act." The government could not be charged with any *direct* wrongful act, such as a trespass, but only with the harmful consequences (sonic boom) of an act (flying) that was not tortious in itself. The Court's statutory construction might well be met with the answer that the required wrongful action was the creation of the sonic boom, not the flying of an airplane. Yet even if this interpretation of the statute is incorrect, it only establishes that the FTCA itself is unconstitutional as applied.

Congress may have long thought that liability for governmental torts is a matter of legislative grace, even though compensation for government takings of private property is constitutionally required. Indeed, the theory of sovereign immunity rests upon a modification of the ancient proposition of English law that the king could do no wrong. In the American context the principle must be transformed to meet the demands of constitutional government, but its absolutist origins are well revealed in the classic justification offered by Holmes: "A sovereign is exempt from suit, not because of any formal conception or obsolete theory, but on the logical and practical ground that there can be no legal right as against the authority that makes the law on which the right depends."[16] Sovereign immunity thus depends upon an absolute power of the government that is wholly inconsistent with the theory of the state which the eminent domain clause presupposes. If the state obtains its authority only from the rights of those whom it represents, it can never claim exemption from the duty to compensate on the ground that it is the source of all rights. The natural rights theory behind the Constitution precludes that result.

The rights of action afforded under the FTCA should be regarded not as a matter of legislative grace, but as constitutionally mandated under the takings clause. The conclusion may appear radical, but it is supported not only in principle but also by a diverse range of authority. In *Armstrong v. United States,*[17] the United States was the prospective purchaser of a large number of boats from Rice Shipbuilding Corporation, its prime contractor. Armstrong was a subcontractor which furnished services and materials for the boats, to which it attached a lien valid in all respects under Maine law. The United States in its original contract inserted a provision giving it the right to call for the "transfer and delivery" of the boats in the event that the contractor, Rice, fell into default on its obligations. Rice's undertaking was in turn secured by a para-

16. Kawananakoa v. Polyblank, 205 U.S. 349 (1907).
17. 364 U.S. 40 (1960).

mount lien placed upon the property, which secured the government's progress payments upon the vessels. When Rice went into default the government demanded and got the transfer and delivery of the boats. Then it interposed the defense of sovereign immunity, thereby preventing Armstrong from foreclosing or otherwise enforcing his valid lien. The Supreme Court assumed that priority of liens lay with the government, but it recognized that this did not dispose of Armstrong's taking claim. The boats could well have been worth more than the government's lien, so the plea of sovereign immunity, if respected, would wipe out a junior lien, which itself was property protected by the eminent domaint clause from taking by foreclosure without compensation.

Justice Black knew that in holding for Armstrong he was treading on sensitive ground. He quite consciously refused to explore the question of whether there was any sense in the asserted distinction "between what destructions of property by lawful government action are compensable 'takings' and what destructions are 'consequential' and therefore not compensable,"[18] but only after alluding to a theme manifest in the FTCA, that in *Armstrong* the government demanded the unencumbered title to the boats by interposing the defense of sovereign immunity, "which no private purchaser could have done."[19] Armstrong's claim reaches constitutional status, so it cannot be simply barred by statute, because the takings clause imposes necessary limits on the doctrine of sovereign immunity. It is not that the doctrine is abrogated altogether, for the government always may hold free of lien or charge any *particular* assets it identifies. But while it can extinguish liens, it must pay for what it has taken out of general revenues.

The question then arises whether it is possible to confine the logic of the *Armstrong* to its "special" facts. Here two grounds of limitation might be proposed. First, the opinion could be said to apply only to cases in which there are liens and not fee interests. This is at best odd, for if any lien, which by definition is only a partial interest, is covered by the clause, the fee must be covered *a fortiori*. The second point is that in *Armstrong* the lien was destroyed, but the thing was not. What difference can this make to the plaintiff's loss? *Pumpelly* is correct in equating the destruction of a thing with its taking, so it can hardly matter whether the

18. Id. at 48. The passage is followed by a string citation of cases, including Pennsylvania Coal Co. v. Mahon, 260 U.S. 393 (1922), discussed in Chapter 6; United States v. Causby, 328 U.S. 256 (1946), discussed below; and United States v. Central Eureka Mining Co., 357 U.S. 155 (1958), discussed in Chapter 8.

19. 364 U.S. at 48.

protected interest is a lien or an equity, or both combined. If the flooded property in *Pumpelly* were mortgaged, surely the full loss would remain compensable even though the payments would have to be made to the mortgagee to the extent of his interest.

Any effort to narrowly confine the principles in *Armstrong* flounders as well when set against the inverse condemnation cases, arising both before and after passage of the FTCA, which show anew the vanishing thinness of a line between trespass and conversion. In *Keokuk & Hamilton Bridge Co. v. United States*,[20] the plaintiff's bridge was damaged but not destroyed when the United States engaged in blasting operations to widen the navigable river spanned by the bridge. "The work was done in the usual way and with more than ordinary care,"[21] and Justice Holmes, speaking for a unanimous court, held that there was no remedy against the United States because the damage was both repairable and not deliberate. Noting that in cases of navigation improvements it was difficult to draw the line between torts and takings, he concluded that "this is an ordinary case of incidental damage which if inflicted by a private individual might be a tort but which could be nothing else."[22]

The decision only shows, however, that the line itself is not worth maintaining, because it makes compensation turn on either the defendant's mental state or the size of the injury. Again the theory of limited representative government determines the outcome. As the eminent domain clause makes actionable against the government conduct actionable against a private party, Holmes's reason for denying relief better explains why that relief should be granted. As there is no principled distinction between torts and takings, the two reasons proffered are relevant, if at all, only on other issues. The size of the loss goes to the question of damages, with the wrong established; the deliberate nature of the harm precludes contributory negligence and similar defenses and may be evidence on the question of punitive damages. Either alone or in combination, these two factors do not deflect the application of the eminent domain clause.

After the passage of the FTCA, much of the pressure on the tort/taking distinction is reduced, but the point continues to be litigated, often for procedural reasons. *Myers v. United States*[23] illustrates the basic problem. The plaintiffs owned land over which the government had con-

20. 260 U.S. 125 (1922).
21. Id. at 126.
22. Id. at 127.
23. 323 F.2d 580 (9th Cir. 1963).

demned a right of way. The gist of the plaintiffs' action was that the government contractors had not kept their activities within the condemned right of way but had entered upon and damaged the contiguous land that the plaintiffs had retained. Their complaint alleged destruction of the plaintiffs' own road, loss of gravel, destruction of the surface of the retained lands, damage to plaintiffs' agricultural and garden tracts, and impairment of access to public roads. The plaintiffs' claim for compensation was *not* at issue. The case only asked whether the action "sounded in tort," in which case the suit proceeded under the FTCA with proper venue in Alaska, or whether it arose as an action "upon the Constitution . . . not sounding in tort,"[24] in which case the Tucker Act[25] vested exclusive jurisdiction in the Court of Claims. In deciding in favor of Court of Claims jurisdiction, the Ninth Circuit wrote as follows:

> It is clear to us that the claims of the appellants asserted against the United States are to recover damages for the taking for public use of property claimed to be owned by the appellants, without the institution of condemnation proceedings. The repeated characterization by the appellants of the taking by the United States as one of trespass and the commission of waste upon the lands in question does not convert the claims to cases sounding in tort and thereby confer jurisdiction on the District Court under the Federal Tort Claims Act. The Fifth Amendment to the Constitution prohibits the taking of private property for public use without just compensation. To us the claims of the appellants against the United States are founded upon the Constitution, and the acts of the United States complained of are in the nature of inverse condemnation.[26]

As a basic proposition, so long as the United States is prepared to honor its constitutional obligations, it can choose the particular forum in which the claims are presented. In this sense, it has the power to distinguish between takings and torts. What is odd is the court's insistence that the plaintiffs spoke falsely in charging the government with trespass and waste. Looking at the matter solely as one of statutory construction, it appears that the FTCA is a better home for the suit than the Tucker Act. Yet the very fact that the Court of Claims had jurisdiction in *Myers* shows that partial takings, here the use and destruction of private property, are of constitutional dimension, which the various limitations of the FTCA, including that stressed in *Laird v. Nelms,* cannot defeat by

24. Id. at 582.
25. 28 U.S.C. 1491 (1982).
26. 323 F.2d at 583.

fiat. All tort actions against the government are founded upon the Constitution, whether or not they "sound in tort" under the Tucker Act. The Tucker Act therefore cannot be viewed solely as a matter of legislative grace, but as the chosen means to vindicate a set of individual entitlements that the Constitution itself protects. If the act were repealed tomorrow, the government's obligations under the eminent domain clause would not be diminished one iota. Even if the plaintiff is denied the federal forum under the statute, recourse can be had under the Fifth Amendment itself, either in federal courts or, if necessary, in state courts.

This same conclusion is fortified by cases in which constitutional causes of action for damages have been inferred under other clauses of the Constitution. The most important of the relevant authorities in this connection is *Bivens v. Six Unknown Federal Narcotics Agents.*[27] In that case the Supreme Court held that the plaintiff stated a valid federal cause of action under the Fourth Amendment against the defendant federal agents, who, acting under color of state law and without probable cause, invaded his apartment and arrested him for narcotics violations. The Supreme Court conceded that there was no explicit authorization of the private damage action under the Constitution itself, but it was quite prepared to infer one because of the need to protect individuals against the trespasses and other wrongs of state officials. In making the argument for this position, Justice Brennan noted, in ways that parallel my central theme, that under the Fourth Amendment the individual had greater rights of protection against the state than against other private parties. Private defendants are not armed with search warrants and can, in some cases at least, be repelled by the police acting on behalf of the aggrieved party. By casting the claim on the constitutional level, the plaintiff, of course, was able to avoid the various limitations on recovery against the United States available under the FTCA in suits alleging the wrongful conduct of its officers.[28] Yet if the actions are required under the Constitution against the officers, there is no reason why similar suits should not be brought against the government as their employer.

Bivens is not the only Supreme Court case in which private causes of action have been inferred under the various specific guarantees of the Constitution. *Butz v. Economou*[29] recognized a private cause of action under the First Amendment; *Davis v. Passman*[30] did so with a claim based

27. 403 U.S. 388 (1971).
28. FTCA, 28 U.S.C. § 2680(h) (1982).
29. 438 U.S. 478 (1978).
30. 442 U.S. 228 (1979).

upon the equal protection dimension of the due process clause of the Fifth Amendment in a sex discrimination case against a congressman; and *Carlson v. Green*[31] did the same under the cruel and unusual punishment clause of the Eighth Amendment in a suit against the Federal Bureau of Prisons. Private actions under the eminent domain clause are *a fortiori*, where the "just compensation" language invites the damages remedy that it fails to provide in so many words, subject only to those limitations that can be justified by the police power or by implicit in-kind compensation doctrines.[32]

Proximate Causation

The issue of proximate causation arises in all types of takings cases. In ordinary conversion suits the defendant is typically charged with taking the plaintiff's property with his own hands, but this paradigmatic case does not determine the outer limits of liability. If the defendant sets a trap into which an innocent plaintiff drops his own chattel, the defendant cannot keep the chattel on the ground that he obtained the property by trap instead of by force. Similarly, if a defendant falsely tells the plaintiff that he can leave his goods in defendant's care but then refuses to return them, he has taken them. However, the limit of liability is passed if the defendant says he will not return the goods if handed over to him: the case is a gift rather than a taking, so the truth or falsity of the spoken words sets the jurisdictional limits of the takings clause.[33]

In all conversion cases it is strictly necessary to take into account all actions besides those of the defendant that are needed to complete the transfer of possession from plaintiff to defendant. Yet the length of the

31. 446 U.S. 14 (1980).

32. If it could be shown, for example, that making the District of Columbia Circuit the sole place for Tucker Act cases imposed no disproportionate burden, then that venue rule could not be challenged on taking grounds. Yet it seems very hard to explain what, besides government favoritism, accounts for the result when external physical harm is inflicted by the government at some distant location. The balance of convenience points heavily for venue at the place of injury. It is far easier to understand why venue rests in Washington, D.C., where central regulatory and administrative actions are involved. See generally, Cass R. Sunstein, "Participation, Public Law, and Venue Reform," 49 *U. Chi. L. Rev.* 976 (1982).

33. Note the parallel under the First Amendment, where truthful statements are rightly given far greater protection than false ones. See, e.g., Gertz v. United States, 418 U.S. 323 (1974) (per Powell, J.).

journey does not change the relative rights between the parties, so long as the intermediate steps in the transfer are induced only by the defendant's force or misrepresentation. By the central premise of representative government, the same rules apply when the government stands in the shoes of a private defendant.

The same extension of causal chains can work in cases of destruction as well, thereby injecting the thorny tort issue of proximate causation into the law of eminent domain. All theories of causation are bound to stumble on difficult cases at the margin. The possibility of marginal error does not, however, imply that an adequate theory of causation—even causation by the state—exhausts its power with the damage inflicted by the direct use of force. Although causation begins with trespass, no private system has ever been content to make trespass the *entire* law of tort. In both common and civil law, causation must embrace some instance of indirect harm or consequential damages. Consider the exact parallels to the conversion cases above. The defendant hurts the plaintiff not by striking him directly but by setting a spring gun or trap that the plaintiff triggers. Or the defendant does not injure the plaintiff but tells him there is a safe path out of the bottom of the canyon when there is not. The extension of the causal chain must be made. The Romans prohibited by statute the "killing" of slaves and certain animals.[34] Yet even when they were pushed by the inherent logic of the situation to create the "analogous" action (like the action on the case) to control parallel situations when the defendant furnished a cause of death, as by offering the plaintiff poison on the pretext that it was medicine.[35] Cases under the "equity" of a statute are also cases under the equity of the Constitution.

Indirect causation receives proper treatment in *Eaton v. B. C. & M. R.R.,*[36] a New Hampshire eminent domain case decided shortly after and in the spirit of *Pumpelly*. In *Eaton* the defendant railroad, acting under public authorization, made a large cut in the ridge of a hill, in consequence of which natural water intermittently flooded the plaintiff's land, reducing its fitness for cultivation. The close connection between the public law of eminent domain and the private law of tort was revealed in the first sentence of the opinion. "It is virtually conceded that, if the cut through the ridge had been made by a private landowner, who had acquired no rights from the plaintiff or from the legisla-

34. See *Dig. Just.* 9.2. For the complete text and analysis, see F. H. Lawson, *Negligence in the Civil Law* (1950).
35. *Dig. Just.* 9.2.7.6.—9.2.9.3.
36. 51 N.H. 504 (1872).

ture, he would be liable for the damages sought to be recovered in this action."[37]

The court faithfully applied this premise to the proximate cause issue. It noted that it is wholly immaterial whether the plaintiff proceeds upon a trespass theory or, owing to the causal intervention of natural forces, upon theory patterned upon the rule in *Rylands v. Fletcher*.[38] Judge Smith made all the right causal arguments; he rejected the argument that the water had come "naturally" upon the plaintiff's land, given that the defendant had "so dealt with the soil" that had previously held the waters in check. "If," he noted, "the ridge still remained in its natural condition, could the defendants pump up the flood water into a spout on the top of the ridge, and thence, by means of the spout, pour it directly on the plaintiff's land? If not, how can they maintain a canal through which the water by the force of gravitation will inevitably find its way to the plaintiff's land?"[39] That the harm involved is remedied under an action on the case and not under the writ of trespass has no bearing on the constitutional question, as there is no reason to believe that " 'the framers of the constitution meant to entangle their meaning in the mazes' of the refined technical distinctions by which the common law system of actions is 'perplexed and incumbered.' "[40] If the defendant had purchased the right from the plaintiff before the harm had taken place, he could be said to have acquired "a flowage easement, and the result is scarcely better for the defendant because the flooding took place without the previous purchase of the limited right."[41] In essence, the damage to the land was a partial taking of the land, for even though the plaintiff was left in possession, he was deprived of its ordinary use, one of the major incidents of ownership.

It is, however, all too easy to lose sight of the basic principles of eminent domain and to return to the arid formalities exposed by *Pumpelly* and *Eaton*. In particular, it seems clear that the law relating to air easements and the like has not benefited in the slightest from the earlier analysis of the flooding cases. The seeds of confusion were planted in *United States v. Causby*,[42] where the court held that the government was obligated to compensate private landowners for the taking of an overflight easement when military planes routinely entered the plaintiff's

37. Id. at 506–507.
38. See Fletcher v. Rylands, 1 Ex. 265, aff'd sub nom, Rylands v. Fletcher, L.R. 3 H.L. 330 (1868).
39. 51 N.H. at 513–514.
40. Id. at 520.
41. Id. at 516.
42. 328 U.S. 256 (1946).

airspace in the course of landing and taking off. The entry itself was treated as an ordinary trespass (and hence taking) of airspace for which the inconvenience and disturbance to the landowner was but one component of actionable damages. The unfortunate implication of the rationale is that the entrance into protected airspace, not the disturbance it generated, forms the gist of the government wrong.

Errors in principle, however, lead easily to errors in result. In *Batten v. United States*,[43] the question, as stated by the court, was "whether a taking of property, compensable under the Fifth Amendment, occurs when there is no physical invasion of the affected property but the operation and maintenance of military jet aircraft on an Air Force Base of the United States produce noise, vibration, and smoke which interfere with the use and enjoyment of property."[44] The court answered the question in the negative, largely by insisting upon the exploded distinction between the taking of property, on the one hand, and mere damage to property, on the other.[45] The court denied recovery with the announcement that "[t]he record shows nothing more than interference with the use and enjoyment."[46] Yet that is precisely the reason why compensation *should* be awarded. One of the least defensible of all nineteenth-century tort distinctions was that between damage by blasting, governed by a strict liability rule, and damage by vibration and the like, governed by a negligence rule.[47] The court in *Batten* has taken this distinction one better at a constitutional level, for in its own view the classification of the nature and source of harm now goes not merely to the question whether negligence must be alleged and proved, but to the much larger question of whether any recovery will be granted *at all*.

To be sure, *Batten* does allow for some play in the joints by noting that

43. 306 F.2d 580 (10th Cir. 1962).

44. Id. at 581.

45. The case tends to belie the assertion that the omission of the "or damaged" language has had no effect on the adjudication under the eminent domain clause. See Bruce A. Ackerman, *Private Property and the Constitution* 191 (1977).

46. 306 F.2d at 585.

47. The key nineteenth-century cases are Hay v. Cohoes Co., 2 N.Y. 159 (1848), authorizing strict liability actions for blasting damage, and Booth v. Rome, W. & O.T.R.R. Co., 140 N.Y. 267, 35 N.E. 592 (1893). The distinction was laid to rest in Spano v. Perini Corp., 25 N.Y.2d 11, 250 N.E.2d 31, 302 N.Y.S. 527 (1969), which authorized strict liability actions for both blasting and vibration damages. The doctrinal situation, however, has not yet come to rest in New York, because Copart Industries, Inc. v. Consolidated Edison Co., 41 N.Y.2d 564, 362 N.E.2d 968, 394 N.Y.S.2d 169 (1977), points toward adoption of a negligence standard in nuisance cases that are distinguished only with difficulty from the ultrahazardous cases.

compensation is required for some cases, as in *Richard v. Washington Terminal Co.*,[48] where recovery was allowed because smoke and fumes were driven out of a tunnel by an exhaust fan and directed across plaintiff's property. *Richard* is far more important than this grudging concession to principle might suggest, because it indicates, in the way foreshadowed by *Pumpelly,* how the integrity of the eminent domain clause is preserved only if takings include damage and destruction. The concession only reinforces the central point, for *Richard* requires that all nuisances be treated as "physical invasions" and therefore as takings prima facie compensated under the eminent domain clause. To insist, the court does in *Batten,* that ordinary nuisances are not physical invasions is to act not only against sound theory but also against the uniform judgment, both ancient and modern, on the status of ordinary nuisances. It cannot be that the tort of nuisance is foreign to the eminent domain clause that is on its face designed to protect private property. There has been a welcome retreat from the *Batten* position in the case law[49] and some recognition at the legislative level that it produces inexcusable, indeed outrageous, results.[50] It is all too tempting to regard any retreat from the "no compensation" position as a matter of legislative grace and not of constitutional command, as if nuisances raised matters of fairness that somehow fall outside the scope of the eminent domain clause. What is needed, however, is not an erratic and unprincipled temporizing but the complete repudiation of *Batten* and the philosophy it incorporates, as a matter both of common law and of constitutional doctrine. Full compensation is prima facie required.

Consequential Damages

In both public and private cases, the problem of causation extends to the issue of consequential damages: what losses stemming from the original wrong should also be compensated? Situations that present this problem are common, in that both the taking and the destruction of private property may result in a plaintiff losing profits and business goodwill

48. 233 U.S. 56 (1913), discussed in Chapter 16.

49. See, e.g., Thornburg v. Port of Portland, 233 Or. 178, 376 P.2d 100 (1962); Aaron v. City of Los Angeles, 40 Cal. App. 3d 471, 115 Cal. Rptr. 162 (1974).

50. See the newspaper account in Lindsey, "Jet Noise in Los Angeles Is Dooming 1,994 Homes," *New York Times,* July 21, 1971 at 1, col. 3, reprinted in Charles Donahue, Thomas E. Kauper, and Peter W. Martin, *Cases and Materials on Property* 382 (1974). See also Aviation Safety and Noise Abatement Act of 1979, Pub.L. No. 96–193, 94 Stat. 50 (codified in various sections of 49 U.S.C.).

and incurring the expenses of relocation and attorney's fees.[51] The most extreme case is the condemnation of a large tract of land, which destroys not only many small businesses and homes but also the sense of community. Detroit's use of the eminent domain power to condemn the Poletown neighborhood to make way for a General Motors plant is but one illustration of the problem.[52] To compensate for the loss of land values without regard for the associational deprivations is again to use tests of remoteness of damage that are utterly inappropriate for private defendants and, by implication, for the government as well. Nonetheless, the courts uniformly deny all such claims on the textual ground that the government has gone into possession of the land alone but has not *taken* the additional items of loss. The emphasis is thus upon the values that have been transferred to the government and not those that are lost to the owner when the government is unable to use them in its own business. "If the business was destroyed, the destruction was an unintended incident of the taking of land."[53] While the general rule remains that "the question is what has the owner lost, not what has the taker gained,"[54] consequential damages of all sorts have been excluded from its purview on the ground that the government need only pay for that which it gets.

Yet the exclusion of consequential damages from the plaintiff's losses in eminent domain cases cannot be defended. The eminent domain clause, like all provisions in the Constitution, is not designed to protect the thing owned; it is designed to protect the owner of the thing.[55] If

---

51. Note, "Eminent Domain Valuations in an Age of Redevelopment: Incidental Losses," 67 *Yale L.J.* 61 (1957).

52. See, e.g., Poletown Neighborhood Council v. City of Detroit, 410 Mich. 616, 304 N.W.2d 455 (1981). For discussion, see Frank I. Michelman, "Property as a Constitutional Right," 38 *Wash. & Lee L. Rev.* 1097 (1981). The central doctrinal questions concern public use, on which see Chapter 12.

53. Mitchell v. United States, 267 U.S. 341 (1925); see also Kimball Laundry Co. v. United States, 338 U.S. 1 (1949). At issue in the case was whether the government, which had made a temporary taking of appellant's laundry, was required to compensate for the loss of its route values, which were of great value to the company but of no value to the government. The court allowed compensation for the "transferable value their temporary use may have had." Id. at 16. The dissent, relying upon *Mitchell*, would have denied recovery completely. The majority's grudging concession is far too restrictive, as the transferable value of the rights may have been far less than their value in use. The proper measure of the loss is the present value of the income stream during the period of occupation, plus any loss in the value of the route system upon termination.

54. Boston Chamber of Commerce v. City of Boston, 217 U.S. 189 (1910).

55. The point dates from W. Blackstone, *Commentaries* 139: "In this and similar cases the legislature alone can, and indeed frequently does, interpose,

therefore it is the *loss* to the owner which functions as the proper measure of compensation, then all consequential losses attributable to the admitted taking—including destruction—are recoverable, just as they are routinely recoverable against a private defendant. If the destruction of property itself is a taking under the eminent domain clause, then the infliction of consequential losses is a partial taking that the clause also reaches. As a matter of justice, the individual plaintiff is not made whole when these consequential losses are systematically ignored. As a matter of general social welfare, the rule invites the government to embark on programs where the expected losses exceed the probable social gains, making all persons net losers in the long run.[56]

The injustice—for such it is—of the current rule is widely recognized in the decided cases and the academic literature.[57] But this broad academic consensus on the basic point has not been matched by a judicial willingness to overturn established doctrine. One recent case that illustrates the extent to which modern "progressive" courts are prepared to indulge in sterile analysis to suppress their own sense of justice is *Community Redevelopment Agency of Los Angeles v. Abrams.*[58] There the plaintiff was an elderly pharmacist whose place of business was condemned by the redevelopment agency as part of a comprehensive plan for urban renewal. The agency paid for the land taken but balked at compensating Abrams for two additional heads of damage: loss of business goodwill and destruction of his stock of ethical or prescription, drugs. The loss of business goodwill could be attributed to the condemnation because the urban renewal program had dispersed Abrams's former clientele, and his old age and questionable health made it difficult, if not impossible,

---

and compel the individual to acquiesce. But how does it interpose and compel? Not by absolutely stripping the subject of his property in an arbitrary manner; but by giving him a full indemnification and equivalent for the injury thereby sustained. The public is now considered as an individual, treating with an individual for an exchange. All the legislature does, is to oblige the owner to alienate his possessions for a reasonable price; and even this is an exertion of power, which the legislature indulges with caution, and which nothing but the legislature can perform." Note that the "full indemnification and equivalent for the injury thereby sustained" should cover consequential damages.

56. Note, supra note 51; see also Gideon Kanner, "When is 'Property' not 'Property Itself': A Critical Examination of the Bases of Denial of Compensation for Loss of Goodwill in Eminent Domain," 6 *Cal. W. L. Rev.* 57 (1969).

57. See Chapters 17-19 for the implications that follow from systematic undercompensation.

58. 15 Cal. 3d 813, 543 P.2d 905, 126 Cal. Rptr. 473 (1975).

for him to begin his business again in a new location. The ethical drugs were destroyed because an applicable California health regulation required that all such drugs, once removed from their sealed containers, be opened and inspected by state authorities before being resold to another pharmacist, a procedure that in this case cost more than the market value of the drugs themselves.

The court denied both heads of compensation, even though no private defendant could escape payment if he forcibly ejected an owner from his place of business.[59] The case for compensation by the state, moreover, becomes perfectly clear in light of the specious tort analogies invoked by the California Supreme Court—surely no defendant's jurisdiction in torts cases—to deny recovery. At one point the court attributed the plaintiff's loss to his own weakened condition. The argument fails as a factual matter, for the dispersal of the plaintiff's clientele could not have been prevented even by a plaintiff in the full vigor of his youth. Nor does it matter that younger owners might have further mitigated the losses. In California, as everywhere else, the tortfeasor takes his victim as he finds him, be it for his thin skull or for his old age.[60] The government stands in no better position.

The denial of the claim for the loss of the ethical drugs fares little better. The plaintiff destroyed those drugs under compulsion of state action; between the party that destroys under the threats of another and the party that makes the threat, the loss should properly lie upon the threatener, even though he is more distant in both time and space from the harm: he forced me to harm myself.[61] The position is not controversial in any system that understands duress. Overly restrictive theories of causation universally rejected in tort contexts should not be called in to aid the government in eminent domain cases. Goodwill and consequential damages are part of the covered losses and prima facie are compensable as such.

The question of consequential damages also arises with the expert appraisal and litigation fees individual property owners incur during the

---

59. United States v. Miller, 317 U.S. 369 (1943); United States v. Reynolds, 297 U.S. 14, 16 (1970).

60. See, e.g., Warren A. Seavey, "Mr. Justice Cardozo and the Law of Torts," 39 *Colum L. Rev.* 20, 32–33; 52 *Harv. L. Rev.* 372, 384–385; 48 *Yale. L.J.* 390, 402–403 (1939).

61. See, generally, Richard A. Epstein, "A Theory of Strict Liability," 2 *J. Legal Stud.* 151, 174–177 (1973). The only difficult point here is whether compulsion by a third party should excuse the person who acted under it. But where the compulsion is by the party against whom the loss is to be charged, the case is too obvious to require authority.

course of condemnation. The received legal doctrine on this point follows from the central proposition of Justice Brewer in *Monongahela*[62] that compensation is tendered only for the "property taken" and not for the losses sustained by the owner. As the government does not keep the litigation and appraisal fees spent by the private party, it follows under the orthodox analysis that the government is not required to compensate for their loss.[63] One justification of this result rests upon the observation that the private owner normally has to bear all these costs when land is sold in the voluntary market, so the net recovery is the price paid less the expenses of sale. Nonetheless, the analogy is wholly inappropriate, given that the sale to the government under its eminent domain power is involuntary. In the voluntary market the simple fact that the seller has entered into the transaction is evidence that he regards the net price as a fair equivalent for the property surrendered. No such inference can be drawn where the sale is involuntary, for it is clear that the owner prefers the stream of income derived from the use of property to the net condemnation proceeds. In short, it follows that the owner is not indifferent between the property lost and the compensation tendered, as the basic theory of the takings clause requires.[64]

62. Monongahela Navigation Co. v. United States, 148 U.S. 312 (1893).

63. For a recent reaffirmation of the dominant position, see United States v. Bodcaw Co., 440 U.S. 202 (1979). *Bodcaw* involved a case in which the court of appeals had sustained an increase in award to cover costs of securing land appraisals needed to show, as was in fact the case, that the government offer of compensation was inadequate. See United States v. 1,380.09 Acres of Land, 574 F.2d 238 (5th Cir. 1978). The Supreme Court reversed, noting that these expenses were routinely incurred and thus hardly distinguishable from the litigation and expert witness expenses for which recovery is routinely denied. Its own brief opinion justified the result solely by an appeal to precedent, without probing into the hard questions raised by the issue. "Perhaps it would be fair or efficient to compensate a landowner for all the costs he incurs as a result of a condemnation action." 440 U.S. at 204, citing Douglas Ayer, "Allocating the Costs of Determining 'Just Compensation,'" 21 *Stan. L. Rev.* 693 (1969). But if fairness and efficiency are ignored, then what can justify the result?

64. Note one further complication on the matter. In the normal private suit in this country, legal fees are not recoverable in ordinary tort actions, so the government claims only the same benefits that are routinely available to private defendants. Two responses are possible. First, the rule in the private area is wrong in principle, so the English rule on costs—winner take all—should prevail. Second, the situation with government is distinguishable because its decision to condemn is deliberate, and thus it always gets the advantage of the no-compensation rule, in contrast to the private cases, where each side has an equal chance of being plaintiff or defendant. See Chapter 14 for a discussion of the disproportionate impact tests that this rule suggests.

The only real question therefore is to determine how to take into account these additional expenses. There is an obvious risk in compensating the individual owner for whatever expenses are incurred in valuing the property or in resisting the takeover, for the private owner will be tempted to spend lavishly if the government must pick up the bill. One possible solution is to scrutinize the expenses for the reasonableness on a case-by-case basis, so that efforts to resist a takeover on the ground that it is not for public use will be disallowed if the land is taken for a highway. The case-by-case method has the advantage of capturing the variation in costs associated with different types of properties. Yet it has the corresponding disadvantage of increasing the administrative costs for the system and of allowing the introduction of error. It might be preferable to develop administratively routine formulas to increase the awards paid for different classes of property to take into account these costs. This might also allow individual owners to prove additional expenses so long as they are prepared to compensate the government if their own claims are adjudged inflated or unreasonable. There can be serious disagreement about how the details of any such compensation system will work. But the range of options is sufficiently well defined that, no matter which is chosen, the outcome will be more consistent with the constitutional text than the current rules routinely denying such compensation.

5   Partial Takings:
The Unity of Ownership

The Conservation of Rights

The proper treatment of partial takings is a matter of sufficient importance and difficulty to receive separate treatment. The central thesis itself is easily stated. The protection afforded by the eminent domain clause to each part of an endowment of private property is equal to the protection it affords the whole—no more and no less. No matter how the basic entitlements contained within the bundle of ownership rights are divided and no matter how many times the division takes place, all of the pieces together, and each of them individually, fall within the scope of the eminent domain clause. A rule of the conservation of entitlements lies behind the clause. If A and B have their own set of entitlements, then no matter how they combine what they have, their rights against the rest of the world—or the state—are neither diminished nor increased.

The proposition seems straightforward enough where the state takes two acres of land from a four-acre parcel. Prima facie, compensation must be paid for the land taken no matter how much land the owner retains. The same principles apply no matter what form of division is imposed. Let the government remove any of the incidents of ownership, let it diminish the rights of the owner in any fashion, then it has prima facie brought itself within the scope of the eminent domain clause, no matter how small the alteration and no matter how general its application.

To take any other position leads quickly to a maze of contradictions. The air rights of Blackacre are owned by A, while the ground rights are owned by B. If the government condemns the air rights, then A is prima facie entitled to compensation. Does it make the slightest difference if A sells his rights to B before the government acts? To be sure, the sale converts what was a complete taking from A into a partial taking from B, but it cannot alter the characterization of the underlying rights or of the government action, even if a different person is now entitled to compensation. In the case of the four-acre plot of land, what is decisive is that which is taken, not that which is retained. It matters not if the claimant owns only the two acres taken or the full four acres: the obligation to compensate is constant in either case. Just as two private parties should not be able by joint contrivance to increase the government's obligation to compensate for property taken, neither should the way they pool or divide their interests diminish that obligation. To adopt any other position is to demand a theory of property rights that tells *how many* things are subject to private ownership, which in turn inspires a pointless shell game each time governmental force is directed against the private owner. The takings clause says, "Nor shall private property be taken for public use, without just compensation." It means, "nor shall private property, in whole or in part, be taken for public use, without just compensation."

There is yet another way to show that the protection of the eminent domain clause extends to each stick in the bundle as well as to the bundle itself. Consider two possible cases. In the first the state takes land outright and then returns it subject to certain new restrictions as to its permissible use. In the second case the state does not take the land outright but imposes by decree the identical use restrictions upon its owner. There is no question but that the first scenario is covered by the eminent domain clause. Here the taking is complete and the compensation is but partial, for the land when newly subjected to restrictions cannot be equal in value to the land in its unencumbered state. What possible difference could it make to the state obligation if the state bypasses the formal taking and compresses the two steps into one? The difference is no more powerful here than it was in the case of inverse condemnation of flowage rights.[1] It is possible to argue that the eminent domain clause reaches complete takings with partial compensation, but leaves wholly untouched partial takings without any compensation at all?

The Unity of Ownership

What then are the rights of ownership? To this question the traditional answer given by both common and civil law systems is that the rights of

1. See the discussion of *Pumpelly* in Chapter 4.

ownership in a given thing consist in a set of rights of infinite duration, good against the rest of the world: with three separate incidents: possession, use, and disposition. The categorization here is not a novel one. It is found, for example, in the Roman texts that speak of the *ius possendi*, the *ius utendi*, and the *ius abutendi*, the "right to abuse," which was quickly construed to cover the right of disposition.[2] It is just this trinity of rights that Blackstone mentioned in his own account of property rights.[3]

The statement of the Supreme Court in *United States v. General Motors Corp.* gives a good summary of the received jurisprudential wisdom:

> The critical terms [of the eminent domain clause] are "property," "taken" and "just compensation." It is conceivable that the first was used in its vulgar and untechnical sense of the physical thing with respect to which the citizen exercises rights recognized by law. On the other hand, it may have been employed in a more accurate sense to denote the group of rights inhering in the citizen's relation to the physical thing, as the right to possess, use and dispose of it. In point of fact, the construction given the phrase has been the latter.[4]

The very fact that this bundle of rights has been understood to comprise ownership of a particular thing should be decisive in the constitutional context. There is no reason to think that private property, as an undefined term in the Constitution, was to be understood in a way completely at variance with the accepted usages of that time or was to mean bare possession, with which it had long been contrasted under both the English and Roman law of real property.[5]

The historical account is, however, fortified by an analytical treatment of the same conception. Here the matter might be approached in two separate ways. First, it might be asked what *more* could be incorporated into the notion of ownership. To be sure, any single owner might ask for the right to control the possession, use, and disposition of things claimed by others. But when it is realized that ownership is a general conception, this broad claim necessarily entrenches upon the like

2. See, for example, J. K. B. M. Nicholas, *An Introduction to Roman Law* 154 (1962), noting the classification and noting that limitations can exist on private ownership rights so created.

3. See Chapter 4.

4. 323 U.S. 373, 377–378 (1945). For a more comprehensive list of incidents that boil down to the critical three, see also A. M. Honoré, "Ownership," in *Oxford Essays in Jurisprudence* 107 (A. G. Guest ed. 1961).

5. On the English law, see A. W. Brian Simpson, "The Ratio Decidendi of a Case and the Doctrine of Binding Precedent," in Nicholas, supra note 2, at 148; on the Roman law, see Nicholas at 98–157, esp. 107–115, 153–157.

rights of other parties. The idea of ownership entails that whatever uses are permitted must fall within the exclusive province of the owner. The class of permitted uses in question is defined in a *substantive* manner to respect natural boundaries, such that each person can do with his own land what he pleases so long as he does not physically invade the land of another.[6] To add any more sticks to the bundle of ownership is to take them from other individuals with equal claim to legal protection. Possession, use (as limited by the physical invasion test), and disposition form the outer limits of ownership, both in common and in technical usage.

The second question is the obverse of the first. What sticks may be taken out of the bundle? It is impossible to find a coherent account of ownership that can make do without any of its traditional elements. Suppose that X is the owner of Blackacre. Is it possible to think that his ownership interests are of less than infinite temporal duration, especially when they are acquired by original occupation and not by grant? If they are of finite duration, when do they end, and who is entitled to obtain possession of the interests, and by what principle, when the time is up? The system cannot be well defined if possible rights remain to be parceled out but no one is able to acquire them. As the state cannot simply acquire rights by declaration alone, then the future value of the thing is simply beyond the powers of human appropriation.

Similarly, possession, use and disposition do not form a random list of incidents. Instead they lie at the core of a comprehensive and coherent idea of ownership. The right way to think about these incidents is to ask what ownership means if any of them are removed. Is it sensible to have a notion of ownership without the right of possession? If so, who can possess the land in question, and why is he not the owner? Suppose exclusive possession is recognized as an essential incident of ownership; what should be done about the question of use? If the owner cannot use the land in question, who can? If it is someone who is not in possession, how do we decide which person it is? And what does it mean to use but not to possess? Any effort to lodge possession in one person and rights of use in another creates a high degree of incoherence with no return payoff. Any viable conception of ownership that embraces the right of possession must embrace the right of use as well.

There is still the status of the right of disposition. Resources owned by one person might be better deployed by another. If the owner cannot make the transfer, must the land remain where it is, or may some other

6. For qualifications, see Chapter 14.

person—by who knows what warrant—sells the land that neither he or his purchaser is entitled to possess or to use? The first-possession rule does not give possession and use to one person, leaving the incident of disposition without a home. The unity of incidents is an inseparable part of the concept of ownership.

In large measure the first-possession doctrine is a necessary complement to the Lockean theory in which individual rights are never grounded in the commands of the state. First possession is a simple and universal rule of conduct that operates as the source of individual rights, good against the rest of the world. The first-possession rule firmly grounds individual claims of ownership especially in a world in which all individuals own their own labor. Possession does not come without an expenditure of resources, and their expenditure makes clear the exclusivity of ownership. Think what would happen if the rule were the first one to look at property could claim to be its owner. In the end, therefore, it cannot sensibly be supposed that the private property referred to in the Constitution is shorn of any of the incidents that lend it coherence. Linking rights of possession, use, and disposition into a single bundle of rights offers powerful utilitarian advantages. More complex schemes only lead to indefinite specifications of the original rights, which in turn hamper the coordinated use and transfer of all resources.

There is then a unitary conception of ownership which flows comfortably from the doctrine of original acquisition. Still to be explained is how the complex division of ownership rights arises from this simple original position. Here the key is the right of disposition, by which the original rights of use and possession can be transferred, pooled, and divided at the pleasure of buyer and seller, donor and donee, mortgagor and mortgagee, and so on.[7] There is under the Constitution no reason to distinguish between rights acquired through original (or adverse) possession and rights acquired through grant. Both can be owned, and both can be taken, be it by a private party or by the state. What is true of a fee simple sold in a private transaction is also true of a lease, easement, mortgage, life estate, or future interest. It is true of bare land or improved property, of mineral interests, and of air rights. It is true of property solely owned and jointly owned, no matter what the form of

---

7. What Thomas Grey, supra Chapter 3, note 1, called the disintegration of private property is nothing of the sort. Ownership rights no longer remain in their original bundles because the costs of transfers have been lowered in ways that increase the frequency of transfers. It is a tribute to the power of the system that so many permutations have been devised for the original set of rights.

ownership. It is true of patents, copyrights, trade secrets, and other forms of intangible wealth, which have value in use and disposition even if they cannot be reduced to physical possession. There is no hierarchy among incidents, no degrees of ownership. There is a partial taking of property if possession is removed, and use and disposition remain; if use is removed, and possession and disposition remain; or if disposition is removed, and use and possession remain. Nor is there a requirement that the loss of the incident be total; partial losses of single incidents may determine the measure of damages but may not negate the taking. Any deprivation of rights is a taking, regardless of how it is effected or the damages it causes. The question to be asked is, "What has been taken?" not "What has been retained?" It is best to review the matter incident by incident. The next chapter is concerned with possession and use; Chapter 7 is concerned with disposition.

6   Possession and Use

Possession

The notion of exclusive possession, which is implicit in the basic conception of private property, accounts for one of the most important takings cases in the Supreme Court literature, *Pennsylvania Coal Co. v. Mahon.*[1] There the owner of land containing coal deposits deeded the surface interest but expressly reserved the rights to remove all the coal underneath the surface. The deed itself contained language by which the buyers (for themselves and their assigns) waived all rights to damage in the event that the surface fell. Sometime after the original conveyance, Pennsylvania passed the Kohler Act, which forbade any mining that caused damage to the surface owner. The Supreme Court held the statute as a taking of the mining company's interest, which it clearly is. The case itself contains elaborate language by Holmes, which he later regretted in correspondence, that where regulation goes "too far" it will be treated as a taking for which compensation must be paid.[2] Owing to the clarity of the grant, however, the case is an easy one. Before the statute the coal company was in possession of a mineral estate. After the statute was passed, the interest itself was lost. "If [the city's] representatives have been

1. 260 U.S. 393 (1922).
2. See 2 *Holmes-Pollock Letters: The Correspondence of Mr. Justice Holmes and Sir Frederick Pollock 1874–1932* 108, (Mark DeWolfe Howe ed. 1941). The letter belies the assertion in Bruce A. Ackerman, *Private Property and the Constitution* 163–167 (1977), that the case posed insuperable philosophical difficulties for Holmes. Indeed, the opinion shows all the signs of having been dashed off in a great hurry.

so short sighted as to acquire only surface rights without the right of support, we see no more authority for supplying the latter without compensation than there was for taking the right of way in the first place and refusing to pay for it because the public wanted it very much."[3] All else is superfluous; the case is easy, although the opinion has generated an enormous amount of scholarship.[4]

Other, more recent cases of equal ease, however, indicate how the Supreme Court has been able to escape this simple conclusion. In *Penn Central Transportation Co. v. City of New York*,[5] the issue before the court was whether the City of New York, acting pursuant to its landmark preservation statute, was entitled to prevent the owners of Grand Central Terminal from constructing a new office tower over the current structure. Here there is no question about remote reaches of the *ad coelum* doctrine, because the owners claimed the right to occupy only airspace that could be effectively occupied.[6] The Supreme Court, however, decided that so long as the use of the existing structures was not impaired, the city could wholly prohibit the occupation and use of the airspace without payment of compensation. The court, speaking through Justice Brennan, held that the state may exclude persons from the occupation of part of what they own and still not come under a prima facie obligation to pay compensation. It did attempt to dress up this bald conclusion with a contention that it was a "fallacy" to assume that the loss of any particular right of easement constituted a taking of property. But the so-called fallacy is really an affirmation of the standard conceptions of property applied everywhere and at all times in the United States: ownership is divisible. The air rights over the existing building were property just as much as the air rights already occupied by the existing structure. Justification and implicit compensation are still matters to be considered, but the case is clearly caught by the clause.[7]

A similar treatment of the right of exclusive possession is found in the more recent Supreme Court case of *PruneYard Shopping Center v. Robins*.[8]

3. 260 U.S. 393, 415 (1922).

4. For a review of the materials, see Carol M. Rose, "*Mahon* Reconstructed: Why the Takings Issue Is Still a Muddle," 57 *S. Cal. L. Rev.* 561 (1984). On the facts of *Mahon,* one could try to make a police power justification for the taking, but it is impossible to find any external harm; see Chapter 8. So, too, there is no credible argument for implicit in-kind compensation, even though the statute is general on its face. See Chapter 14.

5. 438 U.S. 104 (1978).

6. See, e.g., Federick Pollock, *The Law of Torts* 362 (13th ed. 1929).

7. See Chapters 9 and 11.

8. 447 U.S. 74 (1980).

There the appellees entered a large shopping center owned by the appellants and erected a booth in order to collect signatures in opposition to an anti-Zionist resolution passed by the United Nations. There was no interference (apart from the fact of partial occupation) with the business of the shopping center, but the views endorsed by the appellees were not the views of the owners of the shopping center.

The Rehnquist opinion reveals its intellectual weakness at every turn. Nowhere does the court offer a coherent account of the incidents of ownership, including exclusive possession. In private cases no injunction against entry is dependent upon showing actual damages. The entry itself is the violation of the right, for which the injunction is available for redress, even if no damages can or should be awarded. It therefore follows that any demonstration about the negligible impairment of the appellants' rights is wholly beside the point, just as it would be in a private dispute. The entire matter of "investment backed expectations" does not go to the taking issue as such; it only goes to the issue of reliance damages, when, as, and if relevant.

It is well and good to note that the shopping center is not a private home and that invitations had been issued to many to come onto the land for many purposes. That is all quite irrelevant. The idea of property embraces the absolute right to exclude. Whatever the status of others, there is *no* invitation to *these* plaintiffs. The Lockean theory controls. No private person could force his way into the shopping center without the consent of its owners. Nothing therefore allows the state to place conditions upon the owners' right to admit or exclude, or to insist that if A is admitted to the property, then B must be admitted as well. The restrictions that the state places upon the exclusive possession of land constitute a partial taking for which compensation is prima facie required.

Justice Marshall had some sense of the intellectual problem when he noted that some *normative* conception has to underlie the constitutional interpretation of private property, lest a constitutional command be defeated by perpetual legislative redefinition of its subject matter.[9] Yet his mistaken concurrence offered no such alternative construct that would allow him to respect the external authority of the constitutional text and decide this case in favor of the demonstrators. I am not quarreling with the importance of the First Amendment's political guarantees, but it is mistaken to argue that the exercise of this freedom—unlike the exercise of any other freedom—gives the appellee the right to appropriate the

9. Id. at 93–94.

land of another for his own use, any more than the First Amendment gives a political candidate the right to use his neighbor's telephone free of charge. If *PruneYard* represents the best that can be done for private property, then an artful judge of a different persuasion could with perfect probity interpret the First Amendment as nothing more than a solemn guarantee of the right to exchange social pleasantries with close family friends—but not, of course, on private property. Freedom of speech gives one the right to talk in ways that are unpleasant to others, without any justification for so doing. So too, private property gives the right to exclude others *without* the need for any justification. Indeed, it is the ability to act at will and without need for justification within some domain which is the essence of freedom, be it of speech or of property.

Use

The treatment of the incident of use follows a parallel line. The early decisions in *Pumpelly, Eaton,* and *Richards*[10] are best understood as vindications of the constitutional rights to use property in connection with certain forms of tortious invasions, patterned on theories similar to that of *Rylands v. Fletcher.*[11] The errors in *Batten*[12] are likewise easily understood as the court's refusal to protect the incident of use, as separate from both possession and disposition, against interference by nuisances. All those cases involve easements, but the same point can be made in connection with government actions to impose restrictions on use that in private contexts could be imposed by covenant. If the state, as owner of a large office building, prevents by law all construction on land that lies between the building and the ocean, it has taken an interest in private property. Again a powerful theory of private rights—here of restrictive covenants—governs the situation.[13] That the government has not taken physical possession of the land is neither here nor there. It clearly will enter the land by force if the covenant it has created by fiat is not respected by the parties who are subject to it. The government's position is unique only in that it can force exchanges where private defendants could be enjoined. But whether we deal with total or with partial

10. See discussion in Chapter 4.
11. L.R. 3 H.L. 330 (1868).
12. See Chapter 4.
13. See, e.g., Southern California Edison Co. v. Bourgerie, 9 Cal. 3d 169, 507 P.2d 964, 107 Cal. Rptr. 76 (1973), so deciding with respect to a building restriction. See, generally, William B. Stoebuck, *Nontrespassory Takings in Eminent Domain* (1977).

interests in land, we cannot avoid the compensation requirement when the owner is deprived of rights.

Possession and Use: Water Rights

The analysis of the rights to possession and use has thus far referred only to land. The analysis can be extended with equal force to water rights cases. The rights in question are, in riparian jurisdictions, typically incident to the owners of the river banks or shore; the loss of these rights, therefore, is best understood as a partial taking of a larger interest in private property. In water cases the fresh obstacle stems from the obvious but important point that the initial distribution of rights in and over water cannot be specified as precisely as for ordinary real estate or chattels. Yet some account of those property rights is needed to determine whether certain state activities constitute, in whole or in part, a taking of private property, or whether, in the alternative, they work to the disadvantage of the aggrieved party without infringing upon any vested rights. To note the necessity for an account of original entitlements over water is not to provide such an account, a point forcefully made in the well-known passage from Justice Jackson's opinion in *United States v. Willow River Power Co.*, where dam construction resulted in the loss of generating power from a headwater. Jackson wrote:

> It is clear, of course, that a head of water has value and that the Company has an economic interest in keeping the St. Croix [the river blocked up in the case] at the lower level. But not all economic interests are "property rights"; only those economic advantages are "rights" which have the law back of them, and only when they are so recognized may courts compel others to forebear from interfering with them or to compensate for their invasion.[14]

The first proposition—that it is necessary to distinguish between entitlements and advantages—cannot be denied. But the second proposition—that advantage becomes an entitlement only when the court says it is—does not follow from the first. The second proposition is in fact both incorrect and inconsistent with the eminent domain clause. Although the clause does not contain a definition of private property for water rights, it demands that we isolate some independent normative account. In addressing this task the Supreme Court has given far too

14. 324 U.S. 499, 502 (1945).

much weight to the "navigation servitude," which is said to be both paramount and superior to all the riparian interests with which it conflicts. The dubious pedigree of navigation servitude should be apparent from its supposed origins in the commerce clause. Yet to assert that navigation servitude is paramount is to confuse a grant of *jurisdiction,* however broad,[15] to the federal sovereign with *ownership* of things within that jurisdiction. The Supreme Court itself has recognized that the commerce "clause speaks in terms of power, not of property."[16] Yet all that is taken back in the next sentence: "But the power is a dominant one which can be asserted to the exclusion of any competing or conflicting one. The power is a privilege which we have called 'a dominant servitude' or 'a superior navigation easement.' "[17]

Once this elementary confusion of jurisdiction with entitlement is exposed, how then are initial entitlements determined? Here the central insight is that which organizes the entire discussion of prima facie takings. The government is not vested ipso facto with any rights at all. It is only vested with the rights it derives from the individuals it represents. Far from allowing an ad hoc cleavage between public and private law, it insists on their intimate connection, in water law cases as elsewhere. In order to find the appropriate baseline for judgment, therefore, it is necessary to sort out the original entitlements over water between private parties.

Some cases seem more or less straightforward, because the happenstance of a dispute over water rights does not complicate the specification of original position. Thus, in *Kaiser Aetna v. United States,*[18] the private party at its own expense converted a nonnavigable body into navigable waters. Even though the company took all steps to keep the waters private, the government asserted that its paramount easement extended to them. The claim was rejected on the simple ground that it was difficult, if not impossible, to infer a transfer from private to United States control solely from private development for private gain. A private dirt road does not vest in the government once it has been paved. If the law says that anyone who paves thereby opens his road to public use, there is a partial taking, as a use that was once absolute is now made conditional.[19] So too with water rights.

15. See, e.g., Wickard v. Filburn, 317 U.S. 111 (1942).
16. United States v. Twin City Power Co., 350 U.S. 222, 224 (1956).
17. Id. at 224–225.
18. 444 U.S. 164 (1979).
19. The problem of general laws is further discussed in connection with the defense of assumption of risk. See Chapter 11.

In one sense, *Kaiser Aetna* is unique because it concerns the entitlements over what was in its inception within the exclusive possession and control of a single individual. Most cases involving water rights are more difficult, because the question is who has what entitlements with respect to, say, a river, which in any view is held by many persons in common. The precise nature of the competing claims in water is often difficult to determine because of the persistent tension between three separate theories of water rights: the natural flow theory, the reasonable use theory, and the prior appropriation theory.[20] The differences among the theories, however, have been suppressed in the decided cases, as the paramount navigation servitude has swept everything aside.

Even on a sounder view, the differences among these theories are rarely material. The competing theories of property rights in water are chiefly addressed to the rights as between riparians to divert water for their own use. No theory ever allowed private owners to block or hinder navigation on public waters. The central source of litigation in the eminent domain case has been quite the opposite: to what extent can the government rely on its navigation servitude in order to abridge upon private rights, not only of diversion, but also of access and use? In contrast to cases like *Kaiser Aetna,* one can assume that some easement for the benefit of the public at large does exist, whether by long-standing custom or by some more overtly utilitarian view.

The question, therefore, within both the private law and the eminent domain context is, what is the scope of the navigation easement so created? Here it is instructive to revert to a traditional maxim of water law: *aqua currit quo aqua currere debit*—water ought to flow where in fact it flows. An approach of this sort appears to leap in a single bound the enormous chasm between "is" and "ought" and to embrace a teleologi-

---

20. The first two of these theories are riparian in the sense that ownership of the land carries some interest in the water that passes through it. The theories differ concerning the amount of water that any riparian can withdraw for profitable use. Only minor diversions for domestic purposes are permitted on the natural flow theory, while greater diversions for agriculture and manufacturing, with some harm to neighbors, are permitted under a reasonable use theory. The prior appropriation theory works on very different grounds; ownership of a future water flow is acquired by appropriation of the flow and is not a necessary consequence of ownership of the banks. Each of these theories contains enormous internal complexities, which are admirably set out in Joseph Sax, *Water Law, Planning and Policy* 459–467 (1968). For an exploration of the economic weaknesses of the three systems, see Mason Gaffney, "Economic Aspects of Water Resource Policy," 28 *Am. J. Econ. & Soc.* 131 (1969). For my views, see Richard A. Epstein, "Why Restrain Alienation?" 85 *Colum. L. Rev.* 000,000 (1985).

cal view of inanimate objects, not to mention ecological systems, that is quite out of character with today's tempered skepticism. But there is in fact good reason to recognize the practical strengths of the maxim, even if it does not capture an ultimate truth. That the rule bridges the gap between is and ought is hardly a demerit, for every rule of entitlement so functions. Better there be a connection between is and ought than no connection between ought and anything of interest in the external world. For dealing with the eminent domain clause, it is surely preferable to recognize a system of rights already in place than to invent one to replace it.

The parallels between water law and the first-possession rule with respect to land are instructive. One hidden strength of the rule is that it gives a baseline for analysis that provides a clear foundation for future voluntary transactions and is largely impervious to political manipulation. The relative clarity and certainty that come out of this rule will apply to all types of waterways, letting us avoid the temptation to tailor ad hoc rules once a dispute arises.

Using the natural condition of the water as the baseline of entitlements means that no individual is charged with the affirmative duty of changing the situation for the benefit of others. By the same token, no individual may change the flow in ways that prevent others from using or gaining access to the waters in question. By our major premise the state is still in no better position than the public it represents. This view solidifies the *status quo ante,* but it does not create any partisan advantages between persons or between the government and persons, for all rights and duties run in both directions. Nor does it prevent state-coerced changes that satisfy the ordinary requirements of the eminent domain clause.

Judged by these standards, the government can without compensation enjoin activities by riparians that reduce the ease of passage along navigable rivers, much as it can remove blockages—piers, dams, mills, or whatever—placed along public waterways. But by the same token it cannot cut off use of or access to waters in their original condition unless prima facie it is prepared to compensate those individuals whose rights it has taken. To be sure, this watery baseline leaves some unavoidable gray area that is avoided by recognizing complete and paramount rights in the government. It is, for example, unclear whether government actions to prevent the deterioration of waterways under normal conditions requires compensation, on the ground that routine maintenance is only a succession of small permanent improvements.

Yet the Supreme Court has missed the easy cases, not the hard ones.

One unfortunate line of cases concerns the use of water for power generation, which is made possible when water falls from a higher to a lower level. In keeping with the general theory here, any riparian should be able, so long as he does not interfere with the preexisting flow of water, to take advantage of the height differential to generate power for his own use and benefit. Indeed, in the private context, creating obstacles along the river that remove or limit the height differential are actionable wrongs remediable with damages and injunctions. The public parallel arises when the government has built dams or completed other water reclamation projects that have backed up tail waters to the level of head waters. In the first of the major cases, *United States v. Chandler-Dunbar Water Power Co.*,[21] the Supreme Court held that the government was not required to pay compensation when it raised the levels of waters in a navigable river and thereby rendered inoperable the claimant's power plant that was located on the navigable portion of the river. The case seems clearly wrong, because the government did not seek only to protect the rights in flow it already enjoyed but to expand them beyond their natural contours. *Chandler-Dunbar* was distinguished in *United States v. Cress*,[22] which ordered compensation when the government raised the level of water on a navigable river to the mean high water mark, thus interfering with a mill on a nonnavigable portion of the river. The third case was *Willow River Power*, where the court did not trouble itself to say whether the plaintiff's plant was located on navigable or nonnavigable waters: it seems that the plant was located by the junction of two rivers; with part of the tail waters in navigable waters and part in nonnavigable. Brushing the details aside, the Court in *Willow River Power* held that as precedent *Cress* "must be confined to the facts there disclosed."[23] Again, any independent account of water rights condemns this decision as erroneous.

Lest it be thought that these decisions rest upon some special mystery associated with power generation, the "navigation servitude" has been applied in decided cases to destroy, whether by flooding[24] or by specific government order for removal or alteration,[25] perfectly ordinary property interests, such as improvements constructed between the high and low water marks. The decisions powerfully illustrate the unaccept-

21. 229 U.S. 53 (1913).
22. 243 U.S. 316 (1917).
23. 324 U.S. 499 at 507 (1945).
24. United States v. Chicago, M., St. P. & P. R.R., 312 U.S. 592 (1941).
25. Greenleaf Lumber Co. v. Garrison, 237 U.S. 251 (1915); Union Bridge Co. v. United States 204 U.S. 364 (1907).

able tendency to create two sets of property rules in eminent domain cases, one for ordinary people and one that yields unprincipled advantages to the government.

The story is similar for those cases which involve access from the shore to navigable waters. Here it is well established in private law that individual riparians cannot be denied access across their lands to flowing waters, whether navigable or not. Any blocking or impeding of access by a private property, whether or not a riparian, becomes actionable by the owner, even if he can obtain access to the river from other points open to the general public.[26] These results are no different from those which allow an owner abutting on the highway an action against a third party who blocks his access to the road.[27] Given the constant metaphor of the navigable river as a water highway, the same principles should be applied against the government, but a uniform line of cases starting with *Scranton v. Wheeler*[28] have reached the opposite conclusion that all access rights, total and partial, including the worth of riparian land as a "port site," are subordinate to the navigation easement.[29] The decisions are so clearly wrong under any sensible view of the original entitlements between riparians, on the one hand, and the public at large represented by the government, on the other, that they require no further comment.

It does not follow, however, that compensation should be awarded in all navigation easement cases, given the defensive rights in the public at large. Thus *United States v. Rio Grande Dam & Irrig. Co.*[30] upheld the power

26. See, for example, Rose v. Groves, 5 M. & G. 613, 134 Eng. Rep. 705 (1843); Lyon v. Fishmongers' Co., 1 A.C. 662 (1876).

27. See, for example, Rose v. State, 19 Cal. 2d 713, 123 P. 2d 505 (1942). One question is why that easement of access might arise, and the simplest answer is that it is in the joint interest of the parties ex ante. By granting the access to the private parties, the state both increases the benefit of the roads it creates and reduces the loss sustained by (and hence the compensation payable to) the landowner. The access right is very old and has been recognized as the basis of a private right of action, sounding in nuisance, since at least 1535. Anon. Y.B. Mich. 27 Hen. 8, f. 27, pl. 10 (1535). On access, generally, see Stoebuck, supra note 13.

28. 179 U.S. 141 (1900). See also United States v. Rands, 389 U.S. 121 (1967).

29. On port sites, see 389 U.S. 121. For loss of access to major rivers, see United States v. Commodore Park Inc., 324 U.S. 386 (1945), a case which also denied compensation for the diminished use of land between the low and the high water mark and for the "semi-stagnant" waters created when free flowage was blocked by government improvements. Needless to say, allowing the government to disregard its external harms leads to improvements that, on balance, should never be made.

30. 174 U.S. 690 (1899).

of the United States to enjoin construction of an irrigation project not on the river that threatened the river itself. This case, unlike all the others considered, is correct, because here it was the government, not the private party, who sought to respect the *status quo ante* which delineates the original rights. As with the land-based cases, the principle which begins from natural conditions can be applied neutrally in ways that the bare assertion of a paramount state interest cannot.

7 Rights of Disposition and Contract

Interference with Prospective Advantage

This chapter completes the examination of partial takings by looking at cases where the incidents of possession and use are left untouched while the incident of disposition is taken (or destroyed) in whole or in part. The parity between the state and the private defendant can be maintained as before. If the plaintiff owns certain property, then it is wrongful for any private defendant (by the use of force or the threat thereof) to hinder, block, or condition its transfer to a third party, because that constitutes an interference with prospective advantage, long recognized as a private tort.[1] The right of disposition is a property right, in the same degree and manner as the right to exclusive possession. What a plaintiff demands is noninterference by the rest of the world in his dealings with any third party, X. This claim in no way depends upon a contract with X; at stake is the right to contract with X, which is good against the world. Nor is the owner's claim a "mere" tort right, for as the earlier discussion of conversion and destruction shows, torts themselves are a subclass of takings.

By the major Lockean premise, the state stands in no better position. Let the state impose restrictions or conditions upon the right of disposition, let it block or hinder sale or lease or mortgage, then it too has taken

1. See, e.g., Keeble v. Hickeringill, 11 East 574, 103 Eng. Rep. 1127 (Q.B. 1809). Tarleton v. McGawley, Peake N. P. 205, 170 Eng. Rep. 153 (K.B. 1793). For a general discussion, see Richard A. Epstein, "Intentional Harms," 4 *J. Legal Stud.* 391, 423–442 (1975).

property for which compensation is prima facie required.[2] The nature of the restriction and the conditions associated with it may determine the appropriate level of damages, and the restriction in question may perhaps be justified. But prima facie the situation is indistinguishable from one in which the affected property has been taken outright and returned subject to limitations upon its future disposition: a complete taking with partial compensation.

The analysis of the right of disposition thus far parallels that of possession and use. In one important respect, however, alienation differs from those incidents. Because the interest in alienation is *relational*, it is necessary to examine how government limitations upon it affect both potential sellers (that is, present owners) and potential *purchasers* of the property, while recognizing throughout that the government's rights can never rise above those of the private individuals it represents. Any restriction that in form restricts only disposition by the owner perforce limits the rights of others to acquire property in exchange for their cash, property, and perhaps labor.[3] The takings clause reaches *both* the buyer and the seller, not just the seller. This is not to say that the purchaser's position is identical to the seller's, for constitutional differences do emerge on the separate issue of implicit in-kind compensation.[4]

In sharp contrast to this basic theory, the judicial response to the right of disposition is marked by a general hostility, tempered only by occasional protection of the independent status of the right of disposition—usually the seller's side. This chapter considers three kinds of cases. The first, and easiest, involves government restrictions upon the power to sell private property. The second involves the condemnation of leasehold interests which the tenant holds with the expectation, but not the right, of renewal. The third involves the treatment of goodwill in cases where the aggrieved owner is not dispossessed. Thereafter I discuss the inter-

2. For a similarly broad definition of impairment of contracts, as that phrase is used in art. I, § 10, cl. 1, see the statement of Justice Washington in Green v. Biddle: "Any deviation from its terms, by postponing or accelerating the period of performance which it prescribes, imposing conditions not expressed in the contract, or dispensing with the performance of those which are, however minute, or apparently immaterial, in their effect upon the contract of the parties, impairs its obligation." 21 U.S. (8 Wheat.) 1, 84 (1823).

3. Note that there is some doubt whether personal labor, as opposed to the fruits thereof, is covered by the eminent domain clause; see discussion in Chapter 2. The parallel concern does not arise with respect to the contracts clause, as the language "impairing the obligation of contracts" covers both classes of contracts, without apparent limitation of subject matter.

4. See Chapter 14.

ference of rights under existing contracts, as distinguished from the interference with prospective advantage.

Prohibitions on the Right to Sell

In *Andrus v. Allard*[5] the appellees challenged the regulations under the Eagle Protection Act[6] insofar as they prohibited the sale of any objects which contained eagle feathers, even those from birds which were legally acquired before the government prohibition. The regulations did not prohibit all forms of disposition of the property in question, as "it is crucial that appellees retain the rights to possess and transport their property, and to denote or devise the protected birds."[7] On its facts the case is a simple one. The right of sale is part (perhaps the most valuable part) of the right of disposition. The loss of this right is not merely a diminution in value but is the deprivation of a property right, a partial taking for which compensation is prima facie required. To deflect this simple conclusion, the Supreme Court resorted to its usual arguments. It noted first that "the denial of one traditional property right does not always amount to a taking. At least where an owner possesses a full 'bundle' of property rights, the destruction of one 'strand' of the bundle is not a taking because the aggregate must be viewed in its entirety."[8] But this is inconsistent with the court's oft-stated, and correct, premise that partial takings are covered by the eminent domain clause. The statement also looks to what the owner has retained, when the question is always what he has lost; retention of certain, or even all, beneficial uses are material only to finding the right measure of damages once the taking is established.

Matters are not advanced by urging that compensation should be denied because the estimation of lost profits is clouded in uncertainty. The best estimate of value is surely not zero, and the loss of market value is no more difficult to estimate here than are lost profits in the wide range of contract and tort cases at common law, in which they are routinely allowed. The government cannot prevail simply by denying that the taking has occurred. Whatever difficulties the case presents are with the police power, since the prohibition on the sale of eagle feathers presently owned might be intended to protect feathers on eagles in the public do-

5. 444 U.S. 51 (1979).
6. 54 Stat. 250, § 1 (1940) (codified as amended at 16 U.S.C. § 668(a) [1982]).
7. 444 U.S. at 66.
8. Id. at 65–66.

main, for example by licensing eagle feathers that are already in private hands.[9]

Leasehold Renewals

The question of disposition also arises with leasehold renewals. In the simplest case the tenant has an option to renew from his landlord upon stated terms. As the option is at least a contract right, if not an equitable interest in land enforceable by specific performance, the courts have not had any difficulty in awarding compensation to the tenant for its loss when the land is taken outright. The more difficult and interesting question arises when there is only the expectation of renewal, usually supported by past practice, built into the value of the tenant's lease. An assignee may well pay a price that reflects the value and probability of renewal at the end of the term. Indeed, the expectation may in fact have a substantial value to the tenant even if the landlord will renew only to this tenant: the value in use can be positive, even if the value in exchange is zero. The dominant judicial rule, however, is that the tenant's expectation of renewal is *not* a form of private property that can be taken only with compensation. The most often quoted statement of the rule is that of Holmes in *Emery v. Boston Terminal Co.*:[10]

> Changeable intentions are not an interest in land, and although no doubt such intentions may have added practically to the value of the petitioners' holding, they could not be taken into account in determining what the respondent should pay. They added nothing to the tenants' legal rights, and legal rights are all that must be paid for. Even if such intentions added to the saleable value of the lease, the addition would represent a speculation on a chance, not a legal right.

The insistence that only legal rights must be paid for is surely correct, but they can be found on both sides of the transaction. A third party who takes the land or by lesser means blocks the renewal commits a tort against both landlord and tenant. That action prejudices the *rights* of the tenant to acquire, as well as the rights of the landlord to dispose: it is therefore actionable at the instance of both. The expectation of a suc-

9. See, for the suggestion, Susan Rose Ackerman, "Inalienability and the Theory of Property Rights" 85 *Colum. L Rev.* (1985).
10. 178 Mass. 172, 185, 59 N.E. 763, 765 (1901).

cessful renewal works to the benefit of both lessor and lessee, and therefore the value of their joint right to renew should be reflected in any enhanced compensation award, to be divided between landlord and tenant in accordance with their interest.

The problem assumes a new dimension when the tenant owns certain property, for example, improvements or trade fixtures, which when not taken by the government have no value except in use on the condemned land. In *Almota Farmers Elevator & Warehouse Co. v. United States*,[11] the tenant plaintiff had for about forty-eight years occupied land under a series of leases obtained from the landlord, the operator of the adjacent railroad. When the government condemned the land, the current lease had seven and a half years to run but contained no option for further renewals. While in possession, the tenant had constructed upon the real estate certain improvements whose expected useful life was far in excess of seven and a half years. Owing to their customized nature, the improvements had little salvage value separate from the premises. The government conceded that compensation was owing for the leasehold, including the value of the improvements for the remaining years of the lease. The Supreme Court, despite its general rule of no compensation for "any additional value based on the expectation that the lease might be renewed,"[12] included in the award the market value of the renewal rights in setting the compensation payable for the leasehold interest. The court then sought to distinguish *Almota* from the earlier case of *United States v. Petty Motor Co.*,[13] which on the strength of *Emery* had denied compensation for the expectation of renewal of the ordinary commercial lease. It noted that in *Petty Motor*, "the Court was not dealing with the fair market value of improvements. Unlike *Petty Motor*, there is no question here of creating a legally cognizable value where none existed, or of compensating a mere incorporeal expectation. The petitioner here has constructed the improvements and seeks only their fair market value."[14]

This purported distinction will not do, as it misperceives the law of future interests. Conceptually the improvements under the lease can be divided into two separate assets; the term of years owned by the tenant is distinct from the reversion in the same thing owned by the landlord, even if all the costs of erecting the improvement were borne solely by the ten-

11. 409 U.S. 470 (1973).
12. Id. at 471.
13. 327 U.S. 372 (1946).
14. 409 U.S. at 476.

ant.[15] Compensation to the tenant can never be for an interest owned by the landlord. The tenant cannot be compensated, therefore, for the landlord's reversion in the improvement, even if depreciable, any more than for the landlord's reversion in the land. The tenant can be paid only for expectation of renewal in the improvements, the very ground earlier rejected in *Emery* and *Petty Motor.* The valuable and customized improvements are (along with the prior course of dealing) only evidence that the renewal would very likely have taken place, a point of great importance, but only on the valuation of the plaintiff's rights.

The compensation tendered does not depend upon the tenant's right of being in possession of the property but upon the independent right of disposition. Suppose that just before the initiation of condemnation proceedings, the plaintiff had constructed $100,000 worth of customized equipment to be installed on the condemned land. On the analysis given in *Almota*, its value is noncompensable, even for the duration of the lease, because the improvement in question had not yet been attached to the land. But that result is indefensible. True, the case is complicated because the available uses left open to the tenant are in principle greater than those that remain after the machinery is annexed to the real estate. Yet here the customized nature of the equipment may give it a salvage value, or next best use, of say $15,000. To take into account the (unlikely) possibility of nonrenewal at the expiration of term, some portion of the $85,000 should not be recovered, but it is wholly improper for the tenant to bear the full loss. Although the government has taken only one limited incident out of the plaintiff's bag of ownership, it has taken the one incident that matters. The case against the government remains one of interference with prospective advantage, whether or not annexation has taken place. The takings language of the eminent domain clause reaches this transaction, even if the government insists that the owner remain, or allows him to remain, in possession of his customized equipment.

We can go further. Even if the customized machinery was made by a party never in possession, the same result should apply. The owner of the machinery takes by agreement the risk that the landowner will not extend the favorable lease, but he does not assume the risk of interference by an external force in an advantageous relationship that he wishes to establish. Again the award will be reduced to reflect the greater risk of contracting failure and the larger set of possibilities available for mitiga-

15. See, e.g., Helvering v. Bruun, 309 U.S. 461 (1940). See also Internal Revenue Code § 109 (1984).

tion. But the very fact that one can speak of ways to reduce the compensation award indicates why it is required in principle. In all instances interference with prospective advantage by the use of force is as actionable against the government as it is against all private parties.

Goodwill

Interference with an advantageous relationship is important not only where the two parties have had equal stakes in ongoing business transactions. It is also important for the general question of business goodwill—previously discussed in connection with consequential damages for ordinary takings—where the value of the right of disposition is asymmetrical: of great importance to a single seller and of minor importance to a legion of possible buyers. At the outset, the definition of goodwill rightly directs our attention to the values "beyond the mere value of the capital, stock, funds or property employed therein, in consequence of the general public patronage and encouragement which it receives from constant or habitual customers, on account of its local position or common celebrity, or reputation for skill or affluence, or punctuality, or from other accidental circumstances or necessities. "[16]

This general discussion only sets out the rights vested in the holder of goodwill. Yet as all rights have their correlative duties, it is necessary to specify the actions by other persons that constitute an actionable interference with that goodwill. Here the reification of "goodwill" becomes both uncritical and misleading if it is read to render actionable *any* activities that diminish its value. In fact, goodwill is entitled only to the *limited* protection accorded all other property interests: protection from loss attributable to the defendant's taking. As dispossession is by definition not a possible form of government wrong, the taking occurs by forms of conduct that violate the owner's rights in intangible assets. As the previous analysis showed, a prohibition against takings necessarily entails a prohibition against the use of force directed against the right of disposition as a separate incident of ownership, as the common law actions dealing with economic loss reveal.

There are, of course, many situations where goodwill can be destroyed even though the owner is left in possession of land and personal property. A neighbor barricades the entrance to the owner's business without trespassing upon his land. Where interference takes this form, it is necessary to distinguish between the position of the single owner (usually the

16. Joseph Story, *Partnership* § 99 (7th ed. Wharton 1881).

seller) and the large number of persons (usually buyers) who can no longer do business with him. For each buyer the economic losses sustained are the expected gains from contracting with the barricaded owner. Typically these are small. Still the opportunities for mitigation by each buyer is great, as there are many other sources of supply. Finally, the administrative costs needed to calculate the proper level of compensation is high, especially in relation to the size of the loss. Rectification of the loss through the legal system seems intolerable for these practical reasons, even if the prima facie taking by the neighbor is conceded. Yet they are of little moment when a third party uses force to blockade an owner who retains unchallenged possession and use. The losses are concentrated upon a single individual; these losses will be large and may not be subject to mitigation. The taking of the right of disposition is therefore no longer overwhelmed by practical considerations. That right should be protected, as the normative theory clearly demands, regardless of what is done with the small claims brought by a multiplicity of disappointed prospective contracting partners.[17]

From what has been said, it might be supposed that the "takings" language is infinitely malleable, such that every conceivable government action can be transformed effortlessly into a compensable taking. The theory developed here, however, also places strong, indeed *absolute,* constraints against the proliferation of new causes of action. While goodwill is prima facie protected against loss by force, its diminution or destruction *is* in fact *damnum absque iniuria*—harm without legal injury—when neither of those forbidden means are employed. Where goodwill is lost when customers switch patronage because the owner's performance has slipped or because his competitors have outdone him or because tastes have changed, then the plaintiff, no matter how great the financial loss, does not have even a prima facie claim for compensation. As there is no invasion of rights, there is no reason even to reach the question whether administrative reasons preclude a recovery that should otherwise be allowed in principle. In the private context the voluntary choices of third parties generated the plaintiff's loss, and these cannot be attributed to any wrongful conduct of the defendant who has, after all, only *expanded* the set of legitimate alternatives open to them.[18] The present customers of the owner now have an additional party with whom they can do business. The economic loss of goodwill as such, then, is *never* the touchstone of actionability. It is the use of a forbidden mean—force—that is always

17. See Chapter 17.
18. See Epstein, supra note 1, at 391.

decisive on the normative question of entitlement, be it against a private defendant or against the state.

The issue also has a constitutional dimension. The previous case of *Community Redevelopment Agency of Los Angeles v. Abrams*[19] dealt with a claimant dispossessed by an urban renewal program, whose claim for the loss of goodwill should have been compensable under the eminent domain clause. If the arguments here are correct, then his loss of goodwill would remain compensable even if he had been left in undisturbed possession of his pharmacy while his customers were removed by force from the neighborhood. Surely there is a compensable taking if the pharmacy is walled off by the state so that none can enter. How can it be different if, instead of erecting a wall, the state removes all the customers from their homes? There may be some long-term benefits to urban renewal projects, but it is highly unlikely that (when discounted to present value) they will even begin to offset the losses to the owner.

The intellectual case for compensation of goodwill generally enjoys much scholarly support.[20] Nonetheless, the dominant judicial response, in both the nineteenth and the twentieth century, has been to deny compensation on the ground that the destruction of goodwill is not the taking of "property" for constitutional purposes, whatever its status under the private law. Again it is Holmes who has given voice to the dominant sentiment in his oft-quoted passage in *Sawyer v. Commonwealth*:[21]

It generally has been assumed, we think, that injury to a business is not an appropriation of property which must be paid for. There are many serious pecuniary injuries which may be inflicted without compensation. It would be impracticable to forbid all laws which might result in such damage, unless they provided a *quid pro quo*. No doubt a business may be property in a broad sense of the word, and property of great value. If may be assumed for the purposes of this case that there might be such a taking of it as required compensation. But a business is less tangible in nature and more uncertain in its vicissitudes than the rights which the Constitution undertakes absolutely to protect. It seems to us, in like manner, that the diminution of its value is a vaguer injury than the taking or appropriation with which the Constitution deals. A business might be

19. See Chapter 4.

20. See, e.g., Gideon Kanner, "When Is 'Property' Not 'Property Itself': A Critical Examination of the Bases of Denial of Compensation for the Loss of Goodwill in Eminent Domain," 6 *Cal. W. L. Rev.* 57 (1969).

21. 182 Mass. 245, 247, 65 N.E. 52, 53 (1902).

destroyed by the construction of a more popular street into which travel was diverted, as well as by competition, but there would be as little claim in one case as in the other. It seems to us that the case stands no differently when the business is destroyed by taking the land on which it was carried on, except so far as it may have enhanced the value of the land.

Nonetheless this influential passage misstates the problem. It is simply incorrect to assume that the protection of business goodwill against forcible interference requires, or even suggests, that compensation be awarded for the "construction of a more popular street into which traffic was diverted, as well as by competition." This analogy misconceives the degree of protection accorded goodwill under the private law and then extends that distorted view to defeat the proper constitutional result. Neither new roads nor government competition involve the use of force or misrepresentation to limit the plaintiff's prospective relationships with third parties. These losses are not compensable by private defendants; nor, by the same token, are they compensable by the government. In contrast, the situation is wholly different when an entire neighborhood is uprooted to make way for redevelopment, for the state's use of force is too obvious and too persuasive to be denied, as the Poletown case so vividly shows.[22]

There is also nothing to the argument that goodwill consists of some "vaguer" right that is unworthy of the protection given to private property, which is protected. It is settled that partial takings are subject to the same constitutional protection as total ones. Far from being vague, goodwill is something that can be owned, transferred, protected against interference by (at the very least) deliberate force and misrepresentation by third parties, and, of course, taxed.[23] Goodwill can, moreover, be valued in accordance with standard practices. What possible warrant is there then for denying it the status of private property under the Constitution? The California Supreme Court in *Abrams* thought *Sawyer* was part of the answer; the rest was that goodwill was not property *"in a constitutional sense."*[24] But no explanation is given as to why the constitutional

22. Poletown Neighborhood Council v. City of Detroit, 410 Mich. 616, 304 N.W.2d 455 (1981), referred to in Chapter 4.
23. For example, under California law goodwill may be owned, Cal. [Civ.] Code §655 (West 1982); transferred, Cal. [Bus. & Prof.] Code §14102 (West 1964); and taxed, Cal. Const. Art. 13, § 1. Common law tort remedies are also generally available. For a forceful development of the point, see Kanner, supra note 20, at 65–68.
24. 15 Cal.3d at 819, 543 P.2d at 909, 126 Cal. Rptr. at 480.

sense should differ from the ordinary sense, any more than it does for land, shares, or trade secrets.[25] To justify banishing goodwill from constitutional grace, a court must give some independent normative account of private property which explains why, and how, it is permissible to import into the Constitution meanings wholly at variance with both ordinary and legal conceptions. No rival conception of goodwill was offered in *Sawyer* or *Abrams;* none is available in principle. The practical problems of compensation must be worked out within the framework of the clause, not on the assumption that the eminent domain clause is inapplicable.

The case for extending the constitutional protection of goodwill is only reinforced by examining those proposals to afford it limited protection as a matter of legislative grace. Here the original theoretical framework was provided by Frank Michelman, who advocated a greater role for legislative intervention on precisely this question.[26] Michelman's key assumption was that a "gap" exists in legal doctrine, so that any cash compensation awarded to displaced persons should not be treated as a mere legislative "gift" but rather as a discharge of an "imperfect" obligation that is morally appealing but not constitutionally imposed. To the extent that courts are faced with the hard choice between full compensation and no compensation, Michelman's argument continued, they will opt for the latter. Therefore it is better to permit legislation to split the difference by sanctioning partial awards.

The Michelman analysis bore judicial fruit in *Abrams.* There the California Supreme Court denied the owner's claim for loss of goodwill in part because California legislation—legislation not yet in force when the plaintiff's land was condemned—provided limited compensation to $10,000 per claim where the loss of goodwill stemmed from the dispossession from real property and where the owner was unable to take reasonable steps in mitigation.

The statute bristles with ironies. It directs (with the burden of proof on the claimant) a detailed inquiry into mitigation of damages, an inquiry

25. In Ruckelshaus v. Monsanto Co., 104 S.Ct. 2862 (1984), the court adopted the Restatement definition of trade secrets for constitutional purposes. No other account could work. "The Restatement defines a trade secret as 'any formula, pattern, device or compilation of information which is used in one's business, and which gives him an opportunity to obtain an advantage over competitors who do not know or use it.'" Id. at 2872–2873, citing *Restatement (Second) of Torts* §757, comment b (1977).

26. Frank I. Michelman, "Property, Utility, and Fairness: Comments on the Ethical Foundations of 'Just Compensation' Law," 80 *Harv. L. Rev.* 1165, 1245–1258 (1967).

which courts have said to be intolerable as a constitutional matter. Yet it provides no more guidance on the mitigation issue than the identical constitutional rule. The statute's virtues stem not from its substantive rules but from the procedures, such as arbitration, used to set compensation. But these procedures are consistent with the eminent domain clause, which requires just compensation, and not the judicial forum.[27]

In sustaining the statute, the California court initially held that the statute was to be evaluated under a "good faith standard." The question, however, is not of criminal responsibility or official immunity. It is of government compensation for property taken. No good faith standard is sufficient to protect the government from the obligation to compensate in full when it has taken land for a post office; none should protect it when goodwill is taken to build a housing project. The good faith standard, and the judicial discretion it entails, rests on a major misconception of the nature and source of the state obligation. Compensation for the destruction of goodwill does not owe its force solely to legislative benevolence or to widely shared but uninformed intuitions of fairness. It is the necessary outgrowth of a comprehensive theory of private property. That institution contains no gaps in the fabric of rights. For things reduced to ownership, the rules of property uniquely specify the rights of all persons for all times. The rights so specified are internally consistent, so when all external things are claimed under a rule of first possession, each has one and only one owner. There are no residual sticks in the bundle that move between the private and public domain at legislative whim.

What constitutes a taking of private property is a question that admits to a rigid logical answer, so it is always possible to judge which judicial decisions are clearly right or clearly wrong. On this question (as opposed to the proper means of enforcing the police power) there is simply no room for intellectual disagreement or for judicial deference to the legislature. Once private property is taken, if there is no police power justification, compensation must be provided. As is stated in *Monongahela Navigation Co. v. United States:*

[T]he legislature may determine what private property is needed for public purposes—that is a question of a political and legislative

27. The only issues that could arise are those if the procedures in question are heavily biased to the government, so that the value of the expected remedy is less than what is called for by the full vindication of the right. But cheapness of procedure is not the same as bias. See Chapter 4 for a discussion of the parallel issues under the Tucker Act.

character; but when the taking has been ordered, then the question of compensation is judicial. It does not rest with the public, taking the property through Congress or the legislature, its representative, to say what compensation shall be paid, or even what shall be the rule of compensation. The Constitution has declared that just compensation shall be paid, and the ascertainment of that is a judicial inquiry.[28]

By this standard, the compensation scheme under the California goodwill statute is wholly defective. It gives no principled reason why the loss of goodwill is compensable only when coupled with dispossession. More crucially, not even a good faith standard could excuse the fixed upper limit upon compensation, regardless of the circumstances of the case. No private tort defendant could announce in advance that his liability to strangers will be limited to a fixed amount, be it $10,000 or $1,000,000. Neither can the state.

Taking by Misrepresentation

I now leave cases where the government interferes with the prospective advantage by the use of force to address the legal issues that arise in the rare cases where that same end is achieved by government misrepresentation. Interference by misrepresentation with the right of disposition is typified by the tort of defamation. In dealing with defamation, it is often asked why it is a tort at all, let alone one whose rules—at least before the epic decision in *New York Times v. Sullivan*[29]—are weighted heavily in favor of the plaintiff. The answer to this question comes in two parts. First, the injured plaintiff has a right—a property right good against the world—to enter into advantageous relationships with other individuals, to sell, for example, his goods or services. Second, this right is destroyed or damaged by illicit means when the defendant misrepresents the true state of affairs to a third party, who then chooses not to do business with the plaintiff. The tort of slander of title illustrates the necessary connection between defamation and private property: the defendant challenges the title of the plaintiff, with the result that the property cannot be sold to an otherwise willing buyer.

The traditional strictness of liability in defamation, moreover, is not

28. 148 U.S. 312, 327 (1893). Parallel arguments are raised and discussed in connection with workers' compensation laws in Chapter 16.
29. 376 U.S. 254 (1964).

an unprincipled anomaly, but depends critically upon the exposed position of the plaintiff.[30] Not being part of the original communication between the defendant and the third party, he did not assume the risk of any misrepresentation; more important, he is often powerless to protect himself against the misrepresentation, especially if he does not know that the defendant has spoken to the third party. In private law we can thus trace a clear continuity from conversion to property destruction to interference with prospective advantage to defamation, be it of title, credit, or reputation.

This account of defamation is directly relevant to the law of eminent domain, as *Paul v. Davis*[31] suggests. The plaintiff brought a Section 1983 action against a local sheriff, claiming the defendant had defamed him by referring falsely to him in several newspaper statements as an "active shoplifter." The court first assumed that the plaintiff had a state law remedy for defamation. It thereafter considered the more difficult question of whether there was an independent ground for federal relief because the interest in reputation was a "liberty or property" interest protected under the Fourteenth Amendment, which it appeared to deny,[32] thereby barring the plaintiff's Section 1983 claim.

30. See, on strict liability, E. Hulton & Co. v. Jones (1910) A.C. 20 [H.L.E.]. The prima facie case is hemmed in, of course, with a large number of complex privileges, none of which involves the nonnegligence of the defendant. See William L. Prosser, *Handbook of the Law of Torts* 776–801 (4th ed. 1971). The parallel development of defamation and this analysis of eminent domain should be clear enough.

31. 424 U.S. 693 (1976).

32. There are hints of this approach in *Paul:* "Kentucky law does not extend to [Davis] any legal guarantee of present enjoyment of reputation which has been altered as a result of [Paul's] actions . . . And any harm or injury to that interest . . . does not result in a deprivation of any 'liberty' or 'property' recognized by state or federal law, nor has it worked any change of respondent's status as theretofore recognized under the State's laws. For these reasons we hold that the interest in reputation asserted in this case is neither 'liberty' nor 'property' guaranteed against state deprivation without due process of law." 424 U.S. 693, at 711–712. The quoted passage contains a non sequitur. The first two sentences emphasize that the private remedy precludes the claim that liberty or property has been taken without compensation. Yet the last sentence goes beyond that and indicates that reputation is not liberty or property at all, so the question of its state law protection becomes immaterial to constitutional issues. On this last point, the dissent by Brennan, J., seems persuasive in its assertion that the court's "implication . . . that the existence *vel non* of a state remedy—for example a cause of action for defamation—is relevant to the determination whether there is a cause of action under § 1983, is wholly unfounded." Id. at 715.

Paul v. Davis has been frequently criticized by commentators for the narrow interpretation of the terms "liberty" and "property" in the due process clause of the Fourteenth Amendment.[33] The eminent domain clause is usually not mentioned in the analysis. Yet at the root of the critical discontent is, quite simply, the perception that the situation is no different from one in which the state takes or damages the plaintiff's car. The sentiment is analytically compelled, given the necessary progression from conversion to trespass to interference with prospective advantage to defamation. Defamation by state officials *is* a taking of private property under the law, one that may be justified, perhaps on grounds of official immunity, or compensated by private right of action under state law; but it is a taking nonetheless. *Paul v. Davis,* therefore, may be correct if the remedy at state law was adequate, a matter beyond the scope of this inquiry. But in any event the adequacy of the state remedy is a question that has to be tested against the federal constitutional requirement, given the nexus between that question and the issue of just compensation.

Interference with Contract Rights

The previous sections have demonstrated how the taking of private property reaches government interference with prospective advantage by use of force and misrepresentation. It follows almost *a fortiori,* that contract rights created by a voluntary exchange are protected by the eminent domain clause. The original rights of disposition cannot be protected if the fruits of trade are left exposed to government predation. It is just as tortious to use force or misrepresentation to prevent the performance of a contract once formed as it is to prevent the formation of a contract. An impressive line of cases holds that contract rights are covered by the eminent domain clause.[34]

To make the discussion more concrete, consider a bilateral contract for the sale of goods. Assume that the government demands from the buyer an assignment of his rights against the seller. In principle, the amount of compensation owing for this transfer of rights is the value to the buyer of the seller's performance—the expectation measure. The

33. See Henry Monaghan, "Of 'Liberty' and 'Property,' " 62 *Cornell L. Rev.* 405, 409–410 (1977).

34. See, e.g., Contributors to Pa. Hosp. v. City of Philadelphia, 245 U.S. 20 (1917); Long Island Water Supply Co. v. Brooklyn, 166 U.S. 685 (1897). For a general discussion, see William B. Stoebuck, *Nontrepassory Takings in Eminent Domain* 132–133 (1977).

buyer's costs—represented by the price paid for the goods—are irrelevant here, as in any other eminent domain context: when a house is condemned, its original cost is not the proper measure of compensation. If the contract was a losing one for the buyer, then the state takeover does not permit him to recoup his original costs. If the contract was a profitable one, the state should not be entitled to pocket all his profits, leaving the buyer as though he had never entered the transaction in the first place. As ever, it is the value of what is taken—the right to the seller's performance—not what is retained that determines the measure of compensation.

These contract cases can be complicated in a number of different ways. The interference by force with performance may be partial rather than total, as when performance is allowed to go forward subject to government-imposed restrictions. But the terms of the restrictions mark only a variation upon the basic theme; they do not take the case out of the eminent domain clause. The broad account of what constitutes an impairment of contract set out long ago in *Green v. Biddle* is therefore logically implicated in the idea of partial takings under the eminent domain clause.[35] In that account, any state-mandated alteration of contractural rights constitutes a partial taking of private property. In principle it makes no difference whether the changes are made for the benefit of the creditor or of the debtor. To provide the creditor with protection he did not bargain for, with state aid, permits him to take property he is not entitled to. By the same token, legislation designed to relieve debtors of their contractual burdens is subject to an eminent domain challenge.[36] The situation under such legislation is as though the creditors recovered the money or property owed to them, then had to return it to the original debtor. Some devices for relieving debtors are procedural: a creditor's venue is limited, a statute of limitation is shortened, or a new burden of proof is imposed. Others are substantive: the creditor must delay collecting the debt, accept a lower rate of interest, or revalue the security in question. The ultimate constitutional status of these various restrictions upon creditors' rights depends on whether some compensation is provided for the loss, but the clause reaches them all.[37]

35. See supra note 2.
36. I have discussed the contract clause issues at far greater length in Richard A. Epstein, "Toward a Revitalization of the Contract Clause," 51 *U. Chi. L. Rev.* 703 (1984).
37. See Chapter 15.

The same theme manifests itself in other contexts. If the government compels an assignment of a contract right, it must pay the market value of that right, reduce *pro tanto* to the extent that it discharges the obligations of its assignor. If steel is worth $1,500 per ton, and the claimant has a right to purchase it for $1,000, then the compensation owing the original buyer is $500 per ton if the government relieves the buyer of his obligation by paying the seller for the steel; if it does not, the compensation is $1,500 per ton.

Note the implications for *Omnia Commercial Co. v. United States*,[38] a case that arose out of World War I. The plaintiff had entered into a contract to purchase quantities of steel from a manufacturer at a stated price, which was below the market value of the steel at the time of expected delivery. The plaintiff could have received a positive sum if it had voluntarily assigned its rights and delegated its duties to a third party. The government, through its unquestionable powers of requisition, ordered the steel company to deliver its entire output to the government for the war effort. The government order was treated as the classical type of supervening impossibility that excused the seller from liability under the contract. The question was whether the buyer had an action against the government for the loss of the promised delivery.

The court could have responded to the plaintiff's claim in two distinct ways. The first would be to admit the taking of private property from the plaintiff and to justify that taking, perhaps by referring to public necessity brought on by the war. Yet this approach runs into the strong objection that compensation is required most clearly in war cases, which recall Revolutionary War abuses. The second, more hard-edged, approach would be to deny the taking of private property at all, making it unnecessary to reach the justification issue. The court in *Omnia*, obviously influenced by the public necessity arguments, noted that the plaintiff's case, if upheld, would open the way to an "appalling number" of claims against the state, a problem that could be avoided simply by treating the steel as though it had already been delivered to the purchaser.

The court, however, directed most of its intellectual fire to the threshold taking question. Its initial premise, consistent with the position taken here, was that "[t]he contract in question was property within the meaning of the Fifth Amendment, and if taken for public use the gov-

38. 261 U.S. 502 (1923).

ernment would be liable."[39] But it then held that in this case the government did not "take" the contract in question.

> What was here requisitioned was the future product of the Steel Company, and, since this product in the absence of governmental interference would have been delivered in fulfillment of the contract, the contention seems to be that the contract was so far identified with it that the taking of the former, *ipso facto,* took the latter. This, however, is to confound the contract with its subject-matter. The essence of every executory contract is the obligation which the law imposes upon the parties to perform it . . . Plainly, here there was no acquisition of the obligation or the right to enforce it. If the Steel Company had failed to comply with the requisition, what would have been the remedy? Not enforcement of the contract but enforcement of the statute [whereby a government takeover of the Steel Company would be imposed]. If the government had failed to pay for what it got what would have been the right of the Steel Company? Not to the price fixed by the contract but to the just compensation guaranteed by the Constitution.[40]

The broad promise of the major premise is undone by the errors of its application. For steel unsold by the seller, the government must pay the full market value. Why then should its cost be reduced simply because the contract of sale separates ownership from possession? The only complication, which cannot be ignored, is whether the market price in fact reflects the increased government activity because of the war effort. Yet even if that is the case, the entire difference between contract price and market value need not be attributable to government involvement. And in any event, that argument has as great a force where the steel has been delivered as where it has not.

But none of these refinements go to the issue of whether property has been taken. The government takes private property when it compels an assignment of a contract right from the buyer for less than its fair market value. Surely, then, it "takes" the contract when it chooses not to compel that assignment but to appropriate the contract's subject matter, while giving the buyer in exchange an impossibility defense against the seller that in no way protects his profit from the transaction. That the government acted pursuant to a statute adds nothing to its case but only

39. Id. at 508.
40. Id. at 510–511.

shows the infirmity of the statute itself. The familiar refrain applies: no third party could take the steel without being accountable to the plaintiff for its full value, no matter how much the value exceeded the cost. The admitted, but irrelevant, distinction between interference with the agreement itself and the taking of its subject matter is simply of no avail. A wrong done by the government is still a taking.

8   Taking from Many: Liability Rules, Regulations, and Taxes

Takings from *1* to n

I am now in a position to make a fundamental, though controversial, transition that was hinted at, but not developed, in the earlier chapters. Thus far the discussion has concentrated upon those situations where the government is pitted against isolated individuals who assert that their property has been taken. The question here is, to what extent can this account of basic takings, including partial takings, be carried over to deal with claims by a large number of individuals that their property has been taken by acts which, if done against one of them alone, would be covered by the eminent domain clause?

On this issue there is relatively little guidance from the early historical materials. Locke's second treatise contains no analysis of any of the issues examined here: indeed, it includes no discussion of the three major subjects of this section: taxation, regulation, and modifications of liability rules. Nonetheless, his theory of representative government carries over to the current set of issues. These three forms of government activity are amenable to the same form of analysis as garden-variety takings of land; they cannot be kept in a watertight compartment separate from takings of private property. The Supreme Court has acknowledged this point with its own extensive literature on "regulatory" takings.[1]

1. For one recent example, see Ruckelshaus v. Monsanto Co., 104 S. Ct. 2862 (1984).

The present case law makes a strenuous effort to construct the line between takings and regulation. The impulse behind this received wisdom stems from Holmes's observaton in *Mahon:* "Government hardly could go on if to some extent values incident to property could not be diminished without paying for every such change in the general law."[2] Holmes quickly carves out a broad area for legislative control, but he preserves the tension by noting that the principle of judicial deference must have limits "or the contract and due process clauses are gone."[3]

The position I take here does not begin with Holmes's prudential concern. Instead it starts with the analytical question and moves in the opposite direction. The basic proposition, which accords far greater scope to the eminent domain clause, is perfectly general in form. Prima facie, the greater the numbers, the greater the wrong. What stamps a government action as a taking simpliciter is what it does to the property rights of each individual who is subject to its actions: nothing more or less is relevant, including the conduct of the government in relation to other people. The principles of eminent domain that govern a taking of all of one person's property also govern a taking of part of that property. The principles that determine whether one person's property has been taken, in whole or in part, also determine whether many people's property has been taken in whole or in part.

The coverage of the clause, therefore, is not diminished or eliminated even though, first, the taking (including property destruction) is smaller in size, and second, the range and frequency of persons subject to the taking are simultaneously increased. The clause applies to takings that are narrow and deep and to those that are broad and shallow.

The best way to understand the point is to proceed by increments. It is easy to take property from A when he is identified by name; this taking is not transformed into something else just because the same government action is also directed toward B by name. Or for that matter, toward C, D, E, and so on. Nor is the character of the government action altered if the persons whose property is taken are not designated but are described in ways that allow public officials, for example, judges or sheriffs, to identify them at the time of public seizure. No matter what the form of a legal command, its impact falls upon individual persons. The rules that govern takings from single individuals govern takings from the multitude.

The development of a unified theory for both isolated government ac-

2. Pennsylvania Coal Co. v. Mahon, 260 U.S. 393, 413 (1922).
3. Id. at 413. The reference to the due process clause is to its substantive dimension, where it operates as a takings clause binding against the state.

tions and comprehensive government actions spares us the need of drawing some bright line between two classes of government actions. Certainly when the government takes land for a post office, its obligation to compensate does not depend upon whether it takes two separate but adjacent parcels, or a single parcel under common ownership. Let the numbers vary from one to a thousand landowners, and we move only from land taken for a post office to land taken for a military base or for a public highway. This process of accretion offers no sharp or obvious breakpoint between an individual and a large-number taking. On the question of takings simpliciter, it is not possible to ask how widespread government action must be in order to escape scrutiny under the eminent domain clause, because questions of line and degree are wholly irrelevant to this stage of the inquiry. It is only the character of the government action, measured by the standards applied to private parties, that determines whether there is a taking of private property—of one or of few or of many.

The method of analysis does not change when the takings are partial instead of total. If a certain form of government action regulates the use of an individual tract of land, as by restrictive covenent or lien, then it is prima facie a partial taking of private property. Where that partial taking is directed toward the land of many persons, the generality of the rule is increased, but the nature of its impact upon each affected party remains unchanged. The state may wish to call zoning comprehensive land regulation, but it remains an elaborate network of restrictive covenants imposed upon the regulated land. It may choose to use the expression "real estate taxes," but they remain liens upon the property that is subject to them. The legal status of comprehensive liability rules, as well as of general schemes of taxation and regulation, can receive a clean conceptual answer without annoying fuzziness at the edges. The modern effort to distance the taking clause from general laws cannot be maintained. *All* regulations, *all* taxes, and *all* modifications of liability rules are takings of private property prima facie compensable by the state.

The reasons for this comprehensive approach stem in part from the function of the eminent domain clause. Any theory of constitutional review that covers one form of government behavior while excluding the others invites enormous slippage at the margins. Those who are in control of the state will find in the unregulated forms of conduct effective substitutes for those initiatives called into question under the takings clause. Instead of providing a bulwark against the excesses of government power, a narrow construction of the eminent domain clause simply encourages government officials to redirect their behavior to those forms of exploitation that are beyond constitutional review.[4] No comprehensive theory of government control can tolerate such loopholes for legislative action. As the literal application of the eminent domain clause is consistent with its purpose, there is no warrant for confining its application to isolated takings.

In stating the central thesis, I must stress again that differences in the form and incidence of government takings do often make a difference in the ultimate outcome of any given case, even if they are immaterial to the threshold takings issue. Partial takings from large numbers of persons increase the likelihood (but do not create the certainty) that aggrieved parties will receive implicit in-kind compensation, for there is often overlap between the persons whose property is taken and the persons who are benefited by the takings. Where adequate in-kind compensation is implicit in the governmental scheme, then cash payments are improper even though the clause applies.[5] The first task is to show that the clause covers the three basic types of situations: modification of common law liability rules, taxes, and regulations.

Common Law Liability Rules

There is a strong, if uncritical, shared belief that the eminent domain clause cannot reach so far as to preclude changes in the general substantive law. "No person," Justice Pitney wrote, "has a vested interest in any rule of law entitling him to insist that it shall remain unchanged for his benefit."[6] The sense behind this intuition is that the eminent domain clause does not blunt the inevitable evolution of common law doctrine, a commonplace of our legal tradition. To conclude that the common law is malleable is, within important limits, correct, but the reason stated— that there are no vested rights in liability rules—is mistaken. Ownership is a social concept. A system of private property contains a necessary commitment to the web of rights and duties between the owner and the world. The basic rules of ownership state in general form the types of actions by others that constitute wrongs. The basic rules of liability in-

---

4. See, e.g., Richard A. Epstein, "Taxation, Regulation, and Confiscation," 20 *Osgoode Hall L.J.* 433 (1982); Anthony T. Kronman, "Contract Law and Distributive Justice," 89 *Yale L.J.* 472 (1980); Richard A. Posner, "Taxation by Regulation," 2 *Bell J. Econ. & Management Sci.* 22 (1971).

5. See Chapters 14–15.

6. New York Central R.R. v. White, 243 U.S. 188, 198 (1916).

voked in tort cases concentrate upon the particular party whose conduct has singled him out and thus necessitated some vindication of original ownership rights. The two are opposite sides of the same coin, with no radical separation between them.

Much of modern legal scholarship shows the implicit fusion of property rules and liability rules. One recurrent question concerns the choice of remedies, between reparation and injunctions, on the one hand, and damages, on the other.[7] Should, for example, chattels taken be paid for or returned? The common law system has no cause of action based on ownership as such, and the plaintiff can succeed only because he shows a wrongful act of the defendant, which here takes the form of either dealing with the plaintiff's chattel as though it were his own or of refusing to return it to the plaintiff on demand. The Roman system, in contrast, recognizes a class of actions that are wholly property based—the *vindicatio rei*—where the action is conceived as calling for the reclamation of the thing wholly, without regard to any wrongful conduct of the party in possession.[8] There is, however, no functional distinction between the two systems, because simply by bringing a suit, the plaintiff forces the defendant to refuse to return the thing, which is sufficient to trigger the tort of conversion. The act requirement of the common law tort system is satisifed as a matter of course even in a system that purports to rest rights of action upon ownership as such. The point, moreover, does not apply only to chattels. The traditional real actions for the recovery of land—*novel disseisin* and the writs of right and, later, ejectment—also show the analytical merger of the rules of property and of tort.

The intimacy of property and tort rules can be extended beyond the case in which A's land is occupied by B. There would be a clear affront to the conception of ownership if a plaintiff were told that he was *never* entitled to redress if the defendant deliberately destroyed his property. Concern for ownership as an institution would deepen if it were held that a defendant who took the plaintiff's property by innocent mistake was allowed to keep it precisely because he wanted it, or that a trespasser who entered could, as of right, use the land to advance his own political, artistic, or financial interests against those of the owner.

The general point can be carried to its extreme conclusion without any loss of intellectual force; if you deny the plaintiff the prima facie

7. See Guido Calabresi and A. Douglas Melamed, "Property Rules, Liability Rules, and Inalienability: One View of the Cathedral," 85 *Harv. L. Rev.* 1089 (1972).

8. See Barry Nicholas, *An Introduction to Roman Law* 99–103 (1962).

right to recover against a stranger without proof of negligence, then you have taken a limited property interest; if you deny the plaintiff the right to recover for certain nuisances, then you have created an easement to cause a nuisance. If you allow one man to prevent his neighbor from building on his own land, you have created a restrictive covenant. Allow flooding, and there is a flowage easement. By definition, every liability rule is tied to a correlative property interest that the law protects; to alter the one is necessarily to change the other. The linkage is *not* empirical, it is analytical, a function of the way in which we do use, and must use, all legal language.

Two ways might be suggested to distinguish categorically a modification of liability rules from takings of private property as these terms are ordinarily understood. First, modifications in liability rules are at most minor, as many of the rights in the original ownership bundle remain unchanged even as the liability rules shift. Second, the modifications are general in application and are not directed toward specific persons. These are important differences, which any theory must take into account, but they do not strictly demarcate changes of liability rules from takings simpliciter.

As regards the first point, the extent of modification only shows that there is a partial and not a complete taking. Yet that in turn only demonstrates that the compensation prima facie required is less, or that justification may be easier to come by if only because there is less to justify. It does not demonstrate that no taking has occurred. As regards the second point, the generality of the change in liability rules only shows that many persons are affected by the taking; it does not deny that the taking took place. If an errant driver strikes a school bus, we do not say that he has caused no one harm because he has injured many children instead of one. We think of ways to facilitate permissive joinder and class actions to respond to the more extensive violation of individual rights. The same is true here.

The cases that have grappled with the constitutional issues raised by the adoption of workers' compensation and automobile no-fault laws[9] have faced a problem that is substantive and not verbal. Furthermore, even changes within the system of liability rules—like the subtle nuances in the shift from negligence to strict liability or the reverse—raise in principle serious questions under the eminent domain clause, which will be examined in far greater detail in Chapter 14 in the discussion of implicit in-kind compensation.

9. See, e.g., Pinnick v. Cleary, 360 Mass. 1, 271 N.E.2d 592 (1971).

Taxation

Parallel arguments apply to taxation. Summation is again the key. If the state takes property from A, then that property is still taken even if the state also takes property from B through Z. If the state takes some of A's property, it matters not that it takes only some from B through Z as well. The principle is also unchanged whether the partial taking is measured by metes and bounds, by estates in land, or by the standard incidents of ownership: possession, use, and disposition. The form and breadth of the tax, although vitally important for the complete analysis, count for nothing at this stage of the argument. If certain action directed solely toward one individual is a taking, then cloaking it in the *general* terms of a tax only increases the dimensions of the prima facie government wrong by making it a taking against all parties who fall within the statutory ambit. The process is purely additive. No secret alchemy transforms repeated takings of private property into something else which is constitutionally neutral.

It is therefore sufficient in connection with both taxes and regulation to ask one question: does the theory of takings simpliciter developed for individual owners in the earlier section reach the paradigmatic cases of taxation or regulation as viewed from the vantage point of a single owner? The private analogies to both taxation and regulation are instructive.

The common purpose of all taxes is to raise the revenues necessary to support various state activities. As a first alternative, the state might simply have its agents take some portion of the assets held by private individuals, such as part of their land, crops, or inventory. Mass dispossession of assets in kind is clearly a taking simpliciter whether the system of exaction is sensible or capricious, justified or not. If now the government agent, instead of taking in kind, demands under threat of force that certain designated property be conveyed to the state, the matter is scarcely different. The analogy to the private doctrines of proximate cause and duress of goods is decisive in the case.[10] The thief who says, "your money or your life" has given his victim a choice, but he cannot keep the money on the grounds that the victim gave it to him. The thief's threat of force transforms giving into taking.

Matters do not change if the government sets a monetary sum—call it

10. On the role of compulsion in causation, see Richard A. Epstein, "A Theory of Strict Liability," 2 *J. Legal Stud.* 151, 174–177 (1973). On duress of goods, see John Dawson, "Economic Duress—An Essay in Perspective," 45 *Mich. L. Rev.* 253 (1947).

a tax—which the citizen can discharge from whatever assets he chooses. The element of choice added to this stage simply transforms the case from garden variety coercion—"your money or your life"—to one of duress of goods—"of your possessions, you may keep A or B, but not both." The argument against the government, like that against the private party, is that no person is entitled to force any individual to forfeit one thing in order to keep another, when both are unconditionally his *as of right*. The restricted choice in the duress of goods situation is thus wholly different from the choice involved in a market exchange, where the question is always whether one individual wishes to surrender something he is entitled to keep in order to obtain something to which he has *no* claim of right—that is, to buy what he does not own. So long as the government forces the individual to make some transfer, it does not matter what particular thing is transferred.

Following the private analogies, then, private property has been taken, even under a restrictive view of the eminent domain clause which rejects the equation between loss and destruction of property. With a tax, the government takes property in the narrowest sense of the term, ending up with ownership and possession of that which was once in private hands. Anyone who wants to deny the conclusion need only consider the consequences of not paying taxes. Liens are attached to one's land or bank accounts, which are then taken and sold to satisfy the tax obligation. To be sure, there cannot be, either as a matter of general political theory or of constitutional law, any simple equation between taxation and government theft. Yet the analysis does establish that taxation is prima facie a taking of private property. The legitimacy of taxation does not flow from any artificial narrowing of the phrase "taking of private property," but rather, from the justifications available for all other forms of taking: police power, consent, and compensation, typically either implicit or in kind. What cannot be said is that taxes are simply outside the scope of the eminent domain clause because they are not takings at all, when their effectiveness precisely depends upon coerceive power clothed in official garb.[11]

Regulation

The arguments about taxation and takings carry over with equal force to the government's efforts to regulate the possession, use, and disposi-

11. The point addressed thus far is not historical. Those matters are taken up in greater detail in Chapter 18.

tion of private property. Such regulation is a perfectly commonplace affair in modern American life. Some regulations require owners to allow others to gain access and entry to their property. Land use regulation can limit land to residential, commercial or industrial uses; it can limit the densities of use upon such land; it can prohibit certain types of activities; it can specify the minimum lot size or minimum floor size or maximum heights, side yards, and setbacks for certain classes of improvements; it can designate certain structures as landmarks and insist that the alteration or demolition, in whole or in part, be undertaken only with the approval of certain boards or commissions. Regulations limit the goods that can be sold in commerce and the prices charged for them. The differences among these various forms of regulation are sure to be important in any assessment of their economic consequences or their legal justification. Yet these protean forms of regulation all amount to partial takings of private property.

The point of departure is the land use restriction directed by a private defendant against a single landowner. A tells B not to build a structure over ten feet tall or not to sell or lease without his consent. Such conduct, if backed by the threat of force, would be regarded as tortious on the part of A. In the first situation A compels the de facto conveyance of a restrictive covenant—a recognized property interest—upon B's use of his land which, under the original distribution of property rights between neighbors, he can obtain only by purchase or other voluntary transfer. B could therefore obtain an injunction against A's threat of future harm and damages for the harm that has already been inflicted. The nature of A's precise demands upon B is wholly immaterial to the threshold question of whether there was a prima facie wrong; it is relevant solely to the question of the extent of A's wrong and the remedies appropriate for its redress.

The argument from increments now proceeds as it did before. In the private context A's wrong against B would not change if similar demands, backed by force, were also made against neighbors C through Z. The generality of A's demands only makes him the greater menace; it does not lend legitimacy to acts tortious in their inception. If A is the state, it takes an interest in B's land even if its orders are directed solely toward B. By extension, where the state issues a general directive against many persons similarly situated, it has engaged in a mass partial taking of private property: zoning has no magic, as a word or a process, even though it was unknown in 1791. The wrongs of the government, like those of the private party, are strictly additive.

The same arguments can be made with respect to certain government restrictions upon the ability to *dispose* of private property. Suppose that A tells his neighbor B that he can sell his land only with A's consent or must sell his oil below a certain price fixed by A. The taking of B's property is clear; the only dispute is over the proper measure of damages when injunctive relief is inadequate. It is as if A took the land or oil, paid partial compensation, and resold the property at the price he paid. The lack of profit to A does not disguise the loss to B. If B imposed similar regulations upon all owners of land or oil, his wrongs could only be regarded as cumulative across the class.

When the government is A, it engages on a grand scale in the very conduct which has been adjudged prima facie wrongful if done by a private party. It must, therefore, justify that action to escape the duty of compensation. As with private defendants, the level and the form of the resale restrictions or price controls are details about the extent of the prima facie wrong which are wholly immaterial to the threshold takings issue.

This analysis of land use and price controls has, of course, been rejected countless times by the court. In its place, the dominant line of opinion—one that can again be traced to Justice Holmes in *Mahon*[12]—is that regulation, far from being a subclass of takings, is outside the scope of the eminent domain clause unless it is taken "too far." This general proposition necessarily provokes disputes at the margin. But the task here is not to determine which, if any, of those cases are wrongly decided under prevailing doctrine. Instead it is to insist that today's powerful presumption in favor of regulation has set the margin in the wrong place. The conclusive presumption should be that all regulation, whether or not compensable, falls within the eminent domain clause.

One doctrinal issue among many should be sufficient to illustrate the general point. In deciding whether certain forms of regulation are unreasonable, it is often said that courts should take into account the "diminution in value" brought about by the regulation in question. It is said that the Constitution does not protect "mere economic values" from depreciation by government action. The basic point is that where those diminutions are not so overwhelmingly large, the harm suffered by the individual landowner should be regarded as *damnum absque iniuria*, and hence not compensable by the state.[13]

The conventional wisdom relies on the private analogies developed in this book but, like the analogous treatment of business goodwill, utterly

12. 260 U.S. 393 (1922).

13. See discussion of HFH, Ltd. v. Superior Court in Los Angeles County in Chapter 17.

mistakes their import. Never has *damnum absque iniuria* been applied with such vengeance. Where we deal with cases of competition or the blocking of a view, the extent of the damages is quite immaterial, because the injured party can show no invasion of any incident of ownership by the use of force or the theat thereof. With the various restrictions upon the *rights* to possess, use, and dispose, the doctrine of *damnum absque iniuria* is of no assistance. Now the taking of the restrictive covenant or other interest establishes the basic violation of right, leaving diminution of value only its usual function, to measure damages attributable to the government wrong. These are not just cases of mere "economic values." By any theory they are the loss of property rights.

The effort to mix several questions—takings, justification, compensation—into a single issue necessarily brings about a loss of clarity that works to enlarge the scope of state action. *Andrus v. Allard*[14] indicates how easily rights of disposition can be imported into the public domain. The courts that are unable—or unwilling—to demarcate clear principles of judgment are much more likely to retreat into the frame of mind that allows the legislature free rein. That attitude of deference was largely instrumental, for example, in the decision for the municipality in *Goldblatt v. Town of Hempstead*,[15] where limitations upon the right of the landowner to excavate sand and gravel below the waterline were upheld as a regulation that fell short of a taking, even though it prohibited the "most beneficial use" to which the property had been previously devoted. If all limitations on use constitute partial takings, then *Goldblatt* is wrong, as it is impeached by its own account of the ordinance in question. Judicial deference was also decisive in *United States v. Central Eureka Mining Co.*,[16] where a government order that prohibited the mine from continuing to operate was erroneously regarded as outside the scope of the takings clause because, in the words of the Supreme Court, "the Government did not occupy, use, or in any manner take physical possession of the gold mines or of the equipment connected with them."[17] Again, the description used to free the government only condemns it, by its implicit recognition that the order limited the company's right of use. In *Agins v. City of Tiburon*[18] the Supreme Court did not flinch at extensive land use regulations, under which the appellants could build one to five houses on their five-acre tract. When created by private agreement, a re-

14. See Chapter 7.
15. 369 U.S. 590 (1962).
16. 357 U.S. 155 (1958).
17. Id. at 165–166.
18. 447 U.S. 255 (1980).

strictive covenant is a property interest taken from the owner of the burdened land. That covenant remains an interest in real property when created by zoning. To be sure, there are differences between covenants and zoning on the benefit side. The parties who benefit as of right from private covenants are well identified, while the persons who benefit from zoning normally are not. Yet the takings question asks only what has been taken; the nature and distribution of the benefits conferred become relevant only after the initial taking is acknowledged. The well-nigh conclusive presumption that regulations are "reasonable" simply does not begin to address the hard issues in takings cases. The eminent domain clause does not say, "The private rights of disposition and use are in the public domain." But that is how it is now read.

The above analysis of regulation is reinforced if the question is analyzed in terms of the incentives that the constitutional rules impose upon government. Where regulation of use and disposition is permitted as a matter of course, then the individuals who control the levers of government power can get what they want at reduced expenditure of their own wealth. Therefore, their willingness to take and pay for land for public use will be lessened as close substitutes are made available to them at virtually no charge. The current relaxed approach to regulation skews the incentives for political groups by making one form of state action subject to powerful constitutional control while leaving its close substitutes wholly unregulated. Once taxation, regulation, and modification of liability rules are recognized as interchangeable techniques for social control, then the full panoply of government controls over the possession, use, and disposition of property must be scrutinized under the clause. In short steps we have moved a long way from taking land for the post office.

PART III

Justifications for Takings

9 The Police Power: Ends

The Inherent Powers of the Sovereign

The place of the police power in American constitutional law has always been difficult to determine. The Constitution itself does not contain the phrase. Yet much constitutional law and legal scholarship has been concerned with determining its proper domain, as the issue has arisen persistently in cases under the First Amendment, both due process clauses, the contracts clause, the equal protection clause, and of course, the eminent domain clause.

Although it has been read by implication into all major substantive constitutional guarantees, the police power throughout its history has led a shadowy existence. One source of ambiguity is the unfortunate coincidence that the same term does two very different jobs. First, the police power is associated with a state's delegation of powers to its internal subdivisions—cities, counties, special districts, and the like. Can a city engage in sewage disposal? The question is jurisdictional and turns largely on the terms and conditions of the original state grant to its subdivisions, with no visible federal constitutional component.

The second sense of the police power, germane to this inquiry, involves those grants of power to the federal and state government that survive the explicit limitations found in the Constitution. Although most limitations on government power are stated in categorical terms, the police power is a universal part of constitutional discourse that qualifies the explicit text. What sense could anyone make of the state if the government had *no* power to regulate speech or contract or property, or to distinguish between persons? Why form an organization that could literally do nothing at all? To use the old phrase, the police power remains an inherent attribute of sovereignty at all levels of government. Stated in this form, the concept is fully congruent with the Lockean theory of the state, which requires individuals to leave the state of nature solely to obtain peace and security against possible aggression by their neighbors, as the phrase *police* power itself suggests.[1] It would be a very odd construction of the Constitution that denied both the federal and state governments the minimum capacity to maintain peace and good order when those are the central functions of government itself. The police power does not pose any threat to the theory of representational government. If individuals may justify the use of force in self-defense against their neighbors, so too can the state when it acts on their behalf. The basic theory demands that the police power be read into the Constitution, no matter how stringent the standard of necessary implication for unwritten terms. The purpose of this chapter is to examine the proper ends to which the police power, understood in this second sense, can be properly directed. In the next chapter I explore the permissible means to obtain the ends so defined.

An Antitaking Doctrine

Any adequate account of the ends served by the police power limitation should be congruent with the language and aims of the takings clause. The usual discussions about the police power start with some recognition of its fluidity. A common account of the subject is found in the general language of *Lochner v. New York,* showing the usual caution: "There are, however, certain powers, existing in the sovereignty of each State in the Union, somewhat vaguely termed police powers, the exact description and limitation of which have not been attempted by the courts. Those powers, broadly stated and without, at present, any attempt at a more specific limitation, relate to the safety, health, morals, and general welfare of the public."[2]

In more modern discourse the words "police power" seem to have given way to a more pallid formulation which rejects challenges to a zoning ordinance, for example, when it can be shown that the ordinance

1. See John Locke, *Of Civil Government* ¶136 (1690).
2. 198 U.S. 45, 53 (1905).

"bears any rational relationship to a *legitimate state interest*," which, given the looseness of the language, it almost always does.[3]

Both the traditional and the modern formulations go beyond the original Lockean conception and are too broad to be defended in analytical terms. The legitimate state interest test in vogue today is a bare conclusion, tantamount to asserting that the action is legitimate because it is lawful. The test completely ignores the connection between the police power and the need to maintain peace and good order. As such, the test functions, at best, as a convenient label for serious inquiry, without defining the set of permissible ends of government action.

Even the narrower formulation in *Lochner* contains some verbal imprecision.[4] The reference to "health" and "safety" does not distinguish between harm to strangers, as with aggression and threats to public health, and harms arising out of contracts, where agreement, express or implied, can allocate risk between the parties. Similarly, the reference to the "general welfare" of the people invites confusion between the police power and the distinct public use requirement, with their very different consequences. Meeting the public use limitation does not allow the state to take private property without just compensation. Satisfying the police power limitation, in contrast, does allow the state to take without compensation. The police power cannot be interpreted as an unrestricted grant of state power to act in the public interest, for then the exception will overwhelm the clause.

The relationship between public use and the police power is well cap-

3. Construction Industry Ass'n v. City of Petaluma, 522 F.2d 897, 906 (9th Cir. 1975), *cert. denied* 424 U.S. 934 (1976). The exact context of the language was a challenge to exclusionary zoning provisions under a substantive due process doctrine.

4. I ignore here the "morals" component of the police power. Historically this was directed to gambling, drinking, prostitution, and the like. In part, restrictions on these activities may be justified by the concern that they lead to illness, disease, and harms to others, although here the means-end connections are difficult, if not impossible, to draw. See the discussion of Mugler v. Kansas in Chapter 10. In larger measure, however, such restrictions express a moral consensus about activities that are unworthy in themselves even if they cause no harm to others, and they are often defended in just those terms. In principle one could argue that the notion of private property is designed to exclude just those judgments about the conduct of others, which indeed is what happens when the power of the state to regulate, for example, the use of obscene materials in one's own home is struck down in the name of privacy. See Stanley v. Georgia, 394 U.S. 557 (1969). But no matter what attitude is taken toward this historical dimension of the police power, few important modern economic regulations could be saved by applying it.

tured in an analogy drawn from the private law—the distinction between self-defense and private necessity. Self-defense allows one to inflict harm without compensating the person harmed, while private necessity creates only a conditional privilege, which allows the harm to be inflicted but only upon payment of compensation.[5] The gulf between these two principles does not depend upon the conduct of the reasonable man. In conformity with the radical difference in their consequences, the line between them is a more enduring structural distinction. With self-defense the wrongful conduct of the plaintiff—here the use of force—requires him to forfeit relief, while with private necessity the defendant's needs do not require that the plaintiff forfeit all his rights. So too, in the public context, the peril of foreign aggression gives ample scope for government action as a matter of public necessity, but it does not allow the state to commandeer without compensation the munitions plants needed for the war effort. The state must meet more exacting standards to obtain refuge in the police power limitation than to satisfy the public use requirement.[6] The Supreme Court has obliterated a key structural distinction by holding that the "scope of the 'public use' requirement of the Taking Clause is 'coterminus with the scope of a sovereign's police powers.' "[7]

How, then, should a police power justification for admitted government takings of private property be read into the Constitution? As drafted, the eminent domain clause seems to limit the state to two alternatives: either refrain from taking or pay for the property taken. There are, of course, many situations in which these options suffice. No justification is needed where land is taken for a post office. Yet even in cases of outright dispossession, some government action can be legitimated only by appealing to the police power, as when the state seizes a plant that has repeatedly discharged poisonous chemicals into the city water supply. The demand for a full treatment of the police power becomes even more imperative once the notion of a taking of private property is ex-

---

5. See, for the classical tort cases, Ploof v. Putnam, 81 Vt. 471, 71 A. 188 (1908), which recognized the right of the party in distress to use the property of another, and Vincent v. Lake Erie Transportation Co., 109 Minn. 456, 124 N.W. 221 (1910), requiring compensation therefor. The explicit parallels between the tort and the constitutional law are brought out in Dale W. Broeder, "Torts and Just Compensation: Some Personal Reflections," 17 *Hastings L.J.* 217 (1965).

6. See Chapter 12.

7. See Ruckelshaus v. Monsanto Co., 104 S.Ct. 2862 (1984), quoting Hawaii Housing Authority v. Midkiff, 104 S.Ct. 2321, 2329 (1984).

tended to cover partial takings, including all forms of state regulation and taxation.

The intellectual source of the police power lies in the marriage of precise private law analogues to a general theory of representative government. In the private law the deliberate taking of A's private property by B may create a prima facie case of liability, but it does not preclude B from justifying his own action, as by self-defense. On Lockean grounds that right can then be carried over to the state, which can exercise it on behalf of the individuals who possess it. Where the harm threatens a large portion of the population, the state has the sum of their individual rights. The police power as a ground for legitimate public intervention is, then, exactly the same as when a private party acts on its own behalf. The individual who demands protection against takings by others loses that protection when he himself takes or threatens to take property.

At first blush it might appear that the police power is limited in its scope to use against obvious cases of theft and aggression. Yet this interpretation misses the important point that the taking of private property in the private context covers all forms of wrongful conduct short of total dispossession. This broad account of a taking was invoked to describe the actions of the state in the constitutional context, and it must likewise be invoked when individual rights are at stake. Stated in the language of the Constitution the taking by a citizen justifies the taking in response by the state. In ordinary language the wrong of the citizen justifies conduct otherwise wrongful by the state as representative of and in defense of its other citizens.[8]

It follows, therefore, that the police power permits the state to control partial as well as complete takings by private parties. In addition, it covers all cases of force and misrepresentation, even if they result only in the destruction and not the occupation of property. In a word, the police power gives the state control over the full catalogue of common law wrongs involving force and misrepresentation, deliberate or accidental, against other persons, including private nuisances. In light of the discussion of *Batten*,[9] state-created nuisances are in principle partial takings and are compensable as such. In similar fashion, the linkage between public nuisances and the police power quickly follows from the basic principle of summation used in analyzing large-number takings.[10] Just as the state cannot take from one, so it cannot prima facie take from

8. See Chapter 4.
9. See Chapter 4.
10. See Chapter 5.

many. The same principle applies when the state seeks to regulate private conduct. A public nuisance is understood as a wrong against many individuals, each of whom suffers small compensable harms.[11] The state can control these nuisances, thereby vindicating individual rights for which private enforcement is too costly.

Nonetheless, there are clear limits upon the conception of the police power, which cannot be used to regulate conduct that itself is not wrongful under the tests of force and misrepresentation already developed. As a constitutional matter, one end that falls outside the scope of the takings clause is the redress of competitive losses that are not actionable in principle at the instance of the aggrieved victims. Similarly, the police power cannot be invoked to counter the perceived economic inequality between the parties, without force or misrepresentation, as there is no private wrong to control. The sole function of the police power is to protect individual liberty and private property against all manifestations of force and fraud.

The Nuisance Control Rationale

The most distinctive aspect of the police power under the eminent domain clause has been its antinuisance component. Supreme Court cases have repeatedly referred to control of nuisances as a proper end of the state, and there is no doubt today, as in times past, that this proposition is sound in principle. The other side of the proposition, that the state can act only to control nuisances, is far more controversial. It is important here to trace in some detail the intellectual and legal cross-currents that have led to the decline and fall of the antinuisance conception of the police power. In tracing this development, the initial inquiry is, what kinds of activities constitute nuisances?

EASY AND HARD CASES

It is best to begin with an easy case. In the early case of *Northwestern Fertilizing Co. v. Hyde Park*,[12] the town of Hyde Park passed an ordinance which prevented the defendant from transporting waste and other offensive matter through the streets. The restriction was necessary to protect neighbors from invasion by smells, infestation by insects, and other

11. See, e.g., F. Harper & F. James, *The Law of Torts* ¶1.23 (1956). For a collection of materials, see R. Epstein, C. Gregory, and H. Kalven, *Cases and Materials on the Law of Torts* 629–636 (4th ed. 1984).

12. 97 U.S. 659 (1878).

dangers to their health. Whether looked at from the vantage point of history or from that of pure legal theory, the conduct proscribed was clearly unlawful as an ordinary nuisance. The ordinance could have been sustained without making any elaborate inquiries into the permissible ends of the police power of the sort that arise when it is unclear whether certain activities are nuisances. Compliance with the ordinance by the company is far more costly than for all other private parties, because only it had engaged in the prohibited activities. But its disproportionate burden does not call the ordinance into question, for the entire purpose of tort sanctions is to impose disproportionate burdens upon those persons, private or public, who have transgressed against others. The crucial point is that the burdens, however great, are fully justified.

The only reason *Hyde Park* came before the Supreme Court was that the state had originally chartered the company to transfer the materials across town to prevent other serious health hazards from emerging as the garbage decayed elsewhere.[13] Hyde Park (which acted under authority delegated to it by the state) imposed a ban that fell within the proper scope of the police power, but which was at odds with the prior contract between the state and the firm. So long as it is understood that contract rights are property interests, then compensation should be paid, unless there is some reason to attack the original grant as beyond the delegated powers of the city or to believe that the grant reserved to the city an (implicit) right of revocation without paying compensation.[14]

The relationship between nuisance control and the police power received a very different treatment in *Miller v. Schoene*.[15] There the state cut down the ornamental cedar trees owned by the plaintiff without compensating the owner. The cutting took place pursuant to a statute that authorized the state entomologist, upon appeal from ten freeholders in the vicinity, to determine whether the cedars were a host plant that harbored a fungus dangerous to apple trees growing within two miles of the cedars. It was stipulated that the value of the apple trees saved was far in excess of the value of the cedar trees destroyed.

The Supreme Court upheld the power of the state to cut down the trees without compensating the owner. The decision was far more disturbing for its reasons than for its results. The state took private property, even though the claimant was left in possession of the cut timber. In effect, the state paid for the standing trees with cut timber of far less

13. For the relevant provisions of the charter, see id. at 663.
14. See Chapter 11 for a discussion of this aspect of the case.
15. 276 U.S. 272 (1928).

value. The real issue turns on the scope of the police power, which in turn depends upon whether there was sufficient justification for cutting down the trees. This last inquiry made it imperative for the court to decide whether the claimant's cedar trees were in fact a nuisance to the apple trees. Here, as a matter of private law, the question is close, given the unavoidable murkiness at the margin of the act requirement and physical invasion tests that are part of the general nuisance law. The act requirement is clearly stretched to its limits, especially if the cedar trees were on the landowner's premises.[16] Physical invasion seems difficult to establish, given that the fungus moved from the cedars to the apple trees either by their own motion or by the forces of nature and not by any act of the defendant, unless it could be said that the cedars were planted as a lure or a trap for the fungus. If forced to decide the particular question—did the defendant's cedars constitute a nuisance to apple trees in the vicinity?—I should, with some caution, answer no.

The intellectual difficulty of these narrow points conceals their institutional importance. Some uncertainty must be tolerated at the edges; sound social institutions will never stand or fall on the marginal classification issues that test every legal doctrine. The vital point in the case was the court's pointed refusal to attach any importance to the nuisance determination at all. By saying that "[w]e need not weigh with nicety the question whether the infected cedars constitute a nuisance according to the common law; or whether they may be so declared by the statute,"[17] the court abandoned *all* efforts to distinguish police power from public use or to place principled limitations upon the scope of the police power, a point the landowner's counsel noted in oral argument.[18] From the court's premise, the transformation of eminent domain law swiftly follows. If the question is *not*, "Was there a nuisance created by the owner of the cedar tree?" then the police power issue is collapsed to the purely utilitarian question, "Are the benefits to the apple growers of sufficient magnitude to outweigh the costs in value of the ornamental cedar trees that were ordered cut down?" That is exactly the course the court took when it said that the conflict between the two uses allowed the state, under the guise of the police power, to decide "upon the destruction of one class of property in order to save another which, in the judg-

16. For the common law analogies decided in defendants' favor, see Giles v. Walker, 24 Q.B.D. 656 (1890); Merriam v. McConnell, 31 Ill. App. 2d 241, 175 N.E.2d 293 (1961).

17. 276 U.S. at 280.

18. Id. at 275–276.

ment of the legislature, is of greater value to the public."[19] The confusion between police power and public necessity is complete. The price paid for the error is that the just compensation requirement becomes legislative instead of constitutional.

This fatal preoccupation with questions of value is wholly inconsistent with any theory of property rights. Surely one could not ask the "greater value" question posed by the Supreme Court if the issue were whether the owner or an intruder should have possession of certain lands. Nor could that question be asked if the state wanted the land for itself. The question of relative values would go only to whether it would be prudent for the state to condemn the land and not to whether the state should pay for the land thus condemned. The same principle must apply to a *partial* taking by the state in the form of a state-imposed restrictive covenant against growing cedar trees. Now the good "Kantian" insight must dominate: the greater the state need, the stronger the state obligation to compensate.[20] The compensation requirement of the eminent domain clause is as much concerned with the distribution of gains and losses between two persons as with their aggregate amount. Whatever their general philosophical appeal, the court's crude utilitarian calculations are wholly inappropriate to the internal logic of the clause. In the absence of any wrong by the owner of the cedar trees, the decision not to compensate is nothing more than authorization to transfer property illicitly from one class of citizens to another, as the owner of the cedar trees is left with neither the thing nor its value, when he has done no wrong.[21]

CAUSAL CONFUSION

The hard question now is how questions of value have come to dominate a discussion to which they are so manifestly irrelevant. Here the answer lies in the persistent attacks upon the intellectual coherence, and hence the practical importance, of the nuisance conception. At one level, the term "nuisance" is said to be only a "conclusory label reflecting some social consensus about which property uses ought to be preferred."[22] This position is no more and no less than an assertion that legal doctrine

19. Id. at 279.
20. See Bruce A. Ackerman, *Private Property and the Constitution* ch. 4 (1977).
21. For another analysis, see James M. Buchanan, "Politics, Property, and the Law: An Alternative Interpretation of Miller et al. v. Schoene," 15 *J. Law & Econ.* 439 (1972), which stresses the problems of the political process and the questions of coordination among large numbers of separate actors.
22. Note, "Developments in the Law—Zoning," 91 *Harv. L. Rev.* 1427, 1470-73 (1978).

is so amorphous and unprincipled that it cannot constrain judges even in the simplest cases. A crude utilitarianism thus yields to a cruder legal realism. The asserted incoherence of legal doctrine becomes the entering wedge to allow, encourage, and indeed justify judges to reach whatever result they prefer on any given state of affairs. The principle of legality underlying any constitution presupposes that some sense can be made out of the constitutional order. Yet the question of nuisance is said to be so difficult that the entire mechanism of principled adjudication collapses of its own weight. If words cannot instruct, then commands cannot bind.

The challenge to the nuisance conception of the police power also rests upon more serious intellectual foundations. The now fashionable position is that it is impossible to maintain in constructive fashion the distinction between "causing a harm" on the one hand and "not conferring a benefit" on the other. To talk about preventing harm, the argument goes, it must be possible to identify that activity which is uniquely the cause of the harm. Since all relevant cases involve interactions between at least two parties, it is impossible to say whether the party regulated or the party protected is the cause of the harm in question. The distinction between the preventing of harm and the conferring of a benefit thus collapses, making it necessary to jettison the distinction between public necessity and individual wrongs, including, of course, nuisances.

The academic genesis of this position is, ironically, in the work of Ronald Coase in his classic article, "The Problem of Social Cost."[23] Its application to the constitutional sphere rests in large measure upon the work of Joseph Sax[24] and Frank Michelman,[25] where the argument is used as the central device for expansion of state power, a conclusion that Coase would doubtless find intellectually unacceptable. Sax and Michelman's program seeks to undercut any core conception of private property by removing from ownership all rights over disposition and use. Sax goes so far as to note that the conception of private property is so weak that one cannot use it—centuries of elementary trespass law notwithstanding—to determine whether compensation should be

23. Ronald H. Coase, "The Problem of Social Cost," 3 *J. Law & Econ.* 1 (1960).

24. Joseph Sax, "Takings and the Police Power," 74 *Yale L.J.* 36 (1964) (Sax I); "Takings, Private Property and Public Rights," 81 *Yale L.J.* 149 (1971) (Sax II).

25. Frank I. Michelman, "Property, Utility, and Fairness: Comments on the Ethical Foundations of 'Just Compensation' Law," 80 *Harv. L. Rev.* 1165 (1967).

awarded when the Navy uses private land for target practice.[26] The land could be said to get in the way of the bullets, as the face gets in the way of the fist.

Michelman airs the same doubts about the asserted distinction between "private fault and public benefit":

> For illustration of this approach, let us compare a regulation forbidding continued operation of a brick works which has been annoying residential neighbors with one forbidding an owner of rare meadowland to develop it so as to deprive the public of the benefits of drainage and wildlife conservation. According to the theories we are now to consider, a person affected by the second regulation would have the stronger claim to compensation. But even as to him, the matter is not free of ambiguity. To see this clearly, we can take as a third example a regulation forbidding the erection of billboards along the highway. Shall we construe this regulation as one which prevents the "harms" of roadside blight and distraction, or as one securing the "benefits" of safety and amenity? Shall we say that it prevents the highway abutter from inflicting injury on passing motorists, or that it enhances the value of the public's highway facility? This third example serves to expose one basic difficulty with the method of classifying regulations as compensable or not according to whether they prevent harms or extract benefits. Such a method will not work unless we can establish a benchmark of "neutral" conduct which enables us to say where refusal to confer benefits (not reversible without compensation) slips over into readiness to inflict harms (reversible without compensation).[27]

Michelman illustrates his general remarks with two further cases. The first is *Miller v. Schoene*,[28] and the second is the classic situation of "coming to the nuisance," wherein the brickmaker starts his plant in an isolated region, only to find that the individuals who subsequently move into the area complain of the discomfort and inconvenience from the pollution caused by its operation.

It is never a sound tactic to refute a general proposition with a small group of well-chosen counterexamples. In his treatment of the nuisance cases, Michelman has chosen just those cases that have proved most vexing under the private law. Even if one could establish that these cases

26. Sax II, supra note 24, at 167.
27. Michelman, supra note 25, at 1197.
28. 276 U.S. 272 (1928).

had no clear principled resolution, they would not undermine the basic workability of the general nuisance test as it applies to the vast numbers of ordinary pollution cases (like *Northwestern Fertilizing Co.*) in which filth is discharged into rivers and oil fumes into the air. The physical invasion test as traditionally understood makes short shrift of such cases. Likewise, in the other direction, the construction of a house that interferes with a stranger's view does not constitute a nuisance under any conceivable theory of the subject, again because there has been no physical invasion.

The reason why these cases are so clear is that the central function of a system of private property is to establish the neutral baseline of which Michelman speaks. The function of the *ad coelum* rule is to endow boundary lines with legal significance.[29] To argue, therefore, that we need to bring such a neutral baseline to the eminent domain clause ignores the baseline furnished by the system of private property. So long as we are sure that the vast bulk of the cases falls clearly on one side of the line or the other, we can easily tolerate some ambiguity at the margins: litigation exerts powerful forces to select the most difficult cases for adjudication, no matter what the underlying standard. If the defects of the nuisance theory are thought to be decisive, then so too are the defects in any of the more complicated accounts of the police power limitation that others might wish to advance in its stead. How, for example, could one explicate a notion which turns on an individual's possible notice or "foresight" of the regulation imposed by the state?[30]

In addition, there is no reason to concede the force of Michelman's chosen counterexamples. I have already dealt with *Miller v. Schoene*. Concluding that the harm to the owners of the apple trees shall be regarded as an act of God seems quite defensible under the physical invasion test. Similarly, that test runs into little or no difficulty in the case of advertisements beside the public highway. They cannot be enjoined as public nuisances for the same reason that we cannot demand the destruction of a beautiful home or a fine rock formation because they distract the driving public.

This leaves only the case of "coming to the nuisance." There the resolution of the causal issues is quite clear once we recognize that within the framework of legal analysis the phrase "causing harm to another" is

29. See Donald Wittman, "Liability for Harm or Restitution for Benefit?," 13 *J. Legal Stud.* 57 (1984), on the importance of the baseline in structuring private transactions.

30. See Chapter 10 for discussion. See also Lawrence Berger, "A Policy Analysis of the Taking Problem," 49 *N.Y.U. L. Rev.* 165, 175 (1974).

shorthand for "the use of force or fraud against the person or property of another." Time is irrelevant: the brickmaker has sent fumes from his factory onto the lands of the other party. The case assumes the guise of reciprocity of causation only when one asks, as Michelman does, what type of strategic behavior by one party or the other could have avoided the harmful interaction between the parties. Yet the question of causation, properly defined, is not whether the neighbors or the brickmaker should have purchased lands to serve as a buffer for their own activities.[31] On that issue the problem is indeed symmetrical, and no decision one way or the other can be reached. This point, however, shows not the irrelevance of causal language to legal discourse but the inherent weaknesses of Michelman's relative cost-avoider account of causation, which is systematically unable to distinguish between cause and prevention of harm in clearer cases. Michelman does not explain why we are committed to a test that must necessarily fail, when there are better tests that conform more closely to both ordinary language and constitutional text. Properly understood, the causal question here is only this: did the brickmaker discharge pollution onto the land of his neighbors? That question can be answered by the simple techniques of observation that are available in all such nuisance cases. "Buffers," "foresight," and "perceived compatibility with surroundings" are all beside the point. Once the liability rule is established by independent means, we know who must establish the buffer and who is charged with the consequences of imperfect foresight.

It might be replied that this simple answer leaves unaccounted-for the temporal question of who got there first. The question of timing is in one sense irrelevant, because both plots of land were owned at the outset of the script. The point is clarified by the complete account of the coming-to-nuisance cases, in which the distinctive features of the situation are captured by the proper remedial responses. Thus as a matter of strict entitlement the plaintiff's cause of action accrues the moment the invasions take place, regardless of the extent of the immediate harm. Nonetheless, the action may not be brought because there is a mutually beneficial forced exchange that requires the plaintiff to stay his action until he suffers financial loss, but only in exchange for the waiver of the statute of limitations otherwise available to the defendant.[32] In addition,

---

31. Michelman, supra note 25, at 1243–1244.
32. For a more complete analysis, see Richard A. Epstein, "Nuisance Law: Corrective Justice and Its Utilitarian Constraints," 8 *J. Legal Stud.* 49, 72–73 (1979). Note that prescription played a very heavy role in Sturges v. Bridgman, 11 Ch. D. 852 (1879). *Sturges* in turn plays a very critical role in the account of causation in Coase, supra note 23, at 7–10.

the automatic injunction typically given to any party who is victimized by a nuisance may be delayed (with payment of interim damages) in order to take further into account the reversed temporal order, while an injunction need not be absolute but could require a partial abatement of the nuisance.[33] All these points presuppose, however, that it is possible to give a decisive answer to the question of entitlement: is there a principled account of the antinuisance vision of the police power? Michelman and others say no. I say that the physical invasion account, derived from the takings language, covers the field. The nuisance language may be often misunderstood and misused, but the conception has no inherent weakness that makes misuse inescapable.

The traditional physical invasion test also gives a complete explanation and justification for a case such as *Hadachek v. Sebastian*,[34] which raises the coming-to-nuisance issue in the constitutional vein. In *Hadachek* the defendant owned a valuable brickyard. The parcel had been acquired and developed when the land was outside the city limits of Los Angeles and before any residential housing was built in its immediate vicinity. After the lands had been incorporated into the city, and homes built nearby, Los Angeles passed an ordinance making it a misdemeanor to operate a brickyard in specified areas within the city limits. With his primary business banned, the value of the plaintiff's land was reduced from about $800,000 to $60,000. The Supreme Court upheld the ordinance under a broad version of the police power. Michelman's sympathy for the position of the claimant in this case rests upon the failure to develop a comprehensive account of the police power.[35] The case is misunderstood when it is cited to demonstrate that diminution of value, standing alone, does not furnish a sufficient basis for compensation.[36] The reason relief was properly denied in *Hadachek* was not that the loss in value was "only" 80 or 90 percent; indeed, the loss could have been total. What was crucial was that the defendant's losses, however great, were *justified* by virtue of the nuisance, for which the neighbor's coming to the nuisance was at most a partial offset. *Hadachek,* therefore, lends no principled support to a broad conception of the police power divorced from its antinuisance rationale. Instead the diminution of

33. See, e.g., *Sturges;* Ensign v. Walls, 323 Mich. 49, 34 N.W.2d 549 (1948); Pendoley v. Ferreira, 345 Mass. 309, 187 N.E.2d 142 (1963).

34. 239 U.S. 394 (1915).

35. See Michelman, supra note 25, at 1191 n.55.

36. Haas v. San Francisco, 605 F.2d 1117 (9th Cir. 1979), discussed in Chapter 14.

value has here the same role that it does in tort. It is relevant only on damages once liability is established by some independent criterion.

From Private Nuisance to Environmental Protection

The erosion of the antinuisance account of the police power has invited broader government regulation of environmental matters. It should be evident that some environmental regulation falls within the police power. Air and water polution and the discharge of toxic substances all give rise to the violation of private rights, which the state is empowered to prevent. Nonetheless, the simple invocation of an environmental stake is not sufficient to justify government action under the police power; everything turns on what the state does. Condemnation of land for a national park is but an extreme example of governmental action that may be desirable but outside the scope of the police power. In dealing with intermediate cases, the ultimate question remains as before: is the regulation an attempt to control the defendant's wrong or to provide a public benefit? That the distinction is ignored or obscured is borne out by an examination of three modern programs of environmental control: wetlands, floodway, and strip-mining legislation.

Wetlands regulation prohibits the development, without government approval, of certain designated areas of land in order to preserve the fragile balance of nature. Floodway legislation demands that certain areas be kept undeveloped to facilitate the runoff of excess waters. Strip-mining regulation insists at the very least that private lands on which mining operations take place be returned to their "original contours" or "original productivity" upon completion of the work. All three are subject to serious constitutional infirmities.

WETLANDS

In *Just v. Marinette County*,[37] which is perhaps the leading wetlands case, the Wisconsin Supreme Court sustained the local statute which, among other things, prohibited private owners from using landfill upon certain designated wetlands. The court said:

> This case causes us to reexamine the concepts of public benefit in contrast to public harm and the scope of an owner's right to

37. *56* Wis. 2d 7, 201 N.W.2d 761 (1972).

use of his property. In the instant case we have a restriction on the use of a citizen's property, not to secure a benefit for the public, but to prevent a harm from the change in the natural character of the citizen's property. We start with the premise that lakes and rivers in their natural state are unpolluted and the pollution which now exists is man made. The state of Wisconsin under the trust doctrine has a duty to eradicate the present pollution and to prevent further pollution in its navigable waters. This is not, in a legal sense, a gain or a securing of a benefit by the maintaining of the natural status quo of the environment. What makes this case different from most condemnation or police power zoning cases is the interrelationship of the wetlands, the swamps and the natural environment of shorelands to the purity of the water and to such natural resources as navigation, fishing, and scenic beauty. . . .

Is the ownership of a parcel of land so absolute that man can change its nature to suit any of his purposes? . . . An owner of land has no absolute and unlimited right to change the essential natural character of his land so as to use it for a purpose for which it was unsuited in its natural state and which injures the rights of others. The exercise of the police power in zoning must be reasonable and we think it is not an unreasonable exercise of that power to prevent harm to public rights by limiting the use of private property to its natural uses.

This is not a case where an owner is prevented from using his land for natural and indigenous uses. The uses consistent with the nature of the land are allowed and other uses recognized and still others permitted by special permit. The shoreland zoning ordinance prevents to some extent the changing of the natural character of the land within 1,000 feet of a navigable lake and 300 feet of a navigable river because of such land's interrelation to the contiguous water. The changing of wetlands and swamps to the damage of the general public by upsetting the natural environment and the natural relationship is not a reasonable use of that land which is protected from police power regulation. Changes and filling to some extent are permitted because the extent of such changes and fillings does not cause harm. We realize no case in Wisconsin has yet dealt with shoreland regulations and there are several cases in other states which seem to hold such regulations unconstitutional; but nothing this court has said or held in prior cases indicates that destroying the natural character of a swamp or a wetland so as to make that location available for human habitation is a reasonable use of that land when the new use, although of a more economic value to the owner, causes a harm to the general public.[38]

This extended passage is quite carefully tailored in its effort to bring the wetlands regulation within the traditional scope of the police power. The references to pollution "causing harm" and to the invasion of the "rights of others" are quite consistent with the general plan of folding novel cases into traditional theories. Yet the opinion fails to bring the case within the confines of the antinuisance doctrine. Although the development may pollute the lands owned by the Justs, there is no *tort*, because harm, to be actionable, must be *to another*, not to "the citizen's own property." Yet when the opinion speaks of harm to others, it speaks not of pollution, but solely of the economic and aesthetic losses resulting from removing private land from the general ecological balance. There is no physical invasion created by the landowner's use of the property, but only a desire by the state to use that property as part of an extended wildlife sanctuary. It is impossible to conceive of a successful action that any private owner of real estate or wildlife could maintain if the Justs decided not to use their property in its natural state. The normal bundle of property rights contains no priority for land in its natural condition; it regards use, including development, as one of the standard incidents of ownership.

Stripped of its rhetoric, *Just* is a condemnation of these development rights, and compensation is thus required. That wetlands are preserved only identifies a possible gain to the public; it does not eliminate the constitutional obligation. The true impulse behind these cases is the thought, as well expressed in the similar case of *Sibson v. New Hampshire,*[39] that the landfill activity was "bad for the marsh, and bad for mankind." But wherein lie the rights of the marsh? And when the state wants to use private property to benefit mankind, it announces that it wants to take them, at least in part, for public use. It must therefore pay for the privilege.

FLOOD CONTROL LEGISLATION

The pattern of analysis remains unchanged when we turn to various forms of flood control legislation. Again the police power prevents any riparian from blocking a riverbed or channel that carries off excess wa-

38. 56 Wis. 2d at 16–18, 201 N.W.2d at 767–768.
39. 115 N.H. 124, 126, 336 A.2d 239, 240 (1975).

ters, such as the melting of winter snows.[40] Such blocking is a violation of the riparian rights of others, which can be enjoined and controlled by straightforward application of either the natural flow or reasonable use theory of water rights. But it is quite a different matter when, in the name of flood control, the state, by general legislation or administrative action, designates certain privately held uplands as unfit for construction by their owners without public permission. There is no invasive conduct by the individual landowner, so the most that can be said is that this is a taking of development rights for public use. In *Usdin v. Environmental Protection Department of New Jersey,*[41] the court concluded its elaborate discussion sustaining one such statute by saying that the "act of the DEP must be deemed a proper exercise of a police power to prevent a misuse of nature, rather than an act of a compensable taking."[42] But if looked at in the other way, the case is easy. The restriction of development rights is a partial taking of real property, because the prevention of misfortunes of nature is not the same as the prevention of wrongs by the property owner. The prevention of acts of God does not lie within the police power, even if it satisfies the public use limitation. The decision is no different in principle from one which authorizes the confiscation of A's lumber to build the spillway on B's property.

STRIP MINING

Recent strip-mining legislation, subjected to similar analysis, reveals parallel defects. In *Hodel v. Virginia Surface Mining and Reclamation Ass'n,*[43] the Supreme Court sustained the Surface Mining Control and Reclamation Act of 1977 against a constitutional challenge on its face. The act required that land which is strip mined be restored to its original condition and to its approximate original contours, that efforts be made to separate and stabilize the topsoil, that disturbances to the hydraulic balance and to water quality be minimized, and that mined areas be revegetated. Ninety-five percent of the lands in question were located on slopes in excess of twenty degrees, which meant that restoration would be costly. The district court found that in most cases it was economically and physically impossible to mine the lands in compliance with the stated provisions. It also found that the value of the lands before strip-

40. Allison Dunham, "Flood Control Via the Police Power," 107 *U. Pa. L. Rev.* 1098 (1959).
41. 173 N.J. Super. 311 (1980).
42. Id. at 331.
43. 452 U.S. 264 (1981).

ping was in the neighborhood of $5 to $75 per acre, but that after stripping and leveling its market value was a minimum of $5,000 per acre, and in some cases up to $300,000 per acre. Last, the district court found that compliance with the strip-mining provision increased in material degree the hazards of erosion because of the unstable masses created in restoring the land to its original condition. After struggling within the framework of the applicable Supreme Court decisions, the district court finally held that the complete diminution of property values mandated by the regulations constituted a compensable taking of private property.

The Supreme Court reversed the decision on the ground that the "mere enactment" of such comprehensive legislation could not constitute a taking because "neither the appellees nor the court identified any property in which appellees have an interest that has allegedly been taken by the operation of the Act."[44] The point is a small tour de force in light of explicit findings by the district court that the passage of the statute had forced a number of coal companies to go out of business and a number of miners to lose their jobs.

Nor does the claim that the case was brought prematurely offer any defense against the facial invalidity of this statute. The statute constitutes a taking of all the land it governs, for the right to mine coal, like the right to develop wetlands, is one of the traditional incidents of real estate. Yet the statute requires the landowners to pay extensive sums of money to engage in activities that were once theirs to do as a matter of right. The police power, moreover, wholly fails to reach the case. The simple ownership of land in its natural condition can never be a private nuisance, while the development of the land was found to reduce, or at least to not increase, the likelihood of external harms to others. The simple alteration of privately owned lands does not come within a light year of invasion of another's property. The statute should have been struck down on its face because no possible set of emergent circumstances could justify its application in future cases.

44. Id. at 294.

10 The Police Power: Means

Means Scrutiny:
Uncertainty and Two Kinds of Error

Once the ends of the police power are defined, what means may the state use to achieve them? At the outset it is important to stress that the question of means does not admit of the Cartesian clarity possible for the question of ends, where a clear rights-based theory dictates some results and not others. With means questions, no court can have the complete confidence in its own judgments. The state can impose damages or fines for harms already caused, but determining their amounts is as difficult as determining damages in private suits.

More important, the chief constitutional battleground is over the form of relief—the mix of damages and injunction—possible against future and uncertain harms. Again, the state is vested with the rights of the citizens it represents, but these rights are difficult to state categorically. In principle no person should ever be put in a position where he must exercise the right of self-defense, because aggression is a wrong. When a wrong takes place, the question is what remedies are available to the injured party. Clearly there is an action in damages, but it may come too late, or the defendant may be insolvent. Therefore, the injured party is allowed to use force in self-defense, limited to correcting the original wrong, which leads to difficult questions of excessive or deadly force, good and bad faith, extrasensitive victims, and the like.[1] The law

1. See, e.g., Francis H. Bohlen and John J. Burns, "The Privilege to Protect Property by Dangerous Barriers and Mechanical Devices," 35 *Yale L.J.* 525

tends to suppress these problems by allowing the use of force in self-defense when it is "reasonable," which, no matter how explicated, leaves room in the joints.[2]

A parallel problem exists with nuisance cases. Ideally, no one should commit a nuisance. But in a world of uncertainty and greed, nuisances do occur. The question then arises of what remedies should be available. Abatement of the nuisance is a self-help remedy similar to self-defense against personal aggression. But in any complex system of liability, abatement is of limited use. Where it is inapplicable, the issue is whether damages, permament or partial, or injunctions, conditional or absolute, provide the proper remedy. Again there may be presumptions (such as that in favor of injunctions against substantial harms), but the disagreement on the issue of remedies persists, because of the difficulty of finding appropriate remedies to control future and uncertain harm.[3]

What is true with nuisances and self-defense is also true with breach of contract. In principle, breach should not take place, as parties could in principle purchase releases if transactions costs were zero. But they are not, so when breach takes place, the disagreement is again over the choice of remedies, be it with damages or specific performance or negative injunctions. Again there is no consensus in the case law or the academic literature about the precise mix.[4]

The problems in the private area have inescapable consequences for the structure of constitutional law. One cannot demand of the state any greater precision in its choice of remedies than is demanded of the private persons whom it represents. The constant challenge, therefore, is to balance two kinds of error. Errors of overinclusion occur when the regu-

---

(1926); Richard A. Epstein, "Intentional Harms," 4 *J. Legal Stud.* 391, 41–420 (1975). George P. Fletcher, "Proportionality and the Psychotic Aggressor: A Vignette in Comparative Criminal Theory," 8 *Israel L. Rev.* 367 (1973).

2. See William L. Prosser and W. Page Keeton, *The Law of Torts* ¶19 (5th ed. 1984).

3. On the tort subject, see Richard A. Epstein, "Defense and Subsequent Pleas in a System of Strict Liability," 3 *J. Legal Stud.* 165, 197–201 (1974); A. Mitchell Polinsky, "Controlling Externalities and Protecting Entitlements: Property Right, Liability Rule, and Tax-Subsidy Approaches," 8 *J. Legal Stud.* 1 (1979). For a collection of cases, see Richard A. Epstein, Charles O. Gregory, and Harry Kalven, *Cases and Materials on Torts* 618–629 (4th ed. 1984).

4. See Anthony T. Kronman, "Specific Performance," 45 *U. Chi. L. Rev.* 351 (1978); Alan Schwartz, "The Case for Specific Performance," 89 *Yale L.J.* 271 (1980); William Bishop, "The Choice of Remedy for Breach of Contract," 14 *J. Legal Stud.* 299 (1985).

lation sweeps wider than necessary to control the identified evil; those of underinclusion occur when the regulation does not reach all instances of the evil in question. It is not possible to eliminate both simultaneously, and the effort to minimize their joint impact clearly has constitutional dimension. Suppose a landowner wishes to operate a factory on his premises, thereby raising the risk that harmful pollutants will escape onto a neighbor's land. To enjoin the construction of a factory, whose operation would have inflicted no harm upon the neighbor, is to limit the owner's use of property, and thus to take it in part. Yet to permit the factory to engage in operations that result in harm is to authorize the private taking of property for which compensation may not be available if the defendant is insolvent. Yet to enjoin too quickly may be impermissible if a later and more tailored injunction provides all, or even substantially all, the required relief. The best one can do when facing two types of error under uncertainty is to try to minimize the sum of the errors, with each weighted equally, since each involves a limitation of property rights, which are entitled to constitutional protection.

The question of overbreadth and underbreadth so critical to the constitutional inquiry necessarily imitates the task of balancing hardships that has long been the byword of responsible courts of equity. To look only at the risks the state prevents is to ignore those it has increased. As matters of estimate replace matters of principle, some judicial deference is required. The number of factors that bear on the question of just compensation is large, and they are not uniquely ordered. Any complete inquiry must look not only at the statute itself, but at the uneasy mix of legislative competence and legislative bias, all in an effort to assess whether the remedy chosen fits the evil to be avoided. The task invites difficult marginal cases, for minimizing error does not eliminate it when the subject matter is so diffuse and amorphous. Nonetheless, even after allowances are made for the inherent difficulty of the inquiry, the Supreme Court, here as elsewhere, has set its thumb too heavily on the side of state power. In this area too the rational basis test precludes any serious review of the fit between means and ends. What is needed is an intermediate standard of review that says, as did the court in *Lochner*, "The mere assertion that the subject relates though but in a remote degree to the public health does not necessarily render the enactment valid. The act must have a more direct relation, as a means to an end, and the end itself must be appropriate and legitimate."[5]

5. Lochner v. New York, 198 U.S. 45, 57 (1905).

Stated in another way, the court should defer where it believes that a legislative decision is likely to be more accurate than its own, or more precisely, where it believes that the additional costs of its own extended supervision (often financed at public expense, which is itself a taking from third parties) is not justified by an incremental improvement in fitting means to ends. No test of this form can hope to ferret out all forms of legislative abuse. But the enterprise cannot be attacked as vain and mistaken solely because it is not uniformly successful. The inquiry is worthwhile if it reduces the level of abuse below what it would be in the absence of such increased scrutiny, at least in amounts that justify the increased costs (if any) that are involved.

Nor can intermediate means scrutiny be opposed on the ground that it invites a perpetual and titanic struggle between legislatures and courts. That conclusion rests on the mistaken premise that the output of legislative bodies remains constant regardless of the web of legal rules that determines their institutional role. Both government and private parties, however, can be expected to respond to the signals sent out by the courts. As the level of means scrutiny rises, the expected success of legislative initiatives will be reduced, along with the volume of dubious legislation passed. There doubtless would be a transitional period in which earlier legislation, passed under lax standards of review, was challenged under the more rigorous standards that replaced them. Yet once that interim adjustment was made, the changes in primary governmental activities would be predictable, if not in magnitude, then surely in direction. The courts would continue to adjudicate marginal cases, only the margins would shift with the change in rules, while the overall level of legislation should fall, not rise.[6] The lower levels of legislative activities in turn should mean that far fewer nonconstitutional issues have to be resolved. When the system finds its new equilibrium, the burdens of adjudication should be reduced, even as the subset of cases litigated changes. As a first approximation, increased judicial scrutiny should reduce the demands placed upon the judicial system.

6. See, generally, George L. Priest and Benjamin Klein, "The Selection of Disputes for Litigation," 13 *J. Legal Stud.* 1 (1984); Patricia Munch Danzon and Lee A. Lillard, "Settlement out of Court: The Disposition of Medical Malpractice Claims," 12 *J. Legal Stud.* 345 (1983). The Priest and Klein model indicates in the limit that no matter what the underlying rule of liability, the outcome in litigated cases will split fifty-fifty between plaintiffs and defendants. The Danzon and Lillard model does not have that striking implication, but it also assumes that cases will not be randomly settled, so any change in the legal rule will be met by a change in the response of parties to it.

Applications

The Supreme Court has passed on an enormous number of means question cases, for some variation of the police power theme has surfaced not only under the eminent domain clause, but also under the due process clause, the contracts clause, the equal protection clause, and the First Amendment. In my view, a unified approach to the police power is attractive regardless of the context in which it arises. This chapter tests the strength of this approach by beginning with the early land use cases and then extending the analysis to modern decisions, chiefly in the First Amendment and equal protection areas.

MUGLER AND EUCLID

In *Mugler v. Kansas*,[7] the law under attack prohibited the operation of any brewery within the state of Kansas. The plaintiff alleged that his brewery was constructed before the passage of the statute, that his property was ill-suited to any other use, and that its operation did not constitute a public nuisance. Justice Harlan, speaking for the court, upheld the statute by resorting to a two-pronged argument. He first denied that the government action was a taking because the statute did not remove the plaintiff from the possession of his premises. But that argument is met by the analysis of partial takings, given that the incident of use was impaired.

It is doubtful that the "no taking" argument was persuasive even to the court; if it had been, the detailed consideration of the police power justification that followed would not have been necessary. In dealing with the police power, Harlan's argument was quite simply that the legislature may take steps to control the disease, poverty, and crime held to be the inevitable and injurious consequences of alcoholism. Missing was the necessary constitutional analysis of whether this public nuisance was properly attributable to these defendants. Even today the expansive theories of proximate causation only allow an injured party to reach the immediate supplier of the alcohol—bartenders, social hosts, or retail outlets—but not the original producers.[8] Therefore, allowing the legisla-

---

7. 123 U.S 623 (1887).

8. See, e.g., Vesely v. Sager, 5 Cal.3d 153, 486 P.2d 151, 95 Cal. Rptr. 623 (1971), which allowed a party injured by a drunk driver to maintain an action against the purveyor of the alcoholic beverages. That decision did not allow suit against the manufacturer of the beverages and was itself overturned by statute in California. Cal. [Bus. & Prof.] Code § 25602 (West 1964, 1984 Supp.). Similarly, most of the gun cases are decided the same way, so no action can be brought against the gun manufacturer if the gun is not itself de-

ture to designate these activities as nuisances is to erroneously allow it to define the scope of its own powers.

Suppose, however, that the state's characterization of the manufacture of alcohol as a nuisance is, in fact, sound. The second level of inquiry whether the statute is overbroad—calls for analyzing whether the state's narrower means would achieve substantially the same end. In particular, the court never asked whether limitations upon the purchase or consumption of alcohol—be it by age, place of service, or condition of user—might have done away with a large portion of the social problem without the enormous restrictions imposed upon Mugler's operations. Likewise, the court never asked whether a more stringent set of penalties against drunkenness per se, or against offenses committed by persons in a drunken condition, could have achieved the same effect. The answers to these questions, of course, are not crystal clear, but it is difficult to believe that the blanket prohibition against the manufacture of alcohol, at least in existing plants, could have been sustained when the state had not even explored lesser restrictions upon the sale and distribution of alcohol. If the state must justify its undisputed taking of property, then the decision seems wrong, but if not wrong, then surely at the outer limits of the police power.

In one sense *Mugler* might be dismissed as a sport, attributable to the special place of the temperance movement in the nineteenth century. *Euclid v. Ambler Realty,*[9] which gave virtual carte blanche to modern zoning ordinances, cannot be so characterized. The relevant facts, briefly summarized, are these. The village of Euclid was a small town of some 14 square miles, most of it farmland, just east of Cleveland. Through the center of the town ran two railroads, the Lake Shore and the Nickel Plate. At the time of the ordinance in question the plaintiff owned a 68-acre tract (1,800 by 1,950 feet) of unimproved land between the tracks of the Nickel Plate Railroad and Euclid Avenue. The ordinance limited somewhat more than one third of the plaintiff's tract to the construction of single-family homes, two-family dwellings, or apartments. The land so zoned was in the path of commercial development; the zoning reduced its value by about 75 percent, from $800,000 to $200,000. The answer to the first question, was there a taking simpliciter, is evident: the restrictions on use were a partial taking. The question of compensation

---

fective. See, e.g., Martin v. Harrington Richardson, Inc. 743 F.2d 1200 (7th Cir. 1984).

9. 272 U.S. 365 (1926).

therefore turned on whether the ordinance could be sustained under the police power.

Here the trial judge—who displayed far more good sense on the subject than the Supreme Court—viewed the entire enterprise as an ill-concealed effort to transfer wealth from one set of landowners to another through the medium of regulation.[10] The Supreme Court, however, taking a more expansive approach to the police power, wrote:

> The decisions enumerated in the first group cited above agree that the exclusion of buildings devoted to business, trade, etc., from residential districts, bears a rational relation to the health and safety of the community. Some of the grounds for this conclusion are—promotion of the health and security from injury of children and others by separating dwelling houses from territory devoted to trade and industry; suppression and prevention of disorder; facilitating the extinguishment of fires, and enforcement of street traffic regulations and other general welfare ordinances; aiding the health and safety of the community by excluding from residential areas the confusion and danger of fire, contagion and disorder which in greater or less degree attach to the location of stores, shops and factories. Another ground is that the construction and repair of streets may be rendered easier and less expensive by confining the greater part of the heavy traffic to the streets where business is carried on.[11]

It is not possible to quarrel with the antitort rationales—disease prevention, nuisance control—that are said to motivate the zoning ordinance. But a list of ends does not respond to the overbreadth question: do the asserted means mesh with the permissible ends? Clearly they do not. There is no obvious need to segregate residential from commercial areas. The police power has always functioned where the two were integrated, and there is no obvious connection between the degree of separation and the degree of injury avoided. Any desired separation can be achieved by private means. A single person owned large chunks of the zoned property. That owner had sufficient incentive both to guard against negative spillovers and to ensue the proper distribution between common and separate areas as part of a comprehensive subdivision plan.

Other police power justifications for this comprehensive form of zoning are even more suspect. Fire hazards are a recurrent problem of city

10. See Ambler Realty Co. v. Euclid, 297 F. 307, 315–316 (1924).
11. 272 U.S. at 391.

life, yet they have not led to a total ban against urbanization of development. The question, therefore, is not whether development should be permitted freely, but whether it can be prohibited here when it is allowed as a general matter in most places at most times: the selectivity speaks against a close relationship between means and ends. Private injunctions by interested neighbors still lie in cases of manifest peril. Private damage actions lie thereafter. Third-party liability insurance can be a condition of engaging in dangerous trades. State regulations tailored to the peril at hand—insistence on alarms in public places, bona fide prohibition of flammable materials in construction—can move the control of fire from the private to the public domain within the antinuisance account of the police power. The municipality also has other means to deal with the same problem. It can acquire first-rate firefighting equipment, and it can pass ordinances that give fire prevention paramount rights of way upon the public streets. There is a world of difference between the use of these means and the bald assertion that the only way to prevent fires is to prevent construction of many things that can be burnt.

The other considerations referred to in *Euclid* are scarcely more persuasive. Why is it impossible to construct streets with materials that withstand a high volume of traffic when this is done every day? Must inferior materials be used in the busiest locations when more expensive ones are available? Why aren't special assessments for road repairs, a common nineteenth-century phenomenon, a less intrusive alternative?[12]

There is yet another way to show the constitutional defects of the zoning ordinance in *Euclid:* the restrictions imposed in the given area were not imposed anywhere else within the township. Individuals there remained free to develop their land as they saw fit, now without any competition from their regulated neighbors. The differential treatment, while neither a necessary or a sufficient condition to condemn zoning, is always a powerful telltale sign that the police power has become a cloak for illegitimate ends whose influence overwhelms the stated reasons. That point gains urgency here, where there is no conflict between the evidence of motive and the effects of the ordinance.

Euclid, at the birth of zoning, represents a virtual abandonment of efforts to monitor the overbreadth question in land use cases. The insistence upon the "rational relation," here as elsewhere, carries a legal message that is at variance with ordinary usage. Any fit between ends and means, however weak, will suffice even when superior alternatives

12. See Chapter 18.

are available. Nonetheless, the case suggests guidelines for the appropriate level of judicial oversight. The state must meet a clear burden of justification where it imposes land use restrictions (1) that are designed to regulate parcels already subject to common ownership (or, for that matter, are governed by a network of existing restrictive covenants or similar devices); (2) that apply to still-undeveloped land; (3) that prevent certain individuals from engaging in land uses that are open to others; and (4) that are directed toward particular nuisances which can be largely controlled by more tailored means, be it direct legislative or administrative orders, or private suits for damages and injunctions.

It is of course possible to rebut the presumptions as they are created. Certain lands may well have to be left undeveloped because they contain toxic substances that, if moved or disturbed, could contaminate nearby underground water supplies. Other development ordinances could have some antinuisance grounding. One restriction on land use may have a 90 percent probability of preventing an existing peril while a more limited restriction may be effective in only 10 percent of the cases, so the choice between them will be delicate indeed. Yet by the same token, isolated or infrequent counterexamples can be raised against all presumptions. Without further evidence that the presumption is unsuitable, these examples only show what the term "presumption" implies—that exceptions will arise. They do not discredit the presumptions, or their powerful fit with the cases they govern.

The suggested presumptions clearly imply that most comprehensive zoning ordinances in force today do not have a police power justification insofar as they control matters such as minimum lot sizes for development, building heights, setbacks, ground-to-floor area ratios, growth, and the like. Marginal cases will, of course, remain. Restrictions on halfway houses for juvenile delinquents or released criminals will be hard to deal with, even on a case-by-case basis (shades of *Mugler*), but the initial presumption, I believe, should be that these institutions can operate until there is proof of real danger of crime. Similarly, total prohibitions against tie-ins to sewers and water facilities are difficult to justify, for the state acts as a common carrier that must service all comers on payment of user fees tied to costs of installation or use.

FIRST AMENDMENT: PREFERRED FREEDOMS

The First Amendment cases offer an instructive contrast in their attitude toward the police power. The term "police power" does not often appear, perhaps because of the expansive interpretation given to it in cases involving property rights and economic liberties. Nonetheless, when the question is asked, what limitations are placed upon the First Amendment, the answer is definitive: individual rights of speech can be overridden only by a showing of a "compelling state interest." That idea is then narrowly construed to give great weight to the control of force (such as the incitement to riot) and fraud, as the Lockean "antitaking" account of the police power suggests. The legitimacy of a compelling state interest, however, is only the prelude to a ceaseless inquiry into the state's choice of the fit between means and ends. The asymmetry between granting and denying anticipatory relief is fully understood, so the state's hand is often stayed even where the possibility of violence is close at hand, given that the use of force is itself punishable.[13] Accordingly, overbroad regulation is routinely declared unconstitutional on its face.[14] The plans of the American Nazi Party to demonstrate in Skokie, Illinois,[15] generated a number of lawsuits in which the lower courts struck down a whole range of measures that the township sought to impose upon the demonstrators: permit requirements; time, place, and manner restrictions; and demands for bonding.[16] Where political speech is at stake, anticipatory relief against threats of harm verges on the unconstitutional for reasons of overbreadth alone.

The hostile reception to police power justifications in the more prosaic context of public nuisance also speaks to the powerful contrast between the property and the speech cases. In particular it is instructive to contrast *Mugler* with *Erznoznik v. City of Jacksonville.*[17] This case involved a successful First Amendment challenge to a local ordinance which said: "It shall be unlawful and it is hereby declared a public nuisance for any ticket seller . . . connected with a drive-in theater in the City to exhibit . . . any motion picture . . . in which the human male or female bare buttocks, human female bare breasts, or human bare pubic areas are shown, if such motion picture . . . is visible from any public street or public place."[18]

In striking down this ordinance upon its face, the Supreme Court did not pay the slightest deference to the legislative determination of what

13. For the vacillation in the picketing cases, see Thornhill v. Alabama, 310 U.S. 88 (1940); Teamsters Local 695 v. Vogt, Inc., 354 U.S. 284 (1957).
14. See, e.g., Comment, "The First Amendment Overbreadth Doctrine," 83 *Harv. L. Rev.* 844 (1970).
15. See Collin v. Smith, 447 F. Supp. 676 (N.D. Ill.), *aff'd* 578 F.2d 1197 (7th Cir.), *cert. denied* 439 U.S. 916 (1978).
16. 447 F. Supp. at 681.
17. 422 U.S. 205 (1975).
18. Jacksonville, Fla., Ordinance §330.313 (Jan. 14, 1972), quoted in *Erznoznik,* 422 U.S. at 206–207.

conduct counts as a public nuisance, even though obscenity, like drunkeness, may well have fallen under the "morals" head of the traditional police power. *Mugler* and *Euclid* were not so much as wisps on the horizon. Instead, the judicial examination was completely de novo. The court first noted that the statute was bad because it was overinclusive in its scope. As drafted, "it would bar a film containing a picture of baby's buttocks, the nude body of a war victim, or scenes from a culture in which nudity is indigenous."[19] The court then concluded that the ordinance was underinclusive in relationship to its ends. There was no demonstration that it banned all materials that would be patently offensive if seen from the public street or even patently offensive to children; and there was no demonstration that the ordinance was designed—shades of Michelman's example—to prevent the distraction of drivers on the highway. No assessment was ever made of the frequency with which errors would occur, with and without the statute, or of the likelihood that enforcement of the statute would bend to take atypical cases into account. The mere existence of the gap between means and ends doomed the statute on its face, even though it constituted a trivial restriction upon the interests in freedom of speech (it required the drive-in theater to pay for a new wall) in an area close to the narrow account of the police power, but far removed from the core concerns of the First Amendment.

Erznoznik indicates how the doctrine of preferred freedoms imposes powerful restrictions upon legislative prerogatives. The contrast between the police power inquiry undertaken here and that conducted in passing on the general zoning ordinances sanctioned by *Euclid* is stunning, given that *Erznoznik* is in one sense a land use case. In historical terms *Euclid,* as a creature of its time, rests a close parallel to the "bad tendency" test that was influential in the early days of the First Amendment,[20] but has been so decisively rejected in more recent decisions.[21] Yet the bad tendency test was abandoned in free speech cases because it was inconsistent with the basic structure of the First Amendment. That same inconsistency also makes extreme deference inappropriate in eminent domain cases. Implied exceptions are necessary to make the Constitution intelligible, but they can never be used by indirection to nullify basic substantive guarantees.

The far harder question that remains is whether a single standard for

19. 422 U.S. at 213.
20. Patterson v. Colorado, 205 U.S. 454 (1907); Whitney v. California, 274 U.S. 357 (1927).
21. Brandenburg v. Ohio, 395 U.S. 444 (1969).

means and review should apply to both First Amendment and eminent domain cases. My own (cautious) view is that the unification is probably desirable where some intermediate test of reasonable relationship could be applied in all cases of this sort. But the thesis of this chapter does not depend strictly upon accepting this view of the First Amendment; no matter what view is taken of that issue, intermediate scrutiny is still clearly appropriate in the eminent domain area. The key to raising the standard of view in takings case is to attack the implicit division between preferred freedoms and other residual constitutional rights. Here I do not wish to quarrel with the dominant place of the First Amendment, whether for the marketplace of ideas, self-realization of the individual, or protection of the political processes of government. It is still possible to show that the takings clause should be more resistant to encroachment by the police power of the state.

The first point in the argument is that the two amendments have different contours, even if their police power exceptions are identical. The First Amendment places limits on the state's power of condemnation that are far more stringent than the public use requirement of the eminent domain clause. Thus is it an open and shut issue that the First Amendment effectively prevents the United States from nationalizing the *New York Times,* even if it is prepared to operate it as a government newspaper. By the same token, the First Amendment will not avail if the *New York Times* wishes to resist the application of a general environmental statute designed to prevent the pollution of streams by wastes from the newspaper's production plants, just as it has not served to insulate newspapers from the general minimum wage and collective bargaining statutes.

The reasons are clear enough. In the first case the major beneficiaries of the nationalization are government officials who wish to escape criticism: the potential for abuse is so great that it is not worth the effort to try to identify the rare case in which the nationalization might be justified, given the availability of far less restrictive controls upon the press. In the second case the beneficiary is (or is said to be) the public at large, which has insisted only that newspapers adhere to the ordinary obligations imposed upon everyone else. The level of governmental abuse is thus sufficiently reduced so that the ordinary police power and public use rules work well, even though freedom of speech is in some sense implicated.

A second reason for intermediate scrutiny in free speech cases is that there are powerful interests on both sides of the line. Speech may well receive powerful constitutional protection, but fraud, breach of confidential duties, defamation, treason, and incitement to riot are all very serious offenses that warrant the use of public force even in a society that respects the virtues of limited government. In the trade-off between political speech and treason, why is the intermediate test so inappropriate? The intermediate standard has costs, but it is doubtful that these are decisive in an imperfect world. Intermediate scrutiny always asks, is there some less restrictive alternative available? No major abridgment of speech is apt to survive that question. The intermediate standard allows one to weigh the strength of different forms of speech differently, just as it allows one to weigh differently the interests on the other side. It is better to be aware of the problem and to create responsible subcategories and rebuttable presumptions than it is to pretend that all speech is of equal importance, when it evidently is not.

The third response takes a different form and rests on the proposition that the classical protections for speech and for property have common roots. Lockean defenses of property, for example, evoke the images of personal independence and self-realization in which it has become so fashionable to couch the case for the constitutional guarantees of freedom of speech. The First Amendment argument is that individuals will be able to develop their full potential only if they enjoy a protected realm of autonomy in which they are free to act and experiment for themselves. But a system of private property, which also emphasizes individual autonomy, is designed to serve that same end. Property is defensive, not exploitive.

There is also a political dimension. A nation in which private property is protected contains independent, decentralized sources of power that can be used against the state, reducing thereby the possibility that any group will be able to seize control over the sources of information or the levers of political power. In addition, private property provides the private wealth necessary to support active participation in public debate. Private property, in a word, nourishes freedom of speech, just as freedom of speech nourishes private property. Can anyone find a society in which freedom of speech flourishes where the institution of private property is not tolerated? A country in which there is a free nationalized press? The debate over the extent to which the First Amendment protects individual access to a public forum[22] in the end only amounts to a skirmish at the edges of free speech; the central objective is to guard against government favoritism in disposing of public resources, an issue

22. See, e.g., Geoffrey Stone, "Fora Americana: Speech in Public Places," 1974 *Sup. Ct. Rev.* 233.

with a clear eminent domain dimension. But think of the catastrophe that would result if political speech were banned on private property. The persistent skepticism about the government's role in regulating speech also applies to takings cases.

The need for common police power standards in the two areas is brought to the fore by recent Supreme Court cases that show how closely issues of speech and property are intertwined. For many years there appeared to be no necessary conflict between zoning cases and speech cases because it seemed possible to maintain the categorical division between them. But the clash has become evident, especially with the recent move to expand First Amendment protection to commercial speech. In *Metromedia, Inc. v. City of San Diego*,[23] the city passed a complex ordinance that sharply limited the types of signs that could be posted within city limits. Subject to a long list of exceptions for bus stop signs, temporary political signs, and the like, the ordinance banned all forms of noncommercial billboards and permitted only those commercial billboards that referred to the firm located or services rendered on the site where the sign was posted. The asserted justifications for the restrictions on signs were, first, traffic control and safety and second, aesthetic improvement. The California Supreme Court treated this as a *Euclid* case and found no reason to upset the determination of the city council, even though the ordinance was enacted without any hard evidence that it would achieve its professed goals.

The case received a very different treatment in the United States Supreme Court because the threshold question—was this a land use case or a speech case?—was taken seriously. Six justices, a plurality of four and a concurrence of two, found that more serious scrutiny was required because billboards are used to communciate information and thus fall within the ambit of the First Amendment. Denied the easy "out" of deference, the plurality opinion then held that the ban was unconstitutional for noncommercial speech. It further held that the California Supreme Court could sustain the ban on commercial speech on remand if it so chose. The concurrence of Brennan and Blackmun rejected all fine distinctions and urged that the entire ordinance be struck down on the ground that it was difficult to distinguish between commercial and noncommercial speech and that the ordinance as drafted cut too closely to the heart of the First Amendment.

Under the analysis that I have advanced here the case does have one clear outcome. The regulation is a taking of private property as well as a

23. 453 U.S. 490 (1981).

restriction on the freedom of speech. As the sharp cleavage between property and speech cases is no longer viable, the restrictions so imposed must be justified in all their aspects. Here the asserted justifications are insufficient both as to ends and to means. The aesthetic concerns raised by the ordinance are largely outside the antitaking limits of the police power. A taking for public use would require compensation, possibly implicit, to the parties affected.[24] The traffic safety point suffers incurably from the same overbreadth objections that weigh against most comprehensive zoning ordinances. The state's burden is enormous in light of the wealth of other means available such as restrictions on the shape, color, or lighting of signs, or direct control over vehicles and drivers. The classification issue that divided the Supreme Court did not have to be addressed, at least here. To be sure, the question remains whether the billboards, either commercial or noncommercial can be condemned. But the condemnation, if allowed, may well require cash payment, a point sufficient to dim the state's ardor to regulate.

DUE PROCESS CASES: FUNDAMENTAL RIGHTS

As my examination of *Mugler* and *Euclid* indicates, the due process clause has been the home of much takings law, so it is not surprising that conflict between private property and the police power continues to be played out in this arena. One illustration of *Euclid*'s hold on current Supreme Court thinking is *City of Pittsburgh v. ALCO Parking Corp.*[25] At issue was the constitutionality of a 20 percent gross receipts tax imposed upon the owners of private garages that directly competed with the city. I have already established that this tax is a prima facie taking; the question here has strictly to do with police power justification. Reminiscent of *Euclid,* the city contended, and the court agreed, that the tax, falling as it did upon suburban commuters, was an appropriate means to charge them for the damage done to city roads.

The end is legitimate, but the means chosen are not. All the relevant questions were left unexamined. Why did the city not impose the fee upon suburban cars that parked in city garages? Why did it impose the fee upon city cars that parked in private garages? What was the correlation between the amount of the charge and the amount of the damage caused? Did the suburbanites bring benefits to the city that were captured by sales, property, or other taxes? Were the alternative modes of taxation workable? In ignoring these issues, what shines through from the record is that the city's methods were chosen for their anticompeti-

24. See Chapter 14.
25. 417 U.S. 369 (1974).

tive effect upon private firms. If the burden—any kind of burden—were placed upon the city to justify the tax, it would be struck down in a short trial followed by a directed verdict. The proper question can never be whether it is possible for the state to utter words that refer to a police power rationale. The question must be whether the tax retains any reasonable relationship to the antitaking and antinuisance ends of the police power.

Challenges under the due process clause need not always meet such a fate. In particular, the magic of fundamental rights, which have such decisive power under the First Amendment, can reach other forms of land use regulation. *Village of Belle Terre v. Boraas*[26] and *Moore v. City of East Cleveland*[27] together illustrate the central point. In *Belle Terre* the challenged restriction on land use forbade the occupancy of any single-family dwelling by more than two persons who were unrelated by blood, adoption, or marriage. The challenged restriction in *Moore* was adopted with the same general purpose but was drawn to make it illegal for a grandmother to share her apartment with her two grandchildren who were only cousins to each other. Under the *Euclid* standard the zoning regulation in *Belle Terre* was sustained. But if, as Justice Marshall argued in dissent, interests in privacy and associational freedom, especially within the family, were preferred, then quick work can be made of the zoning ordinance on the prosaic ground that there is no fit between the admitted evil and its proposed remedy. Thus in *Belle Terre* Marshall wrote:

A variety of justifications have been proffered in support of the village's ordinance. It is claimed that the ordinance controls population density, prevents noise, traffic and parking problems, and preserves the rent structure of the community and its attractiveness to families. As I noted earlier, these are all legitimate and substantial interests of government. But I think it clear that the means chosen to accomplish these purposes are both overinclusive and underinclusive, and that the asserted goals could be as effectively achieved by means of an ordinance that did not discriminate on the basis of constitutionally protected choices of lifestyle. The ordinance imposes no restriction whatsoever on the number of persons who may live in a house, as long as they are related by marital or sanguinary bonds—presumably no matter how distant their relationship. Nor does the ordinance restrict the number of income

26. 416 U.S. 1 (1974).
27. 431 U.S. 494 (1977).

earners who may contribute to rent in such a household, or the number of automobiles that may be maintained by its occupants. In that sense the ordinance is underinclusive. On the other hand, the statute restricts the number of unrelated persons who may live in a home to no more than two. It would therefore prevent three unrelated people from occupying a dwelling even if among them they had but one income and no vehicles. While an extended family of a dozen or more might live in a small bungalow, three elderly and retired persons could not occupy the large manor house next door. Thus the statute is also grossly overinclusive to accomplish its intended purposes.[28]

That approach bore fruit in *Moore,* where the standard of review articulated in *Euclid* was rejected by Justice Powell, who then found it easy to dispose of the ordinance in question:

> When thus examined, this ordinance cannot survive. The city seeks to justify it as a means of preventing overcrowding, minimizing traffic and parking congestion, and avoiding an undue financial burden on East Cleveland's school system. Although these are legitimate goals, the ordinance before us serves them marginally, at best. For example, the ordinance permits any family consisting only of husband, wife, and unmarried children to live together, even if the family contains a half dozen licensed drivers, each with his or her own car. At the same time it forbids an adult brother and sister to share a household, even if both faithfully use public transportation. The ordinance would permit a grandmother to live with a single dependent son and children, even if his school-age children number a dozen, yet it forces Mrs. Moore to find another dwelling for her grandson John, simply because of the presence of his uncle and cousin in the same household. We need not labor the point. Section 1341.08 has but a tenuous relation to alleviation of the conditions mentioned by the city.[29]

The justifications put forward in these two cases under the due process clause are similar to those which were advanced in *Euclid,* yet in both instances they were disposed of in a well-reasoned paragraph. The contrast between Powell's treatment of the police power in *ALCO* and *Moore* could hardly be more dramatic. The central point, however, is that the dissent in *Belle Terre* and the decision in *Moore* are both flawed by the insistence that some fundamental right must be identified before the

28. 416 U.S. at 18–19.
29. 431 U.S. at 499–500.

statute is subject to any judicial scrutiny. The weakness does not depend on where the line is drawn between ordinary and fundamental rights; it is in the effort to draw any such distinction at all. Under the proper analysis all rights are, as it were, fundamental. Neither the due process clause nor the takings clause draws any distinction among the types of property interests they protect. All such interests are treated as a piece and all are subject to the unified application of the police power rules.

EQUAL PROTECTION: ECONOMIC LIBERTIES

The choice of proper means under the police power has also arisen in the modern equal protection context, to which my analysis extends. In *Minnesota v. Clover Leaf Creamery Co.*, the Minnesota legislature had "enacted a statute banning the retail sale of milk in plastic nonreturnable, nonrefillable containers, but permitting such sale in other nonreturnable, nonrefillable containers, such as paperboard milk cartons."[30] The statute rested upon a legislative finding "that the use of nonreturnable, nonrefillable containers for the packaging of milk and other milk products presented a solid waste management problem for the state, promotes energy waste, and depletes natural resources." After an extensive trial, the Minnesota District Court found that the "actual basis" of the statute "was to promote the economic interests of certain segments of the local dairy and pulpwood industries at the expense of the economic interests of other segments of the dairy industry and the plastics industry."[31]

The United States Supreme Court sustained the statute on an equal protection analysis, in which the classification of various milk containers was judged only under the relaxed "rational basis" test appropriate when there is no suspect classification or fundamental right in issue. The court looked only at what the proponents of the statute said on its behalf, ignoring all the testimony (including that which was undisputed) that had been introduced against the statute. Speaking through Justice Brennan, the court sustained the statute by showing that state pollution agencies supported its passage, that empirical studies had been done on its behalf, and that the bill was "designed to prevent the beginning of another system of nonreturnables" that would be very difficult to stop once it was in place.[32] With the evidence so marshaled, judicial deference alone was sufficient to sustain the statute.

30. 449 U.S. 456, 458 (1981). The statute is 1977 Minn. Laws, ch. 268, Minn. Stat. § 116F.21 (1978).
31. 449 U.S. at 471 n.15.
32. Id. at 465.

Clover Leaf takes on a very different form when treated as an eminent domain case subject to intermediate means scrutiny. In the first place there is no question but that the statute—a ban on the right of disposition—is a taking of private property from the firms that wish to market milk in plastic containers. The question then is whether a police power justification sustains the statute. The statute first runs into that question on the selection of ends. To be sure, "solid waste management" comports perfectly with the antitaking account of the police power, especially with the leaching of toxic substances into the subsoil and underground water supplies. But what of the means? The differential treatment between the two types of containers is now relevant evidence that the means were chosen not to satisfy the stated ends but to fulfill the impermissible purpose of wealth transfer between rival groups of producers. To rephrase the legislature's point, once the new product is allowed into the market, it will be very difficult for an inferior rival to maintain its market share.

Evidence of improper motive is not conclusive, but a fuller examination of the record here leaves no doubt but that where there is smoke there is fire. The Minnesota Supreme Court, in its able opinion,[33] marshaled the expert evidence, wholly ignored by the United States Supreme Court, that showed the superiority of plastic containers. (1) Plastic goods are inert, but paper goods are subject to rapid decay when cracked or bent. The paper goods become sources of bacteriological contamination in landfills; plastic goods do not. (2) Inert plastics do not generate methane gas and hence reduce the risk of explosion. In contrast, methane gas is produced by the decomposition of paper products. (3) The evidence (including decisive cross-examination of state studies funded by paper interests) undercuts any argument that plastic containers require more landfill space than paper products. (4) Plastic goods can be better disposed of by incineration, because they emit fewer toxic substances into the atmosphere when burnt while simultaneously generating more heat.

The evidence, then, seems clear enough, but the case against the statute becomes still more compelling when it is noted that the remedy chosen for the (mis)perceived ill was a *total ban* on the use of plastic products. In truth, even if plastics presented a greater hazard than paper goods, the case is hardly one of imminent peril, and the state need only impose a tax, collected at the point of sale, that measures the expected costs of the plastic containers upon the environment. Yet here too a similar cal-

33. Clover Leaf Creamery Co. v. State, 289 N.W.2d 79, 82–94 (1979).

culation must be made for the competing paper goods. On the evidence presented one cannot pass on the soundness of the two taxes in all situations, but if a greater tax is laid upon a lesser peril, plastic goods, then the tax must be struck down. The only hard case, therefore, is that in which the tax imposed badly misestimates the differential external effects of the rival substances, which at some point becomes too fine a call for judicial control. By that point the potential gains from the legislative suppression of rival products will also be reduced, and there should follow a sharp reduction in the level of rent-seeking efforts for impermissible legislative advantages. The equal protection cases, then, fall into place under a comprehensive theory of eminent domain, which explains why the usual standard of judicial deference applied to economic regulation cannot be defended.

11 Consent and
         Assumption of Risk

In this chapter I turn to a second class of affirmative defenses, consent and assumption of risk, which, on the strength of the analogies to private law, allow the state to take private property without paying compensation. As with the police power, these twin defenses presuppose that the individual owner has made a prima facie case that his private property has been taken. Assumption of risk typically applies to takings (including destruction) that are accidental. Consent applies to deliberate takings. Despite this difference, which is identical to the difference in private law, I treat these defenses similarly, because the words and conduct of aggrieved individuals make it proper to conclude that the taking of private property—complete or partial—by another should be treated as if it were self-inflicted. Incorporation of these defenses is easy within the Lockean framework, which expressly allows the taking of property with actual consent. The critical question concerns the scope of these defenses after their place is conceded.

Consent

The proper role of consent has been the source of much confusion in private law. First there is the delicate line between implied consent and no consent at all, and second there is the question of whether the consent, if given, may be vitiated by duress, misrepresentation, or perhaps incapacity.[1] Most of the difficulties, especially in personal injury cases, have stemmed from the inability to make unique characterizations of what are, in fact, informal transactions where consent has been reluctantly given, perhaps by a person whose weakness of mind or will is evident. Within the framework of eminent domain law, however, there are few, if any, occasions where individuals want to make gifts to government out of general benevolence. The key cases for our discussion, therefore, are those in which the consent to the taking is embedded in some larger transaction which, at least in part, is for the benefit of the individual owner who is resisting the government's action.

The dominant pattern is well illustrated by *United States v. Fuller.*[2] The respondent ranchers used government property adjacent to their own lands to graze cattle under permission granted them pursuant to the Taylor Act. The terms of the act, and the agreements entered into under it, made it explicit that the grants were revocable at the will of the government, unencumbered by considerations of estoppel or reliance. In fact, the government generally acted as if the grazing rights had a quasi-proprietary status, similar to that of broadcast licenses. The apparent permanence of the rights was reflected in the higher market price of the lands to which the grazing rights were attached. In the instant case, however, the government condemned the ranchers' land after first terminating their grazing rights on adjacent federal land. Thereafter it resisted paying for the additional value attributable to the loss of these rights.

The government's action was correctly upheld by the United States Supreme Court. As the court pointed out, the government already had a way to take back the grazing rights without resorting to its eminent domain powers. Consistent with the powers of any private grantor, it could exercise its proprietary rights under the original grant deed. No private citizen can be held to pay for things he could take as of right; the same is true for the government, which stands in his stead. Canceling the grazing rights without taking the affected lands would not generate a compensable claim, so cancellation followed by the taking should not require a different result. It matters not that the respondent could have gotten additional compensation for the sale of the grazing rights to a third party. The key point is that the grazing rights were, given the terms of the grant, not his to sell, so the buyer pays only for the expectation that the grazing rights will not be terminated, not for the rights them-

1. For a general discussion of these issues, see William L. Prosser, *Handbook of the Law of Torts* § 18 (4th ed. 1971).
2. 409 U.S. 488 (1973).

selves. When the rights are terminated, the diminution in value suffered by the landowner (or his transferee) is nonrecoverable from the government. Owing to the terms of the lease, the landowner cannot show that his economic losses were consequent to the deprivation of a right.

From the vantage point of doctrine, *Fuller* is a case in which the *prior consent* of the owner blocks the claim for compensation under the clause, even if thereafter some property interest is taken by the state. This is a clear distinction between *Fuller* and its companion case, *Almota Farmers Elevator & Warehouse v. United States.*[3] In *Almota* the government could not claim to act qua landlord or grantor when it denied the condemnee compensation for the expectation of a leasehold renewal from his private landlord. *Almota* was therefore a three-party situation, in which the lessee could claim a taking of property by virtue of the government's interference with its advantageous relationships with another private party. *Fuller* involves only the exercise of government powers pursuant to a grant.

Note too that it is not possible to undermine the decision in *Fuller* by arguing that the consent was vitiated. The respondents were in principle entitled to show (again as a constitutional matter) that their consent had been vitiated by fraud or duress, but such a claim is quite unsupported on the facts of the case. The only possible line they could argue is some form of economic duress, but that in turn should receive the same short, negative response it properly receives in private law contexts.[4] The grazing rights were not thrust upon the respondent; they could have declined them if they chose. The fact that they grazed cattle on federal lands for a limited period hints of a subsidy to which, if anything, they are wholly

---

3. 409 U.S. 470 (1973). See Chapter 7.

4. For my views on the subject, see Richard A. Epstein, "Unconscionability: A Critical Reappraisal," 18 *J. L. & Econ.* 293 (1975). The rival view, which in this context *expands* the obligation of the state under the eminent domain power, recognizes the existence of the defense in very limited circumstances but cannot find an effective and clear line between the impermissible forms of economic duress and hard bargaining. See, generally, John P. Dawson, "Economic Duress—An Essay in Perspective," 45 *Mich. L. Rev.* 253 (1947). A key element of both the traditional position that I defend and the reform advocated by Dawson is that duress is made out in the cases of so-called duress of goods. The problem arises typically when a customer is made to pay an overcharge to recover from a tailor goods he is otherwise entitled to. The point of the doctrine is that threatening breach of contract to obtain some collateral financial advantage is a form of duress. The doctrine can be easily generalized from the context of hire, e.g., to all service contracts, but that generalization still maintains the sharp line between duress and hard bargaining, which is wholly obliterated when duress of goods is unnecessarily transformed into an instance of inequality of bargaining power.

unentitled and which hardly makes a case for its constitutional perpetuation.

In order to establish some form of duress, economic or otherwise, it is necessary to show one of two things: that the grazing rights were accepted under terms of imminent necessity or, by analogy to the private law doctrine of duress of goods, that the respondent, in accepting the grazing rights, was forced to choose between two benefits, both unconditionally his as of right. Because the case does not remotely raise either issue, the loss remains noncompensable, even after all the exceptions to consent are given their due. What the respondents have gained by the grant they have lost by the exercise of powers contained in the grant. For that they cannot complain.

As approached here, *Fuller* resolves itself into the familiar question: what is the appropriate construction of a grant deed with the state as grantor and a private party as grantee? In the normal case the best rule of construction is to try to honor the intention of both parties as gathered from the text as a whole. The hallmark of interpretation is mutual benefit, not favoritism to one side or the other. This principle protects the state against the charge that all grants should be construed against it because of its superior economic power. Conversely, the principle protects private parties against the claim that the special needs of the state translate themselves into extraordinary claims of right.

It may seem odd, and even regrettable, that matters of contract construction rise to the constitutional level. But as the defense of consent is constitutional, so are its scope and effect. The problem cannot be avoided under the contracts clause, as illustrated by cases such as *Charles River Bridge v. Warren Bridge.*[5] Nor can the conclusion be avoided under the eminent domain clause, given that grants of property are created by contract language with the state. Owing to the absence of any powerful and unique theory of contract interpretation, it seems best to recognize that no single rule of construction is unequivocally dominant. It is pointless to demand of constitutional litigation a precision that the best legal theory cannot supply. Yet even if the permissible area of disagreement is wide and deep, it is still possible to detect a bias in interpretation

---

5. 36 U.S. (11 Pet.) 420 (1837). A solid defense of Story's position, which argued that the original franchise grant carried with it an implicit promise of exclusivity (needed to promote the investment of the first franchisee) is found in James McClellan, *Joseph Story and the American Constitution* 215–226 (1971). Story's position in essence is for neutral interpretation that does not afford the state the type of advantages the Crown received in England, at least when it made grants without return consideration. Id. at 219–220.

in some cases for the parochial interests of government, a bias that displaces any even-handed pursuit of common contractual meaning.

Northwestern Fertilizing Co. v. Hyde Park[6] shows the interpretative problems that arise. Under an enactment of the Illinois General Assembly, the fertilizing company received a grant that authorized it to build in south Chicago "chemical and other works . . . for the purpose of manufacturing and converting dead animals and other animal matter into an agricultural fertilizer, and into other chemical products"[7] and to establish the necessary depots at other places in the city of Chicago to collect and carry the animal waste to its own chemical works. In accordance with the terms of the original grant, the company built its works at a place then "swampy and nearly uninhabitable,"[8] which in time became the village of Hyde Park. Some three years later, the officials of Hyde Park adopted an ordinance that prohibited the collection and transfer of animal waste or other unwholesome and offensive material "into or through" Hyde Park. The ordinance carried a $50 fine for each offense. The question was whether the charter protected the company against the imposition of the fine.

The court started with the strong presumption that the grant passed as few rights as possible to the company; indeed, it read the grant almost as if it could be terminated at will by the legislature. The court decided that nothing in the grant prevented the village from insisting that the plant relocate elsewhere on the south side of Chicago *even after* construction was completed and the plant was in operation. Moreover, it decided that the collection depots already in place could be closed down, thereby forcing the company to abandon its rail network for costly and untried alternatives. This interpretation mocked the company's reliance interest and ignored the language of the charter, which gave to the company, not to the city, control over plant location. No private grant would receive such a crabbed construction, which foredooms the grantee to a losing proposition. No state grant should be construed differently.

The issue is not whether the state can prevent the nuisance under the police power; it is whether compensation must be paid to undo the original grant. Note the analogy: outright grants of the fee made by the state may be undone, but only under the eminent domain power, unless there is a reservation in the original grant. The special problem in *Hyde Park*

---

6. 97 U.S. 659, 663–664 (1878), considered in Chapter 9 in connection with the police power.

7. Id. at 663.

8. Id. at 664.

was that the grant authorized the commission of a nuisance against private parties who are not party to the grant and therefore by ordinary principles are not bound by its terms. Yet to that general principle there is a powerful exception applicable to the state as the agent of the public at large. The state grant binds the public in any dispute with the grantee. Individual citizens may have a grievance against the public body that issued the franchise, but they cannot attack the grant directly. It is true that individual citizens are prejudiced by the nuisances, but so can they be prejudiced by sales of government property. Unless citizens are bound by the legislature by a form of imperfect agency, representative government itself cannot go forward. The state therefore binds its citizens and can revoke the grant only by repurchase. To strive to defeat grants by false construction is likely to be self-defeating for the state in the long run, because it undermines government efforts to trade on its reputation for fair dealing and good faith. Yet the case against the state rests less upon these prudential considerations and more on the simple truth that the eminent domain clause as applied to this case requires payment of compensation for *this* wrong, wholly independent of the future consequences of government behavior.

Assumption of Risk

The second thread in the law of eminent domain is assumption of risk, which is admitted as a defense in the private tort law with either negligence or strict liability rules. The state, therefore, in its representative role, can claim the benefit of this defense in eminent domain cases. The real issue concerns the proper scope and construction of the defense, and here we find another of those unexplained and unwarranted cleavages between the public and the private law. The defense of assumption of risk is today in disfavor everywhere under the private law,[9] yet it has obtained a new lease on life in the eminent domain context. The irony is manifest, as assumption of risk receives a broader construction in the public context than it ever did in personal injury cases during its heyday in nineteenth-century common law.

The defense occupies a very narrow position under the modern law, which insists not only that the plaintiff's assumption of risk be established in fact, but also that the risk be "unreasonable" in principle. The

9. See, generally, Prosser, supra note 1, at § 68, 439–457. Perhaps the leading case for the narrow construction of the doctrine is Meistrich v. Casino Arena Attractions, Inc., 31 N.J. 4, 155 A.2d 90 (1959).

defense can be triggered only if the plaintiff had specific knowledge of the very dangerous condition or instrumentality that caused his harm. The doctrine maintains that the risk is assumed only after the opposite party has given extensive warnings and disclosure about the probable consequences of certain behavior. Today the defense may be set aside upon a demonstration of economic duress, broadly defined, or of inequality of bargaining power, so all-pervasive.

In theory, this narrow modern version of assumption of risk would allow courts to read a key government defense out of the eminent domain clause, further limiting state power. But that approach would be unprincipled, because these modern accounts of assumption of risk in the private law are themselves misguided and erroneous, spurred in large measure by the effort to provide full compensation to all injured parties. A demonstration of these modern errors is, however, not an essential part of my program here.[10] The robust nineteenth-century versions of the defense work to the advantage of the state in eminent domain cases. Therefore, it is sufficient in the constitutional context to show that assumption of risk receives a far broad account than it has ever received under private law.

As conceived at the height of laissez-faire, the assumption-of-risk defense was typically used to bar a worker's action against his employer for accidents arising out of and in the course of employment. The defense often rested upon express agreement and could be set aside on grounds of fraud or duress, but not, of course, on any version of economic duress.[11] The defense could also be *implied* under the circumstances, as when a worker entered into dangerous employment with notice of the general types of risk to be encountered.[12] Yet here the role of notice was

10. For my views, see Richard A. Epstein, "Defenses and Subsequent Pleas in a System of Strict Liability," 3 *J. Legal Stud.* 165, 185–201 (1974).

11. The classic article is Francis Bohlen, "Voluntary Assumption of Risk," 20 *Harv. L. Rev.* 14 (1906). For a typical case law account, see Lamson v. American Axe & Tool Co., 177 Mass. 144, 58 N.E.585 (1900). There were at least some express waivers of tort actions, often accompanied by both workers and employers contributing to a private workers' compensation fund. See, e.g., Griffiths v. Early of Dudley, 9 Q.B.D. 357 (1882); Clements v. London & Northeastern Railway [1894] 2 Q.B. 482. For a discussion of these cases, see Richard A. Epstein, "The Historical Origins and Economic Structures of Workers' Compensation Law," 16 *Ga. L. Rev.* 775 (1982). For a different view on assumption of risk, see Robert L. Rabin, "The Historical Development of the Fault Principle: A Reinterpretation," 15 *Ga. L. Rev.* 925 (1981).

12. For expressions of the dominant view, see St. Louis Cordage v. Miller, 126 F. 495 (8th Cir. 1903); Titus v. Bradford, B. & K.R.R., 136 Pa. 618, 20 A. 517 (1890). For the English view, see Smith v. Baker & Sons [1891] A.C. 325.

sharply circumscribed, because simply giving notice of risk was never taken as the equivalent of the worker's assumption of it. *Volenti non fit iniuria*, not *scienti non fit iniuria* (consent, not knowledge, bars recovery) was the watchword.[13] The distinction turned on the antecedent distribution of rights between the parties. Assumption of risk required some waiver, express or implied, of the *rights* of recovery that an injured party prima facie had against the defendant.

This waiver often could be found in the employment context because the prospective employee was, whatever his economic prospects, not bound by legal duty to accept the employment, nor was he in a position to compel the employer to offer him the job. The worker had sole ownership of his labor; the employer, of his premises and capital. Given this undisputed distribution of rights, an accurate inference could be that the worker surrendered his rights to bodily integrity against certain accidents in exchange for the wage tendered by the employer. The precise terms of that exchange were often difficult to approximate at the margin: for example, did the worker assume the risk of any latent hazard that was known to and correctable by the employer? Should the defense be overriden (as it generally was) where the worker complained about the dangerous conditions to the employer, who in turn promised to fix it? These details need not trouble us here, for it is enough to show the place of the defense in ordinary consensual arrangements, which could be extended to other relationships, such as invitor-invitee[14] and driver-passenger.

However, in many cases notice of possible harm does not even begin to show an assumption of risk. Thus the plaintiff who stands on his own front steps may be on notice of the dangers created by motorists using the public highway. He has a set of choices which would enable him to avoid the risk at some cost if he so chose. Yet this does not establish as-

13. See, e.g., Thomas v. Quartermaine, 18 Q.B.D. 685 (1887), where the proposition is accepted by both the majority and dissent but applied in very different fashions.

14. As noted in Fletcher v. Rylands, L.R. 1 Ex. 265, 286 (1866), "Persons who by the licence of the owner pass near the warehouses where goods are being raised or lowered, certainly do so subject to the inevitable risk of accident." On the duties of landowners to entrants generally, compare Robert Addie & Sons (Collieries), Ltd. v. Dumbreck [1929] A.C. 358, defending the rigid classification of trespassers, invitees, and licensees, with Rowland v. Christian, 69 Cal. 2d 108, 433 P.2d 561, 70 Cal. Rptr. 97 (1968), abandoning the classification and imposing a uniform duty to exercise reasonable care under the circumstances, which still takes into account the status of the entrant.

sumption of risk. The central point is that the individual plaintiff has *both* the right to use his own land and the right to his own physical integrity. No notice of a possible wrong by another can force him to abandon without compensation one entitlement in order to save the other. The position of the plaintiff in this tort context is precisely parallel to that of the aggrieved customer in the case of duress of goods. The defendant's wrong may call forth a duty to mitigate the loss, but it does not establish that there was no compensable loss at all.[15]

The basic structure of the argument remains unchanged when assumption of risk is raised in the eminent domain context. Where there is a waiver of right, for example as part of an antecedent transaction between the private owner and the state, the defense should apply. But where there is only notice by the state, coupled with a restriction of the range of choices previously available to the owner of right, there is no absolute defense at all. The state in these "inverse condemnation" cases can force the exchange and thereby compel the individual owner to mitigate his losses, but it cannot escape the obligation to pay some compensation at some time.

Under the modern law, notice by the state is treated as creating an absolute defense instead of being limited to mitigation of damages. An instructive passage by Michelman illustrates the basic confusion:

Suppose I buy scenic land along the highway during the height of public discussion about the possibility of forbidding all development of such land, and the market clearly reflects awareness that future restrictions are a significant possibility. If restrictions are ultimately adopted, have I a claim to be compensated in the amount of the difference between the land's value with restrictions and its value without them? Surely this would be a weak claim. I bought land which I knew might be subjected to restrictions; and the price I paid should have been discounted by the possibility that restrictions would be imposed. Since I got exactly what I meant to buy, it perhaps can be said that society has effected no redistribution so far as I am concerned, any more than it does when it refuses to refund the price of my losing sweepstakes ticket.[16]

---

15. See *Restatement (Second) of Torts* § 496E (1965). See also Marshall v. Ranne, 511 S.W.2d 255 (Tex. 1974).

16. Frank I. Michelman, "Property, Utility and Fairness," 80 *Harv. L. Rev.* 1165, 1238 (1967). The passage was quoted in HFH, Ltd. v. Superior Court, 15 Cal. 3d 508, 521, 125 Cal. Rptr. 365, 374, 542 P.2d 237, 246 (1975).

Michelman's asserted analogy between the holder of the sweepstakes ticket and the owner of the land fails, as it ignores the initial distribution of rights between the parties. With the sweepstakes, there is simply an exchange of entitlements between two parties. The one gives up money he owns in exchange for the chance of winning a larger sum; the other takes the smaller sum and conditionally obligates itself to pay a larger one. There is no question of third-party rights. If the buyer of the ticket loses the bet, his agreement bars his right to collect. His position is no different from that of the rancher in *United States v. Fuller* who finds that he is no longer able to avail himself of grazing rights held at the will of the state.

The situation with the land use restrictions is quite different. Now we have a three-party transaction—buyer, seller, and state—which is analogous not to *Fuller* but to *Almota Farmers Elevator*. In this case of threatened restrictions, the original owner of the land does not hold his title at the pleasure of the state. Instead, he has rights that are good against the state; there is no reason why he cannot convey to his purchaser whatever rights he has against the state. If the present owner has a good right of action against the state, he can assign it to the purchaser of the land.

The concern with notice can be put more generally. If notice is sufficient to defeat the obligation to compensate, then the eminent domain provision has no force or effect. If notice of possible government action is sufficient to deny compensation for a partial taking of private property, say development rights, then it is sufficient to deny it for a complete taking of property. All that is necessary is that purchasers be aware that the government may act to take over their land in entirety, perhaps by a general declaration that all land henceforth will be subject to condemnation at a price equal to its value on the date the statute is passed, without any allowance for future improvements. Thereafter, private parties cannot object to the outright confiscation of their property because they could have reduced the purchase price at the outset. This in essence is Michelman's argument, but it has the relationship between prices and rights backward. We do not use prices to determine rights; we use rights to determine prices. If the original owner's cause of action against the state is transferable with the land, the price will reflect the rights that existed against the state both before and after the announcement of restrictions. If that protection is rejected, the price of the land plummets, as it does today.

To put the point another way, Michelman's argument is defective, because it fails to account for the transaction from the points of view of the seller and of the buyer. Michelman notes that the purchaser does not need the cause of action because he is in a position to take into account the risk of government regulation by reducing the purchase price. Even if adjustments in the price paid can protect the buyer against the risk, what then protects the *seller* against a capital loss upon enactment of the restriction, itself a partial taking, which is thereafter realized through the sale to a third party? Why is it that he must bear the loss when it is the state that has threatened to take private property?

In truth, the owner does not waive his rights simply because he retains possession of the land while discussion of the land use restrictions are under way. If this were so, the government could gain title over land by announcing its intention to regulate or, for that matter, to confiscate it. No private party obtains rights by simply declaring a refusal to pay, and the state fares no better under our theory of representative government. If the present landowner can resist any simple imposition of a state lien upon his property, then he can avoid his capital loss by transferring his rights against the state along with the sale. To be sure, it is not certain that this transfer of rights will take place. Nonetheless, the seller and the purchaser are not obliged to arrange their joint affairs to minimize the state's financial burdens. The proper implication is that they have organized their affairs to maximize their own joint welfare, not that of strangers or the public at large. The purchaser wants to be in a position to challenge the regulation after he has possession, and the seller wants to be out of the transaction. The sensible strategy is for the seller to transfer his cause of action to the buyer, not retain it, and certainly not to yield it to the state without consideration. Where the contract of sale assigns the right of action to either buyer or seller, then its terms should be respected. Where it does not, the fair implication must be that the seller's rights against the state go to the purchaser. The right to resist government regulation is reflected in the price paid to the seller. It does not get lost in the shuffle.

Michelman does not address these issues, but he is aware that there are some limitations to his notice argument; in a footnote to the quoted passage he says that the point should be treated "gingerly." But even that qualification does not save the position.[17] Suppose the state publishes a map showing the land over which it has plans to construct highways in the next twenty years. The state also announces that any person

17. Michelman, supra note 16, at 1238 n.124, which then discusses the case of the "administrative official, who, lacking regulatory authority but wishing to hold down the eventual cost" of highway construction, tries to discourage private development along his proposed route.

who improves his land does so at his own risk and that the compensation paid when condemnation takes place will not reflect the cost or value of the improvements so made.[18] The correct analysis of this case follows directly from what has been said above. By its announcement, the state has sought to convert actions that are now open to an individual as of right into actions he can take only if he is prepared to assume the risk of loss. This represents an unprincipled demand that he sacrifice one of his entitlements—compensation for property taken—in order to protect another entitlement—exercise of his development rights. The notice given is but another variation of the resort to an illicit conception of assumption of risk, which allows the government to obtain rights by simple assertion.[19]

In principle only two choices should be open to the government. First, it can treat the announcement as a taking of private property, to wit, development rights. Second, it can give the announcement no legal force and effect at all, even though private parties may take it into account in planning their own affairs. On the first view, there is an immediate taking for which compensation, measured by the loss of the development rights, is prima facie due. When the land is subsequently occupied, compensation must be made for whatever rights the original owner retained upon the first taking, measured by their market value at the time of occupation. In essence, two successive partial takings together encom-

18. See, e.g., Pennsylvania State Highway Law of June 1, 1945, P.L. 1242, Pa. Stat. Ann. tit. 36 § 670.219 (Purdon 1961): "No owner or occupier of lands, buildings, or improvements shall erect any building or make any improvements within the limits of any State highway the width and lines of which have been established and recorded as provided in this section, and if any such erection or improvement shall be made no allowance shall be had therefor by the assessment of damages." In Commonwealth v. Spear, 38 Pa. D. & C.2d 210 (1965), the statute was held to be a taking of the right to use, thereby allowing the plaintiff to initiate the state procedures for setting damages. The relationship between assumption of risk and notice was not discussed.

19. For similar views on these advance notice cases, see Jack L. Knetsch and Thomas E. Borcherding, "Expropriation of Private Property and the Basis for Compensation," 29 *U. Toronto L. J.* 237, 243 (1979), noting the welfare losses associated with schemes that allow the government to condemn without payment of improvements made after certain notice is given and concluding, in line with the text, that "a strategy of advance purchase of development rights would seem far preferable to the disruptions associated with a failure to make full value payments to expropriated owners." The authors note the possible risk that if full compensation is made for improvements, private owners might have an incentive to erect expensive structures in order to claim large awards. The possibility is in all events slight, especially since any compensation award is based upon value and not upon cost of construction.

pass the fee: the first is the taking of the development rights, and the second the taking of the land minus these rights. On the second view, there is no immediate taking and hence no immediate obligation to compensate. Similarly, there is no immediate restriction upon development rights, so the state must pay for the land with all improvements, even those made after notice is given, when, as, and if it is condemned. The great failing of the present law is that it allows the government to operate without any constraint on its obligation to compensate when it speaks now and takes later. A principled defense in takings cases is distorted far beyond its useful and proper limits.

PART IV

Public Use and Just Compensation

12 Public Use

The Invisible Public Use Clause

The next question concerns the nature and function of the public use limitation in the eminent domain clause. To judge from the cases and the scholarship on the subject, this chapter largely deals with an empty question. The Supreme Court gave the limitation a mortal blow in *Berman v. Parker* when it noted that "the concept of the public welfare is broad and inclusive" enough to allow the use of the eminent domain power to achieve any end otherwise within the authority of Congress.[1] "The rights of these property owners are satisfied when they receive that just compensation which the Fifth Amendment exacts as the price of the taking."[2] In *Hawaii Housing Authority v. Midkiff*,[3] the court drove the theme home with two broad propositions. First, "[t]he 'public use' requirement is thus coterminous with the scope of a sovereign's police powers."[4] Second, "where the exercise of the eminent domain power is rationally related to a conceivable public purpose, the court has never held a compensated taking to be proscribed by the Public Use Clause."[5]

1. 348 U.S. 26, 33 (1954), sustaining the comprehensive condemnation of blighted areas for public housing projects. For a more detailed discussion, see below.
2. Id. at 36.
3. 104 S.Ct. 2321 (1984). The attitude toward the public use clause taken in *Midkiff* was reaffirmed in Ruckelshaus v. Monsanto Co., 104 S.Ct. 2862, 2879–2880 (1984).
4. 104 S.Ct. at 2329.
5. Id. at 2329–2330.

Scholarly commentators have rivaled each other in their efforts to read the limitation out of the Constitution. Bruce Ackerman, in *Private Property and the Constitution,* dismissed the entire issue in a footnote with the observation that "any state purpose otherwise constitutional should qualify as sufficiently 'public' to justify a taking."[6] As early as 1949 a well-written note in the *Yale Law Journal* observed: "The conclusion that follows is that so far as the federal courts are concerned neither state legislatures nor Congress need be concerned about the public use test in any of its ramifications."[7]

Public Use and the Division of the Social Surplus

There is good reason to believe that the received wisdom, which trivializes the public use limitation, is incorrect. At a minimum the public use requirement is a strict limitation upon the power of government to take private property. That meaning is hardly captured by the present rendition, for the expression "conceivable public purpose" suggests that the court, in its search for a "rational basis," can supply a purpose the legislature itself missed.[8] I believe the public use limitation is an integral part of the eminent domain clause. The best way to approach the problem is as a matter of political theory, to show how the public use language fits in with the Lockean conception of the state, which is generated by a set of forced exchanges among all individual citizens. One critical question that arises is, "Who gets the surplus?" Under the Hobbesian conception of government, the sovereign was free to appropriate as much of the sur-

6. Bruce A. Ackerman, *Private Property and the Constitution* 190 n.5 (1977), citing Berman v. Parker, 348 U.S. 26. Elsewhere Ackerman has written: "What we are talking about mostly is a confrontation with private property on the constitutional level: that part of the constitution that says cryptically, 'nor shall private property be taken . . . without just compensation.' " Bruce Ackerman, "The Jurisprudence of Just Compensation," 7 *Environmental Law* 509, 510 (1977). The ellipses tell more than a volume about Ackerman's comprehensive vision of the clause, as the omitted words are "for public use."

7. Note, "The Public Use Limitation on Eminent Domain: An Advance Requiem," 58 *Yale L.J.* 599, 613–614 (1949).

8. The point is suggested by a passage in *Midkiff:* "To be sure, the Court's cases have repeatedly stated that 'one person's property may not be taken for the benefit of another private person without a justifying public purpose, even though compensation be paid . . .' Thus, in Missouri Pacific R. Co. v. Nebraska, where the 'order in question was not, *and was not claimed to be,* . . . a taking of private property for a public use under the right of eminent domain,' the Court invalidated a compensated taking of property for lack of a justifying purpose" (emphasis in original). 104 S.Ct. at 2329.

plus as it could get. In the Lockean world, however, the sovereign is to be fully constrained, so that the lives, liberties, and estates of the citizens may be preserved. The tangible measure of that constraint is that principled as well as prudential limits are placed upon the appropriation of surplus by the sovereign, that is, by any group of persons who control the monopoly of state power. Locke's own account is deficient in that it does not consider how the sovereign obtains the funds necessary to preserve its monopoly of force; for example, Locke does not consider the question of taxation in any depth. But that omission can be made good without undermining his basic insight. The sovereign is allowed to take from the citizens only those funds that are necessary to operate the state. The rest of the surplus subject to that tax lien should be divided among all citizens, pro rata in accordance with their private holdings. However, all persons do not get the same amount, for the principle of proration requires that those who make the largest investment in the state receive from it the largest return. This pro rata distribution has, it must be stressed, an important allocative function because it does not skew the incentives of private parties in the choice between public and private control over human affairs.[9] For example, if each person received an equal portion of the general gain, there would be an incentive for persons with smaller shares to force matters into the public area, where they would be relative gainers. Keeping the gains pro rata minimizes the possibilities of strategic gamemanship, which otherwise would tend to diminish the size of the surplus. The political situation is more stable if each person receives the same rate of return from an investment in social governance.

The numerical example from Chapter 1 makes the point clear. If the sum of all wealth in the state of nature is 100 and that in society is 150, then there is a potential surplus of 50, which must be distributed. If the costs of keeping order are 20, then the surplus is 30. If there are ten persons in the society, on average each one obtains 3 units of surplus from the successful organization of political life, even though some persons may receive 5 units of gain and others only 1.

The surplus created by political life is distributed not only at the formation of the state but also during the course of its operation. When the

9. For the parallel point about the shift between nonbankruptcy and bankruptcy arenas for litigation, see Thomas Jackson, "Translating Assets and Liabilities to the Bankruptcy Forum," 14 *J. Legal Stud.* 73, 75 (1985). "But although collectivization [into bankruptcy courts] introduces new concerns to be weighed, bankruptcy law should strive to accomplish the transition in a way that minimizes the dislocations from moving from one regime to another."

state acquires private property for public use, the public use requirement should ensure the "fair" allocation of surplus by preventing any group from appropriating more than a pro rata share. Takings for private use are therefore forbidden because the takers get to keep the full surplus, even if just compensation is paid. And it goes almost without saying that the clause does not allow takings for private use without any compensation at all. Only takings for public use are allowed.

We can obtain a better sense of how the eminent domain clause regulates the distribution of the surplus by looking at the close analogies between private and public law. In the law of real property a powerful rule says that an intruder cannot take over private property simply because he is prepared to pay the owner a price equal to its fair market value. The owner is normally entitled to enjoin the takeover before it occurs or to recover the land if it has occurred.[10] This remedial choice reflects a judgment that a property owner is entitled to keep from expropriation the surplus value his property would have in the hands of another. In sharp contrast, the state's exercise of its eminent domain power forces the private party to accept damages by way of just compensation, equal to the owner's best use of the property before condemnation. The state is thereby allowed to capture without negotiation all the transactional surplus, but only for the benefit of the public at large.

A simple illustration shows the contrast. A may own property which he is prepared to sell for $100. B may wish to acquire that property and is prepared to pay up to $150 for it. If there are no rival buyers for the property, the sale price for the property will be some figure between $100 and $150, depending on the negotiating skills of the two parties. If B could resort to the eminent domain power he could cut short the process of negotiation and acquire the property for $100, thereby appropriating the surplus. What is true of the fee simple is also true of easements and other lesser interests in land, all of which are subject to constitutional protection. The public use limitation prevents B from using the state's eminent domain power to capture the surplus. The principal (B) cannot avail himself of the distinctive powers of his agent, the state, and the state can exercise its eminent domain powers only when it discharges a public function which precludes the skewed distribution of the surplus created. This basic theme, the need to control the

10. The historical origins of this rule, in connection with the various actions for the recovery of real property, are outlined in Frederic W. Maitland, *The Forms of Action at Common Law* (reprinted 1936).

private use of eminent domain, finds a powerful echo in the private law of nuisance, in which the clear preference for injunctive relief rests upon the proposition that the common law (including equity) does not countenance the private right of eminent domain.[11]

At first blush there seem to be good reasons to question the soundness of a public use limitation upon legislative power. In particular, the limitation might appear to have adverse efficiency consequences, because it prevents the state from making a quick and easy transfer of the property from one party to another. If direct state transfers could be done without cost, more of the surplus could be preserved by abandoning the public use limitation and relying upon the just compensation requirement alone. The state could order a transfer of the property and eliminate the extra costs of negotiation. Yet this simple analysis is incomplete because it ignores the costs of alternative ways of proceeding. If A obtains any knowledge of B's designs on his property, the battle over the surplus is simply transferred into a different arena. Now both A and B will expend resources not only in negotiating with each other, but also in influencing legislative outcomes. Indeed, if A and B are able to find other parties who are similarly situated, a comprehensive legislative solution only increases the stakes of the game, as the presence of additional players leads to coalitions whose actions only increase the costs of legislative solution. The one-on-one bargaining situation becomes an m-against-n situation, where the strategic possibilities are far more complex. The public use limitation helps curb those abuses, for by controlling the disposition of the surplus it limits the scope of partisan activities. The obvious problem is to make the public use limitation work on the continuum between one-on-one and m-on-n situations. The simple rules of summation I developed in the account of the taking of private property are not suitable for drawing out the constitutional line between public and private uses.

11. See, e.g., Boomer v. Atlantic Cement Co. (Jasen, J., dissenting), 26 N.Y.2d 219, 231, 257 N.E.2d 870, 876, 309 N.Y.S.2d 312, 321 (1970): "Nor is it constitutionally permissible to impose servitude on land, without consent of the owner, by payment of permanent damages where the continuing impairment of the land is for a private use. This is made clear by the State Constitution . . . which provides that '[p]rivate property shall not be taken for *public use* without just compensation' (emphasis added [in original]). It is, of course, significant that the section makes no mention of taking for a *private* use." Note that the theme is also of importance in Morton Horwitz, *The Transformation of American Law: 1780–1860* ch. 3 (1977), whose critique of nineteenth-century law rests in large part upon the proposition that the powers of eminent domain should be narrowly confined.

What techniques, then, might be used to avoid, or at least moderate, the line-drawing problem?

Public Use and Public Goods

One promising approach is to equate public use with the economic theory of public goods.[12] While the terminology is modern, it is directed toward the very problem that confronted both Hobbes and Locke: the coordinated actions of separate parties when time, space, and large numbers are insuperable barriers to the ideal consensual solution. The advantage of the economic theory, moreover, is that it allows us to express more explicitly ideas whose full implications may have been imperfectly understood. It is an aid to the original interpretation that takes the words "public use" and shows the consequences that flow from their use. While all of these consequences were doubtless not specifically intended by the framers, the doctrine that emerges is consistent with the general pattern of their argument and the words in which they expressed it. The language of public use invites the theory of public goods.

Under the standard theory of public goods, two elements are uneasily conjoined. First, the element of exclusivity, so critical to the idea of private property, cannot be satisfied in the provision of any public good. National defense, for example, satisfies the nonexclusivity requirement in a fairly strict way because the act of providing protection for one citizen also provides it for his neighbor. The second element has to do with the costs of the additional protection. The purest of all public goods are those where the marginal cost of any extra unit of protection is zero. In most cases (including national defense) there is usually some positive cost to extending protection to other individuals, if not with the second person, then surely with the nth. Yet even this obstacle is not absolute, for in most cases the good cannot be privatized because the costs of excluding the nth party far exceed any benefits the excluding parties might hope to obtain.

The borderline difficulties with the economic account of public goods should caution us against using this account uncritically in construing the eminent domain clause. Yet it is one thing to note marginal ambiguities and another to insist that they destroy the worth of the concept altogether. A large core of activities falls within this conception of public goods, so the economic conception, however interpreted, easily legiti-

12. On the economics of public goods, see Mancur Olson, *The Logic of Collective Action: Public Goods and the Theory of Groups* (1965).

mates the state's exercise of its eminent domain power. Thus the taking of a piece of land for a lighthouse or a naval shore installation cannot give rise to the abuse in which one individual calls upon the state to do something he is unable to do himself. The property taken remains in the control of the United States, and no private party subsequently obtains an undivided interest in the condemned property. The way in which the property is held and used provides a powerful guarantee that the surplus will not be appropriated any individual but will be divided among the public at large, in roughly pro rata shares. If only a portion of the public benefits from the lighthouse, then in principle a system of special assessments could ensure the proper matching of costs and benefits.[13] So, too, the taxation of private wealth to acquire the land by purchase is also for a public use. The same is true of the salaries of military officials or the purchase of supplies. It matters not that the government transfers, as it must, property or revenues from or to individual persons, whether as employees or suppliers, so long as it is done in aid of providing a classic public good.

This lean account of public goods identifies only one class of cases that satisfy the constitutional command. Nonetheless, this account is too narrow for constitutional purposes, as it would exclude, for example, the condemnation of lands for a public highway or a public park. To be sure, these cases differ in important ways from the first class of public goods. Those goods are public because of the nature of the benefit provided: a citizen is protected by the military whether he likes it or not. In contrast to military or police protection, highways and parks (especially the latter) furnish benefits that the individual citizen is able to refuse if he wants to. Highways and parks are also illustrative of cases where the marginal cost of servicing additional individuals is in practice always positive. Private toll roads and parks are easily organized, so public parks and toll roads could be made private if the government chose to abandon them. The property in these cases is public only because the government chooses to provide the service. Yet the eminent domain power can surely be used to acquire land or other property for these purposes.[14]

13. See Chapter 18.

14. See, e.g., City of Oakland v. Oakland Raiders, 32 Cal. 3rd 60, 646 P.2d 835, 183 Cal. Rptr. 673 (1982). Note that if condemnation is allowed, Oakland will have to pay for the value of the football franchise in Los Angeles, under the market value test. Oakland may also be unable to enforce the personal service contracts with the players or meet the league rules for membership. These conditions are sufficient to doom the takeover, even if public use is satisfied.

The key point is that a second sense of public use is operative here. The highways and parks are operated under the conditions appropriate to common carriers: the service is open to all who meet the minimum requirements of fitness to be served, and some nondiscriminatory fee may be charged for the use. So long as all individuals have the *right* to use the facility on these terms, then the public use requirement is satisfied, even if all individuals cannot simultaneously use it.

The dominant rule has a number of features that are congruent with the basic concern over proper distribution of the surplus. The universal access and nondiscrimination provisions are designed to ensure that no single individual or small group of individuals (be it franchisee or user) is able to capture the entire surplus to the exclusion of others. Restricting the use of public facilities to persons who meet the minimum conditions of decorum and good behavior prevents the diversion of a large portion of the surplus to paying for the costly conduct of a small number of persons.

There is a further sense in which the public use language does not limit the powers of the state: there is no need for continued government ownership of the property after condemnation. As part of a unified transaction, the property taken can immediately be conveyed to private parties subject to the appropriate common carrier restrictions.[15] The position applies not only to garden variety takings of private property, but also to the full range of partial takings outlined above. Thus in *Teleprompter Co. v. Loretto*,[16] New York City licensed the Teleprompter Company to acquire whatever easements were necessary to install its cable television wires in private residential buildings. While each individual connection might be thought of as a private benefit to the party who acquired the service, the terms of the original grant required the firm to

---

15. See, e.g., Munn v. Illinois, 94 U.S. 113 (1877), a case concerning the ability of the state of Illinois to fix maximum charges for the storage of grain. In the course of his opinion, Waite, C.J., noted that traditional common carrier obligations imposed upon a party receiving a legal monopoly the obligation to charge only reasonable fees for the services rendered, where the restriction on the power to charge what one sees fit is the quid pro quo for the monopoly in question. See Allnutt v. Inglis, 12 East 525, 104 Eng. Rep. 206 (1810), referred to in *Munn,* for an English decision that makes the essential point. The fatal weakness of the *Munn* opinion is that it assumes that an effortless transformation can be made between services provided under the protection of a legal monopoly and those that are "affected by the public interest," without ever exploring the enormous differences between the two conceptions.

16. 458 U.S. 419 (1982).

offer its service on a nondiscriminatory basis to all comers at an appropriate price. The infringement of the rights of exclusive possession makes it clear that the company's actions are takings of private property, although the Supreme Court had some doubts—misplaced—on this point. But the taking is for a public use, even though by a private party.

The same analysis applies to other common social institutions. Systems of land recordation in effect alter the priority of title and thus take the property of those parties who fail to register. Yet these are takings for public use, since all owners and prospective purchasers of land have access to the recordation systems.[17] In the same vein I have already argued that modifications in liability rules must be understood as partial takings: everyone who sues or is sued takes the benefit or burden of the rule of general application. Similarly, the ordinary statute of limitations, including that applicable to adverse possession cases, satisfies the public use requirement in that it applies universally to all the cases it governs. To be sure, proper recordation or a statute of limitations may mean more to some people than it does to others, but by the same token people will value government defense in different ways, and access to a public park or highway will doubtless have different values to different persons. These differences in value are an inherent property of all public goods. To assume that they turn such transactions into transactions for private use is to treat the eminent domain clause as a complete bar against government takings, which is manifestly inconsistent with its effort to set a screen through which some takings safely pass while others fail. For the question of public use, public right of access is sufficient to allow the state to go forward. The value of that access is relevant, if at all, only to the question of whether proper compensation has been paid.

Private Takings for the Public Use

The critical issue is how much beyond these limited cases it is possible to go without running afoul of the public use limitation. One question is whether the requirement is satisfied by showing that the taking creates some indirect benefits in which the entire public shares. Suppose, for example, that the state takes property which is then conveyed to some firm to be used in its ordinary course of business; the public obtains benefits in the form of lower prices for the firm's output. Suppose too that the

17. See Texaco, Inc. v. Short, 454 U.S. 516 (1982), also analyzed in Richard A. Epstein, "Not Deference, but Doctrine: The Eminent Domain Clause," 1982 *Sup. Ct. Rev.* 351, at 365–369.

firm sells its goods to all comers. Each person then shares in the benefits in much the same way in which each person benefits when firms, often natural monopolies, operate under common carrier restrictions. Why should great attention be paid to the structure of legal obligation when the practice is uniformly one of general service, to the benefit not only of the proprietor but of the public at large? As the Massachusetts Supreme Judicial Court said in an early case: "Who ever heard of a refusal?" and then added: "And it is among the most pleasant considerations attending this branch of the subject, that the interest or benefit arising from manufacturing establishments is distributed quite as much, and oftentimes more, among the laborers and operatives, than among the proprietors of the works."[18]

But this argument runs too swiftly for its own good, for the account makes it very difficult to identify *any* instance where a taking of private property with full compensation flunks the public use test. Presumably the taking occurs only because the property in its new private use will have a value equal to or greater than its former use. Some portion of the public will always benefit from the transaction (just as others will lose) because of the resulting changes in relative prices. To allow this form of indirect public *benefit* to satisfy the requirement for a public use is to make the requirement wholly empty.

THE MILL ACTS

The effort to escape the constitutional impasse created by the public use limitation developed during the extensive nineteenth-century litigation over the constitutionality of the mill acts. Under these statutes the state authorized any private riparian to erect a dam which backed up the water behind it in order to create a "head" for the operation of a mill. The statutes were often hedged about with limitations upon the dam builder's rights of action: usually a jury was empowered to limit the height of a dam, to define the times and circumstances of flooding, and to protect the heads of dams already in place.[19] The builder of the dam

18. See, e.g., Boston & Roxbury Mill Corp. v. Newman, 29 Mass. (12 Pick.) 467, 477 (1832). The exact distribution of gain will vary from case to case, largely depending upon the elasticity of demand for the various factors of production.

19. See Miller v. Troost, 14 Minn. 365, 369 (1869), where the operative provision stated, "No mill dam shall be erected or maintained under the provisions of this chapter, to the injury of any water power previously improved." The court held that the provision protected dams that were still under construction, in order to protect the reliance interest of the first builder.

was required to pay compensation to the upstream owners whose property was flooded, usually in an amount determined as part of the original jury proceeding. In some instances the level of compensation payable was in excess of the actual losses sustained from the flooding. Notwithstanding these procedural and substantive protections, the mill acts operated in derogation of the common law rights of other riparians by removing their rights to injunctive relief and self-help against the flooding, as well as by eliminating punitive damages, and in many cases, the recovery of permanent damages.[20]

The judicial response to the mill acts was one of genuine puzzlement and uncertainty. In some cases judges sought to evade the charge against the mill acts by pretending that they did not involve the taking of private property at all. No less a figure than Lemuel Shaw insisted that the eminent domain power was not implicated because the state did not take the land, because only the private party who erected the dam had to pay compensation.[21] The United States Supreme Court tried to evade the full force of the public use language by treating the mill acts as a mere "regulation" whose constitutionality could be sustained without any explicit response to the public use limitation.

> The question whether the erection and maintenance of mills for manufacturing purposes under a general mill act . . . can be upheld as a taking, by delegation of the right of eminent domain, of private property for public use, in the constitutional sense, is so important and far reaching, that it does not become this court to express an opinion upon it, when not required for the determination of the rights for the parties before it. We prefer to rest the decision of this case upon the ground that such a statute, considered as regulating the manner in which the rights of proprietors of lands adjacent to a stream may be asserted and enjoyed, with due regard to the interests of all, and to the public good, is within the constitutional power of the legislature.[22]

Wholly absent is an explanation of how the confrontation with the eminent domain clause can be avoided. The court's implicit assumption is that the clause confers additional powers on the state, when the actual

20. See Horwitz, supra note 11, at 48.
21. See Murdock v. Stickney, 62 Mass. (8 Cush.) 113, 116 (1851). The point is consistent with the concern with special assessments in Chapter 18.
22. Head v. Amoskeag Mfg. Co., 113 U.S. 9, 20–21 (1885). *Head* also contains a compilation of all the mill acts. Id., note at 17.

function of the clause is to limit the powers the state possesses. The verbal recharacterization of takings as regulation simply will not work, as the more candid opinions recognized in grappling with the public use question.[23] To be sure, with many early statutes the public use test could be satisfied. Grist mills, for example, were public under the tests noted above because their proprietors were required to process the grain of all comers on a nondiscriminatory basis.[24] Later statutes, however, such as that in *Head*, authorized the damming of water for manufacturing purposes, thereby negating any public right of use. In time the unmistakable trend of the decisions was to uphold the statutes, often with severe misgivings about the results.[25]

The question fairly raised by these mill act cases, and the source of the uneasiness of the courts that addressed it, was simply this: if takings under the mill acts are for public use, what takings are for private use? In *Dayton Mining Co. v. Seawell*,[26] the court was faced with a constitutional challenge on the public use doctrine to a statute which allowed mine owners to condemn lands so they could build roads to transport needed materials and supplies to their mines. The statute was sustained on the strength of the kindred mill act cases in an opinion notable for its anxious effort to show the continued vitality of the public use limitation after the statute was upheld.

> The truth is, that there is a wide distinction between railroad and hotels, and, also, between the business of mining and that of conducting theaters. A railroad, to be successfully operated, must be constructed upon the most feasible and direct route; it cannot run around the land of every individual who refuses to dispose of his private property upon reasonable terms. In such cases the law interferes, and takes the private property of the citizen upon payment

23. See, e.g., Boston & Roxbury Mill Corp. v. Newman, 29 Mass. (12 Pick.) 467, 479–482 (1832); Miller v. Troost, 14 Minn. 365 (1869).

24. Head v. Amoskeag Mfg. Co., 113 U.S. 9, 18–19 (1885): "The principal objects, no doubt, of the earlier acts were grist mills; and it has generally been admitted, even by those courts which have entertained the most restricted view of the legislative power, that a grist mill which grinds for all comers, at tolls fixed by law, is for a public use."

25. For the reluctance, see Miller v. Troost, 14 Minn. 365, 369 (1869): "To say the least, such a law goes to the extreme limit of legislative power, and had not similar laws, in States having constitutional restraints similar to ours, been uniformly sustained by the courts, we should hesitate long before upholding this one."

26. 11 Nev. 394 (1876).

of a just compensation, in order to promote an interest of great
public benefit to the community, which could not be carried on
without the exercise of this power of eminent domain. The same
principle applies to the business of mining; but it cannot reasonably
be applied to the building of hotels or theaters. In the building of
hotels and theaters the location is not necessarily confined to any
particular spot, and it is always within the reach of capital to make
the proper selection, and never within the power of any individual,
or individuals, however stubborn or unreasonable, to prevent the
erection of such buildings. The object for which private property is
to be taken must not only be of great public benefit and for the
paramount interest of the community, but the necessity must exist
for the exercise of the right of eminent domain.[27]

Note the implicit tension that these cases create. There is a strong
sense that a mill creates some overall resource benefit and therefore
should be allowed to go forward. So too with the mining easement.
There is also a sense that the structure of the situation hampers voluntary transactions because the basic resource, be it water or minerals, is
locked in place by nature so that its owners are not free to conduct their
business wherever they please. Yet on the other hand there is the sense
that the original owner of the condemned land is stripped of his land at
its market price, solely for the benefit of another and in derogation of his
own autonomy. The key to understanding these cases follows from these
two points: necessity and division of the surplus. First there is an effort to
limit the class of forced exchanges to those which are induced by some
situational necessity. There is a clear perception that greater latitude is
allowed for exchanges in which the party who initiates the exchange is
constrained by external circumstances; that external constraint reduces
the likelihood that one person can simply assert his will and dominion
over the property of another.

But it is an open question whether the simple presence of the situational necessity is sufficient to satisfy the demands of the public use language. This point presents some difficulty, but in my view, more than
necessity is needed to meet the public use requirement. The basic theory
of public use demands that in forced exchanges the surplus must be
evenly divided. That requirement can be carried over from national defense to mines and mills if some provision is made to divide between the
two parties the surplus created by the movement of resources from one

27. Id. at 411.

private owner to another. The public use requirement is satisfied only when efforts are made to replicate in the transfer situation the same distribution of costs and benefits that is found with normal public goods.

This position is at variance with the received wisdom, but it is supported by a closer look at the mill act cases themselves. One important strand is found in *Head*, where Justice Gray noted that the partition of a joint tenancy on the petition of a dissatisfied joint tenant is in essence a taking of private property for private use, in which the surrender of an undivided interest in one part of the whole is compensation for the receipt of an exclusive interest in another part.[28] That point is surely correct, but the remedy is structured to avoid the problems of the mill acts or the easement by necessity in the mining cases. With the partition of a joint tenancy, neither side can appropriate the surplus to his own use, as the equal division of the property by value necessarily entails an equal division of any surplus obtained from disentangling private interests. The "public" here is the two parties, each with his pro rata share of the gain, to the extent that ordinary institutions can provide it.

The pivotal role of the surplus is strikingly confirmed in the structure of the New Hampshire Mill Act. Although the point was not relied upon in *Head,* the New Hampshire statute fixed the compensation payable to the owner of flooded land at 50 percent *above* the market value of the land, thereby ensuring a division of the surplus brought about by the forced exchange.[29] One could quarrel with the precise amount of the bonus, but not with the evident statutory intention to divide the surplus, even though the asymmetrical positions of the private owners precluded the automatic division available in the partition example. Note also the constraints on statutory choice. The 50 percent figure is surely substantial. To set it higher could well render the statute useless if the benefit to the mill owner is less than the premium payable. Nor is any higher figure needed typically to vindicate the subjective value that landowers attach to farmland or riparian rights, since such property tends to be commercial and not personal. (Indeed, without the statute, subjective values may not be vindicated because the sales could not take place.) Similarly, there is danger in setting the figure lower. One risk is that the lower figure could foster coerced takeovers even where the promise of

28. 113 U.S. 9, 21–22 (1885).
29. New Hampshire Mill Act, 1868 N.H. Laws ch. 20 § 3, set out in *Head,* 113 U.S. at 10–11. My thanks to Robert Ellickson for stressing the importance of that provision.

social gain is small. In addition, if the size of the surplus is small, then voluntary negotiations are more likely to be successful, because there is less incentive to hold out for major gains. The 50 percent figure may not be perfect, but it is far from arbitrary: perhaps a 25 percent premium is better, or perhaps 75 percent. But in these circumstances one should not demand perfect precision because there is no way to provide it.

Other features that lend coherence to the statutory scheme have constitutional significance. Any party can seek to raise a dam under the statute, so its benefits are not confined to some select and preferred group. In addition, the size of the dam is set not by the party himself, but by a determination of three disinterested parties, who are required to report their findings to a court after their original view and estimate.[30] The possibility of abuse is thereby curbed because the party who initiates the taking cannot consummate it by unilateral action. Nor is it a reproach against the mill acts that they reduce the amount of cash paid for flooded land by the benefits conferred upon the servient land by flooding, so long as these are accurately valued, and the surplus is fully preserved.[31] The statute thus responds to necessity, curbs avarice and ambition, and provides for some surplus division that works to the advantage of its victims. It can be upheld without resorting to the vague language of indirect social benefit, which abandons the public use limitation to the political process. In sharp contrast the Nevada mining statute in *Dayton* should be struck down, because it places no restraint upon the mining company's behavior and makes no provision for the surplus, as the mining firm can internalize all the gain from the improved allocation of resources.[32] The same analysis extends to all easements by necessity, where the private takeover meets the public use requirement only upon a fair division of the surplus, subject to some third-party control which limits the ability of the owner of the dominant tenement to define the easement solely for his own advantage.[33]

30. New Hampshire Mill Act, 1868 N.H. Laws ch. 20 §§ 2 & 3.
31. See, e.g., Avery v. Van Deusen, 22 Mass. (5 Pick.) 182 (1827), where the jury was properly instructed to set off against the damage caused by the sawdust and chips that floated upon the plaintiff's meadow the benefits from irrigation to plaintiff's land. See Horwitz, supra note 11, at 50–51, which treats this as another sign of the injustice of the mill acts, because it reduces the sums to be paid by the developer. But the position is consistent with much of eminent domain law on implicit compensation, as in the highway cases. See Chapter 13.
32. 1875 Nev. Stat. 111, § 14, codified in Nev. Comp. Laws § 296 (1900).
33. See, e.g., Othen v. Rosier, 148 Tex. 485, 226 S.W.2d 622 (1950).

RENT CONTROL, URBAN RENEWAL, AND LAND REFORM

RENT CONTROL   The mill acts and related cases mark a watershed in the Supreme Court treatment of the public use limitation. Their examination of the question was serious and responsible, and the result was correct. Yet the want of any theory to explain the connection between public use and private ownership led to an erosion of the public use principle that has set the course of later cases. One area that shows the trend is the rent control statutes that first reached the Supreme Court shortly after the end of World War I. In *Block v. Hirsh*,[34] the plaintiff, Hirsh, sought to recover possession of a cellar and first-floor apartment after Block's lease expired. The defendant claimed that he was entitled to remain in the apartment under the District of Columbia rent statute, passed in response to the emergency wartime conditions. The statute permitted a tenant to remain in possession of premises so long as he paid the rent fixed by the lease, as modified by a rental commission. The statute did allow the landlord to recover the premises for use as his family residence after thirty days' notice. The plaintiff wanted the property for personal use but refused to give the statutory notice, claiming instead that the statute was invalid, in part because it authorized the taking of "private property for private use."

In a five-to-four decision, Justice Holmes upheld the statute as a proper exercise of the police power for "civilized" societies in wartime conditions. Holmes was evasive on the threshold issue of whether there was a taking at all or only some regulation under the police power. On the latter view, it may not be necessary (if regulations and takings fall in separate compartments) to address the public use question at all. But Holmes found that the statute, even if it did not work a taking, nonetheless satisfied the public use requirement. His first argument invoked the familiar line of judicial deference, which is, as ever, inappropriate on a matter of constitutional fact. His second depended upon the sudden influx of persons into Washington, D.C., which he claimed made it in the public interest to regulate rents. "The space in Washington is necessarily monopolized in comparatively few hands,"[35] a point that reveals an elementary confusion of monopoly with unanticipated changes in demand

34. 256 U.S. 135 (1921). See also the companion case of Marcus Feldman Holding Co. v. Brown, 256 U.S. 170 (1921), sustaining a comparable rent control law of New York City. The cases are perhaps more notable for their broad construction of the police power, on which see Chapters 9 and 10.
35. Block v. Hirsh, 256 U.S. 135, 156 (1921).

in a competitive market attributable to exogenous shocks. (Holmes sustained a statute that reduced the supply of housing available in the market by placing a ceiling on the price to be charged.) Finally, he echoed the familiar theme of private necessity by noting, "[H]ousing is a necessary of life."[36]

The constitutional text, however, requires a good deal more than a reference to the public interest. The taking itself is clear, given that the landlord's reversion was taken by the government and transferred to the tenant. But where is the public use? The government does not keep or use the property, nor is the tenant subject to any form of common carrier regulation. The leasehold property simply goes from landlord to tenant. According to my analysis of the mill acts, the public use condition is satisfied only if (1) there is a bilateral monopoly born of necessity, and (2) if some effort is made to divide the surplus between landlord and tenant. The rent control statute fails on both counts. To be sure, any negotiation for renewal of a lease contains some element of holdout, because both the landlord and the tenant have at risk specific capital that the other side seeks to capture in negotiation. Unlike the mill and mining cases, however, here the holdout problem is not severe. Both sides are subject to the risk of holdout, while the size of the potential gains is sharply constrained by competitive alternatives, whether or not prices are rising. Both sides can gain through economizing on transaction costs by renewing the lease for some intermediate level of rent. Indeed, the usual pattern, even with unique properties, is that found in *Almota*[37]— quick, if not automatic, renewal. In rental housing the same result is achieved in the market by the simple expedient of charging current tenants no more than new ones. The case of necessity is weak, almost vanishing.

The rent control statute fails on the second ground for it made no allowance for a premium, doubtless because no tenant would ever invoke it. Indeed, the rental fixed was below market value in an effort to spare tenants the burden of market increases wholly independent of the holdout problem. There is simply no good reason to upset private transactions by state takings if no sizable gains can thus be generated. If the premium cannot be paid, then there is no private necessity sufficient to justify government intervention in the name of public use. The rent control statute (and others like it) should be struck down in its entirety because it violates the public use requirement.

36. Id.
37. See Chapter 7.

URBAN RENEWAL A second class of cases concerned with extensive public efforts to redevelop land, which can run the full range from slum clearance to neighborhood beautification. The nineteenth-century view, abstractly considered, was that it was a perversion of the public use doctrine to acquire land by condemnation for these purposes.[38] When faced with a direct challenge to public housing programs, however, the courts quickly went the other way. The decisive case sustaining the government power was *Berman v. Parker,* decided in 1954,[39] which sustained against public use objections a comprehensive redevelopment plan designed to rid a section of the District of Columbia of its slum housing. The plaintiff owned a department store, which was not in a dangerous or unusable condition in the designated area. His structure was taken over and resold to another party for private use under the master plan.

A thorough opinion in a three-judge district court decision, *Schneider v. District of Columbia,*[40] expressed enormous uneasiness about the constitutionality of the statute. *Schneider* first held that private property could be taken to abate slum conditions, present or reasonably expected, even if the property thereafter was conveyed into private hands. But it split the difference by refusing to allow properties to be taken and reconveyed solely to create "a well-balanced community" in "blighted" areas. "One man's land cannot be seized by the Government and sold to another man merely in order that the purchaser may build upon it a better house or a house which better meets the Government's idea of what is appropriate or well-designed."[41]

Speaking for a unaminous Supreme Court,[42] Justice Douglas found that the program met the public use standard because (note the concep-

---

38. "It may be for the public benefit that all the wild lands in the State be improved and cultivated, all the low lands drained, all the unsightly places beautified, all dilapidated buildings replaced by new; because all these things tend to give an aspect of beauty, thrift, and comfort to the country, and thereby to invite settlement, increase the value of lands, and gratify the public taste; but the common law has never sanctioned an appropriation of property based upon these considerations alone; and any such appropriation must therefore be held to be forbidden by our constitutions." Thomas M. Cooley, *Constitutional Limitations* 532–533 (1868).

39. 348 U.S. 26 (1954). Many earlier decisions presaged its result. One influential case was Matter of New York City Housing Authority v. Muller, 270 N.Y. 333 (1936), sustaining State Housing Law, L. 1926, ch. 823; amended L. 1934, ch. 4, authorizing projects for the clearing and reconstruction of slum areas.

40. 117 F. Supp 705 (D.D.C. 1953).

41. Id. at 724.

42. Berman v. Parker, 348 U.S. 26 (1954).

---

tual confusion) it fell within the police power. The case, however, does not fall under the first two heads of public use: no pure public good is provided, nor is there any universal right of access to the plaintiff's property after the conveyance. In the end, therefore, community redevelopment plans rest on the necessity argument. As was said in an earlier New York case: "To eliminate the inherent evil and to provide housing facilities at low cost—the two things necessarily go together—require large scale operations which can be carried out only where there is power to deal *in invitum* with the occasional greedy owner seeking excessive profit by holding out."[43]

In one sense this "necessity" argument has greater bite with comprehensive development programs than with rent control statutes: holdouts can exist whenever the government seeks to assemble parcels of land under separate ownership. Yet there is a sense in which the necessity here is created not by the inherent nature of resources, as was the case with mines, mills, and nuisances, but by the state's desire to transfer property between private parties. But even if the necessity exists, where is the even division of the surplus that could save the statute? Far from paying any kind of premium, redevelopment statutes refuse to make proper compensation for relocation expenses or loss of goodwill. The statute runs afoul of the public use requirement.

Berman is in a sense an extreme case, because the condemned property was left in its original condition. But the situation is not improved when slum property is converted into public housing projects, where financial and other eligibility restrictions are imposed upon the candidates for rental. Here we are a long way from the common carrier situation. Far from their being an effort to ensure an even distribution of the social surplus, the financial and other eligibility conditions are now meant to prevent universal access at a nondiscriminatory price. The projects are only public because the the government has chosen to operate them, which again is argument by assertion. Looked at on their own merits, the programs depend upon the taking of private property for private use, here on a massive scale.

Once *Berman v. Parker* is on the books, the question remains whether any condemnation of land can be attacked for want of a public purpose. The *Poletown* case[44] shows that one state court allowed government to

43. New York City Housing Authority v. Muller, 270 N.Y. 333, 341–342 (1936).
44. Poletown Neighborhood Council v. City of Detroit, 410 Mich. 616, 304 N.W.2d 455 (1981).

condemn vast tracts of land, not for slum clearance, but for the ownership and use of General Motors, all in the name of stimulating employment. Yet no surplus was paid to the landowners, who were not
compensated fully for their enormous consequential losses.

LAND REFORM In *Hawaii Housing Authority v. Midkiff*,[45] Hawaii had
passed a land reform statute that allowed a local commission to designate certain properties in which residents under long-term leases were
allowed to purchase the fee from their landlord without his consent, notwithstanding any contrary term in the lease.[46] The compensation payable was in an amount not less than the sum of (1) the present value of
the remaining payments under the lease, and (2) the discounted market
value of the reversion.[47] The Supreme Court first noted that Hawaiian
titles dated back to the ancient royal families. It then continued:

> In the mid-1960's, after extensive hearings, the Hawaii Legislature
> discovered that, while the State and Federal Governments owned
> almost 49% of the State's land, another 47% was in the hands of
> only 72 private landowners ... The legislature further found that
> 18 landowners, with tracts of 21,000 acres or more, owned more
> than 40% of this land and that, on Oahu, the most urbanized of the
> islands, 22 landowners owned 72.5% of the fee simple titles. The leg-
> islature concluded that concentrated land ownership was responsi-
> ble for skewing the State's residential fee simple market, inflating
> land prices, and injuring the public tranquility and welfare.[48]

Notwithstanding this history, the Ninth Circuit had struck down the
act as "a naked attempt on the part of the state of Hawaii to take the
private property of A and transfer it to B solely for B's private use and
benefit."[49] The Supreme Court reversed, placing heavy reliance upon
Berman v. Parker because this taking was "rationally related to any conceivable public purpose,"[50] in ending "oligopolistic" control over land
markets, which forced "thousands of homeowners to lease, rather than
buy, the land underneath their homes."[51] "Nor can we condemn as irra-
tional the Act's approach to correcting the land oligopoly problem. The

45. 104 S.Ct. 2321 (1984).
46. Hawaii Land Reform Act, Hawaii Rev. Stat. ch. 516 (1976).
47. Hawaii Rev. Stat. §516-1(14) (1976).
48. 104 S.Ct. at 2325.
49. Midkiff v. Tom, 702 F.2d, 788, 798 (9th Cir. 1983).
50. 104 S.Ct. at 2329.
51. Id. at 2330.

Act presumes that when a sufficiently large number of persons declare that they are willing but unable to buy lots at fair prices the land market is malfunctioning."[52]

The rational basis test again uses false arguments to negate explicit constitutional guarantees. No antitrust expert thinks "oligopoly" because there are "only" seventy or twenty-two or eighteen landowners in a given market. Why then allow the legislature to so find? There is even less reason to find market failure in the simple inability of landlord and tenant to agree upon a price for the renewal of a lease, often long before its expiration. The negotiation of problems concerning only two parties is no more complex than under rent control; in no way does it depend upon the overall structure of the market. The better place to look for land shortages and high prices is in the extensive network of state land use regulations[53] that is today beyond constitutional challenge, even though it facilitates the very oligopolistic practices that land reform statutes are said to counteract.

The case therefore is straightforward. The statute allows tenants as a class to take the reversion from the landlord. These takings do not become something else simply because a large number of tenants is involved. In no individual case is the property used for a pure public good, and in none is there universal right of access. The only way the transfer can take place is if the necessity created by bilateral monopoly is met by an explicit division of the surplus. Yet the bilateral monopoly problem is minor, and the tenant keeps any surplus. Land reform thus runs afoul of the public use limitation, which deserve more respectful treatment than it receives today.

52. Id.
53. "Since Hawaii has one of the strictest land use statutes in the nation and holds most of the 4.1 million acres of land in the state for agricultural or conservation purposes, the impact of the Bishop Estate's leasing policy is magnified." "Hawaiians Foresee Change in Homeowners' Status," *N.Y. Times,* May 31, 1984, at 7.

_13_ Explicit Compensation

Market Value, Not Cost

In this chapter I inquire into the level and form of compensation under the eminent domain clause. I address these questions in connection with takings from single persons or small groups of individuals, who are placed in sharp and total opposition to the state and whose share of the property taken qua citizen is ignored. In principle the ideal solution is to leave the individual owner in a position of indifference between the taking by the government and retention of the property. In _Olson v. United States_[1] it was rightly stated that the owner of the condemned property should be placed "in as good a position pecuniarily as if his property had not been taken. He must be made whole but is not entitled to more. It is the property and not the cost of it that is safeguarded by state and federal constitutions."[2]

Properly understood, this formula requires that compensation be tendered for consequential damages, including some litigation and appraisal expenses.[3] Yet even if these costs are placed to one side, the value of the property, not its cost, determines the amount of compensation to be paid. One measure of value is market value, that is, the price a willing

---

1. 292 U.S. 246 (1934).
2. Id. at 255. The decision itself then disallowed recovery for highly speculative gains that might have been achieved if the private owners could have agreed among themselves to provide flowage easements. The probability here was very low, but the zero estimate biased the result for the government.
3. See Chapter 7.

seller would receive from a willing buyer. Yet market price still contains a systematic bias that underestimates the use value, which is typically in excess of its exchange value. Thus in any condemnation there are two relevant possibilities: either the highest and best use of the property to be condemned lies with the owner or it lies in the hands of another individual. In either case, however, the value should exceed the exchange value, especially with the unique assets that are subject to ordinary condemnation. In the first situation the present owner will not sell at market price because selling will deprive him of the surplus he obtains from present use, perhaps because the property is customized to his own needs or provides him with special locational advantages. Yet the same bias is found in the second possibility as well, because the prospective buyer must pay a price that is greater than the use value to the present owner. To the extent that the prospective buyer's subjective value of the property is greater, there is also an element of real value that is not captured by the market value test.[4] The market value test therefore does not leave the owner indifferent between sale and condemnation where the market is in equilibrium, even if consequential and incidental damages are (wrongly) ignored. And it leaves him indifferent only by ignoring the potential gains to the prospective, if unidentified, purchaser.

The central difficulty of the market value formula for explicit compensation, therefore, is that it denies any compensation for real but subjective values.[5] To avoid this problem, it is possible to resort to alternative measures of compensation. One alternative is to predicate compensation on replacement cost, but this approach has serious dangers of its own.[6] If the replacement cost lies between the general market value and some higher subjective valuation, then compensation is adequate because it permits the owner to duplicate the condemned facilities and thus regain the subjective component of value from his original activities. Yet the owner has no incentive to speak the truth if his subjective value is lower than replacement cost, which exposes the government

4. See, e.g., Jack L. Knetsch and Thomas E. Borcherding, "Expropriation of Private Property and the Basis for Compensation," 29 *U. Toronto L.J.* 237 (1979).

5. For a discussion of the analogous problem in the law of contract, see Timothy Muris, "Cost of Completion or Diminution in Market Value: The Relevance of Subjective Value," 12 *J. Legal Stud.* 379 (1983).

6. See United States v. 546.54 Acres of Land, 441 U.S. 506 (1979), holding that fair market value was the proper measure for the taking of a camp, even though it would cost many times as much to reestablish the camp at a new site, because of new regulations which did not apply to the older institution.

to a serious risk that the owner will simply pocket the money instead of acquiring or constructing the substitute facilities.[7]

Another response to the problem of subjective value as Robert Ellickson, among many, has proposed,[8] is to award a certain bonus value upon condemnation. This bonus can be justified, first, as a balm for the infringement upon autonomy brought about by any forced exchange[9] and, second, as an effort to correct the systematic underestimation of value in the market value test. For these reasons, a 10 percent bonus was used for many years in England in compulsory purchase cases, although its use has been discontinued in recent times.[10]

It is true that no fixed bonus captures the enormous variation among cases. The bonus could correct, however, for the persistent bias of the market value test, even as it generates overcompensation in some cases while tolerating undercompensation in others. Yet so long as there is no systematic bias in the original estimates, then the total burden to the state should fairly reflect the total costs of acquisition, even if some random error remains in individual cases. Bonus values, therefore, have a great deal to recommend them. To be sure, if no bonus values are awarded, the danger of excessive awards is reduced, but the compensation will then, however excusably, fail in its central purpose, as no original owner will be indifferent between retention of the basic property and the substitute award. The case on the constitutional insistence upon bonuses is very close indeed.

The tests for explicit compensation are, however, subject to unambiguous criticism where the compensation tendered is *less* than the market value of the property taken. Given the clear sense of the eminent domain

---

7. See id. at 515–516: "Awarding replacement cost on the theory that respondent would continue to operate the camps for a public purpose would thus provide a windfall if substitute facilities were never acquired, or if acquired, were later sold or converted to another use." The precise analogy under the private law of contracts is where the innocent party in a construction or mining case is awarded damages equal to the cost of completion when that figure is greater than market value, only to pocket the proceeds. See, e.g., Groves v. John Wunder Co., 205 Minn. 163, 286 N.W. 235 (1939), discussed in Muris, supra note 5, at 393.

8. Robert C. Ellickson, "Alternatives to Zoning: Covenants, Nuisance Rules, and Fines as Land Use Controls," 40 *U. Chi. L. Rev.* 681, 736–737 (1973). The suggestion is taken up in Knetsch and Borcherding, supra note 4, at 241.

9. See the discussion of the mill acts in Chapter 12.

10. Comment, "Eminent Domain Valuations in an Age of Redevelopment: Incidental Losses," 67 *Yale L.J.* 61, 66 (1957).

clause, it might be thought that this result could only take place through some unavoidable error in valuation in a given case. Yet today a large number of doctrines set benchmarks for compensation below market value, especially when cost or previous value is used as the benchmark. One illustration of the error is the suggestion in *Penn Central Transp. v. City of New York*,[11] that the state's obligation is discharged whenever it permits the owner of private property to enjoy a "reasonable return" upon his original investment. This appeal to reasonableness is surely reasonable under some circumstances,[12] but this is not one of them. The property owner is deprived of compensation for all or part of the appreciation in market value between the time of his original acquisition or improvement and the date of condemnation.

To see the error implicit in the reasonable return theory, it is sufficient to look at the parallel shift from market value to original cost in the private context, where it is wholly unprincipled. A owns a bicycle that cost $100 but whose value was $500 when B destroyed it; the latter figure measures the compensation that is owed. Surely the wrongdoer would not have to pay the original cost if the property had depreciated in value before the taking or destruction, so there is no reason why he should use the cost figure for appreciated property. The question of cost is relevant, if at all, to the taxes the original owner must pay upon the gain realized in transaction. However, it plays no role whatsoever in sorting out the rights and duties between victim and wrongdoer, except in the unlikely event that cost provides the best estimate of value at the time of destruction. But the principle is clear: value controls. The wrongdoer does not pay $500 if the depreciated bicycle is in the hands of the original owner, but only $100 if it has just been sold to a stranger. The fact of the sale only determines *who* receives the compensation, not *how much* should be paid.

By the central principle of representative government, the government stands in no better position: value is the universal measure of compensation. Owners of depreciated properties do not increase the government obligation by retaining ownership. Owners of appreciated property need not sell their property in order to increase the amount of compensation owed by narrowing the gap between cost and market value. The Supreme Court has in recent years shown a marked fondness for the metaphor of "investment-backed expectations," but this elegant

11. 438 U.S. 104 (1978).
12. See Chapter 17 for a discussion of rate regulation of utilities and other monopolies.

phrase is not a synonym for private property. Nor can it be used to justify a cost-based compensation formula that is in flat contravention of—at least here—the plain meaning of the just compensation requirement. The insistence upon market value as a universal standard applies not only to outright takings but to partial takings as well, including all forms of direct regulation. Both rent control and transferable development schemes show how easy it has been to circumvent the basic standard when the scheme of government intervention has been made complex.

Rent Control

The improper choice of compensation schedules is concretely illustrated by the rent control statutes found, for example, in New York and Washington, D.C.[13] Before the adoption of rent control, certain premises had been let for a stated period of time by a landlord to the tenant. Under the lease the landlord was entitled to regain possession of the premises at the end of the term and to allow the tenant to remain in possession if he agreed to some increase in the rent. (The tenant also could leave if his demands for a reduction were not met.) The statutory schemes insisted that the tenant could compel a renewal of the lease on the old terms, including the old rent, against the will of the landlord. Most statutory schemes modify the rigor of the renewal provision by permitting certain increases, either in accordance with stated schedules or on account of allowable costs incurred by the owner in repairing or improving the leased premises. All these variations are immaterial to the basic question, because none of them corrects a central defect of rent control laws—the renewal of the lease at the option of the tenant on terms that the landlord would reject in a voluntary transaction.

In dealing with the constitutionality of these schemes, Justice Holmes found them warranted under a casual and mistaken account of both the public use limitation and the police power.[14] He never confronted the further question, whether there was a taking for which market value was

13. The basics of the Washington system are outlined in Block v. Hirsh, 256 U.S. 135 (1921), discussed in Chapter 12 in connection with the public use requirement. See also Feldman Holding Co. v. Brown, 256 U.S. 170 (1921), for an account of the early New York rules, which were reintroduced during the Second World War and perpetuated for years thereafter. Many more recent constitutional schemes are based upon freezing rentals at some particular historic level. In principle the analysis is the same, even if the portion of appreciation condemned without compensation is reduced.

14. Block v. Hirsh, 256 U.S. 135 (1921). See discussion in Chapter 12.

paid. To see the just compensation issue that lurks in the background, it is only necessary to recast the transaction in ways that reveal the government's dominant role. In essence, the government (1) takes a leasehold coupled with options to renew at some fixed or formula price, and (2) assigns its interest in the term to the tenant, to whom it then delegates (without recourse) its own duty to make compensation for the property interest so taken.

Functionally, it is as though the government levied a special assessment upon the tenant to purchase his own unit, payable over time instead of in a lump sum.[15] The use of government power shows the basic taking of property. If A's thing is taken by B and handed to C, can B claim that he did not take it at all because he didn't keep it? The private law answer is clear. Far from A having no remedy against B, the presence of C only gives him an alternative source of recovery, on a theory of either restitution or conversion. Rent works just this way with but one complication. The duration of the interest taken from the landlord and given to the tenant is to some extent uncertain, given that the statutory arrangement permits, but does not require, periodic renewals by the tenant.

More concretely, there are two possible ways to characterize the transaction. First, it can be considered a single taking that takes place when the statute confers rights on the individual tenant. Under this view it is necessary to estimate the expected duration of the lease, taking into account the tenant's probable exercise of the renewal rights. There is some chance of nonrenewal, but it is far lower than in the ordinary commercial leasehold arrangement,[16] because the statute is tilted heavily in favor of the tenant, who has the unilateral right of renewal. A perpetual renewal or a renewal for life (depending on the descendability of the right under the statute) therefore seems a good first approximation. Rent control units are not known for fast turnover.

Alternatively, the transaction can be viewed as a series of separate takings, each for a period of time equal to the duration of the fixed term, future options excluded. Each separate lease renewal, then, would require separate government compensation equal to the difference between the discounted value of market rentals and that of statutory rentals for the lease period. By opting for periodic payments, the statutes substitute cost for value. "Reasonable return" on investment is simply a

15. See Chapter 18.
16. See discussion of Almota Farmers Elevator & Warehouse v. United States, 409 U.S. 470 (1973) in Chapter 7.

euphemism for the confiscation of private property, bit by bit and year by year. The disguises involved in the program—the state's refusal to take title, its use of periodic takeovers, the landlord's ability to keep the (ever-receding) reversion, the pass-through of certain costs—are irrelevant, singly or in combination, to the takings question, whatever bearing they have in determining the precise amount of compensation payable by the state. The government could not condemn the fees at less than market price and justify its unwillingness to pay full compensation by reselling the property at its own cost and not for what it was worth. Leases are property just as much as fee interests are, and the same principles of just compensation apply with equal force to both. The rent control laws are in clear violation of the eminent domain clause, because the explicit compensation tendered the landlord is insufficient.

Transferable Development Rights

The arguments against so-called reasonable returns and fair compensation apply with undiminished force to transferable development rights (TDRs), where the proferred compensation is in kind instead of in cash. In-kind compensation is wholly consistent with constitutional principles, so long as it is for market value. But under the "fair compensation" rules closely associated with TDRs,[17] the amount of compensation is defective. By using the TDRs the state—usually through its municipalities— seeks to compensate individual landowners for the loss of their development rights by giving them similar development rights over nearby or adjacent parcels, whose ground rights are retained by the original parcel owners. Thus the state may prevent the construction of an addition over a historic church, while granting the church owners air rights over a nearby parking lot. The purpose of these schemes is to allow the state to undertake worthwhile projects—in particular landmark preservation— that it might not if the full compensation had to be paid. Yet TDRs are premised on the idea that it is "unfair" to make any individual owner bear the full cost of preservation without assistance from the state. "Fair" compensation through TDRs is designed to split the difference so

17. See, e.g., John Costonis, "The Chicago Plan: Incentive Zoning and the Preservation of Urban Landmarks," 85 *Harv. L. Rev.* 574 (1972); John Costonis, "'Fair' Compensation and the Accommodation Power: Antidotes for the Taking Impasse in Land Use Controversies," 75 *Colum. L. Rev.* 1021 (1975).

that some, but not all, of the economic loss to the owner of the restricted site is socialized.

The compromise received constitutional blessing in *Penn Central Transp. v. City of New York.*[18] The Supreme Court, speaking through Justice Brennan, first noted that the loss of the development rights over the existing terminal did not constitute a taking of private property, a conclusion that is wholly incorrect in any regime that recognizes partial takings. Brennan then concluded that the TDRs were "valuable" compensation for the property rights which had *not* been taken.[19] "While these rights may well not have constituted 'just compensation' if a 'taking' had occurred, the rights nevertheless undoubtedly mitigate whatever financial burdens the law has imposed on appellants and, for that reason, are to be taken into account in considering the impact of regulation."[20] The point had already been elaborated in the New York Court of Appeals: "The knowledge that at some future time, when the lease term has run out or the improvements have lost their utility, a larger building could be constructed, should increase the value of the building plot, at least so long as there is a market demand for new construction."[21]

These responses do not begin to meet the constitutional objections. One peculiarity of *Penn Central* is that the air rights to be granted Penn Central were over eight properties, including the Biltmore Hotel, the Waldorf-Astoria, and the Yale Club, that Penn Central already owned. How, it must be asked, is the city in a position to grant these rights to Penn Central as compensation for its landmark preservation statute? To do this, the city must first own the rights, which it acquired not by purchase from Penn Central, but by zoning. The city's compensation for the loss of air rights thus came from its prior uncompensated takings. It is as though A uses money stolen from B to pay B for property purchased from him thereafter.

This difficulty could be avoided by granting Penn Central air rights over structures it did not own, but only by substituting one embarrassment for another. The city would still have to acquire air rights over these properties, which it would do not by payment of compensation to their present owners, but by zoning. Note the irony. If zoning is mere

18. 438 U.S. 104 (1978).
19. On the takings question, see Chapter 6.
20. 438 U.S. at 137.
21. 42 N.Y.2d 324, 335, 366 N.E.2d 1271, 1277, 397 N.Y.2d 914, 920–921 (1977), *aff'd*, 438 U.S. 104 (1978).

regulation, then how can the state then *convey* air rights as compensation to Penn Central? To make TDRs work, we need a theory by which the air rights taken by the state through zoning become property only when they are conveyed by the state. The original confiscation is transparent if the air rights zoned away are then resold for cash, and the matter is not any better when these same air rights are used to acquire other property.

There is also a valuation question, even if the state has perfect title to the air rights offered as compensation. The just compensation requirement still demands that the city pay the fair market value of the property taken. If that compensation is paid in cash, there is no possible quarrel over what the state pays, so the only source of contention is the value of the property condemned. In *Penn Central* the government evaded the constitutional command by paying Penn Central with a set of twisted and contingent rights that cannot be valued sensibly. The state can always compensate with cash, so its unilateral decision to pay with nonstandard coinage properly invites heightened judicial scrutiny. The level of compensation owing is not diminished because payment is made in TDRs or in futures of Kansas winter wheat. Under any impartial estimation of the rights tendered in exchange, the city could not prevail.[22]

The court's defense of its decision in *Penn Central* confirms its internal weaknesses. The court concluded that there was no (compensable) taking because "[t]he restrictions imposed are substantially related to the promotion of the general welfare and not only permit reasonable beneficial use of the landmark site but also afford appellants opportunities further to enhance not only the Terminal site proper but also other properties."[23] But take that sentence point by point. The restrictions are partial takings of property and hence trigger the obligation of just compensation. Promotion of the general welfare by the landmark preservation statute satisfies only the public use inquiry. The retained beneficial use reconfirms that the taking was partial, not that it lay outside the scope of the clause. The opportunity to enhance the terminal or other neighboring properties only shows that some compensation has been tendered for the property taken but does nothing to establish its adequacy. The court stands condemned by its own argument.

22. Even under the best of circumstances, valuations tend to understate the worth of contingent claims when these are taken by the government. See Olson v. United States, 292 U.S. 246 (1934), ignoring the value of flowage easements that could be created only if many different lakeside owners agree to pool their resources. In contrast, contingent building rights are enormously overvalued when granted by the government. It is all part of the same double standard.

23. 438 U.S. at 138.

Interim Takings of Development Rights

In *San Deigo Gas & Electric v. City of San Diego,*[24] the gas company had assembled a large tract of land within the city limits on which it planned to construct a nuclear power plant. The land acquired was not originally zoned for industrial development, but the needed zoning changes were procured after purchase. Before development, however, the city took three actions which led to the instant litigation: it downzoned some of the land from industrial to agricultural, it included a new "open spaces" requirement in its comprehensive plan, and it prepared a map on which the land was designated for purchase by the city upon passage of the appropriate bond issue. San Diego G. & E. contended that these combined actions constituted a taking of private property for which just compensation was owed.

The California Supreme Court had held[25] that all challenges to government regulation under the police power must be brought administratively by way of mandamus. In its view the distinction was justified because of the asserted difference between *takings* of property under the eminent domain clause and *deprivations* of property under the police power, a play upon words that allows the state to escape "interim damages" between imposition of the regulation and its subsequent invalidation as an uncompensated taking. Yet the court's line of argument cannot work. To take a simple example, assume that the government has occupied premises on an indefinite basis. At the onset it may be impossible to determine the length of the government's stay, but there is no question but that compensation must be paid for the period of effective occupation, even if the timing of payment is uncertain.[26] Matters are scarcely different here, for partial takings, even those giving the state restrictive covenants and not direct occupation, are subject to the same rules.

The United States Supreme Court did not formally resolve any of the eminent domain issues, because five justices held that there had been no final judgment from which an appeal was proper.[27] Five Supreme Court justices (Rehnquist plus the dissent) did, however, address the inverse condemnation question.[28] In marked contrast to his *Penn Central* deci-

---

24. 450 U.S. 621 (1981).

25. Agins v. City of Tiburon, 24 Cal. 3d 266, 598 P.2d 25, 157 Cal. Rptr. 372 (1979).

26. See United States v. Westinghouse Co., 339 U.S. 261 (1950).

27. 450 U.S. at 633.

28. On inverse condemnation generally, see Roger Cunningham, "Inverse Condemnation as a Remedy for 'Regulatory Takings,'" 8 *Hastings Const. L.Q.*

sion, Brennan's dissent easily disposed of the arguments of the California Supreme Court. Brennan first noted that just compensation is required no matter how the taking is done, whether by formal condemnation proceedings, occupancy, physical invasion, or regulation. He then noted that the requirement extended to partial takings as well as complete ones, to temporary and indefinite takings as well as permanent ones. Rent control is now easy; *Penn Central*, inexplicable. He also noted that judicial, legislative, or executive policy, in dealing with a fondness for land planning, could not oust the constitutional command. His conclusion was, "Once a court establishes that there was a regulatory 'taking,' the Constitution demands that the government entity pay just compensation for the period commencing on the date the regulation first effected the 'taking,' and ending on the date the government entity chooses to rescind or otherwise amend the regulation."[29]

Brennan's opinion sought to reconcile *San Diego G. & E.* with *Penn Central* on the ground that *Penn Central* only addressed the takings issue proper, and *San Diego G. & E.*, the just compensation question. Yet the effort is at best cosmetic, for the two cases bring wholly different intellectual orientations to the same subject matter. The compensation question in *San Diego G. & E.* arose only because the erroneous strictures on the takings question of *Penn Central* were not followed. The Brennan of *Penn Central* repeatedly insisted that no set formula can decide takings cases; judicial deference was the watchword. The Brennan of *San Diego G. & E.* made no use of that lamentation and considered the takings and the compensation questions in their logical sequence.[30] The two opinions taken together give a textbook example of how the style of decision making influences the outcome of a case. Fuse all the issues of an eminent domain suit into a congealed mass, and discretion is enhanced while compensation is denied. Articulate them with sufficient clarity, and the structure of the argument calls out for compensation.

---

517 (1981), supporting interim damages; Daniel Mandelker, "Land Use Takings: The Compensation Issue," 8 *Hastings Const. L.Q.* 491 (1981), opposing damages. Note that Pumpelly v. Green Bay Co., discussed in Chapter 4, is an inverse condemnation case, as are the highway plan cases discussed in Chapter 11.

29. 450 U.S. at 653.

30. The public use and the police power questions were ignored. The first requirement is satisfied; the police power probably was not raised by the state because direct federal safety control over nuclear power preempted state involvement. See Pacific Gas & Electric v. State Energy Res. Conserv. & Dev. Comm'n., 461 U.S. 190 (1983).

Amortization Statutes for Noncomforming Uses

The problems of explicit compensation have also received inadequate judicial treatment in connection with the many state statutes governing amortization of nonconforming uses. Typically, prior to enactment of a given ordinance, a landowner has used his property as a junk yard, a car repair shop, or a multi-unit dwelling. He may have erected or converted structures in carrying out that occupation. Although the neighbors may not like his use of the property, it cannot be enjoined as a nuisance, either because it is noninvasive in nature or because it is protected by prescription.

Now suppose the government decides to limit these uses. Simple prohibition looks like an uncompensated taking of private property. Yet the neighbors are apt to resist demands for the full compensation that taking ordinarily requires, especially if their gains are less than the losses to the regulated owners.[31] Working under the "fair" compensation framework, amortization statutes allow the existing use to continue for some limited number of years, whereupon the owner must bring it into conformity with the local zoning provisions at his own expense. As with TDRs, the principle behind the statute is that if one splits the difference between the private and the public welfare, the procedure will withstand scrutiny on grounds that its public benefits exceed its private harms.[32]

Yet to speak of any accommodation between private right and public need is to ignore the difference between public use and police power. In essence the statute places strong limitations upon the future uses of both lands and improvements, while leaving the owner the possibility of mitigating by changing his levels of planned expenditures upon repairs and improvements. Nonetheless, two forms of uncompensated loss remain. First, the owner will lose the vaue of his reversion in the structure if its expected life exceeds the permitted period of amortization. To be sure, only the reversion's present discounted value should be compensated, but this figure will hardly be zero, for the real discount rate does not depend upon the level of inflation and runs about 2 percent per year.[33]

31. See, e.g., Comment, "The Elimination of Nonconforming Uses," 1951 *Wis. L. Rev.* 685.

32. See Harbison v. City of Buffalo, 4 N.Y.2d 553, 562–563, 176 N.Y.S.2d 598, 605–606, 152 N.E.2d 42, 47 (1958); People v. Miller, 304 N.Y. 105, 107–108, 106 N.E.2d 34, 35 (1952).

33. The identical point comes up in estimating lost income in personal injury cases. There it is recognized that uncertainty of future inflation is also irrelevant because it affects the discount rate and the future values equally. See Doca v. Marina Mercante Nicaraguense, S.A., 634 F.2d 30 (2d Cir. 1980);

Second, the owner will find the management of his assets more difficult during the limited period in which he is allowed the nonconforming use. Suppose, for example, there is a five-year term allowed in a structure with a fifteen-year life. What is the owner to do if the sensible repairs have an expected ten-year life? To make no repairs at all is to reduce the value of the use or structure during the allowable term. To make the repairs is to sacrifice for nothing their value for the fifth to the tenth year. The needed repairs are thus rendered far more costly because they cannot be tailored to the expected term in which the owner will retain possession.

Once these weaknesses are recognized, there is no obvious way to salvage the statutes. The police power is generally of no value, and there are, to anticipate, no obvious forms of implicit compensation for the owner subject to the requirement, so diminution in market value—the partial taking of use and possession rights being established—represents the minimum level of compensation owed by the state. The various decisions upholding the use of these statutes without compensation point to particular features of a statute that are said to avoid the charge of individual unfairness. In some, but not all, cases the use of the improvement is allowed for its expected life or long enough to permit a "reasonable" return on investment. Other cases of extreme hardship are subject to variance with board approval under local law. But these arguments work no better here than with rent control or landmark preservation. The state which has taken the loaf of bread cannot pay off its obligations by returning a slice of that loaf. All these features may reduce the amount of compensation owing in the particular case, but they cannot hide the confiscation of the reversion, be it of use or structure, be it of a permanent or a wasting asset.

O'Shea v. Riverway Towing, 677 F.2d 1194 (7th Cir. 1982). With both lost income and amortization in question, some estimation must be made of the real shifts in value, be it of improvements or future services, which are, of course, independent of the discount rates.

14 Implicit In-Kind Compensation

Dispensing with Explicit Compensation

Our analysis of the just compensation requirement has thus far been confined to those cases in which the state has been required to tender explicit compensation, either in cash or in kind, for certain types of takings, such as outright takings of land and those resulting from rent control, landmark regulation, and amortization statutes.[1] It does not follow, however, that major government initiatives can go forward only if cash or other property is explicitly transferred to persons whose property has been taken. The Constitution speaks only of "just" compensation, not of the form it must take. In principle, therefore, the state may provide compensation in whatever form it chooses. This proposition indicates the importance of implicit in-kind compensation. Many large-number takings are in the form of regulations, taxation, and modification of liability rules. In these instances, the problem of assessing the impact of the taking, no matter what its form, on each person can be divided into two inquiries. The first asks to what extent the government action limits the person's possession, use, or disposition of property and hence operates as a taking. The second asks to what extent *the restrictions imposed by the general legislation upon the rights of others serve as compensation for the property taken.* The question arises with countless forms of general government action. Are the restrictions upon the rights of creditors to seize

1. See Chapter 12.

the assets of their debtors justified by the like restrictions imposed upon others? Are the restrictions upon the right of an occupier to erect signs on his own property justified by the like restrictions imposed on others? These and countless other cases raise the question of benefits that are implicit under the general legal rule, because they involve neither a separate consideration that is transferred to the regulated parties nor the retention by the regulated party of some portion of what he originally owned. These benefits are also in kind because no cash transfers are made.

These benefits are more likely to take place under statutes of general application because a large number of individuals will be both benefited and burdened by the same rule. In that case the constitutional command for just compensation may be fully satisfied by the operation of the statute itself. Each person whose property is taken by the regulation receives implicit benefits from the parallel takings imposed upon others. Benefits of this sort can often be found. The general creditor who cannot collect from his debtor receives compensation because the parallel restrictions imposed upon other creditors assure that there is a pool of assets available to satisfy claims on a pro rata basis. The landowner who cannot erect a large sign is assured that his neighbor cannot put up a sign that will block his own. So long as the property received by the owner equals or exceeds the value of the property he surrendered, explicit compensation is unnecessary; indeed it is wholly improper over-compensation, which is itself a taking of property from someone else.[2]

These arguments extend beyond the exercise of sovereign power, applying not only to comprehensive regulation and the modification of liability rules, but also to taxes levied to obtain the cash revenues that finance the explicit takings analyzed earlier. In principle, the demand of

2. The importance of implicit compensation crops up in some unexpected quarters. Consider Locke's insistence that the state must provide unbiased judges (*Of Civil Government* ¶13 [1690]). Initially, it seems clear that the takings clause applies to judicial orders. When the state resolves a dispute between A and B, it wrongfully takes property if it makes the incorrect judgment. Forcing A to pay B $100 for a debt not owed takes $100 from A. Not making A pay the $100 when it is owed takes it from B. The demand for unbiased judges therefore translates into a demand that the probability of error be symmetrically distributed, so that each side receives, in the form of erroneous judgments in its favor, ex ante compensation for those erroneous judgments entered against it. So understood, absolute judicial immunity for erroneous judgments still satisfies both the just compensation and the public use requirements, because the legal rule divides the anticipated surplus from collective action.

just compensation is satisfied when two conditions occur simultaneously: (1) the total size of the pie—the sum of the value of all ownership and personal rights—is maintained or increased; and (2) the size of each individual slice of the pie is maintained or increased as well.

Where (2) is satisfied, (1) will necessarily be satisfied as well. However, (1) may be satisfied where (2) is not. In these cases the inquiry must focus on the way (if there is one) in which payments of explicit compensation can bring about a social arrangement satisfying both (1) and (2), taking into account the administrative costs of the move. Standing alone, propositions (1) and (2) do not uniquely distribute any net social surplus, but this surplus has already been accounted for in my treatment of public use, which also mandates pro rata distribution.[3]

The theme of implicit in-kind compensation is recurrent in the law of eminent domain. Holmes hinted at this theme in one of his many propositions in *Pennsylvania Coal Co. v. Mahon,* when he wrote that government action may be sustained where it secures the "average reciprocity of advantage" of all interested parties.[4] It lies at the root of the assertion in *Armstrong v. United States* that explicit compensation is required where burdens are placed upon a few which "in fairness and justice" should be placed upon the public at large.[5] The proposition is closely connected to Sax's instructive distinction between arbitral and entrepreneurial activities; with the former there is greater likelihood that implicit compensation will be provided to potential losers from government action than with the latter.[6] Finally, the implicit in-kind compensation doctrine receives its most sustained and persuasive articulation in Michelman's well-known proposition that rules of general application should be sustained when they work to the long-term advantage of the class burdened by the rules:

> Efficiency-motivated collective measures will regularly inflict on countless people disproportionate burdens which cannot practically be erased by compensation settlements. In the face of this difficulty, it seems we are pleased to believe that we can arrive at an accept-

3. See Chapter 12.
4. 260 U.S. 393, 415 (1922).
5. 364 U.S. 40, 49 (1960). For a detailed discussion of the facts of the case, see Chapter 4.
6. Joseph L. Sax, "Takings and the Police Power," 74 *Yale L.J.* 36 (1964). Sax himself abandoned the distinction in "Takings, Private Property and Public Rights," 81 *Yale L.J.* 149 (1971).

able level of assurance that *over time* the burdens associated with collectively determined improvements will have been distributed "evenly" enough so that everyone will be a net gainer.[7]

While implicit in-kind compensation echoes a recurrent theme that is vital to the eminent domain clause, the issue must again be placed in its proper context. Michelman's formulation seems to treat the question of evenness of burdens over time as though it were the sole key to the eminent domain question. Yet the issue of compensation—and hence of implicit in-kind compensation—can be reached only if there has been a taking of private property, if it is for public use, and if the taking is not justified under the police power or by the doctrines of consent and assumption of risk.

There are instances in which a government action has an enormous disproportionate economic impact without a corresponding duty of state compensation. For example, in cases of *damnum absque injuria,* an individual owner is left worse off by government action that falls short of a taking. Suppose the government erects a large office building that blocks the view of a lake from a large luxury apartment complex, sharply cutting market rents. The economic impact is surely disproportionate, but the government is not obligated to compensate, because the owners of the complex would have no claim for damages, let alone for injunctive relief, against a private neighbor not previously bound by a restrictive covenant. Similarly, there is no cause for compensation if the government terminates the privileges of a single individual in accordance with its reserved powers under grant, as with the grazing rights in *Fuller v. United States.*[8] The harm is concentrated on one person, but compensation is not required because the plaintiff as a licensee at will cannot show that his economic loss was triggered by any violation of his rights.

In addition, some admitted takings, such as the seizure of contaminated dump sites, are justified in full under the police power.[9] The impact in such a case may be massively disproportionate, but the antinuisance rationale may completely justify the government restrictions. Yet compensation is not required, even with the loss clearly established. Michelman was puzzled about the defendant's excavating

7. Frank I. Michelman, "Property, Utility and Fairness: Comments on the Ethical Foundations of 'Just Compensation' Law," 80 *Harv. L. Rev.* 1165, 1225 (1967).

8. See Chapter 11.

9. See Chapters 9 and 10.

activities in *Consolidated Rock Products Co. v. City of Los Angeles*[10]—"an amazing case in which a zoning restriction making no provision for compensation was sustained despite an unimpugned finding that the restriction left the complainant's land utterly unusable for any productive purposes"[11]—but this view rests solely upon his own general theory of compensation, so he fails to appreciate the distinctive and irreducible role of the police power in the constitutional system. The issue of compensation cannot arise until the question of justification has been disposed of. In the typical nuisance prevention case, this question is resolved against the claimant.

Perfect Knowledge and the Pareto Principle

The question of implicit in-kind compensation cannot be considered in isolation from its doctrinal and institutional context. Yet once the threshold issues of taking, justification, and consent are resolved against the government, the case ultimately turns on just compensation. In a world of perfect knowledge and costless measurement, there would be only one correct solution. In each case it would be necessary to identify every person whose property has been taken in whole or in part by government action. Thereafter a precise calculation would be made of the burdens and benefits brought on by that taking. Explicit compensation would be required for the *net* losses sustained by certain parties, and it would be obtained from the *net* gains of others. The public use requirement then divides the total social surplus, net gains over net losses, across all individuals in accordance with their original contributions to the social investment.[12] The system in this form has at least one very desirable property. Each and every dollar of gain from social intervention is in principle uniquely appropriated to some individual by constitutional command, so the problem of rent-seeking and faction is fully counteracted: there are no economic rents to seek.[13]

10. 57 Cal.2d 515, 370 P.2d 342, 20 Cal. Rptr. 638, appeal dismissed, 371 U.S. 36 (1962).

11. Michelman, supra note 7, at 1191 n.55.

12. On the relationship between surplus and public use, see Chapter 12, with particular reference to the mill acts.

13. It might be argued that if there were no rents, then no one would be prepared to provide even pure public interest regulation. Yet this seems unduly pessimistic for two reasons. First, there would be correspondingly little, if any, resistance to this legislation, and second, private groups, such as trade associations, should be able to overcome the free-rider problems that otherwise inhibit the production of good legislation.

A moment's reflection, however, indicates the leaps of faith demanded by this program. Measuring the value of the property taken and the compensation provided in exchange is especially difficult because the benefits of many programs are in the form of public goods, which are notoriously difficult to value. Nor is the task any easier when benefits and burdens are both contingent and uncertain, especially in the absence of any uniform estimate of risk averison, which is apt to vary widely among individuals. In addition, calculating the burdens and benefits is far from costless and generates great political pressures of its own. The sheer number of parties involved indicates that problems of error and measurement, far from being the tail that wags the dog, become for all purposes the dog itself.

A second point is conceptual in form: if the state could have perfect knowledge of each person's private preferences, then the eminent domain clause would *necessarily* forbid any taking of private property which did not maintain or increase the overall level of social wealth. The conclusion here seems odd, if not perverse, because the general assumption is that the eminent domain clause protects only individual rights, leaving to the political branches of government the unique power to decide the utilitarian question of whether to proceed.[14] The conceptual point raises serious questions about the state's power to initiate programs. Nonetheless, the conclusion seems inescapable on formal grounds. The only way to compensate net losers is through tax revenues, but these too are takings of private property that must be compensated. An infinite regress quickly emerges, as the compensation for taxes paid comes from further taxes, which themselves must be compensated. The only way to break the regress is to produce some net social benefit that leaves everyone at least as well off after each round of government takings as they were before. In contrast, where the total wealth is shrunk by government action, there is at least one net loser who can enjoin the taking because he has not been compensated.

When we consider large-number takings, the eminent domain clause exhibits a strong kinship to the standard tests of social welfare developed in the economics literature.[15] The clause does not demand that any takings take place nor that any taking maximize the total level of social

14. This is a point I myself have made; see Richard A. Epstein, "The Next Generation of Legal Scholarship?" 30 *Stan. L. Rev.* 635, 645–646 (1978).

15. For a review of the various formulas, see, generally, Jules Coleman, "Economics and the Law: A Critical Review of the Foundations of the Economic Approach to Law," 94 *Ethics* 649 (1984).

wealth. It does demand that each taking increase the overall level of social wealth. There is a close affinity to the standard Kaldor-Hicks formulation that in principle the winners should compensate the losers in order for one distribution of entitlements to be regarded as preferable to another.[16] Indeed, the takings clause seems even more stringent, given that it requires actual compensation, not hypothetical compensation as the Kaldor-Hicks formula envisions. The clause seems to embody a constitutional Pareto criterion, in which shifts in legal entitlements are possible only if at least one person is made better off, and no person is made worse off. It follows that for any given legislative scheme there are three possible outcomes. First, the program goes forward without any explicit compensation. Second, the program must be enjoined because the net losers from the taking cannot be compensated, thereby highlighting the long-neglected injunctive dimension of the takings clause. Third, the program can go forward only if explicit compensation is paid to some from revenues collected by others.

The choice of responses is a mixture of high principle and particular evidence, not dissimilar to the issues raised in considering the means-ends relationship under the police power. As there are daunting problems of uncertainty, the logical precision demanded on the issue of takings proper cannot be required here. Ideally, a complete doctrine of just compensation would minimize the number of uncompensated takings, which in turn would minimize (the sum of) the errors of estimation and the administrative costs of operating the system, each of which may be dependent upon the other. In this, given the inherent uncertainties in the process, the legislature must be afforded some discretion. In order to choose from the three possible outcomes in any particular case, it is necessary to obtain evidence, usually indirect, of the overall size of the social pie and the size of each of its slices. No single form of evidence will do this job, and in many cases the evidence will be conflicting. The marginal embarrassments could, in principle, be cured by better evidence, but until that evidence is forthcoming, we must learn to live with the hard cases born of imperfect knowledge.

Rather than bemoan fate, however, it is best to consider the various types of evidence that can be marshaled on the compensation question in all large-number takings cases. The first type upon which we can rely is general economic theory, which can be used to estimate in qualitative fashion the wealth effects of particular government programs. The sec-

16. Id.

ond type is redistributive motive, showing what the supporters of government actions intend to gain by programs paid for disproportionately by other citizens. The third type of evidence is the impact of the taking, and the extent of disproportion, upon the parties who are subject to it.

ECONOMIC THEORY:
IN AND OUT OF COMMON POOLS

A large body of literature addresses the efficiency features of government regulation, taxation, and common law rules. In some cases the basic conclusions are controversial, but in many others they are not. One well-established conclusion is that private agreements cannot be expected to fund a sufficient level of classical public goods; holdout problems and transactions costs block voluntary solutions, which in principle everyone would prefer. Any use of taxation and regulation to achieve those ends should be approached with the presumption that those powers create a positive-sum game which, because the required compensation is typically provided, renders them immune from wholesale invalidation. The point is especially powerful in connection with a matter such as the general defense, where it is notoriously difficult to determine the subjective value each person attaches to the state-provided services.

The same presumption applies to other cases where high transaction costs preclude the formation of a well-established system of private property rights. Thus there is a general consensus that exclusive, or at least well-defined, property rights over particular things will expand the size of the social pie. Any system which takes things of value out of a common pool and subjects them to well-defined rights should in principle be able to generate sufficient wealth to satisfy the compensation requirement of the eminent domain clause.

I will mention only two very important categories. First, there is widespread agreement that resources which are naturally found in a common pool, such as oil and gas, are rendered more valuable if subjected to well-defined systems of rights. Blanket invalidation of rules intended to alleviate common-pool problems should therefore occur very rarely in light of the total gains the rules produce. The question that remains is whether any explicit compensation should be paid, and if so, to and by whom? Second, antitrust laws, which prevent monopoly and foster competition, fall clearly into the same class. If transaction costs were zero, the competitive outcome would always prevail because it would produce more goods and services: customers could outbid competitors or at least induce new competitors to enter the business. Monopoly therefore can be understood as a negative-sum game which the antitrust laws, at least in their prospective application, are designed to overcome.[17]

Legislation, however, often works in reverse by taking well-defined property rights away from individual owners and placing them in a new common pool. To take an extreme example, assume a society with ten persons, each of whom has well-defined rights in one-tenth of the social wealth. The state then decides to nationalize all private property and to give each person in exchange a one-in-ten chance of getting the entire social pie. Given that most persons are risk averse, the value of the rights created will be less than their value before being placed in the common pool. If the subsequent division of property is by political decision instead of lottery, rent-seeking combines with risk aversion to reduce the levels of wealth even further. The negative-sum game could be enjoined even if all individuals were subjected to the same legal treatment. Indeed, the real question is, how could a scheme this stark be passed in the first place? Yet the same analysis applies to legislation that seeks to abolish property rights in a more limited compass. Suppose the government announces in advance that it will take any land needed for a highway without paying compensation. In a risk-neutral world without rent seeking, this scheme should pass constitutional muster. Risk-neutral people are indifferent to uncertainty, while the absence of rent seeking prevents factional gains. The random selection of highway sites should not therefore diminish the total size of the pie or skew its distribution. All are fully compensated. But in the world we know, a general statute that subjected all persons to an equal risk of condemnation without compensation would necessarily fail.[18] The lottery ticket given by the state does not have a value equal to the property rights it displaces. The value of property depends not only on what there is in the world but on the configuration of the ownership rights to it.

MOTIVE

However, real-world cases are rarely this stark, because honest disagreement may arise over the effects of various types of takings. In real cases direct economic evidence may be far weaker than it is in the extreme cases just given. Evidence on motive is influential in eminent domain

17. For a more extensive account of my views on the antitrust law, see Richard A. Epstein, "Private Property and the Public Domain: The Case of Antitrust," in *Ethics, Economics, and the Law*, NOMOS 24 (1982).

18. See, generally, Lawrence Blume and Daniel L. Rubinfield, "Compensation for Takings: An Economic Analysis," 72 Calif. L. Rev. 569 (1984), for a discussion of the insurance rationales behind the compensation requirement.

cases precisely because it allows courts to examine legislative enactments even when they have no reliable direct information about their social and economic consequences. The relevance of motive is clear enough and is easily stated: parties that seek redistribution through government action usually know what they are doing. When they say they wish to take from others to benefit themselves, chances are they mean what they say and that they sufficiently understand the means-end connections to do it right. No one has ever accused the dairy lobby of lacking informed self-interest. Identifying parties that are acting from partisan motive provides some evidence of an uncompensated taking. The motive itself can be explicit and naked,[19] or it can be dressed up and disguised. It can be mixed with legitimate motives, either primary or incidental. Evidence of motive should never be conclusive on the question of just compensation but to take a phrase from the negligence literature, it constructs a foxhole that provides some shelter against the fire of conflicting evidence coming from all directions.[20]

DISPROPORTIONATE IMPACT

The disproportionate impact test is central to the eminent domain literature because frequently it is not possible to judge whether certain kinds of government activities increase or decrease the size of the social pie. This test offers a way to pass upon the soundness of legislation when direct measurement is not possible; because it is underinclusive, the disproportionate impact test necessarily affords the state some discretion in the way it conducts public affairs. The simplest way to understand the centrality of the test to the law of eminent domain is to assume that the social pie remains constant in size even after private property is taken for public use. Then the initial assumption can be relaxed, and the test can be examined under the alternative assumptions that the change in resource use has either increased or decreased social wealth, often in some unidentified manner.

The disproportionate impact test is of central importance even in the simplest one-to-one case, the taking of land for a post office. There the

19. See Cass R. Sunstein, "Naked Preferences and the Constitution," 84 *Colum. L. Rev.* 1689 (1984), demonstrating how the theme runs through the full range of constitutional provisions.

20. The foxhole metaphor comes from the courts' inability to fasten upon a single test for negligence in ordinary tort actions. "Local usage and general custom, either singly or in combination, will not justify or excuse negligence. They are merely foxholes in one of the battlefields of law, providing shelter, but not complete protection against charges of negligence." Bimberg v. Northern Pacific Ry., 217 Minn. 187, 192, 14 N.W.2d 410, 413 (1944).

normal assumption is that the individual citizen is on one side of the transaction and the state is on the other, so the case is properly treated as one of me and thee. In truth this sharp opposition is a (justified) simplification of the true situation, for the individual landowner, who is also a taxpayer, is on both sides of the transaction. To understand his position completely, one must take into account not only his private loss but also his proportionate share of the tax liability (itself a taking) used to fund the purchase and his share of the benefits from the public use of the property.

Therefore the owner of the property in fact stands on both sides of the transaction, but his interests are heavily weighted on one side. The isolated takings case is invariably one of disproportionate impact. If the city of Chicago takes my land for a new city hall, the fraction of my land lost is 1, while my fraction of the money tendered by the city is perhaps one part in a million. I may gain or lose in my capacity as a taxpayer, but my financial interest qua citizen is dwarfed by my individual stake. Explicit compensation is required because the size of the overlap is so small that I am left worse off without my land even if I benefit pro rata with other citizens from the new city hall. Since by assumption the property value is the same in public as in private hands, the effect of compensation is to ensure that the relative wealth among individuals is left unchanged.[21]

To take a private analogy, suppose a plaintiff with $100 in General Motors stock sues the company for the destruction of his car caused by a General Motors employee. The shareholder is in fact on both sides of the case, but his stake qua shareholder is so small that explicit compensation (which he pays in tiny part and receives in full) is required to balance the accounts. The victim's fractional interest in the corporation is automatically taken into account by his proportionate share of the decrease in the corporation's net worth. All things being equal, the G.M. shareholder might prefer to recover the same dollar amount from Ford if he did not own shares in that company. But the difference between the two cases is so small that it does not merit attention.

The dynamics are very different with a taking of property from a large number of individuals. Although the fraction of the taking that is

21. There is a close parallel here to the economic discussion of agency costs. See, e.g., Michael C. Jensen and William H. Meckling, "Theory of the Firm: Managerial Behavior, Agency Costs, and Ownership Structure," 3 *J. Fin. Econ.* 305 (1976), where it is noted that individual incentives are skewed where a person must bear the full costs of certain actions while receiving only part of the benefits, or where he bears only part of the costs and obtains all of the benefits.

funded by each individual owner does not increase, the amount each one loses is vastly reduced. In more formal terms, the value of the property taken is m, which is far less than 1; m and n are of the same order of magnitude and in the limiting case are identical.

To revert to the previous example, assume that the city wishes to build upon land which by some quirk is held in a tenancy in common by all the city's residents in equal proportion, and assume that its value is constant in public or private hands. The city takes the land and pays each resident for his interest out of general revenues. Here again the owners are on both sides of the transaction. But now their fractional interests on each side are equal in magnitude, at least in the simplest case in which everyone shares equally in the gains from the new city hall. Each resident's percentage of the transaction as loser is n less than 1, multiplied by the value of the land, which is also the exact fraction of the gain. Under these circumstances it quickly becomes clear that payment of explicit compensation serves no intelligible function because it cannot change the net worth of any Chicago resident nor, *a fortiori*, their relative positions. If the city pays excessive compensation, the portion of wealth in private hands increases, but the gain is precisely offset by the decrease in each person's fractional share of the city's cash reserves. If the city pays inadequate compensation, then each person's private loss is precisely offset by his fraction of the gains left in the city account. Under these circumstances the payment of compensation is a matter of indifference even if it is costless to implement.[22]

Precisely because the net worth of every individual is uninfluenced by the amount of compensation paid, administrative issues come to dominate the decision. Not paying anyone anything is well nigh costless and produces a gain which in the first instance is shared pro rata by the group, leaving everyone better off. The program of perfect compensation outlined earlier is implemented by a set of perfectly offsetting debits and credits. Explicit compensation is always needed when an individual has the full gain or loss on one side of the transaction and the tiny fraction on the other. In contrast, no explicit compensation is needed when all individuals have the same fractional interests on both sides of the

22. Public debt and public funds are subject to political pressures that private wealth and private debts escape. But even the preference for private over collective wealth makes a difference on the narrow point here, for the city could always recoup the extra compensation by increasing its overall levels of taxation. Similarly, if too little money is paid, the difference could be adjusted by reducing future taxes or by expending the saved revenues on some other public project. Note that the same debate can occur over Social Security, if it is believed that public and private savings are substitutes for each other.

transaction. The precise private analogy is to pro rata contributions to or distributions by corporations, which, tax consequences apart, have no financial consequences for the various shareholders.[23]

The two polar extremes, therefore, are 1 versus n and n versus n. Between them lie an infinite number of variations in which either contributions or distributions are out of phase with the overall holdings. In one simple variation the state takes twice as much (homogeneous) land from each member of one group as it does from each member of the other group, but every person receives the identical compensation. Conversely, each person could lose the same amount of land, with the members of one group receiving twice as much compensation as the members of the other group. In either case the transaction can be broken down into two transactions, one proportionate and the other not. In principle, no explicit transfer payments are required for the proportionate part, but they are strictly required for the other part. In non-pro rata cases the levels of compensation paid are no longer a matter of indifference to the participants. The system of automatically offsetting debits and credits will work in part but not in full.

Take the simple case in which one person owns land worth $100 which is condemned by the city, consisting of two citizens, each of whom derives an equal benefit from the public use. The only proper result is for the second citizen to pay $50 in cash (or kind) to offset his one-half interest in the public good. It makes no difference whether this is achieved by levying $50 in taxes from both A and B and paying the full sum to A, or by having B make a simple transfer payment (or special assessment) of $50 to A. It is obviously critical that the valuations of assets be accurate in order to determine the proper level of transfer payments. Therefore valuation is critical in the ordinary eminent domain case and largely immaterial in large-number takings.

Assuming that social wealth does not remain constant after property is taken, what should be done when it is impossible to determine whether a shift of property from private to public hands increases or decreases the total net worth? Here the objective is to find some method of

23. For a detailed exposition of the rules of pro rata and non-pro rata distributions in the corporate tax area, see Boris I. Bittker and James E. Eustace, *Federal Income Taxation of Corporations and Shareholders* (4th ed. 1979). The central theme throughout is that paper and property adjustments that do not affect relative holdings have no tax consequences at all, while those which do affect relative shares can create taxable gain or loss, as the case may be. The rules there are a perfect road map for the eminent domain law considered here, where the individual citizen's stake is analogous to the individual holding in the shares of the corporation.

structuring incentives so that only beneficial transactions take place. In this context the disproportionate impact test exerts a powerful and welcome influence. The test limits the power of any individual actor to obtain the net benefits by taking advantage of any persistent bias in the operation of the legal system. To demand additional contributions from others he must make additional contributions himself. To obtain additional benefits for himself, he has to be prepared to tender them to others. By keeping all individuals in lockstep with each other, the disproportionate impact in large-numbered cases limits the misuse of legislative power. Where widespread legislation has no disproportionate impact, it may create some form of social loss, for nothing prevents a mistaken government program from leaving everyone worse off. The proportionate form of the program thus dictates that there will be no— or, allowing for some dispersion in outcomes, few—net winners. The political process, therefore, is now subject to a built-in constraint against the creation of negative wealth effects, for no one stands to gain by universally unwise government action. The great peril of political life arises where some group receives a large enough increase in its share of the total pie to offset the shrinkage in the size of the pie as a whole.[24] Because the total pie has shrunk, the gains to the successful faction must be offset by an even greater loss to the rest of the population. It is just that loss that the disproportionate impact test seeks to avoid by preventing any coalition from subverting the public good.

Desirable political consequences follow from the disproportionate impact test, which has no bite where it is not needed. There is good reason to rely upon the political process to correct the original errors of resource allocation brought about by the private law. In contrast, where the effects are disproportionate, a winning coalition could obtain laws that inflict heavy losses upon losers. The requirement of explicit compensa-

24. More formally, let V be the value of the total pie in a well-organized society and V^* ($< V$) its value when rent seeking occurs; let n be the percentage of the total pie held by one group, and $(1-n)$ the fraction held by the second group before legislation with disproportionate impact is passed. After that legislation is passed, the fraction held by the first group will be equal to $(n + x)$, and that of the second group $(1 - n - x)$, where x is the fraction of relative wealth shifted by the legislation. The net worth of the winners after legislation exceeds their net worth before it, or $(n + x)V^* > nV$. This result will happen if the winners have calculated their sums correctly. For the winners, the gain in share offsets the loss in the size of the pie. For the losers the economic effects are always unambiguous, and usually large, because $(1 - n - x)V^* < (1 - n)V$. A group cannot win if it has a smaller share of a smaller pie. Note that the social loss equals $V - V^*$. The disproportionate impact test is designed to minimize that loss.

tion to the losers now helps ensure that the political game will have a positive sum. In both pro rata and non–pro rata cases, therefore, the system is endowed with a set of structural incentives that minimizes these allocative errors, even when there is no direct knowledge of whether certain takings produce net social gains or net losses. In other words, the disproportionate impact test creates a precise link between each individual welfare function and the social welfare function, so that the latter is simply a multiple of the former. It follows (from the simple calculus) that an individual constrained by the disproportionate impact test will necessarily maximize his own welfare if he endorses government initiatives that maximize aggregate social welfare as well.[25]

Step Transactions

We should not underestimate the hidden difficulties involved in isolating the evils that the disproportionate impact test is designed to combat. In particular, the test will function only when we have some independent knowledge of the scope of any transaction.[26] To revert to the simplest case, assume that citizens in group A are made to contribute property for the sole use of those in group B. This transaction looks like a taking without just compensation, so far as it goes. But what happens if there is a parallel transaction of equal value in which the individuals in group B are required to contribute property for the sole benefit of those in group A? Should the two transactions be considered in isolation or together? Separately considered, both transactions require compensation. Viewed together, however, the overall situation may be regarded as benign, as the takings in the one case are offset by the takings in the other, leaving members of both groups better off.

Yet how should a court decide which sets of transactions are to be linked? Some answers can be suggested. Where the two transactions can be "stepped"—treated as part of a unified whole—because both are part of a common plan, then the result seems clear. The state should be able

25. The proof is straightforward. Find any social welfare function $F(x)$. By the disproportionate impact test, the individual function $f(x) = kF(x)$, with k less than one. The first derivatives will equal zero at the same point for both functions, which therefore have the same maximum point.

26. The point is also noted in Frank I. Michelman, "Politics and Values or What's Really Wrong with Rationality Review," 13 *Creighton L. Rev.* 487, 499–500 (1979), in his discussion of the "stream of legislation," which also takes a skeptical view of integrating separate transactions, each of which is alone defective.

to group the transactions together and to claim that the imbalance of the one is offset by the opposite imbalance of the other. But what if the two laws are passed independently? It is now tempting to say that so long as the combined effect is benign, it is appropriate to step the transaction to meet the standards of proportionate impact by showing that there exists a larger group with more benign description. The generalized linkage of separate legislative enactments is, however, a trap of constitutional dimensions. One point is that the benefits and burdens of the two separate packages may not be of the same magnitude. Nor is there a neat separation of persons into groups. While many individuals gain under one statute and lose under the other, some other persons will either lose or gain in both. The statutes are linked, but only after the fact; each part of the package was acted upon independently and bears the influence of factional efforts, which the compensation requirement is meant to combat. The abuses are additive, in fact, but they are treated as offsetting as a matter of law when the political dynamic is ignored. In the limit, a court could place all legislative initiatives past and future into a single hopper and proclaim that the benefits and burdens are always proportionate, thereby gutting the takings clause for general regulation.

Here general economic theory limits the scope of the disproportionate impact test. Where each separate statute bears the sign of a negative sum game, then their totality yields only a larger negative sum. If the losses from each statute are 10, then the losses of the two taken together are 20, not 0. The only way to combat this error (which by definition leaves uncompensated takings) is to follow the linkages only as far as the legislature makes them explicit, which typically will be program by program or statute by statute. Infrequently, some connections between statutes will be missed. However, the error costs are far lower if the disproportionate impact test is used to evaluate each government program on its own terms. The fidelity to the constitutional provision is therefore far greater.

Generalization, Equal Protection, and Representation

The above analysis of disproportionate impact has important implications for the role of *generalization* in both legal and ethical theory. Under the traditional view, the generality of a rule is often thought to be a good thing, because it prevents individuals from being singled out for special abuse. Yet no one thinks that generalization is always a good thing: the rules of racial segregation and religious persecution were consciously written in very general form. The disproportionate impact test provides a good explanation of why generalization, while relevant to ethical inquiry, is not a complete substitute for substantive ethical propositions. So long as government action constitutes a taking *and* a giving to the same individuals in the same proportions, all is well. The very generality of the rule, in Rawls's phrase, places all individuals behind the veil of ignorance so that, being benefited and burdened, they will not be able to prefer their own interests to those of others. Many common law rules have just this character.[27] But generalization, far from being a fail-safe protection against individual abuse, can be transformed into a mass mode of exploitation. Government action may be very general in its articulation and application, but it may impose all of the burdens on one class and all of the benefits on another, imposing uncompensated takings of private property on a grand scale.

The general proposition yields a strong but not conclusive presumption that general legislation is confiscatory in two classes of cases, which predictably have increased in frequency as the judicial control of legislative action has diminished. Retroactive legislation is one such presumptive evil. Because one person has undertaken actions that another has not, the costs to the first of the ostensibly neutral law are far greater than the benefits he receives in exchange. The government action never takes place on a blank slate, since the legal rights of all persons are well defined before the legislation is passed. Even with prospective legislation, individual rights are lost, and in some instances the loss can be quite large. Prospective legislation never refers to the situation "ex ante," where ex ante means before the acquisition of entitlements. Legislation is prospective only in the sense that it precedes the particular action (say, constructing a building), which a person had a right to take before the legislation abridging it was passed.

The companion to retroactive legislation is special or class legislation that mismatches the burden to one person of losing property with the benefits conferred in exchange on another. As with retroactive laws, special legislation calls for heightened scrutiny because it gives powerful evidence of inadequate compensation for loss of rights. The burdens may be concentrated and the benefits diffuse, or vice versa. But no matter whether we deal with subsidies from general revenues or special taxes

27. See Chapter 17. For a discussion of the same point in another context, see Richard A. Epstein, "The Social Consequences of Common Law Rules," 95 *Harv. L. Rev.* 1717 (1982).

on oil and gas, the mismatch of benefits and burdens is a clear sign of uncompensated takings. As a first approximation, the formula for sound general legislation is simple: special burdens for special benefits; general burdens for general benefits. Retroactive and special legislation often violate this presumption. Both of these types of schemes have long been characterized as unfair on intuitive grounds, but these intuitions have a strict analytical basis, just as they have a secure constitutional anchor to the just compensation requirement of the eminent domain clause.

The difficulty of making abstract judgments about general legislation also shows the close linkage between equal protection and the law of eminent domain.[28] The analysis under the two provisions is consistent in two important ways. The modern view of equal protection, roughly speaking, has two requirements. First, the classification of persons or actions that the state chooses must be related to some legitimate state end. Without some constraint, the state could choose whatever end it wanted. All state actions would be valid because they would have a reasonable, indeed perfect, relationship to this end chosen, however bizarre.[29] If the state wants to give subsidies to blue-eyed babes born in New York, the statute will perfectly adjust means to ends, rendering the equal protection provision a complete nullity and allowing disproportionate taxes to prevail. The class of ends therefore must be constrained for the equal protection doctrine to be intelligible.

The second part of the modern theory makes a powerful distinction in the degree of means-ends scrutiny brought to different kinds of government actions. Thus, again broadly speaking, a suspect classification such as race or national origin is subject to a high degree of means-ends scrutiny, while classifications which involve mere economic relationships are subject to a very deferential standard of review, as in *Clover Leaf.*[30] An area such as sex-based classification is subject to an uneasy level of intermediate review.

The eminent domain clause suggests a very different role for a theory

28. It also shows how it is possible to lend content to the general ethical injunction to treat like cases alike, but given the substantive dimension to the inquiry that prevents the formula from being an empty one, as argued in Peter Westen, "The Empty Idea of Equality," 95 *Harv. L. Rev.* 537 (1982).

29. See, e.g., Cass R. Sunstein, "Public Values, Private Interests, and the Equal Protection Clause," 1982 *Sup. Ct. Rev.* 127,129-131. Sunstein notes that one purpose of the equal protection clause is to prevent the formation of legislative factions, a result that seems to be in tension with his willingness to tolerate the low level of scrutiny under the rational basis test. Id. at 131-135.

30. See Chapter 10.

of equal protection. The takings clause contains *within itelf* the substantive standards that differentiate between the legitimate and illegitimate ends of government behavior. Any form of taking is legitimate if justified by the police power (which has its own constrained set of ends).[31] But when that justification fails, compensation must be provided, which in the context of general prospective legislation may be implicit and in kind. At this point the disproportionate impact test tracks the equal treatment requirement in the equal protection clause but endows it with its necessary set of substantive ends. With the protection of property established, there is no more reason here than with the analysis of the police power to reserve greater scrutiny for cases in which there is a suspect classification or a fundamental right. Where property-based claims are involved, it is quite sufficient to identify a class of individuals that will profit by the taking of another's property.

In the examples previously given, a simple equal protection inquiry might allow only racial divisions in Chicago to trigger a judicial examination of the disparate impacts of the city's taxing and regulatory programs. Yet so long as it is possible to identify any class of individuals who are, for whatever reason, the victims of disproportionate legislation, this class can claim (1) that its property has been taken, and (2) that insufficient compensation has been tendered for it in exchange. A systematic wealth transfer from the north side to the south side of Chicago, or the reverse, should be sufficient, if demonstrated with the same clarity as the racial division. The disproportionate impact, not the boundaries of the classes or the motives for setting those boundaries, becomes the dispositive issue.

Within this uniform framework certain cases may properly receive stricter scrutiny than others, if only because it is easier to identify the relevant class of abuses. Thus the demands on the state should be very stiff in racial cases because the dynamics of interest group politics make it very likely that redistributive coalitions will form along racial lines. Sexual classifications should be treated somewhat more cautiously because it is somewhat less likely that coalitions will form for redistributive ends.[32] On the other hand, it may be almost impossible to trace the collection of tax revenues and expenditures for street cleaning in Chicago, so the level of judicial control should (arguably) be lower.[33] In all cases,

31. See Chapter 9.

32. Indeed, sex classifications may be appropriate in many instances to prevent redistribution, as with the life insurance and annuity cases. See Chapter 19.

33. See the discussion of special assessments in Chapter 18.

the ultimate question is whether the taking has been compensated. The differences in group types only lend strength, greater or lesser, to the disproportionate impact test, which in turn provides evidence of compensation when direct measurement is beyond the judicial ken.

The arguments just developed bear a striking resemblance to the view of general constitutional interpretation put foward by John Ely in his book *Democracy and Distrust*.[34] Ely first tries to demonstrate that no clause-bound approach will solve the central problems of constitutional interpretation. He then seeks to show that many of the most difficult constitutional provisions are best understood as efforts first, as with the First Amendment, to keep open the access of all groups to the political process, and second, as with equal protection, to prevent the dominant groups within any legislature from converting the political process to an instrument of their own ends.

Ely's analysis in this book is quite puzzling, for the Constitution contains large numbers of substantive guarantees that on their face at least are not directed to matters of structure and process.[35] My analysis here, however, suggests that there is at least one way to bridge the gap between two sets of concerns, ironically enough by the clause-bound interpretation that Ely dismisses. The political process is intimately and rigorously tied to the eminent domain clause in all large-number takings situations. Any efforts by one group to manipulate the political process against another group in matters of taxation or regulation, for example, will be caught by the just compensation requirement, for which disproportionate impact and corrupt motive are useful surrogates. The question of representation-enforcing remedies is not an extraconstitutional value read into various constitutional clauses. It is instead relevant evidence on the question of whether certain schemes bring about an illicit redistribution of private property from A to B, expressly prohibited by the takings clause. Where the legislative process is skewed, there is greater opportunity for factions to operate, which makes forbidden results more likely. Ely relies on property cases to show the improper consequences of inadequate representation, traditionally attacked under the due process clause.[36] But he pays scant attention to the doctrinal home of the property cases because he accepts the modern framework of pre-

34. John H. Ely, *Democracy and Distrust* (1980).

35. See Laurence H. Tribe, "The Puzzling Persistence of Process Based Constitutional Theories," 89 *Yale L.J.* 1063 (1980).

36. See, e.g., Ervine's Appeal, 16 Pa. 256 (1851), cited by Ely, supra note 34, at 81.

ferred freedoms and fundamental rights, which relegates the takings clause to the fringes of constitutional interpretation.[37] Yet there is no obvious or proper way to cabin the disproportionate impact test to a small class of cases or to deny the powerful link between legislative breakdown and insufficient compensation. The next four chapters show the way in which the economic theory of property rights and the motive tests work both in harmony and in conflict in evaluating particular legislative and common law innovations.

37. Ely's short discussion of the clause is found at 96–97, and its implications are not probed or tested. After one paragraph on the central purpose of the clause, he turns to a discussion of the reconstruction amendments. Similarly, his discussion of the famous footnote 4 in United States v. Carolene Products, 304 U.S. 144 (1938), is extensive but does not challenge the line between economic liberties and other rights guaranteed by the Constitution. See Ely, supra note 34, at 75–77, 151–153.

15   Property and the Common Pool

The basic analysis of implicit in-kind compensation applies to every form of taking identified in the first chapters of this book. The working out of the system depends, however, on linking the general theory to particular institutional arrangements as developed both at common law and by legislation. There is no shortcut in this enterprise, as the power of the theory is revealed only by the unity it imposes on the many separate areas of doctrine and practice. In organizing the inquiry it is useful to recall that common law classification identifies three separate types of rules: those for the acquisition of private property, those for the protection of private property, and those for the transfer of private property. This chapter addresses the question of how, and to what extent, the rules for implicit in-kind compensation permit flexibility in relation to control of the common pool, with either the original acquisition of property or its subsequent control and division.

Common Pools: First Possession

The standard rule for the acquisition of private property at common law is that of first possession. Implicit in that rule is the assumption that in the original position each person owns his own labor, and no person owns anything external to himself. The rule of first possession then matches individual persons with external things.[1] Yet this rule cannot be

1. See, for Anglo-American law, Pierson v. Post, 3 Caines 175 (1805), 2

defended as a necessary truth about the legal relationship between possession and ownership: no legal rule has that desirable property.[2] The
first-possession rule, however, does have certain very attractive utilitarian features that account for its persistence over time. It allows the transition from no ownership to ownership to take place without conscious
government interference or authorization, and this is critical to a Lockean theory that regards the state as the protector of property rights but
not as their source. The rule also ensures that each bit of property will
have only one exclusive owner, who can then see that it is well exploited, either by use or by sale.[3] In addition, by imposing a minimal
standard for the acquisition of property, the rule tends to reduce acquisition costs far below what they would be if extensive use or development of a thing (such as planting trees in order to perfect a homestead)
was required to perfect ownership.[4] The first-possession rule as applied
to land also facilitates the use of easy devices—such as surveys or
fences—so that the original owner can give notice of his claim to the rest
of the world, thereby reducing conflicts in ownership claims. Finally,
with durable property, chiefly land, the first-possession rule has one
especially desirable feature: it creates no incentive to reduce the value of
the thing in order to keep the thing for itself.

This last point shows the weakness of the first-possession rule in cases
not dealing with raw land, where the act of individual acquisition tends
to reduce the value of those natural resources that remain in the common pool; for example, with fisheries and with oil and gas, unrestrained
private acquisition tends to reduce the value of the whole. Each person
finds it in his own interest to destroy the common pool resource because
he bears only a tiny fraction of the losses sustained to the pool itself while
keeping the full gains of that fraction of the pool he has taken for his
own use. When that basic pattern is repeated countless times by all persons, all are left worse off than they would have been if their conduct
had been governed by some form of mutual restraint. In principle the

---

Am. Dec. 264 (1886). For the civil law tradition, see Gaius, *Institutes* II, 66 (de
Zuleuta trans. 1945).

2. See Richard A. Epstein, "Possession as the Root of Title," 13 *Ga. L. Rev.*
1221 (1979).

3. For a theoretical statement of how virtually all restitution and liability
rules can be explained as devices to minimize the transaction costs of obtaining the right incentives, see Donald Wittman, "Liability for Harm or Restitution for Benefit?" 13 *J. Legal Stud.* 57 (1984).

4. See Laura Ingalls Wilder, *The First Four Years* (1949), on the difficulty of
keeping trees alive on land where they are not naturally found.

parties could make a comprehensive agreement to oust the first-possession rules for wasting resources. But such a contract would be faced with the same insuperable obstacles that prevent the consensual formation of society at large, given the familiar trinity of high transaction costs, free-rider questions, and holdouts.

Because these negotiated solutions typically fail, collective solutions are required, so long as there are no constitutional impediments to action. One approach insists that there is really no problem at all, that so long as things remain unowned, no one can claim a deprivation of property rights solely because the state decrees its common ownership over the thing in question.[5] This argument will not work. As always, the state is only the agent of the individuals whom it benefits in any given transaction. Its only unique power is to force exchanges upon provision of just compensation. If a state decree vested title in the state, then a similar declaration must vest title in a private individual, which is what the first-possession rule precludes. The ipse dixit cannot achieve the desired position, because the state cannot rise above the citizens it represents.[6]

Indeed it could hardly be otherwise. The fatal objection to the declaration theory of private ownership is that it cannot explain how either a private party or the government can obtain *exclusive* rights to anything. The first-possession rule requires external acts and imposes positive costs

5. See discussion in Chapters 1 and 2.
6. The Supreme Court has made the same point in connection with the power of the state to keep wild animals from being traded in interstate commerce. Geer v. Connecticut, 161 U.S. 519 (1895), sustained a statute providing that "no person shall at any time kill any woodcock, ruffed grouse or quail for the purpose of conveying the same beyond the limits of this State, etc.," in part on the ground that the state had title to wild animals not reduced to possession. That proposition was strongly attacked by Field, J., in his dissent, id. at 538–540. Eventually his views prevailed, so restrictions on the sale of fish and wild animals are now governed by the same rules applicable to the commerce clause generally.

The explicit repudiation of ownership created by government assertion is found in a passage in Douglas v. Seacoast Products, Inc., 431 U.S. 265, 284 (1977): "A state does not stand in the same position as the owner of a private game preserve, and it is pure fantasy to talk of "owning" wild fish, birds, or animals. Neither the States nor the Federal Government, any more than a hopeful fisherman or hunter, has title to these creatures until they are reduced to possession by skillful capture." The passage was cited with approval in Hughes v. Oklahoma, 441 U.S. 322, 334–335 (1979), overruling *Geer* and rejecting the theory that state ownership may be acquired by declaration. See generally Walter Hellerstein, "Hughes v. Oklahoma: The Court, The Commerce Clause, and State Control of Natural Resources," 1979 *Sup. Ct. Rev.* 51.

upon those who take them. While everyone can "grab," everyone's grab is subject to the rival grabs of other persons, whom he cannot hinder by the use of force. In contrast, there is no cost to making declarations, nor is there any obvious way to sort out their priority. Declarations alone preclude the exclusive ownership of anything while establishing joint ownership of nothing.

If, therefore, only first possession establishes private rights good against the world, then the property rights it creates are protected by the eminent domain clause against state declarations to the contrary: the right of acquisition is itself a property right, good against the world. In addition, if no private person may use force to prevent any individual from taking unowned things, then the police power does not place the state in any better position. There is no private wrong to control when private parties take unowned things.[7]

The case then turns squarely on the question of whether the common pool regulation provides implicit in-kind compensation to those whose property it takes. There is strong reason to believe that it does. Initially the allocative effects of this regulation are apt to increase the total size of the pie. The public use requirement imposes no barrier to public regulation, given the obvious holdout problems in the original position, so long as no private party by unilateral action can obtain a disproportionate share of the surplus created. So long as the gains are shared in rough proportion to the losses, the pooling arrangements should be sustained. Here it is sufficient to trace how implicit in-kind compensation works with legislation in three disparate contexts—oil and gas exploration, public waters, and bankruptcy—that have a common underlying structure.

OIL AND GAS

The genesis of the common pool problem in the oil and gas cases may be briefly summarized. Early on, the common law judges applied the first-possession rule to oil and gas located under land of several different landowners. In light of the "fugitive" nature of oil, no person had absolute title to any oil, wherever located, in the pool until he took it out of the ground and reduced it to his separate possession.[8] By the "owner-

---

7. See Chapter 5.
8. Many of the references here are contained in the excellent collection of materials in C. Donahue, T. Kauper, and P. Martin, *Property: An Introduction to the Concept and the Institution* 325–359 (1974). See also Hammonds v. Central Kentucky Natural Gas Co., 75 S.W.2d 204 (1934).

ship" variation of the basic rule, the landowner owned the oil in place, but his title was subject to defeasance if a neighboring owner first reduced the oil to possession. By the competing "nonownership" rule, every landowner was said to have a profit a prendre, an exclusive right to drill for oil on his own property, but not defeasible ownership of the oil in place.[9] Both rules recognized the physical obstacles to any system that gives absolute rights of ownership of oil based on its original underground location; because oil and gas move continually, no one can know whether these resources are his when they come out of the ground. Both rules also had the desirable effect of ensuring that oil and gas once removed from the ground had a unique and easily identified owner, vested with the exclusive rights of possession, use, and disposition.

The differences between the two formulations have influenced the outcome of cases on a number of difficult points of law concerning taxation, conversion, information, and the like.[10] Yet these differences are dwarfed by a weakness shared by both rules: neither addresses the common pool problem. Both rules induce each owner to take as much oil out of the pool as quickly as possible, thereby destroying much of its productive capacity. Consistent with the absolute nature of property rights, no private party could prevent the wasteful or malicious destruction of the pool by any one person who had an interest in it; although malice may make bad acts worse, it does not convert these actions into ones that involve the use of force or fraud.[11] Acts that are lawful without malice remain lawful with it, so long as one applies only the basic takings doctrine without forced exchanges.

There is much to criticize in this pattern of ownership, but no amount of criticism can deny that individual claims under first possession, whether of specific oil or the right to acquire oil in place, are as fully vested as those found in land. In the limit, for example, the state could not claim the entire pool to the exclusion of *all* the surface landowners solely because the oil was still in place. If complete takings are subject to constitutional scrutiny, then so too are partial takings, whether by legislative, executive or judicial action. Implicit in-kind compensation is again the key.

9. See Westmoreland & Cambria Natural Gas Co. v. DeWitt, 130 Pa. 235, 18 A. 724 (1899); Ohio Oil Co. v. Indiana (No. 1), 177 U.S. 190 (1899).

10. See Westmoreland & Cambria Natural Gas Co. v. DeWitt, 130 Pa. 235, 249-250, 18 A. 724, 725 (1889); Stephens County v. Mid-Kansas Oil & Gas Co., 113 Tex. 160, 254 S.W. 290 (1923).

11. For expressions of the dominant attitude generally, see Mayor of Bradford v. Pickles [1895] A.C. 587; Allen v. Flood [1898] A.C. 1. For its application in oil cases see, e.g., Hague v. Wheeler, 157 Pa. St. 324 (1893).

Consider first the implicit in-kind compensation in the judicial liability rule that prevents waste of oil and gas from wells drilled in the common pool. In *Elliff v. Texon Drilling Co.*,[12] the plantiffs sued for damage to their royalty and mineral interests in a certain oil pool when the defendant's "blowout," allegedly caused by his negligence, damaged the plaintiff's production. The traditional first-possession rule afford no protection to the lost interest because of the simple syllogism: no ownership, no tort claim.[13] Yet the court was able to impose an affirmative obligation—here for the exercise of reasonable care in drilling—whose breach was the source of a tort action for damages. Ex ante (that is, before the occurrence of the loss) the negligence rule in question worked for the benefit of all against all; ex ante the available production from the well is increased and not reduced. Owing to the surplus thereby created, the liability rule generates its own compensation. Owing to its neutral application, there is no problem with either disproportionate impact or the public use requirement. Indeed, if the court had gone immediately from a "no liability" to a strict liability position, the analysis would be precisely the same on both the compensation and public use questions, for this more rigorous rule has the same reciprocal benefits as the negligence alternative. The choice between those two rules is utilitarian: which most increases the size of the pie? Either rule is consistent with the eminent domain clause, which fosters but does not compel overall social improvements. No matter which rule is chosen, the combination of a surplus over the original common law no-liability position and the disproportionate impact test puts the compensation question to rest.

The same type of argument can also justify various legislative enactments that fashion a more radical redefinition of rights than is obtainable at common law. In *Ohio Oil Co. v. Indiana (No. 1)*[14] the state of

---

12. 146 Tex. 575, 210 S.W.2d 558 (1948).

13. For a view that there is no connection between property and tort, see Richard A. Posner, "Epstein's Tort Theory," 8 *J. Legal Stud.* 457 (1979), which does not explain why there is no prima facie case whenever anyone finds himself worse off by the actions of another, e.g., the case of competition. The powerful part of Posner's claim is that once we introduce a common pool system, we have new owners and therefore new tort claimants. Deciding what parties to vest with private rights of action is no mean trick. See, e.g., Pruitt v. Allied Chemical Corp., 523 F. Supp. 975 (E.D.Va. 1981), where commercial fishermen, wholesalers and distributors, restaurant owners, and their many employees all sought to maintain tort actions for harm caused by oil spills. See also Richard A. Epstein, "The Principles of Environmental Protection: The Case of Superfund," 2 *Cato J.* 9 (1982), in defense of unified government controls, without any private suits not based on traditional ownership claims.

14. 177 U.S. 190 (1899).

Indiana passed legislation which required any person who drilled oil to provide pipes, receptacles, or other facilities sufficient to contain the first two days of oil flow from a well. The rule operates in derogation of a vested property interest under both the ownership and nonownership versions of the first-possession rule. Yet notwithstanding the prima facie taking, the act provides ample implicit in-kind compensation. The impact of the statute is proportionate, and economic theory offers good reason to believe that the statute will increase overall levels of production.

This analysis justifies even more extreme forms of legislative intervention. Thus many states have passed statutes regulating the spacing of oil wells or providing for unitization of common fields,[15] in order to prevent excessive drilling, which is still possible under the crude common law tort mechanisms of *Elliff*. Again the burdens to each owner are offset by the promise of greater benefits. Again the disproportionate impact test warrants the constitutionality of the system and indicates where compensation is required. Thus, if unitization statutes eliminate certain owners from the common pool, the impact may be disproportionate. But in that case, compensation for the lost property interest is required.[16] So too it should be possible to attack any scheme for giving the participants different shares of the original pool from those they could reasonably obtain under the first-possession rule.[17] Here a certain degree of discretion must be allowed, given the incurable uncertainties as to the physical distribution of the oil and the surface owners' ability to reach it. But any system that tries reasonably and in good faith to take into account both the surface area and the thickness of each person's share of the pool should normally withstand any constitutional challenge, as has in fact been the case.[18] Common pool questions invite administrative solutions to handle the complex calculations of the property lost and the benefits

15. Howard Williams and Charles Meyers, *Oil and Gas*, vol. 6 (1984).

16. See C. Donahue, Jr., Thomas E. Kauper, and Peter W. Martin, *Property* 357 (1974), noting that typically the excluded landowner receives "a share in the royalty interest of adjoining drillers proportionate to his share of the oil deposits underlying his tract."

17. Such a result could take place under certain systems in which small owners do not labor under the same common pool restrictions applied to larger ones. See James H. Keahey, "The Texas Mineral Interest Pooling Act: End of an Era," 4 *Nat. Res. Lawyer* 359 (1971), for a discussion of the abuses under Rule 37 of the Texas Railroad Commission, which suspended the minimum area restrictions for small drillers.

18. See, e.g., Railroad Comm'n v. Rowan & Nichols, 310 U.S. 573 (1940); 311 U.S. 570 (1941); Pickens v. Railroad Comm'n, 387 S.W.2d 87 (Tex. 1965).

received in exchange. Nothing in the eminent domain clause either compels this solution or prevents it.

PUBLIC WATERS

The analysis of oil and gas rules extends to common pool questions arising from the use of public waters. In *Rossmiller v. State*,[19] a criminal case, the accused was prosecuted under a state statute that in relevant part provided first that "ice formed upon meandered lakes . . . of the state belongs to the state as property."[20] It then enacted a licensing scheme, enforced by criminal sanctions, that prevented the cutting and shipping of ice without payment to the state of a royalty of ten cents per ton, which monies were paid into the common school fund. The court struck down the statute, holding that the ice upon the public waters of the state was not the property of the state ab initio and could not be converted into public property by simple declaration. The court then (properly) found that the police power limitation was not sufficient to prevent the appropriation of ice by private parties, whether for use or for sale, for domestic or commercial purposes. It also insisted that the state could not claim ownership of the property "for its own use as entity," for use "is vested in the people of the state as a class."[21] In the court's view the situation was "unchangeable," in that "every one within the state [has] the right to enjoy [the beneficial use of public waters] so long as he does not invade the like right of another, without any interference by claim of paramount right to the subject thereof."[22] The court accordingly concluded that any statute that sought to change this legal order was necessarily unconstitutional.

Rossmiller was sound in its perception that the statute worked a taking, here of the right to obtain the unowned ice, which could not be curtailed under the police power limitation. The tax in question may have been ten cents today, but it could be ten dollars tomorrow, and in either case it was a partial taking of a previously unconditional property right—a nonexclusive profit *a prendre*. Yet these property rights are no more "unchangeable" than any other, as forced exchanges are the very essence of the eminent domain power. The question therefore is compensation, which may be found because we deal with common pool legislation. If

19. 114 Wis. 169, 89 N.W. 839 (1902) (discussing Wis. ch. 470, Laws of 1901).
20. Id at 172, 89 N.W. at 841.
21. Id at 188, 89 N.W. at 844.
22. Id. at 188, 89 N.W. at 844.

the revenues obtained from ice-cutting licenses are used "to replenish the public treasury," then the bulk of the public receives ample compensation, so ownership by declaration should suffice—in the absence of disproportionate impact. But for Rossmiller and the other entrepreneurs who made substantial capital investments in ice farming prior to passage, disproportionate impact can easily be found. Their losses included not only the speculative profits from entering into a novel line of business, but the more definite and substantial losses in going-conern value. In principle there is a difficult question of how to measure the required compensation. One answer might well be the reduced value of the business, as measured either by the previous investment that is lost or by the expected profits that are no longer obtainable. Yet for these purposes it hardly matters. As the state provided no mechanism to assure any compensation, the statute should be invalid and the criminal prosecution to no effect.

The analysis of the compensation question raised in *Rossmiller* has obvious relevance to the modern question of fisheries. There is no question that the state can prevent unlimited fishing in its waters, but the compensation point will not go away. Those who have made substantial investment in reliance upon the current distribution of rights have to be compensated for their losses. In most instances it seems difficult, if only for political reasons, to make cash payments to the fishermen who must labor under the new regulations. But compensation could be provided in the form of substitute rights to fish under the new regime, equal to the value of what has been lost. Here the compensation should take into account the prior vulnerability of individual fishermen to exhaustion of the fishery, again an issue of valuation and not entitlement. That administrative problems will arise seems clear enough. But they cannot be avoided by the hard line that finds vested rights only in the fish captured. That limited view is precluded by the constitutional status of the first-possession rule, which *Rossmiller,* for all its weaknesses, well understood.

BANKRUPTCY AND INSOLVENCY STATUTES

Implicit in-kind compensation also plays a key role in the analysis of the bankruptcy and insolvency laws, where common pool problems frequently arise. Insolvency demands that the legal system determine the priorities for distributing the assets of the debtor's estate among secured and nonsecured creditors, with the given that some creditors will receive less than full satisfaction. At common law the common pool problem arises as follows. The debtor who pays one general creditor in full in order to stave off bankruptcy has not committed a tort against his other creditors, who are thereby left with worthless claims against the debtor's estate, which formed a common pool of wealth for the general creditors.[23] The payment of a debt does not amount to the use of force or fraud against a rival creditor, nor is it a conveyance of specific property owned by other creditors, none of whom have perfected a security interest in any particular piece of property.

This common law system has the virtue of simplicity, but it also labors under the disadvantages associated with common pool problems where nothing is owned in the original position. All creditors have some inchoate claim to the debtor's assets, and none has a specific claim to any particular asset. As the property rights among the parties are ill-defined, individual creditors are encouraged to press their claims with full vigor at the earliest sign of trouble. While the debtor may well survive if only one creditor behaves in this fashion, he will likely fail if all his creditors seek to protect their interests by demanding immediate payment. In the effort to meet his obligations piecemeal, the debtor may disrupt his own business, reducing its total value to the detriment of other creditors. In principle, each creditor may agree to stay his hand if the others do the same, so that all can share the gains from preserving the debtor's business as a going concern. Nonetheless, the familiar problems of high transaction costs (locating all the other general creditors), free riders (let someone else organize the campaign), and holdouts (I'll join, but only for more than my pro rata share) often doom that enterprise to failure.

To meet this problem, bankruptcy statutes often impose a creditors' bargain that restricts the rights of individual creditors unilaterally to remove assets from the common pool. Of special note, the trustee in bankruptcy may set aside as voidable preferences those payments made to a particular general creditor by a hard-pressed debtor.[24] The exact contours of the trustee's ability to set aside preferences is not always easy to specify. The common pool approach, with its attendant costs, is not needed when the debtor is fully able to pay his debts as they mature. Accordingly, in the ordinary course of business there is reason to set aside the payment of debts before the threat of insolvency looms. In order to distinguish between payments that can and those that cannot be set aside, the statutes contain fixed periods, once 120, and now 90, days before bankruptcy, before which payments of obligations are inde-

23. Shelly v. Boothe, 73 Mo. 74 (1880).
24. Thomas H. Jackson, "Bankruptcy, Non-Bankruptcy Entitlements, and the Creditor's Bargain," 91 *Yale L.J.* 857 (1982).

feasible against the trustee in bankruptcy, as representative of the other creditors. These statutes have, however, equivocated on the question of whether a preference is voidable only if the creditor knew of the debtor's distressed position.[25] All of these preference arrangements do not seem equally desirable (knowledge, for example, should be irrelevant here, if only for administrative reasons), but their small differences in execution do not control the basic constitutional question. Bankruptcy statutes that coordinate the actions of separate general creditors are constitutional insofar as they overcome a common pool problem without creating any bias for or against any class of general creditors.

The cases have reached the proper result but often under the wrong theory. In particular, the pooling features of bankruptcy statutes are not constitutional simply because no creditor has any property right in the debtor's assets, so there is literally nothing to be taken under the eminent domain clause. In *Dames & Moore v. Regan*,[26] arising out of the Iranian hostage crisis, President Carter issued an order that stayed all claims brought in United States courts against the state of Iran and government-owned enterprises and required them to be heard before an international arbitration tribunal. In dealing with one aspect of the executive order, Justice Rehnquist argued that the general creditors had no property interests in their claims because the president had suspended their rights of action before any liens were perfected. Yet the distinction between perfected and unperfected liens is not a distinction between property and no property. It is no different from the distinction between vested and contingent remainders: both are property, albeit in different forms and with different values.[27] To assume otherwise is to allow the legislature to make property rights by declaration, as impermissible here as in other common pool situations.

To test the general status of unsecured claims, assume that the statute

25. Under the earlier bankruptcy statute, ¶ 60 of the Bankruptcy Act of 1898, the period was 120 days, but the power of the trustee only reached those preferences paid when the preferred creditor had knowledge of the debtor's difficulties. The current law (¶ 547 of the Bankruptcy Code), which calls for a 90-day period without the knowledge requirement, is probably superior because of its simplicity.

26. 453 U.S. 654 (1981).

27. See, e.g., James S. Rodgers, "The Impairment of Secured Creditors' Rights in Reorganization: A Study of the Relationship between the Fifth Amendment and the Bankruptcy Clause," 96 *Harv. L. Rev.* 973, 988–995 (1983), rightly deriding the importance of any difference in property claims between secured and unsecured creditors. The proper inference to draw, however, is that both forms of interest are protected, not that neither is.

barred the claims of *all* unsecured creditors and transferred the funds of bankrupt debtors to the public treasury. Could one say that no property interests have been taken? How does this differ from a statute that confiscates all property held under a trust which gives the trustee the power to designate beneficiaries from a limited class? What if a statute simply said that all actions for unsecured debts were abolished? The point is that unsecured creditors do have a property interest, albeit contingent in a common pool, in which they, and not the public at large, are the only members. Their relationship to each other is very complicated, just as with the surface owners over a pool of oil and gas. Yet it is one thing to reorganize creditors' rights inter se and quite another to transfer these same rights to third parties. The "no taking" account reaches the right result with preference legislation, but it guarantees the wrong result whenever forced transfers are made to persons outside of the original pool.[28]

In order to escape the common pool problems associated with default, many lenders seek to obtain security for their loans, which gives them priority over general creditors. At common law the only modes of security were possessory, requiring the creditor to take physical possession of chattels, go into occupation of land, or take possession of the deeds and other evidence of title. That system is very cumbersome because it opens up the high risks of creditor misbehavior, as by the creditor who sells the land held as security to a third party. In addition, it makes it difficult, if not impossible, for the same property to serve as collateral for two or more loans by different creditors, each of whom cannot have exclusive possession. To overcome these difficulties the legal system has introduced various systems of registration that order the competing claims by time of perfection. But the state is under no obligation to create the system in the first place, even though it could not (without compensation) abolish the awkward possessory modes of securing debts created by self-help. Yet the present system of recordation is so manifestly superior in sorting out priorities to the common law system it replaces that its own

---

28. In addition, the eminent domain clause does prevent the retroactive invalidation or subordination (a partial taking) of existing liens. See, e.g., 11 U.S.C., ¶ 552(b), which provides for a retroactive release of nonpurchase money, nonpossessory security interests of household furnishings, and the like. The statute was sustained in Matter of Gifford, 688 F.2d 447 (7th Cir. 1982). The statute was construed (in the teeth of its language) to apply only prospectively in United States v. Security Industrial Bank, 459 U.S. 70 (1982), to avoid the constitutional challenges that were rejected in *Gifford*.

constitutionality is simply beyond challenge by any of our tests of implicit in-kind compensation.[29]

Once the system of secured credit is in place, one theoretical question is whether it can be abolished tomorrow without anything being put in its place except for the original security interests available at common law. In principle the original statute could be drafted as though it created a contract among all citizens, so that its repeal would constitute a breach. Yet there seems no reason to treat this statute differently from any other, so its repeal simply removes benefits that the state was under no obligation to provide in the first place, where everyone was on notice that the benefits were contingent at the outset. So understood, the case is but a complex variant of the grazing rights cases, such as *Fuller v. United States*.[30]

Nonetheless it seems impermissible for legislation to allow only some individuals to have access to the system in question. Selective access subordinates the common law modes of security held by some individuals to the statutory claims of those allowed into the system. That subordination is a taking of private property that is no different from reversing the order of first and second mortgages by statute. The limited access negates any argument that the taking is for a public use, while the disproportionate impact test shows that the scheme would fail for want of just compensation as well.[31]

29. See Chapter 14.
30. 409 U.S. 488 (1973). See Chapter 14.
31. The solution here is an effort to escape a dilemma posed by Rodgers, supra note 27. On the one hand, he is unable to decide whether the "property rights held by secured creditors are in some sense anterior to the positive law," 96 *Harv. L. Rev.* at 987, or whether government could render "nugatory" all protections of property simply by announcing that all legal rules are subject to change. Id. at 988 n. 61. The approach taken in the text indicates that the state need not generate the obvious gains from recordation, but that if it does, it must divide the surplus evenly by allowing for universal access.

16 Tort

The principle of implicit in-kind compensation, relevant to the common pool cases, also plays a vital role when property rights are unique and well defined. This chapter uses that principle to examine the manifold variations that both common law and statute make from the original fixed set of property entitlements in physical injury cases. The chapter covers nuisance, general tort rules between strangers, and harms arising out of consensual arrangements, in both their prospective and retroactive application.

Nuisances

INVASIVE NUISANCES AND BILATERAL MONOPOLIES

The rules of tort are designed to redress violations of the rights of ownership, acquired under the first possession rule, against the actions of others. In order to operate the system, it is necessary to determine the rights that ownership entails. Here the original common law rules specified the correct normative result. Ownership was claimed for all times, and it embraced the maxim *cuius est solum eius est usque ad coelum et usque ad inferos* (loosely translated as "whosoever owns the earth owns from the heavens to the depths"). By that rule every invasion, however minute, of the protected space is an actionable wrong remediable both by damages and injunction. Conversely, if there is no physical invasion, there is an unassailable exercise of property rights, even if everyone else is left worse off in consequence. The invasion line has a sharp black and white quality that gives property rights their Cartesian appeal. Clear lines let people know where they stand, and they help persons recombine their original rights in voluntary transactions.

Yet the system must give at the edges, as unquestioned adherence to the physical invasion test could generate substantial welfare losses. Even the judges most committed to the protection of private property[1] recognized that it was ultimately self-destructive in utilitarian terms to make physical invasion the sole touchstone of tortious liability. Much of the law of nuisance is designed to indicate where the physical invasion principle gives way in both directions, by denying liability in cases of some invasion and imposing it in others where no invasion has taken place. In large part the modifications of nuisance law are based upon a mixture of utilitarian and distributive considerations: everyone will be better off by relaxing the absolute conceptions that drive the system of private property.

To begin with the simplest case, total respect for absolute exclusivity invites everyone to sue, not only for damages but also for injunctive relief from the countless trifling invasions of property, be it by noise, dust, or fumes. The object of these suits will uniformly be, not the prevention of the trivial harm, but the extraction of some portion of the economic rents otherwise attributable to gainful use of land. If a defendant's action benefits him $1,000, while its invasive aspect costs the plaintiff $1, then the (now familiar) holdout value of a demand for injunctive relief is enormous. But as every property owner will be both plaintiff and defendant part of the time, all parties lose over the long run because of the repeating nature of the game. Analytically the situation is indistinguishable from the common pool problem of the last chapter. As before, some coercive device is needed to stop the negative-sum game.

One possibility is to deny the problem and to say that low-level invasions are not "really" invasions at all, so the plaintiff loses because there is no prima facie violation of his rights. But that solution fails because it denies the very proposition which the eminent domain clause asserts, that there is some natural and unique set of entitlements that are pro-

---

1. The best illustration is Baron Bramwell, who was one of the few common law judges with an explicit laissez faire ideology, which led him to adopt strict liability rules in Fletcher v. Rylands, 3 Hurl. & C. 774 (Ex. 1865), *aff'd* Fletcher v. Rylands, L.R. 1 Ex. 265 (1866), *aff'd sub nom.* Rylands v. Fletcher, L.R. 3 H.L. 330 (1868). Just two years earlier Bramwell had made what is still the best formulation of the implicit in-kind compensation rules in Bamford v. Turnley, 3 B. & S 66, 122 Eng. Rep. 27 (Ex. 1862).

tected under a system of private property. If not all invasions of another's property are regarded as violations of right, then why is any physical invasion so regarded? If physical invasion is wholly irrelevant, then what content is left to the eminent domain clause? We are then easily driven to the same skeptical orientation on causality that led to the intellectual annihilation of the police power. Again the only question that can ever be asked is what set of socially determined entitlements maximizes social welfare. The exclusive concern with consequences necessarily obliterates the original benchmark, the original property rights, which determine who must pay compensation to whom, and how much. This approach leaves only the question of whether government actions are permissible, but it has no place for the question of whether permissible actions generate an obligation to compensate.

As with the common pool, then, the takings question cannot be evaded by pretending that it does not exist. Nonetheless, three common law doctrines, the so-called "live and let live" rule, the locality rule, and the distinction between general and special damages are all designed to prevent endless holdout suits for injunctive relief, indeed even for damages.[2]

LIVE AND LET LIVE

In the live and let live situation, the general rule provides that certain low-level interferences normally associated with ongoing household or business activities shall not be privately actionable. The rule easily satisfies all the tests for adequate implicit in-kind compensation. As with the common pool, high transaction costs block voluntary renegotiation of property rights, given the large number of parties.[3] Similarly, as the banned suits would be brought solely for their holdout value, we can be confident that the value of the activities undertaken will exceed, for each individual and in the aggregate, the value of the curtailed rights of action. In addition, it is highly unlikely that the gains created by the prohibition create differential benefits for one class of individuals at the

2. See Richard A. Epstein, "Nuisance Law: Corrective Justice and Its Utilitarian Constraints," 8 *J. Legal Stud.* 49, 82–90 (1979), for a more detailed exposition of the doctrines and their relationship to the general formula.

3. See Guido Calabresi and A. Douglas Melamed, "Property Rules, Liability Rules, and Inalienability: One View of the Cathedral," 85 *Harv. L. Rev.* 1089 (1972), for a discussion of these factors in setting up a system of property rights and tort actions. Their article has no constitutional component, but the general relationships it identifies have the generality and permanence that are required of constitutional principles.

expense of another. The rule simultaneously sweeps in a vast number of different activities; one person will now be able to cook, the next will be able to practice the violin, and so on down the line. The high frequency of low-level activities swept into the rule effectively eliminates the possibility of its disproportionate impact. The point is reinforced when the two built-in limitations are made express. First, special or substantial damages are not brought within the operation of the rule, but are themselves the object of suits for damages and injunctions by aggrieved parties.[4] Second, the total prohibition does not protect activities undertaken with malice, here defined in its ordinary sense of actions taken with ill will to other individuals.

The live and let live rule cannot be defended by showing that low-level invasions not actuated by malice are not invasions when in fact they are. The rule cannot be defended by resorting improperly to a Coasian definition of causation, which in its nihilistic way undermines the system of property rights in its entirety.[5] Instead it concedes the force of the original wrong but identifies the implicit in-kind compensation as the freedom of action created by the rule. Indeed, one attractive feature of the live and let live rule is that the forced exchanges it sanctions are not initiated unilaterally by any private party. There is, therefore, an even division of the surplus, similar to that found in partition cases, without the need for bonus payments, as are required with the mill acts.[6] Whether the question of implicit in-kind compensation is judged by the economic theory of property rights, by a concern with partisan motive, or by the disproportionate impact test, the rule easily meets all constitutional standards.

LOCALITY RULE

This analysis can be extended to cover the locality rule, which provides that in deciding whether certain conduct gives rise to an actionable nuisance, it is necessary to take into account the extent to which the conduct differs in kind and intensity from other conduct within the same locale. As stated, the rule is designed to prevent the single owner of a private home from enjoining all manufacturing in an industrial district or all use of the rails or highways. As with the live and let live rule, the theme is that everyone who suffers the limited nuisances of others is fully compensated by the parallel right to inflict limited nuisances upon

4. See, e.g., Colls v. Home & Colonial Stores [1904] A.C. 179.
5. See Chapter 9 for discussion.
6. See Chapter 12.

others. It differs from that rule only insofar as it tolerates a higher level of interference within a narrower territorial base. Within the constitutional framework established here, these two conditions go together hand in glove. The greater homogeneity within a local region tends to ensure that the higher levels of interference are offset by higher levels of compensation, thereby preserving the position of all parties in roughly equal proportions.

The wide variation in levels of invasive activities, however, makes the rule more problematic than live and let live, because some individuals may think themselves net losers under the system. Nonetheless, this does not undermine the soundness of the basic scheme, for there is nothing in the rule which ex ante biases its application in favor of any single individual or determinate class. Those who find the land unattractive to use may still realize large gains from selling it to a third party who can take advantage of the environment. And if the level of inconvenience rises too high, the common law rule on actionability can be changed, or direct regulation can be introduced to limit nuisance-like activities to the point where they provide a net benefit to all members of the group. Because the expected gains and losses are distributed evenly across the members of a class, the disproportionate impact rule insulates the locality rule from challenge under either the public use or the just compensation clause of the Constitution.

GENERAL AND SPECIAL DAMAGES

Parallel arguments help account for the persistence of the distinction between general and special damages both at common law and under the Constitution. As developed in private law, general damages not compensable by private action must satisfy two conditions. First, the injury must be widespread in extent, and second, it must be insubstantial in nature (common examples are cases of "mere" fright by persons who witness an accident or of delays in traffic on the public highway).[7] Nonetheless, to avoid large welfare losses the state provides a system of direct administrative controls—fines, inspections, police enforcement—to counter the risk of nuisance. Yet private action is preserved for special harms to avoid the disproportionate impact of large injuries, especially in cases of personal injury and complete loss of access to public highways,[8] which if left unredressed would create opportunities for all persons to inflict disproportionate losses upon their neighbors. The di-

7. See Epstein, supra note 2, at 99–101.
8. Anon., Y.B. Mich. 27 Hen. 8, f. 27, pl. 10 (1535).

chotomy between general and special damages is not perfect and is tested most severely when there is only a partial loss of access to public ways, where disproportionate impact is hardest to measure.[9]

The constitutional decisions on these issues are essentially a repeat of the common law adjudication. There is, for example, the same reluctance to award compensation for partial loss of access,[10] and the distinction between general and special damages rightly remains important. *Richards v. Washington Terminal*[11] illustrates the parallels to the private law distinction. The plaintiff suffered substantial damages from the dust, noise, and vibrations brought by the defendant's construction activities, which were conducted under statutory authorization. The court accepted the defendant's argument that its conduct was generally privileged against suites for general damages, but it awarded compensation for special damages. The stated reason for the distinction, that property is not "taken" (in the required sense of damaged or destroyed)[12] when the injury is low-level and widespread, is incorrect. The takings question proper does not admit of degree, as all partial takings are covered regardless of extent. Injury there was, but its limited severity and breadth suggested that its victims on the whole, were better off because of the benefits that would be conferred by the completed construction project: this explains why repairs on public streets do not normally call for compensation, even though they involve private access rights, which are protected from public taking.[13] This rough balance of cost and benefit—of property taken and property received—is wholly absent with Richard's special damages, so the cash compensation therein provided was necessary to redress the balance. The case reached the right result through the wrong argument: simply deciding whether a "taking of private property" has occurred cannot do all the jobs needed to apply the takings clause.

9. See, e.g., Smith v. City of Boston, 61 Mass. (7 Cush.) 254 (1851), where the claim for relief was denied in a case of partial loss of access. For different views of the case, see Richard A. Epstein, "The Social Consequences of Common Law Rules," 95 *Harv. L. Rev.* 1717, 1732 (1982); M. Horwitz, *The Transformation of American Law* 77–78 (1977).

10. See, e.g., Malone v. Commonwealth, 378 Mass. 74, 389 N.E.2d 975 (1979).

11. 233 U.S. 546 (1913).

12. Id. at 551–552.

13. See Transportation Co. v. Chicago, 99 U.S. 635 (1878), in which the decision in Pumpelly v. Green Bay Co., 80 U.S. (13 Wall.) 166 (1871), discussed in Chapter 4, was limited in an unprincipled way because the judges failed to see the power of the disproportionate impact test.

Richards was distinguished in *Batten v. United States*,[14] where compensation was not awarded for nuisances inflicted by flying aircraft upon large numbers of landowners. The difference between the two cases is that the damages in *Richards* were confined to a single person while those in *Batten* were imposed upon a large number of individuals. But damages are not converted from special to general solely because they are inflicted upon a large number of individuals. Any individual landowner's loss could have equaled or exceeded that of the single plaintiff in *Richards*. To excuse payment of explicit compensation, it is necessary to show that the landowners who were harmed by the nuisance—received substantial *matching* benefits—a finding effectively precluded by the net diminution in the value of their land, and the obvious intention of operating the military base for the benefit of the public at large, and not just the immediate neighbors of the base.

A proper matching of benefits and burdens is more fully appreciated in *Swetland v. Curtiss Airports Corp.*,[15] where the plaintiff sought to enjoin the construction of a nearby airport as a private nuisance. The court's response was to enjoin low overflights as a nuisance, while allowing high overflights to continue without compensation. The decision follows easily from both the overall wealth effects and the disproportionate impact test, even if the plaintiff's air rights originally extended to the highest reaches of the heavens under the *ad coelum* doctrine.[16] The plaintiff's only value in the higher airspace is the holdout value to air transportation. Yet the benefits he derives, direct or indirect, from cheaper goods and services because of air transport, leaves him in a better position than he would have been in if there had been no use of the airspace at all. (It is wholly irrelevant that he would prefer to have both the benefits of air transportation and the rights of exclusion over his own property, for that would constitute a double payment.) The cost to the landowner of the low-overflight nuisance, however, is far greater and is not shared by all the property owners, let alone by the public at large. Even if the plaintiff were better off with both the air service and the uncompensated nui-

14. 306 F.2d 580 (10th Cir. 1962).
15. 41 F.2d 929 (N.D. Ohio 1930), as modified 55 F.2d 201 (6th Cir. 1932).
16. That point itself has been contested, because it has been urged that as possession lies at the root of title, the landowner owns only the area that is subject to effective occupation. See, e.g., Frederick Pollock, *The Law of Torts* 362 (13th ed. 1929). For a more recent discussion, see Bruce Ackerman, *Private Property and the Constitution* 118–123 (1977), criticized in Richard A. Epstein, "The Next Generation of Legal Scholarship?" 30 *Stan. L. Rev.* 635, 650–652 (1978).

sance, he would (contrary to the mandate of the public use limitation) receive only a tiny portion of the surplus created by air transportation. The distinction between high and low overflights, then, is in perfect accord with both the common law distinction between general and special damages and the constitutional underpinnings of the eminent domain clause.

NONINVASIVE NUISANCE: SPITE FENCES

The logic of implicit in-kind compensation also accounts for cases where the defendant's noninvasive conduct is actionable. In principle the physical invasion test allows any individual to build without limit on his own property so long as there is no entrance, direct or indirect, upon the property of another. Yet from the late nineteenth century on, the case law has allowed a property owner to enjoin a neighbor's construction of "spite fences" intended solely to block his view or light.[17] The spite fence cases deviate from traditional common law rules of liability both by abandoning the physical invasion test and by making liability turn on malice, or motive, which is generally regarded as irrelevant in most other contexts. Yet relaxing the invasion requirement while insisting upon proof of malice go hand in glove, as the same theory operative in the live and let live cases is at work here. The restriction on land use so defined is fully compensated by the parallel limitations imposed upon the property of others, for before construction of a spite fence the gains and losses are proportionate. The basic rule on spite fences is not applicable to all forms of land use: it is not possible, for example, to have a neighbor's house or shed ripped down solely on the ground that it was erected with malice.[18] By limiting sharply the use values that are subject to forced exchanges, the rule reduces the likelihood of substantial redistributions of wealth between private parties. In principle, the low transaction costs between neighbors cut against the need for the rule, but the rule may be justified as a response to a possible bilateral monopoly problem which still allows the parties to bargain their way to an alternative distribution of rights. The overall gains from this rule are more difficult to assess but are probably positive. The rule clearly passes muster, given its proportionate impact and the want of any redistributive motive.

The close kinship of common law and constitutional adjudication is

17. See, e.g., Flaherty v. Moran, 81 Mich. 52, 45 N.W. 381 (1890).
18. Kuzniak v. Kozminski, 107 Mich. 444, 65 N.W. 275 (1895).

well illustrated by the early Massachusetts case of *Rideout v. Knox,*[19] in which Holmes sustained a spite fence statute that declared any fence "unnecessarily exceeding six feet in height, maliciously erected or maintained for the purpose of annoying the owners of adjoining property" to be a private nuisance. The statute placed limitations upon the noninvasive use of property that worked a taking simpliciter not within the ends of the police power. Nonetheless the statute met the requirements of implicit in-kind compensation. The scope of the permitted forced exchanges are sharply limited because fences lower than six feet are governed by the common law rule and those over it are subject to suit on proof of malice. True, after the erection of a fence it may be possible to identify substantial wealth shifts between the parties. Yet the crucial time for measurement is ex ante, at the time of passage of the statute, when shifts are much more difficult to detect. *Rideout v. Knox* also suggests proper limitations upon the power of the state to readjust property rights between neighbors.

> It may be assumed that under our constitution the legislature would not have power to prohibit putting up or maintaining stores or houses with malicious intent, and thus to make a large part of the property of the commonwealth dependent upon what a jury might find to have been the past or present motives of the owner. But it does not follow that the rule is the same for a boundary fence, unnecessarily built more than six feet high. It may be said that the difference is only one of degree. Most differences are, when nicely analyzed. At any rate, difference of degree is one of the distinctions by which the right of the legislature to exercise the police power is determined.[20]

The difference between spite houses and spite fences does not rest on the ground that one is a taking simpliciter and the other is not, and it does not rest on the police power, as Holmes suggests. Nor are the questions of degree—stressed with such fondness by Holmes—simply an unanalyzable part of the human condition. Instead the case tracks the common law rules for spite fences, with the single clarification that no common law rule can provide: a number, here six feet, below which the inquiry cannot run. The case, therefore, is best understood as a textbook application of the disproportionate impact test. Spite fence statutes do not

19. 148 Mass. 368, 19 N.E. 390 (1889).
20. Id. at 369, 19 N.E. at 392.

hold out the power of abuse in application that is found in a prohibition on spite houses.

SUPPORT RIGHTS

The common law rules of lateral support also show the power of the disproportionate impact test for noninvasive nuisances. By a well-nigh universal rule, each landowner has a duty of lateral support to the property of a neighbor. The obligation of support extends only to land in its natural condition and not to improvements, present or future. Easements for the land are reciprocal and thus provide implicit in-kind compensation for each other. Improvements are excluded from the duty of lateral support because of the disproportionate burdens that must result when one party acts strategically by building early to obtain more extensive easements over the land of others. Nonetheless, once construction has taken place there are still reciprocal affirmative duties, now of giving notice before excavating, which at low cost to the new builder allows the holder of the dominant tenement to mitigate losses by shoring up a structure or purchasing a support easement. At every point the rules increase overall efficiency while improving the position of each of the parties. This historic exception to the absolute no-invasion rule is beyond any eminent domain attack.

General Liability Rules

The bargaining problems so evident in the nuisance area are, if anything, more acute with the general tort liability rules governing harms between strangers. In principle any set of rules created may be contracted out by a set of complete contracts governing all contingencies between persons. In practice these contingent contracts will never be formed because of the impossible barriers to transactions. It is therefore necessary to ask what possible transformation of liability rules from the original strict liability position is consistent with the just compensation requirement of the eminent domain clause.[21] It is possible to consider the situation under two heads. The first involves modification of the liability rules in cases where the defendant inflicts harm upon another by force or misrepresentation, the traditional misfeasance case. The second involves the converse case, where the general rule of nonliability is modified where the defendant has not caused harm in either of these two senses, the traditional nonfeasance cases.

21. See Chapter 4.

MISFEASANCE

In approaching the question of liability for misfeasance, it is instructive to begin with the extreme case that simply abolishes all tort actions for damages to person or property. One possible advantage of this extreme position is that it drives administrative costs to zero. But this regime promises widespread catastrophe; its incentive effects are so disastrous that everyone would be worse off from unbridled aggression, which government, under the Lockean theory, is designed to counteract. As a formal matter the universal repeal of tort doctrine would seem to have no disproportionate impacts. Yet when the focus is upon actual impacts, even the disproportionate impact test cannot justify this solution, given the differential opportunities for mischief it creates and the overall reduction in wealth it promises. As with spite houses, the destabilization of property rights would be far too great to provide implicit compensation, no matter what approach was taken.

The unsoundness of the extreme position does not rule out, however, a whole host of intermediate adjustments, whether by statute or at common law. Consider the perennial conflict between systems of negligence and those of strict liability. Suppose, as I have argued, the idea of ownership necessarily entails a strict liability standard in all tort cases between strangers. Still it does not follow that a shift from strict liability to negligence must be invalidated unless explicit compensation is made to net losers under the new system. In particular it is mistaken to judge the soundness of the shift by looking ex post (after the accident) at a plaintiff whose claim is denied solely because he cannot prove negligence. The proper point of reference is prior to accidents, where it appears that the net wealth effects attributable to the shift in liability rules are small, perhaps negligible. The direction of the shift, moreover, is still heavily debated in an enormous academic literature.[22]

As the concern of net social benefit offers relatively little guidance on the choice of rules, far greater weight must be attached to the two concerns: motive and disproportionate impact, with the latter belied by the marginal effects of any rule change upon the holdings of any given individual.[23] In order for the liability rule to matter, there must first be some accident which generates a lawsuit whose outcome hinges on the choice

22. See, e.g., Richard A. Epstein, "A Theory of Strict Liability," 2 *J. Legal Stud.* 151 (1973); George P. Fletcher, "Fairness and Utility in Tort Law," 85 *Harv. L. Rev.* 537 (1972); Richard A. Posner, "A Theory of Negligence," 1 *J. Legal Stud.* 29 (1972).

23. For a more detailed statement of the descriptive argument shorn of its constitutional implications, see Epstein, supra note 9, at 1717.

of the rule. But accidents are uncommon occurrences for most people, while the principles of negligence and strict liability converge in the large majority of stranger cases. In some instances the negligence standard is toughened by the articulation of a high standard of care or by the use of res ipsa loquitur, with negligence presumed from the occurrence of the accident. Similarly, strict liability principles may be attenuated when the defendant's conduct is excused because of the intervention of a third party. Not only is the gap between the rules small, but before an accident most persons do not know which rule will work in their favor, as they cannot predict whether a lawsuit will cast them in the role of plaintiff or defendant. Given the determinants of the situation, most people in fact operate behind a veil of ignorance, which keeps them from manipulating the system for their own advantage. The Rawlsian ideal no longer depends upon the hypothetical construct of individuals who do not have knowledge of their personal situation; external circumstances create the only veil that is needed.

The attractions of the disproportionate impact rule become even greater when one considers direct judicial examination of the relative welfare effects of the two rules. Empirical evidence on the incidence of the two rules is nearly impossible to find, for there are no market transactions to provide any telltale traces of clues about which rule is generally preferred. Insistence on explicit compensation raises the question of who should pay what to whom. To nullify common law discretion on this by constitutional fiat fixes the original set of rights so as to preclude the forced exchanges that the takings clause itself invites. On this question the difference between what is wise and what is constitutional is vital, as the broad generalization of common law liability rules here does furnish a powerful safeguard against mischief. The stakes are small, given the issue in controversy, and there is a large overlap between the individuals benefited and those burdened by any shift in liability rules. The devices of political self-correction work very well here. The only proper constitutional treatment is to allow these two basic liability rules to resonate freely with one another. A court can move from strict liability to negligence or from negligence to strict liability without offending the eminent domain clause. It can also adopt any intermediate position—res ipsa loquitur or similar presumptions of negligence from proof of causation—that makes the two systems converge. The result stands, moreover, even if one denies that the strict liability rule is necessarily built into the conception of ownership. Let negligence be the starting point, and the strict liability rule satisfies the tests for implicit in-kind compensation for reasons parallel to those just developed.

The same analysis can be extended to other tort doctrines. The merits of the foresight and directness tests of causation,[24] for example, raise deep questions about the use of language and the fairness of outcomes in individual cases. Endless ebbs and flows can be detected in the decided cases. But these passing choices, even on fundamental doctrine, do not raise any concern under the eminent domain clause, no matter which—if any—view of causation a strict system of property rights is thought to entail. Generalization on all stranger cases in the absence of political manipulation guarantees implicit in-kind compensation.

Contributory negligence and comparative negligence present even more acute dilemmas, as there is no natural or unique way for the best legal theory to weigh the relative importance of the wrongful conduct of the two parties (whether by negligence or by simple causation). In principle either the contributory negligence or the comparative negligence rule represents a taking of private property, even if no one can (as yet) identify the proper baseline rule. Yet the embarrassment is of no practical consequence to the constitutional inquiry. If one rule is that required by a proper view of the tort system, its alternative can be justified under the disproportionate impact test, again for the reasons set out above.

NONFEASANCE

The nonfeasance cases are based on the good Samaritan question—is a person obliged to rescue a stranger from imminent peril not caused by the rescuer? In contrast to the misfeasance cases, the question now is whether the legal system can expand the degree of protection beyond that set by the original distribution of ownership rights, which stresses the gulf between hurting someone by the use of force or fraud and not helping someone ("failure" to help begs the duty question) who is threatened by external forces not created by the defendant.

Begin with an extreme case that is the converse of total abolishing of the tort system. Suppose the legislature enacted a statute which made everyone strictly liable for failing to rescue a stranger from imminent peril. The statute, read literally, holds that it is immaterial what costs a defendant must incur in order to make the rescue; it is a matter of com-

24. The major cases are, In re Polemis [1921] 3 K.B. 560; Overseas Tankship (U.K.) Ltd. v. Morts Dock and Engineering Co., Ltd. (The Wagon Mound [No. 1]) [1961] A.C. 388 (H.L.E.). See, generally, H. L. A. Hart and A. M. Honore, *Causation in the Law* (1959); for a collection of materials on causation, see Richard A. Epstein, Charles O. Gregory, and Harry Kalven, Jr., *Cases and Materials on Torts* ch. 5 (4th ed. 1984).

plete indifference whether the defendant stands at the top of the bridge with the rope in hand or is asleep in his bed a thousand miles away. This type of statute would be unconstitutional because of its overall wealth effects, for it would allow every plaintiff to pick at random some person of means to hold categorically liable. While the statute may be neutral on its face, its impact is certainly quite the opposite, given its open invitation to strategic behavior, so the test fails because of its disproportionate impact, in the unlikely event of its legislative passage.

Yet the extreme case does not resolve the intermediate situations, such as those where a duty of "easy" rescue is imposed only on parties who could act at "little or no cost or inconvenience."[25] The phrasing of the rule is designed to limit the greatest abuses of application, but it invites a host of unanswered questions—contributory negligence by the plaintiff, objective misperception of the risk—that have never been faced because the proposal has never been adopted even in this age of ever-expanding tort liability. Nonetheless I would sustain the proposal, confident that precisely because its effects are not disproportionate it could never gain acceptance as a general statement of obligation between strangers. Even though ex ante certain individuals might stand to gain or lose from the easy rescue rule, they will not be able to identify themselves; if they can, the potential gains are in all likelihood less than the organizing costs of any coalition that might wish to capture them. Under these restricted conditions, the generalization of the legal rule itself offers solid protection against any disguised governmental confiscation.

Limitations on Actions

At common law, once an obligation is created, it remains in existence indefinitely unless it is discharged or released. The passage of time does not confer additional rights upon the plaintiff nor does it impose additional obligations upon the defendant. Only actions between the parties can change their legal relation. However, every legal system contains

25. See, e.g., James Barr Ames, "Law and Morals," 22 *Harv. L. Rev.* 97, 113 (1908), who stated his "working rule" as follows: "One who fails to interfere to save another from impending death or great bodily harm, when he might do so with little or no inconvenience to himself, and the death or great bodily harm follows as a consequence of his inaction, shall be punished criminally and shall make compensation to the party injured or to his widow and children in the case of death." See also, Ernest J. Weinrib, "The Case for a Duty to Rescue," 90 *Yale L.J.* 247 (1980), where the phrase "easy" rescue appears.

statutes of limitation whose central function is to bar these rights of action, as the common law does not, solely because of the passage of time.

The application of the eminent domain clause to these statutes is clear. The rights of property include the right of redress for future as well as past harms. Any statute limiting that redress is as much a taking of private property as any other modification of a common law liability rule. But no one has ever seriously challenged either the wisdom or constitutionality of statutes of limitation. The justifications for the common view are not hard to find. Statutes of limitation are welcome because they provide general improvement; disputes are kept from festering, and cases are tried before parties die and evidence becomes stale. The statutes are of public record, and in broad outline their existence is of common knowledge. Giving notice to injured parties therefore is not a problem, and once it is given they can typically meet the statutory command at very lost cost. Doctrines that prevent a statute of limitation from running in cases where the actions should be allowed, as when the plaintiffs are infants or insane persons unable to sue on their own behalf. The limitation period differs among classes of cases: between real and personal property, between conversion and trespass, between intentional and negligent harms. Yet the precise categorization of actions by type is not likely to work ex ante any systematic shift in wealth across members of the population because the classifications do not reflect any obvious social grouping. The power to mitigate losses (by suing on time) is virtually absolute, and where a statute does bar a cause of action, it is difficult for any person to predict in advance whether he will be the aggrieved plaintiff or the contented defendant.

The constitutional case for these statutes is overpowering. Any shifts in wealth worked by the statutes will be small, randomly created, and overshadowed by the overall increase in the size of the pie. The worst-off members under the new legal regime will be better off than they were under the old. All three measures of implicit compensation are satisfied. The direct economic evidence shows an overall increase in wealth, there is no redistributive motive, and there is a total want of disproportionate impact.

More complex issues arise where the legislature by statute limits, not the time in which a cause of action may be brought, but the amount of money that can be recovered by a successful claimant or paid by a responsible party. An important limitation of this sort is contained in the Price-Anderson statute, which limits the recovery of all victims of nuclear accident to $560,000,000 from both private and government sources (augmented by an indefinite promise that "Congress will take whatever action is deemed necessary and appropriate to protect the public from the consequences of a disaster of such magnitude") no matter what the severity of their injuries. The limitation is clearly a partial taking. The critical question is whether the statute affords sufficient implicit in-kind compensation.

The constitutionality of Price-Anderson was challenged in *Duke Power Co. v. Carolina Environmental Study Group, Inc.*,[26] where the Supreme Court used a takings analysis even though it did not formally proceed under the eminent domain clause. Initially the court equivocated on the question of whether any quid pro quo was required, given its own precedents that "[a] person has no property, no vested interest, in any rule of the common law" that has already been considered and rejected.[27] But it then addressed the matter in detail, consistent with this analysis of implicit in-kind compensation.[28] The court found that quid pro quo in the advantages the statute gave to plaintiffs who were not required to prove negligence, enabling them to overcome questions of third-party intervention or to contest affirmative defenses based on contributory negligence or assumption of risk. In addition, the regulatory restraints reduced the likelihood of an incident in the first place and thus provided further benefits to offset the damage limitation.

There is no question that this package of benefits could be worth a good deal to prospective plaintiffs, and that the reduction in rates resulting from the company's protection from suit affords all purchasers of electrical power further benefits. But the proper question is not whether the statue confers some benefits, it is whether the benefits are equal to or greater than the loss of a possible right of action for unlimited damages. Addressing the question cannot be avoided, even though it demands inquiry into matters of degree. In the limit the statute is surely bad if it limits total recovery to $100, while it is doubtless good if it permits recoveries up to $10 billion.

The intermediate cases raise the hard questions. With utilities (and shareholders) on one side and the public on the other, the case does not

26. 438 U.S. 59 (1978).

27. Id. at 88 n.32. The quotation is from Second Employers' Liability Cases, 223 U.S. 1, 50 (1912), and derives from Munn v. Illinois, 94 U.S. 113, 134 (1877). For criticism, see Chapter 8.

28. Note that the assets of the utilities far exceeded the $60,000,000 for which they were placed at risk under the statute. The question here does not go away with limited liability, and the Price-Anderson Act cannot be viewed simply as a scheme of mandatory insurance for the protection of strangers. The assets of the firm are insulated from suit by the statute.

present the picture of reciprocal rights and duties found in the oil and gas or the live and let live cases. The disproportionate impact test does not save the statute, even as it does not invalidate it. It is very difficult to determine the value of the other benefits afforded by the statute. In adopting strict liability standards the statute may only conform to the general strict liability rule for ultrahazardous activities at common law.[29] The abrogation of the defense of causal intervention may only duplicate the effect of the general common law.[30] Contributory negligence and assumption of risk have had only limited roles to play in these cases, even when they were unquestionably accepted within the common law framework. More important, it is surely not a point in favor of the statute that the original 1957 aggregate limit has not been adjusted for inflation over the past twenty-five years.

The terms of the bargain may therefore have radically changed, so it is possible that Price-Anderson was constitutional when passed but is not today. The problems here run in every direction, for one risk of simply raising the aggregate limit is that it invites juries to inflate awards. However, a more complex structure might control this problem without depriving individual plaintiffs of the proper levels of compensation. Other insurance limits could be written on a per plaintiff or per family basis. Limits for wrongful death cases could be made explicit, either by number or by formula. In personal injury actions separate limits could be directed to medical expenses or to pain and suffering, especially for psychic damages. The details of these alternative systems would require far more information than is presented in *Duke Power*. Nonetheless, because the just compensation requirement applies, the problem of valuation is far more insistent than was recognized by the Supreme Court. The global judgment that some substantial value is given in return may suffice under the relaxed modern standards, but it is inappropriate under the eminent domain clause.

Workers' Compensation Laws

The workers' compensation cases show the uneasy overlap between the laws of contract and of tort. In general discussion, compensation laws are thought to be a substitute for the tort laws that previously governed industrial accidents, which accounts for their treatment here. Yet they differ from other tort matters considered in that they seek to regulate

29. See *Restatement (Second) of Torts* §§ 519–520 (1977).
30. See id. § 522. See also Yukon Equipment, Inc. v. Fireman's Fund Insurance Co., 585 P.2d 1206 (Alas. 1978).

relations, not between strangers, but between individuals who have entered into consensual arrangements with each other, where the agreements can expressly, as well as implicitly, allocate the risk of loss or accidental injury.

Workers' compensation laws are now found in every jurisdiction. Adopted for the most part during the first quarter of the twentieth century, these laws reworked the entire structure of employer-employee relations.[31] Under the previous common law regime, individual employers and workers were free to bargain over all terms and conditions of employment, including compensation for work-related injuries. In the absence of any agreement, the general tort-like rules fashioned at common law imposed upon the employer a general duty to furnish the employee with a reasonable safe place of work. As offsets, the employer had three independent defenses: assumption of risk, contributory negligence, and common employment.[32] The workers' compensation law undid the old common law regime and expanded the number of industrial accidents for which the employer could be required to pay compensation, while simultaneously limiting the amount of compensation required for each such accident.

To implement this end, the following structural reforms were introduced. First, the employer's negligence, or lack thereof was made irrelevant to the compensation question. The new test of liability was whether the accident "arose out of and in the course of employment." Second, the trilogy of common law defenses was abolished, so that only deliberate self-infliction of injury barred the worker's claim. The explicit quid pro quo for this expanded employer liability took two forms. First, the employee's tort remedy against the employer was eliminated by the so-called "exclusive remedy" provision of the statute. Second, the compensation paid for covered injuries was less than a successful plaintiff could

---

31. For a general account of the workers' compensation programs and the changes they wrought on common law rules, see Ives v. South Buffalo Ry. Co., 201 N.Y. 271, 94 N.E. 431 (1911), striking down the New York law; New York Central Railroad Co. v. White, 243 U.S. 188 (1917), sustaining the amended New York law against federal constitutional challenges. For an account of the growth of workers' compensation, see Richard A. Epstein, "The Historical Origins and Economic Structure of Workers' Compensation Law," 16 Ga. L. Rev. 775 (1982).

32. Contributory negligence was roughly the worker's failure to take reasonable care for his own safety. Assumption of risk involved an employee's decision to accept a known risk. The defense of common employment provided that, as between himself and the employer, a worker took the risk of the negligence of his fellow servant.

have recovered for those same injuries at common law. Workers' compensation made no allowance for pain and suffering, and in its early versions placed definite financial limitations on recoveries for both lost wages and medical expenses. If the common law recovery was designed to leave the plaintiff whole, workers' compensation benefits had the more modest goal of cushioning the blow from injury or death. In essence the "compensation bargain" exchanged broader coverage for lower levels of recovery.

As a matter of positive law, workers' compensation statutes which assume this general form are unquestionably immune from constitutional challenge. Historically the position was more complex. The first of the statutes so passed—the New York Workmen's Compensation Law of 1910—was struck down by the New York Court of Appeals in *Ives v. South Buffalo R.R. Co.*[33] Judge Werner's opinion in *Ives* is widely discredited today, and it contains more than its fair share of twists and ironies, but the questions it asks about the workers' compensation statute cannot simply be brushed aside.

Werner's opinion in *Ives* begins with words of praise for the Wainwright Commission, whose comprehensive report detailing the waste and inefficiency of the common law helped secure the passage of the workers' compensation act.[34] The court then quickly concluded that no constitutional obstacles prevented the statutory elimination of the defenses of common employment, assumption of risk, and contributory negligence. But it balked at the statutory regime of liability without fault, which made the employer's liability turn not on its own actions, but upon the status of the employee at the time of injury, which had never been the source of liability even under the strict liability rules of the common law. The court then invoked two fundamental propositions to strike down the statute. The first dealt with the relationship between legislative enactments and constitutional provisions, and the second with the substantive operation of the statute.

The right of property rests not upon philosophical or scientific speculations nor upon the commendable impulses of benevolence or charity, nor yet upon the dictates of natural justice. The right has its foundation in the fundamental law. That can be changed by the

33. 201 N.Y. 271, 94 N.E. 431 (1911).
34. The full title of the commission's report was "Report to the Legislature of the State of New York, by the Commission Appointed under Chapter 513 of the Laws of 1909 to Inquire into the Question of Employers' Liability and Other Matters."

people, but not by legislatures . . . Any other view would lead to the absurdity that the Constitutions protect only those rights which the Legislatures do not take away. If such economic and sociologic arguments as are here advanced in support of this statute can be allowed to subvert the fundamental idea of property, then there is no private right entirely safe, because there is no limitation upon the absolute discretion of legislatures, and the guarantees of the Constitution are a mere waste of words . . . The argument that the risk to an employee should be borne by the employer because it is inherent in the employment, may be economically sound, but it is at war with the legal principle that no employer can be compelled to assume a risk which is inseparable from the work of the employee, and which may exist in spite of a degree of care by the employer far greater than may be exacted by the most drastic law. If it is competent to impose upon an employer, who has omitted no legal duty and has committed no wrong, a liability based solely upon a legislative fiat that his business is inherently dangerous, it is equally competent to visit upon him a special tax for the support of hospitals and other charitable institutions, upon the theory that they are devoted largely to the alleviation of ills primarily due to his business. In its final and simple analysis that is taking the property of A and giving it to B, and that cannot be done under our Constitutions.[35]

In a revealing concurrence, Chief Justice Cullen stated:

I know of no principle on which one can be compelled to indemnify another for loss unless it is based upon contractual obligation or fault. It might as well be argued in support of a law requiring a man to pay his neighbor's debts that the common law requires each man to pay his own debts, and the statute in question was a mere modification of the common law so as to require each to pay his neighbor's debts.[36]

It is hard to quarrel with the court's argument insofar as it rests upon the supremacy of the Constitution. But the force of that observation only establishes that any modification of the liability rules, even if wholly prospective, is tantamount to a taking of private property, as Werner expressly noted. Both opinions in *Ives* are wholly flawed by their failure to address the question of implicit in-kind compensation. Thus

35. 201 N.Y. at 294–296; 94 N.E. at 440 (citations omitted).
36. 201 N.Y. at 318–319; 94 N.E. at 449.

Werner's analogy to special taxes for charity[37] and Cullen's analogy to a general obligation to pay a neighbor's debts both lie very wide of the mark. These examples are of prima facie takings of private property for which there is no implicit in-kind compensation to the owner. The payment of an employer's money to the charity may enhance overall welfare, but there is no matching of benefits and burdens, as it is false to say that hospitals are largely devoted to alleviating ills attributable to the employer's business. The tax, being largely for the benefit of strangers, thus fails under the disproportionate impact test.[38]

Cullen's hypothetical statute for paying another's debts has close parallels to a statute imposing a universal, strict, and unconditional duty of rescue. In form, making everyone pay for his neighbor's debt creates proportionate duties. Yet in practice it creates a stupendous moral hazard by allowing everyone to spend someone else's money. Where A can pledge B's credit, he is able to authorize his own creditor to take B's money instead of having to take it himself. The rule will leave virtually everyone worse off, and it will also create heavily disproportionate impacts if individuals, as would doubtless be the case, differentially exploited the opportunities of expropriation that this extreme rule provides. The motive behind such a statute makes no conceivable sense. The statute thus looks like my earlier examples that abolished tort liability entirely or imposed absolute duties of rescue regardless of circumstances. This rule is struck down under all three measures of implicit in-kind compensation.

The workers' compensation statutes, like other intermediate modifications of liability rules, are a very different matter. Far from being largely for the benefit of strangers, or for no one at all, they are structured as a "compensation" bargain between employer and employee. Under the eminent domain analysis here, that quid pro quo is not a small statutory detail but a relevant source of compensation for the rights lost by the employer. It was the obvious presence of some quid pro quo which persuaded a unanimous United States Supreme Court in *New York Central R.R. v. White*[39] to sustain the statute.

Nonetheless *White* is not as easy as the conventional wisdom has it. Its

37. The reference to "special taxes" here is not accidental or unimportant. See Chapter 18.
38. The question of whether any tax for charitable purposes can survive is considered at greater length in Chapter 19.
39. 243 U.S. 188 (1917), which incidentally was written by Justice Pitney, whose conservatism is evident from Coppage v. Kansas, 236 U.S. 1 (1915), which holds unconstitutional state legislation banning yellow dog contracts.

key question is not whether a quid pro quo exists, since everyone concedes that there was some compensation for the property rights taken. The problem is that the Constitution requires just compensation, which in turn demands an inquiry into whether the statute provides a full and perfect equivalent for the rights taken away. Here the first part of the quid pro quo is explicit: the exclusive remedy provision under the statute. The second is implicit: the ability to vary the wage terms of the contract to compensate for the additional risk the statute casts upon the employer.

Are these two benefits to the employer sufficient in combination? The answer is by no means obvious, for if the compensation system were such a good idea, employers and employees[40] would have adopted some version of it voluntarily. The point is not one of idle speculation, for both the railway and mining industries in England[41] did adopt voluntary compensation schemes and, according to the Wainwright Report, so did many railroads in New York[42] and presumably elsewhere in the nation. However, the statute went beyond what was done before. The capital value of many, if not all, businesses were reduced by this legislative taking, which either imposed an obligation that they had not voluntarily accepted or expanded the scope of the compensation obligations already undertaken. More generally, the argument is that the statute imposes a limitation upon contractual freedom that leaves both parties worse off. By the test of implicit compensation, it follows that the benefits provided under the statute are necessarily insufficient, requiring that it be invalidated.

This argument moves too fast for its own good, however. First, it is not clear that the common law rules on common employment formed an accurate benchmark for liability. In many industries the administrative costs of introducing a compensation system would be too great on a firm

40. The text considers the compensation laws only from the vantage point of the employer. A parallel argument is that they hurt the position of (at least some) employees as well. The difficulty in making that argument here is that the eminent domain clause is limited to private property, which should probably be read not to include the disposition of labor as such. Note that the substantive due process arguments are not subject to this limitation, because they embrace both liberty and property, and hence one is not required to draw the uncertain line between them.

41. For a discussion, see Epstein, supra note 31, at 775, 787–797. The key cases here are Griffiths v. Earl of Dudley, 9 Q.B.D. 357 (1882); Clements v. London & Northwestern Railway [1894] 2 Q.B. 482. The English Workers' Compensation Statute was passed in 1897 (60 & 61 Vict., ch. 37) and served as the prototype for the American statutes.

42. Wainwright Commission Report 35–36.

by firm basis, but these reforms would be embraced by firms if endorsed on a grand scale by legislation. If the only choice were between two coercive regimes—common law and workers' compensation—there is no particular reason to reject workers' compensation in favor of the existing common law solution, especially on constitutional grounds. Indeed, it is far from clear that the common law rules are superior to the statutory scheme. The very fact that many employment contracts opted out of the common law undercuts any claim that its liability rules are ideal, at least for all firms in all industries.

In fact it is easy to identify several features that arguably make compensation systems superior to the common law rules. Their coverage rules for many industrial accidents are often simpler to operate than the common law rules.[43] The compensation system creates a kind of risk sharing between employer and employee whose incentive effects may be superior to those of common law rules. The problem of cost minimization is difficult because both employer and employee are typically in a position to take steps to prevent the accident. The common law rules purport to deal with this problem by coupling full tort damages with the affirmative defenses of contributory negligence, assumption of risk, and perhaps common employment. The compensation system handles this problem by reducing the level of payments while expanding the scope of coverage and truncating the affirmative defenses. In essence, the employer's incentives are preserved by his having to pay some damages, while the worker's are preserved by making the payment only partial. The system therefore tends to control conduct on both sides and may well be attractive to the employer as well as the employee, thereby barring any facile condemnation of the statute as a simple exercise of disguised confiscation.[44]

Sanction for worker's compensation statutes is also troublesome because of the clear difference between this and other (proper) modifications of the common law rules of civil responsibility. The difference is the undeniable element of class conflict, a matter feared since Madison described the perils of "factions" in *Federalist* 10. Oil and gas rules apply to a select group of landowners, largely of the same social class and subject to reciprocal rights and duties. General rules of tort liability apply to

43. The argument is not decisive because the number of cases to process is larger. The two points move in opposite directions, so the ultimate question here is empirical. Yet nothing makes the answer the same for all firms, given their different frequencies and severity of injuries.

44. I deal with these questions in greater depth in Epstein, supra note 31, at 775, 800–803.

everyone at large. Automobile no-fault systems apply to all drivers from all social classes and income brackets and are for that reason alone an easier case at a constitutional level than workers' compensation.[45] No matter how delicately the matter is put, workers' compensation laws apply to two largely discrete classes of individuals—employers and employees—whose intense historical opposition is too plain to bear recounting. Although many, but still a minority, of employers supported the compensation program politically,[46] several (partial) explanations for that behavior do not speak well for the statute. Some employers may have supported these statutes to stave off worse legislation. Other firms may have done so to obtain a competitive advantage over their rivals because their own costs of compliance were lower, perhaps because the higher quality of their work force reduced their compensation liability. Still others may have supported the statute because they believed in its soundness.

In addition, the statutes are suspect because they are justified on the ground that workers as a class suffer from unequal bargaining power, which entitles them to legislative protection. That rationale is *constitutionally* defective because it permits government intervention to shift wealth from one class to another in cases where the classic police power ends of controlling force and fraud are wholly absent. So long as the system of private property contains the right to dispose of acquired wealth, employers must have the right to contract with employees over the terms and conditions of labor, unless it can be shown that some abuse (force and fraud, again) is an integral part of the contracting process or unless compensation (here implicit) is provided for. To use "inequality of bargaining power" to overthrow the right to contract is to sanction endless legislative intervention, because there are differences of relative wealth endowments in virtually all cases, be it of corporations or individuals. The claim that inequalities of wealth undermine contractual choice repeals the principle of freedom of contract under the guise of an exception. No test of inequality of bargaining power can sort contracts into legitimate and illegitimate classes. Nor does the test explain how the thousand gradations of degree in relative wealth are arrayed against a

45. See, e.g., Pinnick v. Cleary, 360 Mass. 1, 271 N.E.2d 592 (1971). While these statutes make dramatic shifts, they do not eliminate tort remedies for willful harms and substantial damages. They also leave in place the full complement of direct traffic regulations, including police enforcement. They seem clearly constitutional even after the quid pro quo is strictly required.

46. See Wainwright Commission Report at 20 for signs of employer support for the compensation programs.

standard that admits only of an all-or-nothing result. No system of private property can condemn bargains solely because of preexisting differences in the wealth or power of the parties. Nor is there any reason to, for no matter what the original set of endowments of each party, both are improved by their right to trade. If contracts are not to the mutual benefit of both parties, then why have they persisted over time in thousands of discrete transactions? Properly understood, a system of private property always protects wealth that has been acquired either by first possession or voluntary agreement. The millionth dollar is protected just as much as, but no more than, the first. The state cannot take property lawfully acquired because its owner has too much of it; for the same reason, it cannot take some part of that property. A limitation on the power to dispose of property is a partial taking. If outright confiscation is not justified by showing that the owner has some "superior" bargaining strength, then a partial taking cannot be so justified either. The frequent refrain of inequality of bargaining power as a reason to invalidate contracts introduces a wild card that blocks any serious discourse.[47] It is wholly inconsistent with any system of private property, even where forced exchanges are allowed.

Still the argument has not reached its final resting place, for the redistributive rationales are not the only ones that can account for the passage of the statute, given the efficiency arguments that can be made on its behalf. At this juncture a possible intermediate position has a good deal to commend it. The basic compensation system is quite unexceptionable insofar as it creates a presumptive alternative to the common law rules of employer liability. But the prohibition against contracting out of the compensation system is itself suspect. In principle, the prohibition could be justified as a reasonable means to control employer fraud, but it is doubtful that the means-end connection can be made in fact, because in most cases employers know what the working conditions

47. There is a sense in which the question might arise. In many bargains, especially as part of ongoing relationships, a surplus may be generated. Inequality of bargaining power can then be said rigorously to exist if one side has a systematic opportunity to exploit more of the surplus than the other. For an elaboration of this point in employment contracts, see Richard A. Epstein, "In Defense of the Contract at Will," 51 *U. Chi. L. Rev.* 947 (1984). In its usual sense, however, the term is used as a synonym for employer domination, which if pressed to its conclusion makes it impossible to explain why workers receive positive wages: why should any employer pay anything if he has a decisive bargaining advantage no matter what the current price level? And once it is recognized that some wages must be paid, why not at the competitive level?

are.[48] Without this police power rationale, the proper constitutional rule gives the employer and employee *by contract* the opportunity to vary the compensation or coverage terms set by the legislature or to scrap the entire system if they find it too costly. The Wainwright Commission rejected this proposal because it "would leave the workman dependent on the whim or favor of the employer."[49] But whim and favor do not explain the emergence of durable private institutions as they existed before the statute. Employers will not casually jettison all compensation systems, because in order to attract and retain desired employees, they must shape a comprehensive benefit package. (For example, employers routinely offer disability protection even for harms that are not work-related.) But subjecting the legislative rules on workers' compensation to variation by contract places an effective check on legislative excesses. If the states make coverage too wide or compensation too extensive, the parties can correct the basic error without losing the substantial benefits of having the basic compensation system in place for those parties who want to use it.

The arguments here are not based simply upon the economic desirability of markets; they also satisfy the constitutional demands of the takings clause. The conventional legal position sustains the constitutionality of workers' compensation statutes solely because their form provides the employer a quid pro quo. Yet the form of the plan, standing alone, does not determine the extent of the compensation, which depends as well on plan particulars: how broad is the coverage and how high are the compensation levels? These plan features, moreover, can easily change over time. A compensation package that was arguably fair to both sides when the legislation was passed may not remain so over the life of the program. Again, these difficulties are largely obviated by subjecting the coverage provisions to variation by contract. The right to

48. The point, for example, was not taken up by the Wainwright Commission, which stressed the fortuitous nature of compensation, the wasteful operation of the tort system, the slowness of settlement, and the antagonism that tort liability fostered between employers and employees. The argument about fraud would have to rest upon a showing that employees' mistakes about working conditions were exploited by employers who effectively misled them about the nature and the size of risks, and this over the (nearly) full range of cases to which the workers' compensation statutes applied. It seems very unlikely that any fraud could succeed, given the intimate involvement of the employees in the plant. The most plausible cases for this rationale are the cumulative trauma cases. Yet here there is often a serious question whether the employer knew of the scope and dimension of the risks.

49. Wainwright Commission Report at 36.

contract is part of the right to property, and by eliminating that right, the workers' compensation statutes (like the Federal Employers Liability Acts)[50] are unconstitutional. The final irony of *Ives* should now be apparent. Blinded by a preoccupation with liability without fault, the opinion's fatal defect was its hasty willingness to permit the abrogation of the common law defenses, including assumption of risk by express contract. By so doing it opened up the possibility that the protection afforded the employer under the statute did not provide the necessary quid pro quo because it gave the legislature carte blanche in setting the required compensation levels.

Retroactive Legislation

GENERAL INVALIDITY

The workers' compensation plans sustained in *White* only covered accidents that occurred after the passage of the statute. In the course of its opinion the court noted that very different considerations would apply to statutes that were retroactive in application.[51] It follows necessarily from my general discussion of implicit in-kind compensation that retroactive legislation should receive very heavy scrutiny. The starting point for the analysis is that any accrued cause of action (or any accrued defense to a cause of action) is a form of property protected by the eminent domain clause. Retroactive legislation strips away the preexisting claim and thereby deprives those individuals who hold the claim of their property. To be sure, these persons receive compensation from any general enactment because they are likewise free of any claim that others might choose to raise against them. However, the existence of some compensation does not guarantee its sufficiency. The great vice of retroactive legislation is that the benefits received in exchange for surrendering rights of action will typically apply only to future claims, where they are just as likely to be burdened as benefited by the rule. The rights taken away will therefore systematically have a greater value than the rights given in exchange. Therefore this represents a well-defined polar situation in

50. Employer's Liability Act, 34 Stat. 232 (1906), struck down on grounds that it went beyond interstate commerce in the Employer's Liability Cases, 207 U.S. 463 (1908). Shortly thereafter a second act was passed, Employer's Liability Act, 35 Stat. 65 (1908), as amended 36 Stat. 291 (1910), which withstood challenge on the same grounds. Second Employers' Liability Cases, 223 U.S. 1 (1912).
51. 243 U.S. at 202.

which incomplete compensation means that the impact of the legislation is disproportionate.

The question of retroactive legislation has come up frequently in the context of employee compensation plans, both for retirement and for industrial compensation. At one time the Supreme Court showed some willingness to invalidate these statutes, as the theory of eminent domain requires. But more recently the court has adopted an uncompromising pattern of deference that has brought in its wake still bolder legislative initiatives. The contrast in jurisprudence is well illustrated by comparing the 1935 case of *Railroad Retirement Board v. Alton R.R.*[52] with the 1975 decision in *Usery v. Turner-Elkhorn Mining Co.*[53] The orientation of the current law is now quite extreme, as virtually all retroactive legislation on economic matters is routinely sustained by the Supreme Court.[54]

In *Alton R.R.* the court invalidated New Deal legislation that, among other things, required the railroads to fund retirement programs for workers who had previously left their employment and to whom the railroads owed no existing obligations, because they had either retired, moved, or been dismissed with cause. The statute also required any railroad that hired any former railroad worker to take previous years of service into account in setting the contribution to the fund, effectively requiring the railroads to pay high wages for experienced workers and preventing those workers from bidding down their own wages. The system did not demand any direct payment from railroads to workers, as the moneys were to be contributed to a common fund operated by the United States government. However, the common fund had no magic effects but only acted as a conduit between the railroads and the employees. The plan did not have a whisper of constitutional plausibility. There is not even a pretense of quid pro quo, as the benefits went all in one direction and the burdens in the other. While the case was argued

52. 295 U.S. 330 (1935).

53. 428 U.S. 1 (1975).

54. See, e.g., Pension Benefit Guaranty Corp. v. R. A. Gray & Co., 104 S.Ct. 2709 (1984), which sustained the Multiemployer Pension Plan Amendments Act of 1980. The act removed the employer's right to withdraw from preexisting multiemployer plans, which were of course contract rights that in principle are protected under the eminent domain clause. It is a sign of the current situation that the case did not involve the question of whether the legislation could limit the rights of withdrawal. The litigated issue was whether the rights of withdrawal could be limited from the date of first consideration of the plan by Congress, some five months before passage. It is a form of retroactivity in the second dimension: the retroactive application of a retroactive law.

formally on "due process" grounds, its inescapable theme was confiscation:

> The statute would take from the railroads' future earnings amounts to be paid for services fully compensated when rendered in accordance with contract, with no thought on the part of either employer or employee that further sums must be provided by the carrier. The provision is not only retroactive in that it resurrects for new burdens transactions long since past and closed; but as to some of the railroad companies it constitutes a naked appropriation of private property upon the basis of transactions with which the owners of the property were never connected. Thus the act denies due process of law by taking the property of one and bestowing it upon another.[55]

Justice Robert's opinion found two elements of the plan constitutionally infirm: the forced contributions to the fund and the insistence that newly hired workers be credited with prior years of experience. In the first, the decisive feature is the loss to the owners (the property taken) and not the form in which the benefits are provided to the workers. As to the second element, any credit for previous work experience is clearly a prospective limitation on contract rights, but that does not save it from constitutional condemnation. The only possible purpose of the provision is to protect existing workers from competition by others not presently in the labor force. As such it cannot provide implicit compensation, either for the railroads or for the workers so taxed, as they receive no benefits under the plan. The decision is clearly right: an easy case.

A very different approach was taken in *Turner-Elkhorn* in its consideration of the black lung disease compensation program. In its original form the statute created a fund for the compensation of workers afflicted with the black lung disease. Contributions to the fund came from general revenues and from special taxes upon the coal mining companies. The original version of the statute covered only those mines that employed the covered workers, but it was later amended to cover all mining companies, largely to redress the competitive imbalance created by the original tax. The constitutional attack on the statute was, as in *Alton R.R.*, grounded upon the takings dimension of the due process clause. But between 1935 and 1976 a major constitutional revolution had occurred. Because "only" economic issues were at stake, the Supreme

55. 295 U.S. at 349–350.

Court applied its new presumption that Congress has virtually plenary power on matters of economic regulation; it sustained the statute, even though it noted that the tax was retroactive, that it could not have any influence on the levels of precaution taken in the years before its passage, and that it did not reach the "excessive profits" of the taxed firms in what had been in any event a competitive industry.

The court stopped short of calling this tax a taking, although it surely was. To speak, as Justice Marshall did, of the statute as simply adjusting "the benefits and burdens" of shared economic life is to ignore the fact that one adjustment was a taking of private property and the other was a giving of that property to someone else. Nor does it make the slightest difference whether one considers the original version of the statute or its amended version, as both versions are subject to the identical condemnation made in *Alton R.R.* As Justice Marshall noted, in *Turner-Elkhorn* the moneys were tied to a particular program, while in *Alton R.R.* the moneys could be spent as the workers pleased. But that is a distinction without a constitutional difference. The ultimate question of implicit in-kind compensation is whether the government action confers a sufficient benefit upon the parties whom it burdens. That reciprocal benefit to the mining companies is not demonstrated by showing that the benefits to third parties are made in kind instead of in cash. To allow the form of the redistribution to govern is to ignore the mandate of the clause, which is to prevent that redistribution from taking place, even in disguised form.

In the revision of the statute the tax was imposed upon firms that were not in business at the time the covered workers sustained their injuries. Yet the change in funding does not alter the constitutional result, for this statute also works an uncompensated taking against a somewhat different class of individuals. To escape these conclusions, the Supreme Court erected its own wall of ignorance by adopting as its major premise the proposition that economic regulation has nothing to do with property rights, when that is just what regulation is all about. By any of the three tests designed to measure the implicit compensation received by the parties burdened, it is clear that the black lung disease program cannot survive any serious constitutional scrutiny.

There remains the difficult question of whether any special benefit program should be funded from general revenues, a matter I take up in Chapter 19. But even if such a program is an acceptable form of government behavior, it is quite indefensible to cast that obligation upon some small proportion of the public which is not responsible for the harm under any theory of obligation. If any individually covered employee were to sue any mine directly, he would be met with a host of defenses, from a general denial of causal connection to assumption of risk or the statute of limitations. The legislature can no more remove these defenses by fiat than it can by fiat create new causes of action: the requirement of reciprocal benefits still remains.

OVERCOMING THE PRESUMPTION

It might be supposed that the eminent domain clause imposes a total ban upon retroactive legislation because of the systematic mismatch of benefits and burdens. However, that conclusion is both overhasty and wrong. The real question is whether implicit in-kind compensation is provided when private rights are removed. As applied to retroactive legislation, this means that the compensation must be substantial because the value of the property taken is substantial. The particulars of any given scheme may reveal how that needed compensation will be supplied at the right level. One example of retroactive legislation with adequate compensation can be drawn from the insurance regulation of cumulative trauma cases under workers' compensation. Another is drawn from the market share liability rules in product liability cases.

INSURANCE COVERAGE   The insurance coverage question arises in determining who is required to pay worker benefits in the cumulative trauma cases, that is, cases where injury results from continued low-level exposure to dangerous substances, as with the inhalation of asbestos. These cases are routinely covered by modern compensation systems. My analysis necessarily assumes both the soundness of the current compensation system and the validity of the individual claims that are brought under it. The question then becomes, which employers, and which insurers of which employers, should be charged with the particular claims? Suppose the original rule provides that compensation should be proportioned in accordance with the length of a worker's employment with his various employers. Proration suffers, however, from great administrative difficulties, because it requires the participation of many insurance carriers and employers in the handling of a single claim. Nonetheless each employer and each insurer has vested contract rights which are undone by state legislation that makes only the last insurer of the last employer (including the employer if self-insured) bear the full insurance obligation for the loss.[56]

56. Ill. Rev. Stat. ch. 73, § 1084 (1977). The specifics of the legislation often rule out employers for whom there has been a very short period of ser-

The insurance coverage legislation in effect places all the compensation obligations in a common pool and then parcels them out in ways that promise to reduce the administrative costs of defense without creating any systematic tilt in favor of one group or another. In practice one firm may find itself worse off, but for these purposes it is sufficient that ex ante every firm may have a positive expected value under the scheme. The retroactive interference with vested rights promises benefits of the same or greater order of magnitude than the costs it imposes and thus passes muster under all three measures for implicit compensation. There still remains some question about the distribution of any administrative savings created under the insurance statute; yet here the public use doctrine is satisfied because no individual firm can appropriate the surplus for its own benefit, given the relatively fixed and automatic operation of the rule.

MARKET SHARE LIABILITY   *Sindell v. Abbott Laboratories*[57] was a product liability case brought by daughters whose mothers had taken the drug DES during pregnancy. The claims alleged that the manufacturers had been negligent in testing and marketing the drug, to the injury of the plaintiffs. The precise issue in *Sindell* was whether these actions could go forward where, owing to the lack of good records in the generation between ingestion and suit, no plaintiff could identify the specific drug company that had supplied the particular tablets to the plaintiff's mother. To overcome this identification hurdle, the court then adopted the principle of market share liability, which allows each DES daughter to recover from the class of DES manufacturers even if she cannot identify the manufacturer that supplied her mother with DES. As before, it is assumed that all other elements of a valid cause of action are established. The market share rule makes manufacturers bear the liability for harms they did not cause while removing from them most of the liability for harms they did cause. Because the defenses to private suits flow from the definition of property rights, the manufacturers are protected under

---

vice, but that refinement only makes the calculations more accurate and thus enhances the constitutionality of the statutes. Note too that the scheme runs into real practical difficulties if applied in futuro because of its troublesome incentive effects, as employers would be reluctant to hire workers with bad medical prospects. See Patricia Danzon, "Tort Reform and the Role of Government in Private Insurance Markets," 13 *J. Leg. Stud.* 517 (1984). The Illinois statute was repealed by P.A. 83–588, § 2, eff. Jan. 1, 1984.

57. 26 Cal.3d 588, 607 P.2d 924, 163 Cal. Rptr. 132 (1980), *cert denied;* E.R. Squibb & Sons, Inc. v. Sindell, 449 U.S. 912 (1980).

the eminent domain clause. (It is as though the state has first extracted the money from them without any justification and then paid it over to the victims.) Each defendant is therefore deprived of its property when forced (as in the insurance schemes just considered) to compensate for harms which it has in no sense created. The rule also operates retroactively, since it was announced not at the time of sale but only after the suits were filed. Yet here implicit in-kind compensation for the retroactive application is *perfect* so long as all manufacturers are joined in the common pool. Each defendant has to pay a small fraction of all claims instead of the total amount of its own claims, but the total liability is identical, even without the matching of plaintiff and defendant, on the assumption—very plausible in the DES cases[58] that the frequency and severity of claims are randomly distributed across manufacturers. It makes no difference whether one defendant pays 10 percent of 100 claims or 100 percent of 10 claims, so long as the expected burdens are not altered thereby.[59]

Sindell took the market share rule beyond its constitutionally permissible contours, however, by holding that any substantial portion of the manufacturers could be required to bear the full costs of injuries to all plaintiffs. The objection to this rule does not depend upon the vagueness of the term "substantial." It would apply with equal force even if some fixed fraction of the market, say 75 percent, was responsible for the losses of the entire class. Rather, the weakness in the result is that pooling arrangements are used to achieve wealth transfers that would be improper in any direct suit brought by an injured party against a drug manufacturer that had not supplied the drug. Pooling is permissible only to overcome the identification problem and not to increase the financial burdens on solvent defendants. The correct result can be achieved only by limiting recovery against each named defendant to its proportionate

58. It is plausible for two reasons. First, the dangerous substance in DES is DES itself, a chemical constant, so there is no concern with impurities or manufacturing processes. Second, most of the claims are small (adenosis), and even where they are not (as in the cancers) they tend to be randomly distributed.

59. Note too that there is a broader pooling effect, so the variance for any given firm is reduced, which provides an additional benefit for risk averse firms. Some additional administrative burdens are uncompensated, but against these must be set the uncompensated losses borne by plaintiffs with valid causes of action who stumble in identifying the supplier. Here it is very difficult to say one should trump the other; even an aggressive theory of eminent domain does not have a great deal to say where the error costs of both solutions are very high and not easily comparable.

share of the total loss. By holding a fraction of the market responsible for the entire loss, the court in *Sindell* introduced a systematic bias of over-compensation that makes firm A pay the debts of firm B. The rule necessarily takes property without just compensation. Both in *Sindell* and in general, the ultimate test of any liability rule is not its retroactivity but the mismatch of benefits and burdens, which is frequently, but not necessarily, associated with retroactive rules.

17 Regulation

Implicit in-kind compensation issues also arise with direct state regulation of the use and disposition of private property. The treatment of this enormous subject can be kept relatively brief, as it builds on the theoretical framework already established. This chapter addresses land use regulation and more comprehensive forms of economic regulation, including wage and price controls, on the assumption that these are all (large-number) takings of private property. I consider here only regulations that are not justified under the police power, so the key question usually is whether the regulation provides for the implicit in-kind compensation required by the Constitution according to the three separate tests already developed.

Land Use Regulations

SOURCES OF DISCONTENT

The need for diligent judicial supervision in land use cases derives in large measure from the persistent risk of faction in local government politics. Although the parties confronted with general liability rules may lie behind the veil of ignorance, quite the opposite is true with land use regulation, as the earlier discussion of *Euclid* indicates.[1] Everyone knows his own position in advance, so there are easily exploitable gains to be made under public control, both from the owners of undeveloped plots and from those who wish to acquire them. One common situation is where

1. See Chapter 10.

developers of low-income housing are prevented from buying land in suburban communities that have strict minimum acreage requirements. The parties thereby excluded are an alliance of the rich and the poor, of the business establishment and of minority racial or ethnic groups.[2] The situation is aggravated because there is no correlation between ownership rights and voting power. The land in question is often vacant or has a single owner; the developer and the prospective purchasers are often outside the jurisdiction and thus do not have voting rights or direct political influence. In this original position the apparent generality of land use regulations is not a safe guide, for it conceals a myriad of possibilities for skewed application. It may be claimed that rich and powerful developers (if such they be) can protect themselves from these risks by effective use of the political process. That may be so, but why should they be required to negotiate the hurdles of the local zoning procedures in order to overcome obstacles to land development that never should have been erected in the first instance?[3]

The risks of intrigue becomes clearer if we recall that most systems of land use control are not normally self-executing. Instead, they set out in very general terms the desired ends—preservation of aesthetic qualities, prevention of urban sprawl, maintenance of individual neighborhoods, or whatever.[4] Thereafter the operation of the system depends upon discrete applications, usually culminating in decisions by a local planning board, often in response to some highly particularized request of local groups. An enormous slippage thus occurs between the articulation of a general principle and its concrete application. In the usual land use controversy, the participants press for their immediate advantage, and their zeal may be heightened if their successful maneuvers frighten off others who wish to challenge local domination.

This state of affairs is confirmed by the common scene of irate neigh-

2. Note too that prospective buyers from the developers stand in a position that differs from that of the developers. To be sure, these local ordinances strip these buyers of the right to acquire property. In most cases, however, these losses should not be compensated because they are too small and diffuse, like the loss of prospective customers when a business is relocated; see Chapter 4. But where individual parties have made substantial investments in acquiring land, the effects are disproportionate, and explicit compensation is in principle required.

3. See, e.g., Harbison v. City of Buffalo, 4 N.Y.2d 553, 564–575, 176 N.Y.S.2d 598, 606–616, 152 N.E.2d 42, 48–54 (1958) (Van Voorhis, J., dissenting).

4. See, e.g., Cal [Gov't] Code § 65302(a) (West 1983).

bors appearing en masse before a zoning board to protest, or insist on, some proposed change in permissible land use. Citizens generally could, if they chose, distinguish between reductions in value that are generated by possible nuisances and those that are not. But because both legitimate and illegitimate forms of activity can reduce their land values, citizens have little incentive to act with self-restraint. Why should they discriminate among their objections, especially when the legal system itself as now constituted ignores the relevant distinctions or brands them as artificial or unintelligible? The rational strategy is to act and to vote out of narrow and immediate self-interest. The protesting citizens will tolerate the requirements for procedural rights of hearing and expert witnesses because they offer opportunities for delay and have no appreciable effect upon the ultimate outcome. Public speeches may expose or obscure the unfairness of local decisions, but the First Amendment, even if respected to its fullest, will alter the outcomes in only a tiny fraction of cases.

The political process is directly connected to the problem of takings. Local boards may take private rights of use and disposition into the public domain without compensation, then parcel them out again to others by majority rule. Zoning stands in stark contrast to a system of private property, which allows a single owner (within the confines of the nuisance limitation) to decide how to use his plot of land. Where property rights are enforced, owners can make choices on efficient land use without having to overcome the conundrums of collective choice. Where the present owner is ill-equipped to develop or use the land, an individual or a firm can easily arrange a sale. Land use regulation places the land back into a modified common pool, where many persons can limit the future use of the land, even though only one person, the owner, can actually use it. Ill-defined rights replace well-defined ones, and transaction cost barriers are likely to exceed the gains that otherwise are obtainable from any shift in land use or ownership. Another negative-sum game.

Strict judicial supervision of the zoning process is therefore appropriate to correct the unstable political situation. The present routine judicial deference to local action is wholly inappropriate. To be sure, uncompensated takings are not the only outcomes of local zoning boards, so it is out of the question to invalidate all zoning per se.[5] Some

5. See Frank I. Michelman, "Political Markets and Community Self-Determination: Competing Judicial Models of Local Government Legitimacy," 53 *Indiana L.J.* 145 (1977–78).

zoning does restrain nuisancelike activities, and some regulations work for the benefit of those who are simultaneously burdened. The discussion of the police power reveals principled limitations on local power. Similarly, the implicit in-kind compensation argument must be answered by the array of techniques already developed: direct measurement of the consequences of regulation, theoretical predictions of economic loss, disproportionate impact tests, and examination of local motive. In many land use situations all these point to the need for explicit compensation, as the following case law discussions illustrate.

APPLICATIONS

It is perhaps appropriate to begin with regulations that should in principle pass constitutional muster. Consider, for example, local controls over the size, shape, and color of new signs, regulations which are far more focused than the total bans on billboards previously discussed.[6] The restriction is an abridgment of property rights not accounted for by the police power. Nonetheless, implicit in-kind compensation can be found in this, which upon examination turns out to be yet another common pool problem. Without the regulation, each individual has the incentive to make his sign as conspicuous as possible, because he will internalize all the gains from its prominent place and bear only a fraction of the associated aesthetic costs. Unilateral efforts to limit sign size will be of little use, as some people will exploit the opportunities created by others' self-restraint. Multiparty contracts cannot be negotiated, given the usual transaction cost constraints. A comprehensive ordinance can control the abuse, while guaranteeing each person the visibility needed for effective use of the signs. Such restrictions are routinely included in shopping center leases, where many shops are leased from a common landlord, for just this reason. The regulation, therefore, cannot be attacked by those who want it to bind others while they remain as free as before. The proper baseline for compensation is whether an owner subject to the restriction is better off than he was before the scheme was imposed, not whether he is better off if unrestrained while others are bound. The details of this regulation will vary from case to case, and one must be alert to see that built-in biases in favor of certain classes of landowners do not create a disproportionate impact that undermines the fairness of the scheme, as might occur if present occupiers are given more extensive sign privileges than newcomers.

This pattern can be applied to more extensive forms of regulation. In

6. See the discussion of *Metromedia, Inc.* in Chapter 10.

Maher v. City of New Orleans[7] the local ordinance required local approval for any alteration of the exterior of certain structures located in the Old French Quarter. In this case a request to raze a structure and construct an apartment unit in its place was denied. The restrictions are a prima facie taking, but the possibilities for in-kind compensation are substantial, because preserving the character of the neighborhood works to the advantage of all the regulated parties. Nonetheless, it does not follow that no compensation is required, because the benefits may extend beyond the regulated owners to others in the area who gain, say, from the increased tourist trade. To make the final constitutional assessment, therefore, it is necessary to ask whether the regulation decreased the values of the regulated structures (reflecting the owner's obligation to repair and maintain) and, if so, whether those decreases were offset, either in whole or in part, by any special reduction in real estate taxes included as part of the regulatory package. No conclusive presumption that the benefits received equal the value of the property taken is appropriate, even where the possibility of reciprocal benefits is manifest. The problem cannot be avoided by pretending that the taking has not taken place.

But in most controversial zoning cases it is improper to deny explicit compensation. The major weaknesses in the received judicial wisdom can be shown by a close examination of three land use cases in California. *HFH, Ltd. v. Superior Court in Los Angeles County*,[8] made a conscious effort to sustain land use regulations on the theory of implicit in-kind compensation. The plaintiff, a limited partnership, had purchased a 5.87-acre plot of land in an agricultural area, which at the time was zoned for commercial use. Five years after purchase, the land had not been developed. At that time the local zoning authority rezoned the land for agricultural uses on a temporary basis, then shortly thereafter zoned it for "low density residential uses," which effectively precluded its intended commercial use. It was stipulated that the land value was reduced from $400,000 to $75,000. Here the court's initial argument was that the reduction in value was *damnum absque iniuria*, a mere diminution in value. That conclusion, however, is wholly untenable, because it treats the loss as though it arose through a change in market conditions, when it was in fact a reflection of the partial taking, here of a state-

---

7. 516 F.2d 1051 (5th Cir. 1975). A similar analysis of the case is found in Donald Wittman, "Liability for Harm or Restitution for Benefits?" 13 *J. Legal Stud.* 57, 75–76 (1984).

8. 15 Cal. 3d 508, 542 P.2d 237, 125 Cal. Rptr. 365 (1975), *cert. denied*, 425 U.S. 904 (1976).

imposed restrictive covenant over the land. Equally weak was the argument that ownership imposes the duty to develop land within some reasonable time after acquisition lest the right be properly lost to state control. The point is not simply that it may be self-defeating for a court with antigrowth inclinations to impose an unnecessary incentive for premature development. It is that ownership gives the right, not the duty, to develop, as well as the right not to develop. No waiver of rights can be inferred simply from the exercise of one or two equally permissible options. The regulation necessarily involves the partial taking, here of development rights.

However, the supposed coup de grace was the court's observation that the value of land for commercial purposes depended at least in part upon the fact that other nearby land had been previously limited to residential uses. In essence, it argued that the plaintiff could not have it both ways: reaping the benefit of the restrictions upon others while escaping their burden. Such an argument is clearly correct when benefits and burdens are part of a single overall package—for to decide otherwise is to let every legislative scheme combating common pool problems unravel at the first sign of dissent. But here the two sets of restrictions were not imposed at the same time nor as part of the same plan. No private party could demand that the owners of the benefited land pay compensation for the enhanced values of those lands on any kind of restitution theory. The position of the state is no better. How, then, is it possible, long after any relevant statute of limitations has run out, to use the benefits conferred as a setoff against the compensation owed for imposing the restrictive covenant?

Suppose, however, that both present and previous restrictions are treated as part of a comprehensive scheme. There is still the strict constitutional obligation to make the best possible measure of their worth. If, for example, it could be demonstrated that the plaintiff's land would have been worth only $380,000 if the nearby land had been unzoned, then the explicit compensation payable by the state should be reduced by $20,000, a far cry from the uncompensated loss of $325,000 sustained by the complaining landowner in *HFH, Ltd.* But there is no evidence that the restrictions on nearby land benefited this parcel at all. If the nearby land had been left unzoned, it could have been devoted to intensive residential development, thereby enhancing the value of plaintiff's land for commercial use. Alternatively, if the neighboring land had been developed commercially, the plaintiff's land for either commercial or residential use may have been worth far more than $40,000: one cannot ignore the possibility that the restrictions on both parcels were imposed for the benefit of third parties not joined in this litigation. The first approximation must be therefore that the cost of the regulation to the landowners was $325,000, which is scarcely changed by taking into account implicit in-kind compensation. And it is wholly improper to erect a conclusive constitutional presumption that the implicit benefits conferred are equal to the losses imposed, when evidence on market values is so emphatic the other way.

Nimbleness in escaping constitutional constraints is also revealed by the Ninth Circuit's decision in *Haas v. City and County of San Francisco.*[9] There the plaintiff was the owner of a large plot of undeveloped land in the Russian Hill area of San Francisco, on which he planned to build a high-rise apartment building. The original purchase price of the land was $1,650,000, with payment conditional upon obtaining a valid site permit from the relevant city agency. While the land was under contract, Haas's first request for permission to build was rejected by the City Planning Commission. The commission then adopted on its own more general height and bulk restrictions which, among other things, restricted construction in the Russian Hill area to buildings lower than 300 feet. Haas then submitted revised plans which conformed to the new requirements, which were approved after a pubic hearing. Thereafter the land sale contract became final; the purchase price was paid to the seller, and a $165,000 commission to the broker. Haas immediately broke ground on the site, only to face a challenge in court from the Russian Hill Improvement Association, a neighborhood group, which sought to stop the construction (by outsiders, no less) on the grounds that the project was subject to the requirements of the 1970 California Environmental Act, as amended. Haas prevailed at trial but lost on appeal; it was held that he was not grandfathered out of the act's requirements because he had not begun substantial on-site construction in time.[10] Back at square one, Haas found himself in more hostile circum-

---

9. 605 F.2d 1117 (9th Cir, 1979).

10. Russian Hill Improvement Ass'n v. Bd. of Permit Appeals, 44 Cal App. 3d 158, 164, 118 Cal. Rptr. 490, 494 (1974). The applicable statutory language grandfathers out of the environmental statute projects on which "substantial construction has been performed and substantial liability for construction and necessary materials have been incurred." Cal [Pub. Res.) Code § 21170(a) (West 1977). The test stated by the statute is incorrect on constitutional grounds, even if only retroactive restrictions can be challenged under the eminent domain clause. The disproportionate impact should include all reliance expenditures, even those which are not made on the physical site. Indeed, one can go further, as even expenditures made to acquire specific parcels of land should be compensable if subsequent restrictions defeat the

stances, for in the interim the City Planning Commission had adopted a general 40-foot height limitation, imposed strict density controls, and downzoned his property from R-5 to R-3. There was no question that the process resulted in a substantial diminution in the value of the land, nor was there any doubt that powerful local prejudices condemned the "out of state" interests that sought to undertake the development.

Whether this was a compensable taking was said to turn on the familiar question of disproportionate impact. Judge Hufstedler, speaking for a unanimous court, addressed the disproportionate impact claim as follows:

> Haas' property has not been singled out from other Russian Hill properties and made to bear a disproportionate economic burden. The record contains not the slightest suggestion that the land use regulations at issue involved "reverse spot" zoning. On the contrary, the land use controls were part of a comprehensive plan for the development of the City to preserve aesthetic values and other general welfare interests of the inhabitants. The land use restrictions "were reasonably related to the implementation of a policy . . . expected to produce a widespread public benefit and applicable to all similarly situated property" . . . All of Haas' neighbors are subject to the same restrictions upon the future development of their property as those imposed upon Haas. To be sure, at the moment, Haas appears to have suffered a disproportionate impact because no other affected landowner has as large a parcel of undeveloped land as does Haas. Nevertheless, all of the landowners in the Russian Hill area are no more able than is Haas to redevelop their property, either alone, or in combination with other landowners, for high-rise apartments.
>
> Haas has suffered a serious economic loss, and a frustration that it is not equally borne by the owners of adjacent parcels. That the loss is heavy and that Haas must bear more than its proportionate share of the burden for the sake of the general welfare, however, did not convert the regulation into a taking.[11]

---

purchase, as these expenditures (like the special improvements in *Almota*, discussed in Chapter 7) had an expected value at least equal to their cost. The import of the California statute is to countenance broad retroactive land use regulation.

11. 605 F.2d at 1121.

In dealing with Hufstedler's argument, it is important to note the two separate ways to attack a partial taking: direct valuation of economic loss or disproportionate impact. By direct valuation, the proper measure is the difference between value before and value after that is attributable to the regulation. Putting aside the effects of previous zoning ordinances, the purchase price of $1,650,000 is credible evidence of market value and should be augmented by the 10 percent broker's fee and other acquisition costs. Haas claimed that the residual value of the land was only $100,000, a figure that seems low, given the substantial market for row and town houses in the Russian Hill area. But even if one doubles that figure, say, it is very difficult to believe that Haas receives some benefit from comprehensive land planning that is not reflected in the value of his land.

To the above, one can reply that in matters of general regulation, the disproportionate impact test replaces direct valuation. The court equivocates on the applicability of the test, denying it at the outset of the quoted passage, only to admit it somewhat grudgingly at the end. But on the facts of the case, the disproportionate impact test also requires explicit compensation, notwithstanding the very rigid approach to the subject taken by the court. To Judge Hufstedler, the decisive question in *Haas* was whether the same *type* of restriction was imposed on both Haas and his immediate neighbors. To be sure, this test is not wholly empty, for Haas would get compensation if his land use were restricted but all the neighbors remained free to construct high rises on their land.

Yet simply because *Haas* does not nullify the disproportionate impact test, it does not follow that the opinion has given that test its due. As ever, the goal is to measure the level of compensation required by indirect means. To rely upon the formal parallelism of the restrictions is to assume that the simple existence of some reciprocal benefits is dispositive. But when the Constitution speaks of just compensation, it makes the *amount,* not the *existence* of compensation, decisive: on this question the evidence of market values is telling against the court. Even if that evidence is ignored, the impact is disproportionate even if the restrictions were neutral on their face, for the costs they imposed upon Haas far exceeded those imposed on his neighbors. Haas wished to build, while they wished to restrain construction. For the neighbors, a nonmarket surplus value in their own land was protected; for Haas, an expectation was dashed. In addition, the neighbors had far fewer opportunities to develop. None of them had incurred any of the reliance costs in acquiring a large parcel for construction, nor had any started construction.[12] Haas had assembled enough land to build the high rise. To do the same, any other builder would have to incur the same assembly cost and might well find himself blocked by a single landowner who refused to yield. Again, Haas had only to worry about empty land while other builders would have to knock down existing houses. The court conceded that Haas's assembly costs "appeared" to put him at a greater disadvantage than others. These are more than mere appearances; he was placed at a greater disadvantage than others. The disproportionate impact test is, therefore, satisfied, and the decision incorrect.

Whatever its failings, *Haas* seems consistent with the current Supreme Court jurisprudence on the subject of land use regulation as developed in *Agins v. City of Tiburon*.[13] The plaintiffs owned some five acres of prime residential land with a view of San Francisco Bay. Acting pursuant to California law, the city developed a plan which restricted the number of houses that could be built on the land to five. Just before the zoning action, the city had authorized the sale of $1.25 million in bonds for the acquisition of property to be held for open space uses. There was no explicit reference to the plaintiff's land in the authorization,[14] but the message is still quite clear. Why should the local government pay $1.25 million to acquire land for open spaces, when at a tiny fraction of the cost it can zone the land to achieve most of its desired end, the restriction of new construction? To be sure, there is a difference in the outcome, as zoning will not permit members of the general public to *use* the land, a valuable right which eminent domain takeover provides. But from the vantage point of the local residents, the relevant question is only this: is it worth paying $1.25 million for the land when the restrictive covenant, which is worth some substantial fraction of the land's value, can be acquired for virtually nothing? The answer seems obvious, especially if the land subject to the restriction can be condemned for its reduced value after a decent interval has passed and some appropriate formalities (a separate hearing, a new decision) are observed.

Justice Powell, writing for the court in *Agins,* shows how the incorrect use of the police power and implicit in-kind compensation arguments can gut the takings clause:

12. In fairness to the court, these elements were stipulated to be irrelevant here, but only because of the collateral estoppel effect of the prior decision in the California state court, 605 F.2d at 1119–1120. They would have been considered if the correct standard had been applied in the earlier litigation.

13. 447 U.S. 255 (1980).

14. Agins v. City of Tiburon, 24 Cal. 3d 266, 270, 598 P.2d 25, 27, 157 Cal. Rptr. 372, 374 (1979).

The zoning ordinances benefit the appellants as well as the public by serving the city's interest in assuring careful and orderly development of residential property with provisions for open-space areas. There is no indication that the appellants' 5-acre tract is the only property affected by the ordinances. Appellants therefore will share with other owners the benefits and burdens of the city's exercise of its police power. In assessing the fairness of the zoning ordinance, these benefits must be considered along with any diminution in market value that the appellants might suffer.[15]

Clear enough, and clearly wrong. First, it is immaterial that other property owners are subject to the zoning regulation. The regulation is still a taking simpliciter, and unless all land in the area is subject to the restriction, there is still an enormous disproportionate impact, as unimproved land is subject to extensive restrictions on use that enhance the value of lands already improved. Certainly there is no claim that no one was benefited by passage of the ordinance, for if everyone would lose, the measure would never pass. The restrictive rules are a government-sponsored restraint of trade.

Second, it is immaterial that the owners "share" in the benefits of the police power. The issue is the extent of the benefits they receive, which must be a full and perfect equivalent of the property surrendered. A nickel's compensation will not discharge a hundred dollar obligation. To treat the mere existence of some benefits as an adequate measure of their value is to indulge in a conclusive presumption that is known to be wrong or, at the very least, contrary to the manifest evidence.

Third, the benefits of the police power should not be "considered along with any diminution in market value that the appellant might suffer."[16] It is not just that these benefits are wholly inadequate. It is instead that they are already embedded in land values when the regulation is imposed. To take them into account separately is to count them twice, to the improper benefit of the state.

HFH, Ltd., Haas, and *Agins* are representative of a uniform line of cases that reveal all that is perverse about the modern eminent domain law. They begin with a narrow interpretation of the taking language, which is then bolstered by an expansive interpretation of the police power and a strained reading of the disproportionate impact requirement. The current law merges doctrinal error with an indefensible deference to local governments.

15. 447 U.S. at 262.
16. Id.

Rate, Price, and Wage Regulations

The general theory of implicit in-kind compensation also applies, with more difficulty, to larger forms of economic regulation. The sources of the problem should be evident, for it is more difficult to calculate the wealth and distributional effects of comprehensive government regulations. Direct compensation is almost impossible because of the inherent complexity of the situation, so in some situations the appropriate remedy for constitutional violation may be total invalidation of the regulation. The intellectual problem would be much simplified if we could state with confidence that all regulation of wages and prices is per se unconstitutional, but that universal judgment cannot be sustained.

I will begin with one area in which government regulation may well be appropriate: railroad and public utility rates. The proper treatment of these issues first came before the Supreme Court in the last part of the nineteenth century, when rapid industrialization made extensive investment in railroads and utilities feasible. In the leading case of *Smyth v. Ames*[17] Nebraska had established a set of tariffs for the transport of persons and freight which, the railroad claimed, deprived it of all opportunity to make a reasonable return on its capital investment. The case was argued under the rubric of the due process clause, but the analysis was vintage eminent domain, for Justice Harlan viewed that the proper issue was whether the rate structure worked a taking of the railroad's property for public use without just compensation.[18]

One might ask why a railroad or utility has to submit to any form of regulation at all. If the price of its service in the marketplace exceeds the regulated price, then (since the eminent domain clause covers rights of disposition) it has made a prima facie showing that it is entitled to compensation for the difference between the market and the regulated return. But this argument misses an important feature about the industries regulated: they have achieved their market position, and perhaps their monopoly position, by virtue of government intervention that allowed them to assemble the necessary interests in land. Railroads typically resorted to government power to obtain the original land grants, and utilities typically can exercise private rights of condemnation and can avail themselves of public rights of way.

17. 169 U.S. 466 (1898). One measure of the importance of the case is that William Jennings Bryan was one of the lawyers representing the state of Nebraska in defending its rate regulation.
18. Id. at 522–527.

The issue can now be joined. All these takings must be for a public use, so the question is, who is entitled to the surplus created by the redeployment of resources under the eminent domain power? If the utilities or railroads could operate in a wholly unregulated fashion, their original shareholders could appropriate the surplus for themselves, in violation of the public use requirement that demands its even distribution.[19]

The question of rate regulation concerns how to both maximize the size of the surplus and ensure its fair division. At a minimum one could argue that the proper response is a simple command of universal, nondiscriminatory service, allowing the regulated firm to set whatever uniform price it chooses. Yet here the dangers are manifest. When the industry is complex, it cannot provide all services at equal unit costs. It costs more to produce electricity at peak hours than at slow times. A nondiscrimination provision therefore creates its own perverse incentive by setting equal prices for goods with unequal costs. The result is overconsumption at peak hours in a system that sells some units at a loss while others generate an enormous profit. Rate setting allows for classification that preserves the ideal of nondiscrimination, while making it flexible enough to guard against the uneven division of the surplus, which a legally assisted monopoly will otherwise generate.

Direct rate regulation is therefore understood as the tail end of a system that confers upon the regulated industry the private power of eminent domain. In one sense it closely resembles the situation already considered with workers' compensation, where the size of the quid pro quo is left to legislative discretion, with little or no constitutional scrutiny by the courts.[20]

19. Even if no regulation exists at the outset, subsequent regulation is allowable, not pursuant to the reserved power of the grant but because the original grant without the restriction was a violation of the rights of others, which is now limited by its belated state assertion. Indeed, the key question is whether the state could recover for the interim profits obtained before the conditions were imposed, a formidable undertaking that often is not worth the candle. See the Conclusion for the complications that flow from efforts to undo past errors.

20. The problems of regulation are sufficiently acute that a strong case could be made to capture the surplus by selling off the state's exclusive rights to operate a public utility by competitive bid to a party that could then charge the monopoly price, for which (given the lump sum payment at the front) it will receive only a competitive return. Yet that proposal may result in insufficient service being provided to some segments of the population. On the strength of present knowledge it seems impossible to say that any such system so dominates traditional regulation that it necessarily supplants it, especially since the eminent domain clause only requires fair division of the surplus and does not impose legislative duties that maximize the size of the surplus.

But rate regulation took the opposite turn historically. The courts recognized that the power of regulation could be converted into the power of confiscation if the state were free to set the rates any way it pleased. The formula of "reasonable return" was therefore an effort to escape both horns of a dilemma. First, it is quite clear that no fixed rates can be set at the outset, as can be done when land is taken for a post office. As with workers' compensation, the once-and-for-all solution cannot take into account the uncertainties that the future holds.[21] Second, the state cannot (because of the dangers of faction) be allowed to set the compensation at whatever level it pleases after the railroads have made their original investment. The system of judicial review worked out in *Smyth v. Ames* represents the intermediate position in a world in which the railroad is allowed to defer payment for its use of the state power to acquire property. In one sense, the decision seems to contradict the general proposition that "value and not cost" should be the measure of compensation. Yet, properly understood, rate-of-return regulation is an effort to provide the competitive return (and the fair distribution of surplus that it entails) in situations where competitive markets have been excluded.

The tasks needed to implement this system are formidable. In *Smyth v. Ames,* for example, the lawyer for the state of Nebraska, defending the rate schedule, stressed that profits should not be allowed "for injudicious contracts, poor engineering, unusually high cost of material, [or] rascality on the part of those engaged in the construction or management of the property."[22] The point is fair, for it notes that while the system may begin life as cost based, losses in value attributable to firm mismanagement should not be passed on to consumers. Thus the rate base should properly be adjusted to take into account the depreciation in value attributable to the sins of management (whose behavior is doubtless influenced by the incentive structure under which it operates). The complications of rate regulation extend to a myriad of other issues; there is constant inquiry as to the proper cost of capital, the level of risk associated with the venture, and the pricing of obligations that the regulated industry must undertake. None of these tasks is easy to discharge where the best guiding formula can speak only of "a reasonable rate of return." Indeed, a powerful case could be made for a simple nondiscrimination provision, on the ground that the error and administrative costs of direct regulation dissipate most, if not all, the surplus available to the natural

21. See Chapter 16.
22. 169 U.S. at 479.

monopoly.[23] This is not the place to defend or attack the specifics of rate regulation in particular industries; I only wish to show here why the system, as outlined in *Smyth v. Ames,* falls within the broad outlines of the constitutional tradition.

In sharp contrast are other forms of regulation, which seek to limit the profits of individual firms whose gains in no way depend upon the state's exercise of the eminent domain power.[24] In these cases today the dominant social response is to ignore the distinction and to assume that rate regulation is justified as a matter of principle, wholly without regard to how the regulated party came by its advantages. This unwillingness to pass on the merits of comprehensive economic regulation is clearly reflected in the decided cases; challenges to zoning decisions at least receive a respectful hearing before they are rejected, but challenges of comprehensive economic regulation are typically dismissed with the back of the hand and an invocation of the ghost of *Lochner.*[25] A closer examination is needed.

Consider first the controls which limit the prices at which commodities can be traded in the open market. It is tempting to succumb to the easy way out and regard the government action as a mere regulation rather than a partial taking. But this approach fails in principle; the decisive question is whether the taking should be regarded as compensated or not. Here there is the same uneasy mix between direct methods of valuation (what happens to the market value shares of regulated companies) and the disproportionate impact test. Again there is no easy or uniform result. Take as the limit a regulation that says every product, regardless of value or previous cost, must be sold for no more than one dollar. If prospective regulation falls within the eminent domain clause, then such a statute must fail, assuming (as ever) that it could be passed

23. See Harold Demsetz, "Why Regulate Utilities?" 11 *J. L. & Econ.* 55 (1968); Richard A. Posner," Natural Monopoly and Its Regulation," 21 *Stan. L. Rev.* 548 (1969).

24. I do not regard limited liability as a sufficient hook on which to predicate comprehensive regulation. Here the universal availability of the privilege means that parties can share pro rata in the gains it supplies, while any externality can be met by the demand for insurance against tort risks. Any effort to use state privilege as a hook for additional regulation is contrary to the demands of the theory, because the likely outcome is that certain individuals, such as those who acquire special charters or privileges, will get more than their pro rata share of the surplus. See Henry Butler, "Nineteenth-Century Jurisdictional Competition in the Granting of Corporate Privileges," 14 *J. Legal Stud.* 129 (1984).

25. Lochner v. New York, 198 U.S. 45 (1905).

in the first place. The utter chaos that would result from this regime renders unnecessary any protracted demonstration of its overall negative impact. Some persons (virtually all) would necessarily be net losers. Indeed, even if disproportionate impact were the only relevant consideration, the statute would still fail, for its severity depends critically on the nature of private holdings. While all persons will be left worse off, some will be hurt more than others. Price controls pass muster only if one looks to their neutral form—that everyone labors under the same one-dollar price restriction—and ignores their economic effects, which leave all parties with uncompensated losses.

In the real world, no one would present such an absurd scheme of price controls, so the constitutional prohibition has no practical bite on legislative behavior. Indeed, the very steps that are needed to make these controls politically feasible are those which bring it into closer conformity with constitutional standards. The base prices are typically linked to historical prices, reflecting the different values of different holdings, and thereby muting the radical shifts in wealth that otherwise might have taken place. But no single regime of control will have the same result with different goods, whose price movements vary widely even in markets with no inflation. The prices of computer goods are steadily falling, those of agricultural produce fluctuate widely, that of photographic film is tied to silver, and so on down the line. There is still the powerful argument that price controls must be struck down because the inherent rigidities so drastically reduce the size of the pie, no matter how equitable the original formula, no matter how lofty the legislative motive. There comes a point where the generality of the statute might save it from constitutional challenge under a (charitable) version of the disproportionate impact test that ignores the inherent imbalances in any system of direct price controls. When price controls are introduced in wartime (with its exogenous shocks), they might be justified as a response to nonmarket windfalls in the first place. But the great reason to accept the constitutionality of the scheme is that—if it is as bad as is commonly believed—in peacetime it will crumble without constitutional invalidation, because just about everyone will work for its elimination.

The matter is very different, however, when selective price controls are applied to one industry but not others. The leading illustrations are the controls that were imposed upon natural gas prices during the 1950s and those on oil and gas prices, which were left in place after the general system of price controls imposed by President Nixon in 1971 was dismantled.[26] Now the disproportionate impact arguments should be decisive in favor of a claim for explicit compensation. There is no question that the regulations are a partial taking; the right of disposition above and beyond a certain price has been removed, even if the other incidents of ownership have been left undisturbed. And although there is implicit compensation, its amount is inadequate, given the disproportionate impact of the regulation. It is immaterial that no single oil company is subject to the rule in question, because when an entire industry is regulated, there is no reciprocal provision of benefits and burdens wholly in the regulated class, in sharp contrast with the common pool regulation. Every party regulated is no better off by virtue of the others being regulated as well. To be sure, there is some indirect overlap. The oil companies' shareholders are also consumers who benefit from the rules. Yet there is no perfect diversification across the two markets; quite the opposite, many consumers have no producer interest and many producers have tiny consumer interests. No evidence suggests that the crazy quilt of regulation will balance out in the long run, even if aggressive use of the step transaction doctrine is permitted to link separate regulatory schemes, each one a negative-sum game.[27] The amount at stake in the controversy is enormous, but the principled response is easy.

The argument can be extended to other forms of direct regulation. General usury laws might be sustained on the strength of the disproportionate impact test, even though the overall wealth effects are surely negative. But any doubts raised in that context disappear concerning selective restrictions on the right to lend at interest. Yet the judicial response, even at the height of the *Lochner* era, was to invoke the canon of judicial deference and a broad account of the police power to sustain (against an equal protection challenge) a Connecticut statute that exempted from its general usury law only national and state banks but not other unsecured lenders.[28]

In the early part of this century there was some willingness to strike down minimum wage or maximum hour laws,[29] as well as federal and

26. See, e.g., Gale Anne Norton, "The Limitless Federal Taxing Power" (paper presented at the Federalist Society Western Regional Conference on Reforming Tax Policy, University of Colorado School of Law, Oct. 14–16, 1983).
27. See Chapter 14.
28. See Griffith v. Connecticut, 218 U.S. 563 (1910).
29. See Adkins v. Children's Hospital, 261 U.S. 525 (1923).

state prohibitions against yellow dog contracts.[30] But this entire line of cases has been largely discredited on the controversial ground that the doctrine of substantive due process does not limit legislative activity on issues of common concern. But the eminent domain argument will not so easily disappear; here it could be asserted by either the employer or the employee. As with the workers' compensation, the prohibitions cut to the heart of freedom of contract. Restrictions on hours or wages are without question limitations upon the power of the employer to dispose of property. The claim of the employee, ironically, might not fit under the eminent domain clause because the restrictions are upon his right to dispose of his labor, not property. Yet the employee is also sharply limited in his right to acquire property by the use of his labor. It is possible, if unlikely, that the "liberty" interests in personal services are covered by the eminent domain clause as well, since they routinely were covered by the principle of freedom of contract as it developed under the law of substantive due process. But for the employer these limitations upon employment contracts are undoubted partial takings, with all the earmarks of class legislation, which requires their complete constitutional invalidation. Just compensation (much less an even division of surplus) is not, and could not, be tendered.

The arguments above apply in general form to all regulations that limit the wages and hours of employment. Indeed the constitutional attack is, far easier here than it is against the workers' compensation statutes because there is no plausible police power claim based upon matters of safety and health. Nor is there any plausible argument that employers misrepresent wage rates: think how supporters of the minimum wage would respond to a bill which required the employer to disclose in writing the contract wage.

The point was well understood by the first Justice Harlan, who had dissented in *Lochner,* in his opinion striking down yellow dog legislation in *Adair.* Because *Adair* is an easy case, it follows that the subsequent social legislation, especially the National Labor Relations Act, with its complex restrictions upon freedom of contract and the exclusive possession of private property, must fail on eminent domain grounds as well.

Collective bargaining is yet another system in which well-defined markets are displaced by complex common pool devices whose overall

30. Adair v. United States, 208 U.S. 161 (1908); Coppage v. Kansas, 236 U.S. 1 (1915).

wealth effects are in all likelihood negative and whose disproportionate impact, especially on established firms, is enormous.[31] The only way to deny the claim is to insist that all prospective regulation of contractual rights is outside the eminent domain clause. But what then of a $1,000 per hour minimum wage statute, a $10 per hour maximum wage statute, a total prohibition against hiring all workers, a complete abolition of all rights of action under private contract, or a statute forbidding the sale of nonunion goods? Placing all rights of disposition outside the class of property rights is one convenient way to deal with these claims. But that approach simply avoids a serious problem by stripping property of one of its essential attributes. Today statutes that eliminate rights of disposition on a wholesale basis would probably be attacked (with uncertain success) under the equal protection or due process clauses, but the new doctrinal home cannot conceal the fact that property is the basis for the claim.

It will be said that my position invalidates much of the twentieth-century legislation, and so it does. But does that make the position wrong in principle? The breadth of my charges shows only that there is a clear pattern of constitutional decisions in a wide diversity of cases. The linkages among the cases tend to make much of the legislation stand and fall together. If my arguments here are correct, then any New Deal economic and social legislation that suffers from the vices of the labor statutes in principle should be consigned to the same constitutional fate. The New Deal *is* inconsistent with the principles of limited government and with the constitutional provisions designed to secure that end. Any attack on this social legislation does not mean that the state cannot continue to govern, or that certain ruinous practices will continue to the detriment of the public at large. The police can function; the courts are open; the army is at the ready; common pools can be contained; holdout problems can be overcome; uncertainty can be handled. But the takings clause is designed to control rent seeking and political faction. It is those practices, and only those practices, that it reaches. The only arguments against this position are more pragmatic, that once we depart from

31. For a more detailed analysis of the relevant issues outside the constitutional context, see Richard A. Epstein, "A Common Law of Labor Relations: A Critique of the New Deal Labor Legislation," 92 *Yale L.J.* 1357 (1983). As the common law arguments there track the constitutional arguments here, there is very little difference in the outcome. There is no answer to Justice Pitney's argument in Coppage v. Kansas, which if anything is too weak because it did not stress sufficiently that the inequalities of wealth that emerge in voluntary transactions come as part of a positive-sum game.

principle, it becomes impossible to return to the path that principle requires. I will consider those arguments after exploring how the eminent domain clause (or at least the takings arguments) applies first to taxation and then to the legislative creation of welfare rights.

_18_ Taxation

To what extent can the takings clause and parallel constitutional provisions limit the government's power to tax? It is a truism that the United States and the several states may impose some taxes upon individual activities within their jurisdiction.[1] The modern view of the subject, repeatedly emphasized in the decided cases, is that in general the power of taxation is plenary.[2] Indeed, the only limitations imposed upon it are found in other constitutional provisions that limit government power generally. A general taxation scheme that imposes differential tax burdens upon blacks and whites, or upon men and women, will be struck down under the equal protection clause, but a uniform, higher-level tax upon both blacks and whites is invulnerable to attack. A special tax upon newspapers will be struck down as a limitation upon the freedom of speech.[3] The proposition that all taxes are subject to scrutiny under the eminent domain clause receives not a whisper of current support. The taxing power is placed in one compartment; the takings power in another. The first power is wholly untouched by the limitations imposed

1. Art. I, § 8, cl. 1 reads: "The Congress shall have Power To lay and collect Taxes, Duties, Imposts and Excises, to pay the Debts and provide for the common Defence and general Welfare of the United States; but all Duties, Imposts and Excises shall be uniform throughout the United States." Analogous powers can be found in all states and are in any event an indispensable attribute of sovereignty.

2. See, e.g., Magnano Co. v. Hamilton, 292 U.S. 40 (1934).

3. See, e.g., Grossjean v. American Press Co., 297 U.S. 233 (1936); Minneapolis Star and Tribune Co. v. Minn. Comm'r of Revenue, 460 U.S. 575 (1983).

upon the other. A confiscatory tax approaching 100 percent will be attacked in vain as arbitrary, but the attack is in the garb of substantive due process, not eminent domain.

Nonetheless the current distinction rests upon a sleight of hand. The point is well made by asking not *whether* the distinction between a tax and a taking should be drawn, but *how* it should be drawn. What constitutes a tax? Nineteenth-century writers began by asserting that the distinction was airtight, then defined taxation as the flip side of confiscation. Thomas Cooley, for example, was "too competent a lawyer to argue that the public-use limitation on the power of eminent domain—a limitation which appeared in almost all state constitutions—was intended to restrict the takings power."[4] Thus chapter 14 of his book *Constitutional Limitations* is titled "The Power of Taxation," while chapter 15 is titled "The Eminent Domain" (chapter 16, to complete the opposition, is called "The Police Power").[5] Yet Cooley insisted that the public use limitation in the eminent domain clause was implicit in the definition of a tax:

Everything that may be done under the name of taxation is not necessarily a tax; and it may happen that an oppressive burden imposed by the government, when it comes to be carefully scrutinized, will prove, instead of a tax, to be an unlawful confiscation of property, unwarranted by a principle of constitutional government.

In the first place, taxation having for its legitimate object the raising of money for the public purposes and proper needs of government, the exaction of moneys from the citizens for other purposes is not a proper exercise of this power, and must therefore be unauthorized.[6]

Cooley's implicit account is that a tax as a general levy is not a wrongful taking. That a single conceptual framework covers both taxes and takings is made still more explicit in Clyde Jacobs's account of the public purpose principle, which flourished in the late nineteenth century:[7]

4. Clyde E. Jacobs, *Law Writers and the Courts* 107 (1954).
5. Thomas M. Cooley, *Constitutional Limitations* (1st ed. 1868).
6. Id. at 479. The passage is discussed at length in Jacobs, supra note 4, at 107–109.
7. See Jacobs, supra note 4, at ch. 5. Jacobs noted that the Supreme Court, by a seven to two vote, "thought sufficiently well of the public purpose restriction to bring it within the scope of due process of the Fourteenth Amendment." Id. at 152–153. See Falbrook Irrigation District v. Bradley, 164 U.S. 112 (1896), where the court had used it to strike down financial assistance to

[T]he public purpose principle was a response to the belief that government powers should not be exercised so as to deprive a person (either natural or corporate) of his property unless he be guilty of a crime or of civil delinquency, or unless he receive some more or less direct compensation for that which was taken from him. The state and federal constitutions had explicitly provided for direct compensation to those persons whose property was taken by the government in the exercise of the power of eminent domain, but no provision had been made for compensatory benefits when property was taken through the avenue of taxation ... The judiciary obviously could not insist that every taxpayer receive equal benefits, nor did the judges ordinarily attempt to measure the amount of taxes against the amount of benefit. But the courts did require that the purposes for which taxes were levied and appropriations were made be such that there was a reasonable prospect that some direct benefit would or could accrue to the taxpayer as a member of the body politic.[8]

All the elements found in the analysis of takings reemerge in the taxation context: takings, justification (in the control of crime or civil delinquency), public use, and implicit compensation. This chapter explores this unitary analysis of taxes and takings. For ease of exposition I put aside all special taxes, such as those on pollutants, that might be justified under the police power, notwithstanding their disproportionate impact. I also put aside until the next chapter all taxes that are used for redistributive purposes. Here I confine my attention to the just compensation and public use limitations, which in this context tend to converge, because public use demands only a fair division of the expected surplus from government action, best measured by the same disproportionate impact test that controls the just compensation question. Here I shall first consider several forms of special taxes that have been imposed at either the federal or state level: special assessments, typically for street and sewer improvements; the more recent windfall profits tax;[9] and the severance taxes imposed upon the extraction of minerals.[10] Thereafter I

---

private manufacturers, Parkersburg v. Brown, 106 U.S. 487 (1882); Cole v. La Grange, 113 U.S. 1 (1885), even though they had allowed such assistance to railroads, a distinction that could be justified by the common carrier status of railroads; see Chapter 7.

8. Jacobs, supra note 4, at 157–158.
9. United States v. Ptasynski, 462 U.S. 74 (1983).
10. Commonwealth Edison Co. v. Montana, 453 U.S. 609 (1981).

examine the constitutional status of other estate and gift taxation and then of the progressive income tax.

Special Assessments

The history of special assessments and their constitutional supervision is long and complex, and I can review it only briefly here.[11] To take a simple model, assume that paving a public street will provide $200 worth of benefits to the individuals whose property abuts it and that the cost of the paving is $100. Assume also that others in the community benefit if the street is paved. In principle, the street should be paved, so the only question is how to finance and supervise the project. One possible response is to rely upon voluntary arrangements by the abutting landowners. Yet because the street is a common pool resource, this contractual arrangement will typically falter because of holdout and free-rider problems. Everyone would prefer the street to be paved without his contribution. The net effect is that the improvement typically will not be made, leaving everyone worse off for the want of public intervention. Under the eminent domain clause, the public use hurdle is easily surmounted so long as the surplus is evenly divided among the affected landowners.[12]

Both the public use and the just compensation questions turn, therefore, on the matching of costs and benefits for abutters, an issue on which measurement problems obviously dominate.[13] Before the Civil War it was common practice to assume the benefits received individually. Some constitutional decisions in the eminent domain tradition demanded this[14] by treating the special taxes as partial takings of the land,

---

11. For a more detailed treatment, see Stephen Diamond, "The Death and Transfiguration of Benefit Taxation: Special Assessments in Nineteenth-Century America," 12 *J. Legal Stud.* 201 (1983).

12. See id. at 209, referring to special assessments for private roads, that is, those "open only to those who paid for them"—which could be for a public purpose if operated under common-carrier-type restrictions.

13. The cases here all concern local improvements, with local benefits. External benefits are apt to dominate with superhighways, for which special assessments are highly inappropriate. Consider the extreme case, in which the new highway makes transportation into the local region costless. To charge the cost of the improvement against the local property is to mismatch benefits and costs if the improvement eliminates the site-bound positive economic rents of the nearby lands.

14. See, e.g., People ex rel. Post v. Mayor of Brooklyn, 6 Bar. 209 (N.Y. Sup. Ct. 1849), rev'd in People ex rel. Griffin v. Mayor of Brooklyn, 4 N.Y. 419 (1851), allowing formula assessments.

---

thereby overcoming the rigid division between the taxing and eminent domain powers. The objection to individualized calculations was that their administrative costs and their general unreliability ate up most, if not all, of the gains from installing the improvement. The point, moreover, carries constitutional weight: if the administrative costs exceed the anticipated surplus, then the special assessment becomes a bonanza for contractors and assessors, while the landowners are left worse off.[15]

The alternative schemes of measurement, which came into increasing prominence toward the end of the nineteenth century, computed changes by some general formula, typically front footage, acreage, or assessed valuation, as a surrogate measure for private benefit received from the tax. A reduction in administrative costs was thus achieved by introducing a less precise system of valuation, whose offsetting advantage was its greater resistance to political abuse. Individualized changes, of course, directly measure the compensation conferred, while formula charges depend upon a disproportionate impact test. It is not surprising that both practice and case law oscillated uneasily between the two measures. The emerging consensus in the early part of the twentieth century favored relaxed judicial intervention, which basically permitted the state to choose between the two measures of benefit conferred. Holmes himself called this choice one of "degree,"[16] because there is no obvious way to show that one method of computing benefits is both cheaper and more accurate than the other for all cases.

The disproportionate impact standard, however, did not result in complete abdication of all judicial scrutiny over special assessments. Instead, the inquiry became transformed into one which asked whether some defect in the overall procedure made it unlikely that an individual owner received his fair share of net benefits (or even net losses) from a given special assessment. The law thus shows anew the linkage between the eminent domain clause and government procedures that the general theory requires. One concern was whether there was a right of hearing on the matter of benefit conferred, at least where benefits are calculated individually.[17] As a substantive matter, constitutional supervision was triggered by strong evidence of a fatal mismatch between benefits and cost. In *Norwood v. Baker*,[18] a street opening case, a special assessment based on front footage was imposed upon a single landowner, who was

---

15. For a discussion of the abuses, see Diamond, supra note 11, at 210–214.
16. Martin v. District of Columbia, 205 U.S. 135, 139 (1907).
17. See, e.g., Londoner v. City & County of Denver, 210 U.S. 373 (1908).
18. 172 U.S. 269 (1898).

required both to compensate herself for the land lost and for the cost to the public treasury of running the valuation. "In our judgment, the exaction from the owner of private property of the cost of a public improvement in substantial excess of the special benefits accruing him is, to the extent of such excess, a taking, under the guise of taxation, of private property for public use without compensation."[19] The nature of the common pool problem is far from self-evident where only a single landowner is involved and that owner is not compensated for his losses in the forced exchange. Yet that decision was quickly and rightly qualified to make it clear that in ordinary circumstances any of the available methods of assessment were constitutionally permissible in the absence of evidence of a mismatch between taxes and benefits.[20] That the caveat was not empty is clear, for example, in *Martin v. District of Columbia*,[21] where Holmes struck down a special assessment imposed upon the landowners for an alley running through their block, on the ground that the costs (including costs of running the assessment) were three times the value of all the land.

The questions of special assessments go beyond the particulars of any individual assessment scheme. One difficult question concerns how the special assessment is integrated with the general property taxes levied within a community. The justification for the special assessment is that the parties within the area obtain a special benefit that requires special burdens. External benefits to outsiders are ignored because they are offset by the external benefits received by the group taxed when roads built elsewhere are similarly financed. To be sure, it is not necessary to finance all the streets in a town by special assessments, for a consistent practice of paying for all street improvements out of general revenues keeps both benefits and burdens in lockstep. The economic arguments as to which mode of operation is best are generally left to the legislature, given the abuses implicit in both regimes and the obvious closeness of the question.

In principle, however, the situation is very different if the state decides to finance some local improvements by special taxes and others of like kind and quality by general revenues, for now the parties who are specially assessed bear a community burden that is not offset by any return benefit. So, too, there is no objection to consistently including in any

19. Id. at 279.
20. French v. Barber Asphalt Paving Co., 181 U.S. 324 (1901). The decision echoed the earlier treatment of Thomas M. Cooley, *Constitutional Limitations* 618 (5th ed. 1883).
21. 205 U.S. 135 (1907).

special assessment a lump sum for the payment of future repairs and expenses. But the case becomes very different if other repairs are financed out of general charges, for the same built-in imbalance reemerges, albeit on a more limited scale. To be sure, the state should be allowed to show that some special benefit to the assessed properties justifies the differential burden. But unless that proof is forthcoming, the disproportionate impact test requires consistent taxing over time across similarly situated parcels. These restraints, moreover, are sufficiently general that they need not give rise to any enormous burdens of litigation. In sum, the whole history of special assessments shows the futility of maintaining a rigid categorical distinction between taxing and takings. The want of extensive litigation today does not show that the earlier restrictions on special assessments have lost all their validity. It only shows that the constitutional requirements are routinely satisfied by the institutional framework used for handling the assessment, whose importance has diminished with changes in technology over time.

Windfall Profits Tax

Special assessments also include taxes that have been imposed upon particular goods and services at the federal level.[22] The windfall profits tax has been challenged under the uniformity clause of the Constitution, "but all Duties, Imposts and Excises shall be uniform throughout the United States."[23] because of the special treatment granted some Alaskan oil. The analysis of uniformity and of the takings clause run on parallel tracks, and both provisions invalidate the tax. In its basic design, the windfall profits tax is imposed upon the difference between the market value of crude oil and the price (according to classification) at which it could be sold under the regime of maximum price regulation in effect at the time of passage.[24] The tax was set at between 60 and 75 percent and has resulted in the collection of billions of dollars because of the wide spread between market and regulated prices.

Standing alone, the tax exerts a clearly disproportionate effect upon

---

22. Much of the following discussion is based upon my treatment of the windfall profits tax in Richard A. Epstein, "Taxation, Regulation, and Confiscation," 20 *Osgoode Hall L.J.* 433, 443–445 (1982), which was published before the 9–0 Supreme Court decision in United States v. Ptasynski, 462 U.S. 74 (1983), sustaining the tax.

23. Art. I, § 8, cl. 1.

24. Crude Oil Windfall Profit Tax of 1980, Pub. L. No. 96–223, 94 Stat. 229 (1980).

the owners of crude oil, because burdens and benefits are mismatched. That its purpose is to do just that is clear from two of its central features. First, large portions of the tax revenue are paid into a general trust fund, which is used for the improvement of transportation, the assistance of the aged, and other social purposes. The very existence of the fund is powerful evidence that the taxes collected do not provide any special benefit to the owners of crude oil on whom it is levied. Second, the tax is constructed to prevent the shifting of the burden to consumers by adjustments in the underlying price,[25] thereby concentrating its effect upon the owners of the oil.

In one sense the tax was a blessing to the producers of crude oil, because it left them better off than they were under the previous regime of rate regulation. Therefore, if those price regulations were constitutional, then there is no principled way that the tax can be attacked as confiscatory by thse whose economic position it improves. But in fact the scheme of selective price controls is an unconstitutional taking of private property, as are limits on the right of disposition in voluntary transactions.[26] The only proper baseline against which to measure the tax is the market price. When that is done, the disproportionate impact is clear enough, as are the negative wealth effects, which guarantee at least some uncompensated losses.

In dealing with this test, however, it might be tempting to say that the taxes' benefits and burdens are so diffused through the public at large that it is quite impossible to learn whether they are systematically matched. Much of the regulated oil is owned by public corporations whose stock ownership is spread across a wide number of individuals via direct or institutional holdings. But if this argument were taken seriously, compensation could be denied when the government takes land held by public corporations. The argument is wrong, whether the confiscation is outright or disguised. Accounting for the pass-through of tax burdens only shows that many persons are on both sides of the line. It does not indicate that all persons are on both sides of the line, much less in equal proportions: if they were, no single group of individuals would support or oppose the tax. In addition, it is easy to identify cases of clear disproportion in persons with extensive holdings in crude oil, say

25. The theory here was that as the tax is on profits only, the seller of the crude oil will maximize his own return by selling at the same level he would have sold at without the tax. The argument as stated ignored at least one important second-order effect. The tax will reduce the total amount of oil produced, and the shift in supply will tend to raise the market price.

26. See Chapter 17.

in the form of working or royalty interests. There is, moreover, no duty for investors to diversify away this political risk in advance, any more than a farmer must buy land in a neighboring state as a hedge against local confiscation for highway construction.[27]

At most there remains the slender possibility that diversification of holdings is so powerful that the effects of the tax are disproportionate when their full economic incidence is understood. But that possibility is far from self-evident, so only one argument for invalidation of the windfall profits tax is that it reduces the likelihood of error in administering the tax law. The best that can be said for the tax is that, with private pass-throughs, it operates in a fashion closely akin to the general revenue tax. But why take the chance that it will not work this way? If the ideal tax is a general revenue tax, then the state should be required to use it. There is surely no reason to allow it to hide between factual uncertainties of its own creation. Nor can it be said that the special tax is needed because a parallel increase in general revenue taxes is politically unacceptable. The disproportionate impact test is used on matters of taxation precisely to resist those political pressures, given that direct judicial supervision of public expenditures is not possible.[28]

The tax must be invalidated because there is no workable scheme to compensate those who are forced to pay. Everyone is made worse if the government must bear the expenses of collecting the tax and then paying out the proceeds to the thousands who may colorably claim it. Any such procedure is sure to produce more error and confusion than a sim-

27. Indeed, there are often offsetting benefits that limit the degree of diversification. For those with real expertise in an area, the gains from specialization usually outweigh the additional risks of engaging in limited activities. That is why there is division of labor within ordinary markets. In any event, the risks to which one should be properly subject are market risks, not the depredations of private citizens or the government.

28. The government is well aware of this problem and has organized the situation so that the tax is collected before it can be constitutionally challenged. Under the applicable law, constitutional challenges to the collection of the tax cannot be raised when the tax is withheld, but only when it is due, after the close of the tax year. Internal Revenue Code §7421 (1984) prohibits suits to restrain assessment or collection of taxes; 28 U.S.C. §2201 (1976) prohibits federal courts from issuing declaratory judgments in federal tax cases. This delay creates a powerful incentive to validate the tax, given that the moneys have already been spent and alternative funds cannot be raised. All of this clearly burdens a constitutional right; the proper regime is one which applies the usual standard to taxing statutes: an injunction against collecting (or, at least, spending the collected moneys) where there is serious doubt of the constitutionality of the tax, coupled with an expedited decision on the merits.

ple nullification of the tax. And the procedure would cost money that must be raised by taking it from someone. As there are sure to be errors in matching payments with proceeds, the injunction would be strictly required even if the legislature were so misguided as to pay individualized compensation, doubtless by formulas that would undercompensate.[29]

The Supreme Court in *United States v. Ptasynski*[30] did not so much as mention the takings arguments, which were effectively undercut by its own precedents. But the issue raised in the case—that the tax was invalid because it was not uniformly imposed, given that some Alaskan oil was not subject to the special tax—bears a close kinship to the disproportionate impact test, even if uniformity under the Constitution only refers to geographical uniformity.[31] There are good reasons why uniformity should be treated as an absolute condition for all taxes it governs. It is a clear way to prevent favoritism between states and the rent-seeking behavior that this can induce, and as the Supreme Court has noted, the provision was enacted in all likelihood with that end in view.[32] More precisely, given that all revenues are fungible, setting taxes is the very type of enterprise in which government discretion is apt to do more harm than good, thereby justifying a powerful per se rule that limits it. The court's conclusion, that "the Uniformity Clause gives Congress wide latitude in deciding what to tax and does not prohibit it from considering geographically isolated problems"[33] is inconsistent with both the language and the structure of the clause, and with the constitutional theory that animates both.

Indeed, *Ptasynski* simply reduces the uniformity clause to the pablum so characteristic of the "rational basis" test generally used for economic liberties, which is no test at all. The court said that Congress may think

29. For a comparison of the compensation arrangements made in the buyout of lands for urban renewal, see Chapter 12.

30. 462 U.S. 74 (1983).

31. See, e.g., the Head Money Cases, 112 U.S. 580 (1884), sustaining a uniform tax on all persons who entered the United States by port but not on those who came by rail; Knowlton v. Moore, 178 U.S. 41 (1900), validating a progressive inheritance tax, discussed below.

32. See 2 Joseph Story, *Commentaries on the Constitution of the United States* § 958 (1833).

33. 462 U.S. at 84. The chief authority for the point was the Regional Rail Reorganization Cases, 419 U.S. 102 (1974), which allowed a bankruptcy reorganization of regional railroads in the face of the uniformity language in the bankruptcy clause, art. I, §8, cl. 4. Even here there is an important difference—money is fungible, railroads as such are not.

it fit to give a break to oil and gas that is especially costly to produce. What conceivable economic justification is there for shifting from low- to high-cost production? Every bit of known theory suggests that the ideal tax should not alter the choices between investments, an end that is admirably served by the uniformity clause. The feeble rationalization given in *Ptasynski* shows how a single incorrect argument can transform a strict prohibition into a blanket license for legislative deals and manipulation between states as well as individuals.[34]

State Severance Taxes and Beyond

The windfall profits tax has as its state analogue the large severance taxes upon various energy sources located within the state. Thus in *Commonwealth Edison v. Montana*,[35] the state imposed a tax equal to 30 percent "of the contract sales" price of all coal sold, whether in intrastate or interstate commerce. The tax itself was based upon value and not upon tonnage, and the amount was effectively equal to seven times the previous tax levels, although no new services were provided to the owners of the property against which the taxes were levied. Because the tax showed the utter want of judicial protection of individual rights against abuses of taxation, *Commonwealth Edison* also turned on federalism questions, in this instance whether the tax imposed a disproportionate burden upon out-of-state consumers.[36]

The special assessment cases give clues to the irregularities of the

---

34. The role of the disproportionate impact test in interstate conflicts is not limited to a proper appreciation of the uniformity clause. The use of nondiscrimination tests to measure whether imported goods are improperly taxed (see Michelin Tire Corp. v. Wages, 423 U.S. 276 [1976]) is yet another application of disproportionate impact, as is the principle of intergovernmental immunity that looks with far greater toleration upon general taxes that are applied in a nondiscriminatory fashion to the other sovereign, be it state or federal. See, e.g., McCulloch v. Maryland, 17 U.S. (4 Wheat.) 316 (1819), noting that the prohibition on state taxation "does not extend to a tax paid by the real property of the bank, in common with other property within the state, nor to a tax imposed on the interest which the citizens of Maryland may hold in this institution, in common with other property of the same description throughout the State." Id. at 436. The theme is developed extensively in John Hart Ely, *Democracy and Distrust* 83–86 (1980), where the nondiscriminatory tax is treated rightly as evidence of the proper functioning of the political process.

35. 453 U.S. 609 (1981).

36. For arguments that it did, see Epstein, *supra* note 22, at 445–449.

Montana severance tax. One sign of its illicit nature was that half of the revenues were placed in a special fund that could be appropriated only by a vote of three-fourths of the members of both houses. A second sign was that the general property and income taxes in the state were reduced, highlighting the shift from general to special taxes as part of an overall plan in which outsiders could not share in the gains pro rata.

A number of arguments could be made to support the constitutionality of the tax, but none of them suffice. The tax was said to encourage the preservation of coal within the state's borders. At most, that argument establishes the public use that allows the taking. It does not begin to establish a police power justification that allows the taking without compensation. Nor can it be argued that the tax is needed to offset the increased benefits that coal products received because of the increased value of their product, for the state can capture that gain in two separate ways: a uniform sales tax based upon value, which will result in a higher yield as prices increase, or a state income tax. The special severance tax, therefore, can be justified only by a showing of special benefits conferred, of which there are none.

The decision in *Commonwealth Edison* might also be defended on the ground that, unless the court refuses to invalidate the tax in the extreme case, it will find itself enmeshed in an endless review of every form of local government taxation. As a general matter, that assertion is clearly false, because a uniform sales tax on all goods will meet whatever constitutional standards are imposed, while allowing the state to reach whatever revenue target it sets. To be sure, there will be some difficult cases. Suppose, for example, the state removes all sales tax from basic food staples. A huge number of individuals and firms are affected, so the pass-through arguments gain in credibility. Although exempting food from taxation may be advertised as an implicit subsidy to low-income individuals,[37] it only invites the type of legislative mischief that uniform levels of taxation avoid, as for example the redistributive struggles between chain food stores and restaurants. Accordingly, such an exemption should be struck down, as should efforts to segregate, for example, general real estate taxes by the type of real estate (residential commercial, manufacturing) subject to the tax. In all cases the uniform level of taxation allows the state to reach any revenue target it chooses, without having to resort to special taxes that invite political intrigue and an overall diminution in wealth.

37. See Chapter 19.

Income Taxation: Progressivity

A more difficult and controversial question is, what limitations does the eminent domain clause (or arguments that imitate its basic structure) place upon the operation of the income tax, insofar as it collects moneys for the provision of pure public goods? As elsewhere, it is impossible to measure benefits and costs directly. We must see whether the income tax produces a disproportionate impact and whether it enlarges the overall pie. The obvious target of this critique is progressive taxation.

The critique here is not taxation as such, nor all the inequities it necessarily produces. When the United States government decides to commit troops in foreign combat, its actions will be supported by some and opposed by others. Nonetheless, the constitutional command for a single foreign policy (with responsibility divided between the president and the Congress) makes it impossible to simultaneously satisfy all points of view. To insist that classic public (nondivisible, nonexclusive) goods provide equal subjective benefits, much less benefits that exceed tax payments, is entirely inconsistent with our (indeed any) system of organized government. Some measure of equality may be provided simply because the government makes an enormous number of collective decisions that are supported by different groups for their own reasons. For some persons the balance will not even out in the long run. The price of collective life is that disappointed citizens cannot obtain tax refunds for unwanted public actions, either case by case or on an aggregated basis.

Nonetheless, it does not follow that there are no constraints on how the government can raise taxes to discharge its public functions. The original Constitution limits the taxing power. Congress has power "to lay and collect Taxes, Duties, Imposts and Excises, to pay the Debts and to provide for the common Defence and general Welfare of the United States."[38] The structure of the clause suggests that the proper objects of taxation are limited in nature, while the references to "common defense" and "general welfare" reinforce the kinship between the constitutional constraint and the standard economic accounts of public goods. Indeed, the "general welfare" of the United States is not an unlimited grant of power; it should be read narrowly, in parallel to the other two heads, public debt and common defense, and in sharp opposition to any system of coerced transfer payments between citizens.

Yet over time the limitations on the taxation power have eroded. In

38. Art. I, §8, cl. 1.

United States v. Butler[39] the court rightly recognized that the general welfare language constrained the objects of taxation.[40] However, it then held that the limit included not only matters intrinsic to the clause but also the exercise of the specific powers granted to Congress elsewhere in Article I. In *Butler* this reading allowed the court to strike down a processing tax imposed under the Agricultural Adjustment Act by taking the view that agriculture was a purely local matter, outside (in 1936) the scope of the commerce clause. In forging this linkage between taxation and commerce, the court neutralized all the internal limitations upon taxation, for within the decade Congress could regulate virtually all economic activities, including all agricultural activities, under the commerce clause.[41]

The developments under the commerce clause and the general welfare clause show once again how easily the Supreme Court can convert a charter of limited government into one of plenary legislative power. But even if the general welfare clause is read narrowly, thus confining the proper object of taxation to the provision of classic public goods, the distribution of the burden across citizens remains critical. That question can be approached either by considering the implicit limits in the idea of taxation, as was done by the nineteenth-century public purpose doctrine, or by considering the eminent domain clause proper, which in principle should limit the power to tax just as it limits the other powers conferred on Congress under Article I.[42]

39. United States v. Butler, 297 U.S. 1 (1936).

40. Even on this point there was controversy, as one position limited the power to tax to ends contained within the very clause and not elsewhere. See the discussion, 247 U.S. at 65–68. In good lawyer's style Justice Roberts resolved the question in favor of the broader view of the clause, which he then found too narrow to sustain the tax in question.

41. See, e.g., Wickard v. Filburn, 317 U.S. 111 (1942).

42. As a matter of history, one could argue that the question of progressivity was settled by the Sixteenth Amendment, passed in 1913, which provides: "Congress shall have power to lay and collect taxes on incomes, from whatever source derived, without apportionment among the several States, and without regard to any census or enumeration." The decision was passed to overrule Pollock v. Farmers Loan and Trust 157 U.S. 429 (1895), which had struck down a progressive income tax but only on the ground that it included a direct tax on property, not apportioned among the states. The Sixteenth Amendment could be read to have reaffirmed *Pollock* insofar as it tolerated progressive taxation, even though on its face it is directed to a very different issue. I believe, however, that the clause should be read as it was written, to say that the power of taxation is no longer limited by the demands to apportion among the states in accordance with a census or enumeration. So read, the Sixteenth Amendment says that fairness between states is no longer

I have shown that no direct measurement of public goods aids in deciding how to allocate the tax burden. But motive and disproportionate
impact still remain. The redistributive motive behind progressive taxation seems too clear to deny. Indeed, the motive is often considered a
central social justification for progressive taxation. But the more important arguments run to impact. The disproportionate impact test necessarily ignores all wealth effects attributable to political disagreement
over issues of war and peace. But there is no similar necessity in avoiding
the possible correlations between income (or wealth) levels and benefits
received. In voluntary markets the tastes of private parties are highly
dependent upon income levels. A similar assumption seems equally
plausible in the context of public goods. A tax that worked on a simple
per capita basis (that is, where the charge was constant regardless of the
level of the income, so that, in principle, the tax could exceed the full
amount of income) does not have any obvious virtue.[43] Quite the contrary, if a capitation tax offers a very bad measure of indirect benefits,
then the mismatch it fosters dooms the tax under the eminent domain
clause as an illicit redistribution to the rich.

What forms of general revenue taxes are permissible? Here the choice
rests essentially between two broad classes of taxes on net income. The
first class consists of proportionate taxes, under which a constant percentage of net income is taxed, from the first dollar of net income to the
last. The second class is that of progressive income taxes. These share
with proportionate income taxes the feature that the total amount of tax
(strictly) increases the total amount of income. General revenue taxes
are also structured with marginal tax rates that, far from being constant,
strictly increase with income and frequently include some zero-tax income at the bottom. Both progressive and proportionate taxes permit
the government to reach any revenue target, for the rate of taxation may
be set as high as Congress wishes. The only formal constraint is distributional. In principle, the proper tax could be progressive if the benefits
from government operations increased more steeply than private in-

---

a concern for the federal tax laws. It does not address fairness between individuals.

43. See Cooley, supra note 20, at 613. "Taxation is the equivalent for the
protection which the government affords to the persons and property of its citizens; and as all alike are protected, so all alike should bear the burden, in
proportion to the interests secured. Taxes by the poll are justly regarded as
odious, and are seldom resorted to for the collection of revenue." In principle
the same passage could be read as an argument against progressive taxation,
perhaps even on constitutional grounds.

come. But there is no real evidence to support that conclusion, and (transfer payments still to one side) there is some intuitive reason to deny it. The interest in bodily security, for example, is probably not linear with income, for people with taxable low incomes may tend to value bodily security highly, especially if they are young with extensive human capital or imputed income.

Suppose, however, that the question is treated as one where no reliable evidence is obtainable on the benefit function. One conclusion might be that any general taxation schedule generated by the political process is permissible and that the Supreme Court in its brief deliberations on the question was correct: the matter of tax schedules falls exclusively within the domain of the legislature, even if taxation is a taking of private property.[44] There is arguably some "direct" benefit provided for the taxes, so even Cooley's formulation does not rule out progressive taxation.

Nonetheless this approach overstates the political consequences of imperfect information on the distribution of public benefits. The absence of a precise benefit schedule does not end the inquiry. Instead, it requires us to take into account second-order considerations in order to minimize the possibilities of error, that is, any mismatch between taxes imposed and indirect benefits received. The uncertainty in individual benefit schedules requires reformulating the fundamental question: what tax schedule, all things considered, minimizes the expected mismatch of taxes and benefits?

For a variety of reasons, the flat tax seems better able to do this than any other possible candidate. At one level it quite literally imposes a proportionate burden upon all sources of income and thus passes the disproportionate impact test which is so critical to this branch of eminent domain law. But the formal equivalence is not necessarily decisive, because in practice the flat tax cannot assure a perfect correspondence between taxes and indirect benefits. Still, the fit is far from random. The flat tax certainly gives a respectable matching, and it is clearly superior to a highly progressive tax, where the redistributive motive is powerful evidence of redistributive effects.[45] In addition, a flat tax dispenses with the need to choose one of an infinite set of arbitrary progressive schedules. Some other baseline (specifying the level of progressivity allowed

44. See, e.g., Walter Blum and Harry Kalven, *The Uneasy Case for Progressive Taxation* (1953).

45. See Michael Graetz, "To Praise the Estate Tax, Not to Bury It," 93 *Yale L.J.* 259, 274–278 (1983). The explicit transfer justifications are discussed in Chapter 19.

regardless of rates) might well be part of a more comprehensive constitutional scheme, but in its absence, the flat tax is the most "natural" approach.

The case for the constitutional flat tax is reinforced when one considers the political dimension. When the degree of progression is allowed to vary freely, an important constitutional bulwark against uncompensated takings is removed. The progressive tax increases the frequency and intensity of legislative rent seeking by increasing the expected gains of factions. The contrast between general tort rules and general tax rules is quite sharp, for most people do not lie behind a veil of ignorance about their expected incomes. Private efforts for political gain will be resisted by prospective losers, generating the typical negative-sum game that the eminent domain clause is designed to forestall. As the pie becomes smaller, the likelihood of having net losers increases. The rigidity and simplicity of the flat tax are the best controls against this possibility. By reducing the gains from rent seeking, it reduces its overall levels. By increasing the size of the pie, the flat tax tends to increase the size of each of its slices. In addition, the system of constant marginal rates simplifies private planning in response to taxation, thus offering additional sources of gain by reducing the levels of tax avoidance both lawful and unlawful. The protection afforded by a flat tax is far from ideal, because there will be some political programs from which one group gains all (or most of) the benefits for which another group is made to pay a proportionate share of the costs. But this point only illustrates the two implicit premises: first, the only way to stop all government abuses is to have perfect knowledge of individual benefit schedules from public goods, and second, a disproportionate impact test is always underinclusive in that it cannot ferret out all types of abuse. Yet the flat tax should not be rejected because it cannot stop all abuse, so long as it can reduce its overall levels.

There is no real cost to reading the eminent domain clause as requiring the flat tax. The flat tax does not place any total revenue constraint upon the government, nor does it hamstring the legislature and the executive from carrying out their constitutional functions, such as appointing judges or in waging war. But no parallel discretion is needed in deciding who should pay salaries or fund armies. Money is perfectly fungible; a dollar is a dollar, regardless of the source. The gains from discretion in funding are likely to be vanishingly small, while the abuses it invites are likely to impose real costs on the system.

The flat tax also imposes minimal demands on the courts, which are not required to run prisons or mental hospitals or to investigate the merits of political decisions. The flat tax has striking parallels to the rule of one man, one vote used in reapportionment cases. It is easy to administer, it provides a better incentive structure for political choice, and it does not replace political choices with judicial decisions either on how much to tax or how to spend the revenues so raised.

In response to the above arguments one could argue that the proper concern is not with nominal rates but with effective rates, and that the effective levels of progression are far lower than those in the tax tables.[46] But these numbers are often very difficult to credit because they do not include the costs taxpayers incur to avoid paying highly progressive taxes—the decline in yield sustained by holders of municipal bonds, the added business risks of tax shelters, and the extensive legal and accounting fees. In addition, it is very odd to defend a progressive tax on the ground that it yields proportionate rates. It is far better to recognize that the case for the flat tax is every bit as robust after these complications are taken into account, for the flat tax still maximizes the likelihood that every individual will be left better off after the tax is imposed.

A second objection takes a different tack: if the progressive income tax is ruled unconstitutional, then the entire structure of the Internal Revenue Code may be fair game for constitutional review. If only proportionate taxes on net income are allowed, then the definition of taxable income becomes a constitutional matter. But it is one thing for the definition of income to become a constitutional matter; it is quite another to insist that any deviation from the ideal definition of income is constitutionally infirm. Quite the opposite: any deviation from an ideal, Haig-Simons definition of income can be tolerated so long as that deviation does not generate any systematic disproportionate impact.[47] Thus there is no constitutional requirement that unrealized appreciation from real estate or stocks be taxed or that future pensions be taken into income before they are paid over, or that accelerated depreciation be allowed (or disallowed) for business property, or that deductions for moving expenses, medical expenses, or casualty losses be required or disallowed.

---

46. See, generally, *Income Tax Schedules, Distribution of Taxpayers and Revenues* (OECD Paris, 1981), which reports, among other things, that in the United States the individual marginal rates for persons in the tenth percentile are 16 percent, while for those in the ninetieth percentile they are 36 percent, no small difference.

47. Henry Simons defined personal income as the "algebraic sum of (1) the market value of rights exercised in consumption and (2) the change in the value of the store of property rights between the beginning and the end of the period in question." Henry C. Simons, *Personal Income Taxation* 50 (1938).

The switch from an income to a consumption tax (by allowing a deduction for savings and for reinvested gains) or back again, is also entirely within the legislative power. Likewise, nothing demands that partnerships be taxed like corporations or like trusts. Trusts, annuities, and pensions need not be taxed at the same time and by the same rules. Partnership income may be passed through, and corporate income may be subject to a double tax, while only retained earnings are taxed to trusts. The only remaining constraint is that all forms of ordinary income, when taxed, are taxed at flat rates. Nor are there any constitutional grounds for attacking the separate treatment of capital assets, property used in the trade or business of the taxpayer, or for using a six-month or a twelve-month holding period for long-term capital gains rates. All are permissible, as the tax law remains free, through the application of general rules, to adopt different treatments for different types of assets. Some might want to tax capital gains at ordinary income rates before gains are realized.[48] Others may argue that realization is an appropriate trigger for taxation, if only to avoid forced sales of assets. Similarly, lower capital gains rates (including zero taxes for reinvested capital) are justified to counter the lock-in effect (arising from the taxpayer's power to determine when gain is realized from an investment) or to neutralize the effects of inflation on capital assets. The gains and losses of these tax rules are so heavily diversified throughout society that it seems pointless to challenge them under any disproportionate impact test.

The results may be quite different for some of the explicit subsidies that are worked into the taxation system. For example, rules that allow percentage depletion in excess of costs seem to create a clear subsidy to mining or oil and gas. Although there is no way to challenge the *timing* of available deductions for capital items (because there is no obvious baseline against which the timing question can be measured), it seems easy enough administratively to strike down the cost recovery in excess of actual expenditures for the very reasons it is condemned in ordinary policy discussions: the rules create a systematic mismatch between burdens and benefits that allows some individuals to pay less than a pro rata share, under any definition of income.

How far the flat tax principle should be pushed is, of course, a difficult question. Suppose it was argued that the deduction for interest on home mortgages creates an implicit subsidy for owners as against renters

---

48. See, e.g., David Slawson, "Taxing as Ordinary Income the Appreciation of Publicly Held Stock," 76 *Yale L.J.* 623 (1967).

that can only be eliminated by either striking out the homeowners' deduction or by creating a like deduction for renters for that portion of rent used to service an underlying mortgage. There may be something to say for this proposal, but it is unclear that it reaches constitutional proportions, for at every stage there is (and has been) enormous freedom of choice to develop land or to acquire housing in either market. The effects here seem so diffuse across the population at large that the current result might well stand, especially as it is so heavily embedded in long-term mortgage arrangements.

Indeed, any more elaborate dissection of particular provisions of the Internal Revenue Code reveals the strength of the constitutional prohibition on progressive taxation. Far from creating ambiguity in the basic tax provisions, the flat-rate tax reduces the need to control other forms of abuse by direct regulation. Because every one faces the same marginal tax rates, for example, the rich no longer obtain a special advantage from investing in tax-free municipal bonds or from making charitable contributions. The tax advantages of the interest deduction for high-income homeowners are similarly reduced, as are the gains from percentage depletion. Splitting of income by gifts and family trusts loses all of its tax attraction if every dollar, from first to last, is subject to the proportionate tax. The few remaining differences between tax regimes are largely eliminated as individuals are free (either directly or through pension trusts and stocks that hold their assets) to diversify their financial holdings and choose investments with the greatest marginal tax advantages. The shift to proportionate taxes can only eliminate the administrative costs of the system (which are takings from everyone) and thereby increase the size of the overall pie, and in all likelihood the size of its individual slices.

But, it may be asked, why worry about progressive taxation when there is no effective way to control deficit financing, on the one hand, or inflation, on the other? The question shows the close relationship between the three devices but, far from showing why it is unimportant to control taxation, it points to the opposite conclusion. Deficit financing and inflation tend to work in a pro rata fashion, so it becomes difficult for any group to exploit that situation for an organized gain. With deficit financing, the costs are reflected in increased interest payments which will be pro rata charges against the public at large if progressive taxation is eliminated. Banning progressive taxes, therefore, introduces a welcome symmetry among the three modes of deficit government finance. As all are borne roughly proportionately, there will be lower factional gains from the choice of financing devices, providing yet another limitation on the potential for abuse. The case for the progressive tax is not "uneasy." It is wrong.

Estate and Gift Taxation

The proper treatment of the various transfer taxes—estate, gift, inheritance—is even easier. As constructed, transfer taxes are usually highly progressive, with large exemptions at the bottom and steeply higher marginal rates thereafter. The redistributive motive furnishes the major explanation for these taxes.[49] Their disproportionate impact is manifest and is without a corresponding special benefit. These taxes are levied upon individuals who are already subject to the full complement of income and excise taxes. If some portion of the common cost is not defrayed by these taxes, then proportionate transfer taxes could make up the difference. Nonetheless, progressive transfer taxes are subject to the same objections as progressive income taxes, both in their failure to match benefits and costs and in the open invitation to economic rent seeking. The recent liberalization of the transfer taxes[50] has reduced the bite by (1) increasing individual exclusions per year to $10,000 per transferor-transferee, (2) introducing (in phases) a $600,000 exemption from estate taxes for the gross estate, and (3) providing a marital deduction for all interspousal transfers. The net effect of these rules is to remove the burden of the transfer tax from all but a tiny fraction of the population, which only intensifies the selective impact, thereby rendering the tax more vulnerable to a takings challenge.

Nonetheless, progressive transfer taxes are a fixed star in the current constitutional firmament, for the challenges to them were easily brushed

---

49. "Theorists have developed a number of other defenses of inheritance taxation. It has been suggested, for example, that the death tax is an appropriate toll charged by the state for use of the probate machinery and for other services in facilitating the transfer of private property at death. Others have argued that the state is collecting a belated fee for protecting the property during the decedent's lifetime, or more cynically, that it is levying a kind of penalty for any tax evasion the decedent may have indulged in during life. Still others assert that the inheritance comes as a windfall; therefore the tax imposes no sacrifice on the heirs, and they have an ability to pay justifies the levy . . . But it is hard to escape the conclusion that today's gift and estate taxes rest squarely on equalitarian foundations, to which these other theories are little more than decorative buttresses." Boris Bittker, *Federal Income, Estate and Gift Taxation* 990–991 (3d ed. 1964).

50. See generally, Economic Recovery Tax Act of 1981, Pub. L. 97–34, 95 Stat. 172, 299 (1981). For a summary and criticism of the provisions, see Graetz, supra note 45.

aside early on. *Magoun v. Illinois Trust & Savings Bank* [51] sustained progressive state inheritance taxes. Shortly thereafter the Supreme Court, in *Knowlton v. Moore*,[52] sustained a progressive federal inheritance tax enacted during the Spanish American War. At the end of World War I, in *New York Trust v. Eisner*,[53] Holmes relied squarely on *Knowlton* to sustain the more highly progressive features of the then recent estate tax.[54] These decisions do not address the takings issue as such, resting only on general declarations that the courts stand ready to intervene in the event of massive government abuse.[55] However, the eminent domain clause is clearly implicated in all these decisions, as is shown by the chief arguments used to sustain these taxes, first in *Magoun* and then in the subsequent cases: "1. An inheritance tax is not one on property, but one on the succession. 2. The right to take property by devise or descent is a creature of the law, and not a natural right—a privilege, and therefore the authority which confers it may impose conditions upon it."[56]

A moment's reflection reveals the infirmities of this position. As regards the first proposition, there is no principled distinction between the right of property and the right of succession. The conception of property includes the exclusive rights of possession, use, and disposition. The right of disposition includes dispositions during life, by gift or by sale, and it includes dispositions at death, which are limited only by the status claims of family members protected, for example, by rules relating to dower and forced shares. There is no residual claim that runs in favor of strangers or of the public at large.

Similarly, the second argument in *Magoun* is but a restatement of naked positivism, utterly inconsistent with a constitutional theory of private property or limited government. The eminent domain clause is designed to limit the power of the legislature; it can achieve that end only if it accepts some natural law account of property that is able to re-

---

51. 170 U.S. 283 (1898).
52. 178 U.S. 41 (1900).
53. 256 U.S. 345 (1921).
54. An estate tax is more progressive than an inheritance tax because in the former the entire wealth of the decedent is lumped together, regardless of the number and identity of the beneficiaries under a will. With an inheritance tax each share is separately taxed, providing for most estates a built-in form of tax splitting. In addition, most inheritance taxes provide for lower tax rates to persons bound to the decedent by blood or marriage, further lowering rates for the typical disposition.
55. See, e.g., Knowlton v. Moore, 178 U.S. at 77.
56. 170 U.S. at 288. The above language was relied upon in Knowlton v. Moore, 178 U.S. at 55.

sist legislative nullification. The positivist account offers no protection for private property at all. If the right of succession is a privilege conferred by the state, then can the same be said of the right of possession or of ordinary sale? "Private property is what the state says it is" is another forbidden *ipse dixit,* inconsistent with all constitutional theory, in taxing matters as elsewhere.

This argument, if it is good against state imposition of progressive transfer taxes, works *a fortiori* against the federal government, for it is no longer possible to entertain the pretext that taxation is the price for exercising a privilege that the government is said to be able to withhold at will. There is no federal power to either grant or withhold the right of inheritance. The federal government is even more plainly required to justify its taking by showing that it falls within one of the permissible categories of public takings. Of this there is not a shadow in the decided cases or the academic literature, given the manifest redistributive purpose.

_19_ Transfer Payments and Welfare Rights

The most casual look at the modern political landscape reveals that while very substantial sums are spent on classic, nonexclusive, public goods, a greater portion of government revenues is devoted to transfer payments. The modern position is that the size and the purpose of these payments raise only political and social issues that are left wholly unconstrained by the Constitution. Yet the question of rights cannot be put aside so easily. Since all tax revenues are property taken from someone, so the claims of the eminent domain clause are both insistent and inescapable. No shortcut allows an evaluation of these programs that bypasses our complete interpretative framework. Are the taxes collected and spent for a public use? Do they meet the police power or consent justification? Is implicit in-kind compensation furnished to those who pay them?

As a matter of first principle, most of these programs suffer fatal constitutional infirmities. But it is one thing to identify past errors and quite another to remedy them, even if we could summon the will to do so. The first part of this chapter explores the constitutional status of transfer programs and welfare rights on the assumption that the challenges are made before the programs are in place. The only question is whether they meet applicable constitutional standards. The second theme is, if these programs are unconstitutional in principle, can they be undone now that they have been in place for several generations, often on an enormous scale? Simple invalidation is virtually impossible because of the social institutions and individual claims that have grown up around long-standing social programs. Are these historical claims so great that continued acquiescence in the status quo is the only responsible course of action? Is there, in other words, a constitutional ratchet whereby errors introduced into the system can never be undone?

Writing on the Blank Slate

The first challenge to modern transfer programs comes from the public use limitation, which prohibits state-coerced transfers of property (including money) from A to B. Programs for social security, unemployment benefits, and ordinarily welfare do not supply pure public goods. If anything, transfer payments are at the opposite pole from common goods such as defense. Nor can transfer payments be understood as akin to common carrier obligations. Common carriers labor under an obligation of universal service, and can exclude only those who fail to observe minimum standards of conduct and decorum. Both the basic principles and its exception are designed to secure a fair division of the surplus across all members of the society. Universal service permits all to share in the gains; the requirement of good behavior prevents any individual customer from seizing unilaterally an excessive share. In contrast, the eligibility requirements for transfer payments are designed to ensure that only a selected group shares in the gains in circumstances where the government regulation is not necessary to overcome the bilateral monopoly problems found, for example, in the mill act cases.[1]

The public use requirement thus seems to stop the entire array of government transfer programs in its tracks, which in one sense is not surprising in light of the original constitutional structure. Wholly apart from the eminent domain clause, nothing in Article I appears to confer upon the federal government the power to make transfer payments, that subject being left to the states (which must struggle with their own takings clauses). Any additional prohibition on transfers contained in the takings clause does not therefore chart a new course for the federal government but only confirms the original constitutional judgment.[2]

1. See Chapter 12.
2. Note, however, that incorporation of the eminent domain clause into the Fourteenth Amendment does present a more dramatic challenge. If states may provide transfer payments, some competition between jurisdictions to keep profitable enterprises will tend to reduce the levels, reducing the importance of the absolute constitutional prohibition. In the text I follow the implications, not for federalism, but for a system that regards transfer payments as an inappropriate function of any government, state or federal.

Money is the most fungible and divisible of assets. Shifting it between private parties is the last activity in which government should be engaged. It is agreed by all that a naked transfer from A to B is forbidden. How then does the transfer become permissible where there is a broad class of people like A and another class like B? The greater the number of parties on both sides of the line, the greater the magnitude of the state wrong, given the evident mismatch of benefits and burdens.

Investing the public use language with such enormous powers may seem arbitrary or worse, considering its pallid role in contemporary constitutional adjudication. Yet one way to understand the strength of this position is to ask whether, if the public use barrier is overcome, transfer payments satisfy the just compensation requirement. With taxation, it was possible to articulate a very simple flat-rate tax that provided for classical public goods, curbed private abuse, and allowed for easy judicial supervision. With a free rein on transfer programs, no parallel constraint limits private abuse or makes judicial supervision workable. The typical benefit program takes cash from taxpayers and provides its recipients with a package of contingent benefits that are notoriously difficult to value, ex ante or ex post. There is no perfect overlap between the parties who pay and the parties who collect. To make matters more difficult, these programs must overcome all the complexities confronting contracting parties in private markets, chiefly the normal insurance risks of adverse selection and moral hazard, within a complex regulatory environment, where the demands for public service make the categorical "no" unheard of. Whether we deal with transfers from city dwellers to farmers or from rich to poor, we set up the familiar cycle of attack and defense so characteristic of rent-seeking behavior, while inviting the usual set of allocative errors at high administrative costs. Given the systematic biases and inefficiencies, the upshot is that there are necessarily some uncompensated losers. A complete ban on transfer programs removes the need to pass on the compensation issue, on which the program will be shipwrecked in any event. It also reaches the right result more cheaply than any case-by-case determination, thereby minimizing the expected number of uncompensated takings to all parties over time. The proposition can be illustrated by any number of social programs, but here I shall confine my attention to unemployment compensation programs and to the recent regulatory efforts to equalize the periodic annuity payments received by men and women, before turning to welfare programs generally.

UNEMPLOYMENT BENEFITS

The constitutionality of unemployment compensation programs was sustained by the Supreme Court in *Carmichael v. Southern Coal & Coke Co.*[3] Alabama imposed a percentage tax upon the monthly payroll of employers who employed eight or more workers for a twenty-week period, the proceeds of which were paid into the Unemployment Trust Fund established by the United States and administered under the Federal Social Security Act.[4] The act exempted those "who employ[ed] agricultural laborers, domestic servants, seamen, insurance agents, or close relatives," and "exclude[d] charitable institutions, interstate railways, or the government of the United States or of any state or political subdivision."[5] In addition the statute provided that the unemployment benefits could be awarded "only after a substantial 'waiting period' of unemployment and then only to the extent of half wages and not more than $15 a week for at most sixteen weeks a year."[6] No one was denied benefits because he was not indigent.

The statute was attacked on a variety of grounds concerning the arbitrariness of its coverage, given the long list of excluded groups, and also on a substantive due process theory that embodied an implicit takings claim. Justice Stone, in sustaining the statute, appealed to the standard constitutional assumption that the government has broad discretion to identify the proper objects of taxation and to distribute the benefits therefrom.[7] He operated on a standard that not only validated this statute, but subsequently made it quite impossible to attack any public benefit program financed by tax revenues, such as medicare (including the 1984 temporary freeze of physicians' fees). The difficult question of public use was answered by an appeal to precedent which gave Congress the power to aid some at the expense of others, buttressed by a catalogue of cases in which special taxes on liquor and other commodities could be used for particular functions, such as public education.[8]

3. 301 U.S. 495 (1937).
4. The Social Security cases revealed a real uneasiness about the federalism questions raised by this complex web of funding provisions. See Steward Machine Co. v. Davis, 30 U.S. 548 (1937).
5. 301 U.S. at 512.
6. Id. at 519.
7. See, e.g., Bell's Gap R.R. Co. v. Pennsylvania, 134 U.S. 232 (1890).
8. 301 U.S. at 522. "Cigarette and tobacco taxes are earmarked, in some states, for school funds and education purposes ... Liquor license fees and taxes are paid into old age pension funds ... Unemployment relief, though financed in most states by special bond issues, has in some instances been fi-

The matter takes on a very different complexion if one takes seriously the constitutionality of tax programs. At first blush, the unemployment compensation taxes come very close to meeting the standards of the disproportionate impact test. The benefits of unemployment compensation are largely shared by both employer and employee, for the employer can capture some portion of the employees' gain by reducing the wages. In addition, the structure of the benefits—with a waiting period and coinsurance—is effective in reducing the moral hazard of employees quitting because they are made better off by the unemployment benefits. Likewise, the limitation of the statute to business with eight or more employees is justifiable on administrative grounds, and as an effort to increase the homogeneity of the insurance pool, given that the excluded workers share in neither the tax nor the benefits. The decision to provide benefits to nonindigent employees, if anything, strengthens the statute by making it more of an insurance and less of a welfare scheme.

However, the statute does not begin to address the concealed but implicit redistribution of wealth within the class of covered employees. As structured, the tax is levied upon the total payroll, so employers and employees in stable work forces end up paying a net subsidy to employees (and of course employers) who worked in high-turnover industries. Justice Sutherland in his informative dissent noted that other unemployment statutes subdivide the overall pool by industry in order to minimize the implicit subsidy—by controlling for the difference between seasonal and nonseasonal workers, for example.[9] Nonetheless, in *Carmichael* Stone rejected any intermediate efforts to police the system, using the standard appeal to judicial deference. He buttressed that point by appealing to police power argument that the statute was an effort to control for external harms since it is impossible to confine the causes of unemployment within one industry, and to account for "competition . . . or . . . tariffs, inventions, changes in fashions or in market or business conditions, for which no employer is responsible."[10] In addition he resorted to an implicit in-kind compensation argument (in ways that parallel the error of Locke's tacit consent argument).[11]

nanced by Gasoline Taxes." Id. at n.14. All the above are presumed constitutional by Stone, but the point was not argued, except with reference to precedent.

9. Id. at 529–531.

10. Id. at 524. Indeed, it is just when the going gets roughest that Stone pronounces that there need be no relationship between benefits and burdens in the area of taxaton, quoted above.

11. See Chapter 2.

The only benefit to which the taxpayer is constitutionally entitled is that derived from his enjoyment of the privileges of living in an organized society, established and safeguarded by the devotion of taxes to public purposes. Any other view would preclude the levying of taxes except as they are used to compensate for the burden on those who pay them, and would involve the abandonment of the most fundamental principle of government—that it exists primarily to provide for the common good.[12]

The argument as stated refers both to the police power and to the theory of implicit benefit. The former is used to explain why the state can check the external effects of competition. Yet there is no obvious reason why a firm which hires additional workers should, on balance, be regarded as having contributed to the external harm of unemployment. To the contrary, Stone's account in *Carmichael* of the sources of unemployment rests upon an erroneous view of causation that leads to a wholly unlimited view of the police power. Begin with Stone's account of competitive injury. Remove the state and we have private conduct, which as a constitutional matter cannot be stamped as tortious in the absence of force or misrepresentation. If a disappointed competitor and his employee have no right of action against their successful rival, then the state as their agent can no longer claim that taxes are a public substitute for a private damage remedy that cannot be collected for administrative reasons. Taxes to redress competitive injuries thus bear no resemblance at all to taxes on pollution, which are substitutes for difficult-to-administer damage actions. In essence Stone's argument fails to respect the basic principle of the takings clause: the only unique power of the state is to force exchanges when voluntary transactions do not work. The antitaking view of the police power does not apply to competitive injuries in the same fashion that it applies to ordinary nuisances.

Nor is the argument better on the second limb, which evaluates the benefits from taxation. If living in society is sufficient benefit for the taxes imposed, then all taxes meet the applicable standard and all constitutional review ceases. Yet there are other ways to examine taxes, even if direct measurement of their benefits is not possible. Unemployment compensation programs fall under the restricted versions of the disproportionate impact test, as some workers and firms are required to subsidize others. Stone sought to defeat the argument by disputing the premise. He wrote: "It is not a valid objection to the present tax, con-

---

12. 301 U.S. at 522–523 (citations omitted).

forming in other respects to the Fourteenth Amendment, and devoted to a public purpose, that the benefits paid and the persons to whom they are paid are unrelated to the persons taxed and the amount of the tax they pay."[13] Yet he never explained why the test is wrong as a matter of theory, even with the vast number of constitutional cases on special assessments that show, at the very least, the relevance of disproportionate impact.

The attacks upon this form of unemployment tax are reinforced by noting their expected overall allocative effects. Paying these benefits may have an adverse effect upon the levels of employment. If an employer must make payments into the compensation fund upon firing a worker, he will be more reluctant to hire workers, especially short-term risky workers, in the first place. Blocking the formation of new jobs cannot reduce unemployment levels. Likewise, as unemployment benefit levels rise, workers will be less likely to seek substitute employment, because they have less to gain from getting new jobs. The impact of the unemployment tax upon capital formation is difficult to assess, but since the tax works as a lien against future earnings, it tends to depress the rate of return on investment, and hence the formation of new businesses and hence new jobs. The indirect harms seem to be quite great, although these were never mentioned in *Carmichael,* which stressed not the truth of the matter, but only what Congress could have found.[14] A system of transfer payments simply cannot be expected to have either positive wealth effects or a proportionate impact, and accordingly it should be struck down.

SEX-BASED ANNUITIES

A similar set of considerations applies to the recent controversy over whether insurance and annuity companies should be allowed to use sex-

13. Id. at 521.

14. See id., Stone, J., at 516–517: "The evils of the attendant social and economic wastage [of permanent unemployment] permeate the entire social structure. Apart from poverty, or a less extreme impairment of the savings . . . and apart from the loss of purchasing power, the legislature could have concluded that unemployment brings in its wake increase in vagrancy and crimes against property, reduction in the number of marriages, deterioration of family life, decline in the birth rate, an increase in illegitimate births, impairment of the health of the unemployed and their families, and malnutrition of their children." But this analysis does not explain why it is a bad idea to provide infinite benefits, because it does not locate the costs of the plans. Note that the reference to the loss of purchasing power from unemployment is now widely understood to be wholly misconceived, because in the aggregate the gains from transfer to some are offset by the losses to others.

based mortality tables in determining pension benefits. Here the implicit transfers arise out of a system of regulation that requires insurers to pay unequal benefits, measured by their expected present value, in exchange for equal contributions. The mismatch between contributions and payments can be attacked in our two familiar ways. It is very clear from the design of the program that impacts will necessarily be disproportionate, with women as a group net winners, and men net losers. (Married couples of roughly equal ages are left unaffected.) In addition, the program of mandated transfers has an overall negative effect upon social wealth, leaving some persons necessarily uncompensated. To make the point clear, consider the fate of the pension program in *City of Los Angeles Dept. of Water and Power v. Manhart.*[15] The original plan adjusted the employees' contributions to take into account the systematic difference between men and women in expected longevity. Since all employees received equal monthly benefits, the women made larger monthly contributions into the plan to offset their greater expected life span.

The court held that the sex-based calculation of employee contributions constituted an illegal form of sex discrimination. Accordingly, it ordered a prospective equalization of monthly payments without changing the benefit levels. One consequence of *Manhart* is that the total (expected) compensation for women becomes higher than it is for men,

---

15. 435 U.S. 702 (1978). The decision has been extensively and critically analyzed, in Spencer L. Kimball, "Reverse Sex Discrimination: *Manhart,*" 1979 *Am. Bar Found. Res. J.* 83; Lea Brilmayer, Richard W. Hekeler, Douglas Laycock, and Teresa A. Sullivan, "Sex Discrimination in Employer-Sponsored Insurance Plans: A Legal and Demographic Analysis," 47 *U. Chi. L. Rev.* 505 (1980). G. J. Benston, "The Economics of Gender Discrimination in Employee Fringe Benefits: *Manhart* Revisited," 49 *U. Chi. L. Rev.* 489 (1982).

The analysis of Brilmayer and her coauthors rests in part on the assumption that life expectancy is not uniquely determinable because there is no unique group to which any individual can be assigned: the life expectancy of a black South Carolina male is fifty-eight years if so classified and seventy years if classified simply as a male. The mistake in their argument is to assume that all classifications are equally good, when they are not. Market processes select the most homogeneous subgroup on which it is possible to obtain aggregate statistical data at reasonable cost. If one insurance company grouped only by sex, a second company would enter the market and sign up males a lower rate. The first insurer would have to recalculate his rates to reflect the different composition of its remaining pool. The process would continue as long as any new entrant could skim off a subgroup with favorable demographic characteristics. Insurance firms simply foreshorten the game at the outset by using the best group classifications obtainable, including those based on sex.

which in turn results in an increase in the demand for male employees relative to female employees. In addition, the court's decision invites countersteps by the firms and employees governed by it. Some male employees can reduce their losses in part by taking pensions not tied to life expectancy, by electing either a large-sum payment upon retirement or (for tax reasons) fixed payments for a definite period. That decision in turn changes the composition of the remaining pool that opts for variable payments by increasing the number of female claimants. The larger fraction of women creates the risk of plan insolvency if the pensions on lifetime annuities are fixed at their original levels. Yet readjustments are hard to make before individuals exercise their pension rights.

These economic and administrative factors led the city of Los Angeles, after *Manhart,* to deny both men and women lifetime annuities,[16] even though this had been the dominant choice for both sexes. Benefits are again equalized between men and women, and no colorable violation of the civil rights act can be found. But *cui bono?* An overwhelming percentage of both men and women have geared their choice of annuities to the lifetimes of themselves and their spouses. That decision reflects a commendable risk aversion, because people fear outliving a fixed-term pension more than they value unconsumed resources to will to their middle-aged children. Now the pooling of lifetime risk is effectively precluded, so ironically the restrictions on voluntary plans, if anything, place greater burdens on women, whose greater life expectancy suggests that there is likely to be a greater variation in the date of expected death. That variation in turn makes it more difficult for women to determine the optimal rate for consuming wealth from a fixed stock of capital. *Everyone* is worse off, in unequal proportions. The only uncertainty lies in the extent of the grievances by men and women; there is no uncertainty about condemning the unisex tables under the takings clause.

WELFARE TRANSFER PAYMENTS

Before considering transfer payments under a welfare system, it is important to note just what is at stake. Welfare transfers, whether in cash or in kind, aid the poor at the expense of the rich, within the limits of practical measurement. Even if welfare payments to the poor were completely proper in principle, vast chunks of the previous analysis remain

16. Jane Bryant Quinn, "The Great Unisex Debate," *Newsweek,* July 4, 1983, at 52.

wholly unchanged, as there is nothing to warrant the capricious redistributions, whether they are to tenants at the expense of landlords, to residents at the expense of outsiders, to debtors at the expense of creditors, to consumers of oil and gas at the expense of producers, or to women at the expense of men (or neither at the expense of both).

The acceptance of transfer payments from rich to poor also changes at least three elements of the previous analysis. First, the public use limitation can no longer block either cash transfer payments from rich to poor or in-kind programs, such as subsidized public housing programs. Second, greater government freedom in taxation is permissible to fund the desired redistribution. Yet this does nothing to strengthen the case for the windfall profits tax or other special forms of income taxation. The obligation to aid the poor must fall on the rich generally, and not some fraction thereof, so the progressive income tax, and only the progressive income tax, is legitimated if redistribution is regarded as the order of the day. Third, and most doubtfully, the various quasi-insurance programs, unemployment benefits, Social Security, and medicare, with their crazy quilt pattern of benefits, may pass muster if their dominant effect is to redistribute wealth from rich to poor.

There is no need to explore the scope of these qualifications, however, if the takings clause in principle prohibits all forms of forced transfer payments for welfare purposes. The argument takes on in the usual sequence the four central issues of the eminent domain clause: takings, justification, public use, and compensation. The first point—takings—is clear, so squaring welfare rights depends upon whether they can run the gauntlet posed by the three remaining points. Clearly, no simple argument will suffice, as there is no classic public good like defense that necessarily requires a collective choice. One obvious justification is the broad consensus that exists today in favor of making public welfare payments. This reduces the political objections to the system, but it does not establish the unanimous consent needed to transform taxes into voluntary contributions. And it certainly does not establish consent to the nature and form of the transfer systems now in place.

The key to welfare's justification rests upon an uneasy union of police power and implicit in-kind compensation arguments. Welfare rights do not mesh easily with the antitaking rationale of the police power: unlike taxes on pollution, welfare payments are not designed to control the wrongful conduct of the parties taxed. But it will be said that they fall within the police power because they are designed to protect against the violence of *others* who will act in antisocial fashion when these benefits are not provided. But this is the very antithesis of a rights-based claim.[17] It clearly justifies the use of force against the wrongdoers and not against their victims. No one would be happy to silence speech because the government cannot control those who would interfere with it, lest casual assertions of the police power become the entering wedge for government repression. That same argument applies here. The police power does not routinely justify penalties upon legitimate acts as an indirect means to control illegitimate ones.

In the end, the case for welfare rights within a system of private property must rest upon implicit in-kind compensation to those who have paid the taxes. One form of that argument traces the police power point. The compensation to the rich is that they are spared the violence that would overcome them if the poor were shut out from the social gains. The peace obtained is worth more than the money paid to obtain it. So viewed, the welfare payment is little more than a strategic bribe that spares the payers the greater costs of police enforcement and control. Yet where the opportunities for individual advancement are left as open as a system of limited government would leave them (for example, without barriers, such as the minimum wage, to entry in labor markets), there is less reason to fear that some permanent underclass will remain a constant threat to the social order. Because individual initiative promises relatively higher returns the propensity for violent activity should be reduced. The proper constitutional response, therefore, is to insist upon the usual level of means scrutiny to justify transfer payments. The first defense against violence should be police measures, which can be modified as exigencies arise.[18] Transfer payments are rarely a suitable means to counteract violence; they are best justified by showing a clear and present danger of social unrest that cannot be handled by conventional techniques. It is hard to quarrel with providing free food in a flood-torn town to reduce the chances of looting, even if that were characterized as a transfer scheme. It is equally hard to see how the same argument justifies the food stamp program as an antidote to revolution.

17. The same argument of possible violence has also been used to justify the National Labor Relations Act, the centerpiece of modern labor law. I have considered the soundness of the argument in that context in Richard A. Epstein, "A Common Law of Labor Relations: A Critique of the New Deal Legislation," 92 *Yale L.B.* 1357 (1983).

18. Similar difficulties undermine the "industrial peace" justifications for the National Labor Relations Act, for which the same response is appropriate. See Epstein, supra note 17, at 1404–1406.

The argument can be carried to still another level, for it can be said that free-rider problems exist in any voluntary welfare system, as in any other system of collective action.[19] The parties who provide the benefits contribute to social stability that is shared by all yet not everyone is required to pay their fair share. The only way to overcome the problem is to require everyone to contribute to fund the public good, here welfare programs. But who determines whether the probable external effects of welfare payments are positive or negative for unwilling contributors? Suppose X thinks that welfare payments are a dreadful mistake because they encourage individuals to survive on handouts instead of fending for themselves. He refuses to support all charitable activities, or any kind or description. If X obtains a political majority, should he be allowed in the name of the police power to ban charitable giving by others? If he cannot, then why can the majority exact his contributions from him? The refusal of any single individual to provide welfare payments does not prevent others from going ahead with their plans. Indeed, virtually all educational, religious, medical, and welfare charities have long operated with the cooperation and financial support of only a tiny fraction of the total population. There are no common pool problems comparable to those found with the exploration of oil and gas; no natural resource will be dissipated if all interested parties are not required to contribute.

A second way to answer the implicit in-kind compensation question is to make an insurance argument, that the eligibility rules for welfare are sufficiently general to allow those who pay today to collect tomorrow if they suffer a reversal of fortune. The mistake here is identical to that made in *Carmichael* and *Haas*.[20] The insurance must be actuarially fair in its terms. It is never sufficient to simply refer to the existence of some return benefits, which are conveniently unvalued. To satisfy the just compensation requirement, it is also necessary to make the best possible estimate of their expected value, which must exceed the payments exacted. If everyone were both risk averse and behind a veil of ignorance, then everyone might be better off with a security net than without it. That conclusion is highly controversial, as any welfare system is likely to impose efficiency losses, because of its negative incentive effects and its substantial administrative costs. Without detailed knowledge of these three relevant quantities—the degree of risk aversion, negative incen-

19. See Frank H. Easterbrook and Daniel R. Fischel, "Auctions and Sunk Costs in Tender Offers," 35 *Stan. L. Rev.* 1 (1982), addressing the free-rider problem in the context of tender offer regulation.

20. See Chapter 17.

tives, and administrative costs—no empirical judgment can be made about the plausibility of welfare rights even under these restrictive conditions, much less those in place today.

Yet the most critical point is that a system of transfer payments is not imposed upon individuals behind a veil of ignorance. In sharp contrast to the situation with general tort rules,[21] all of us today do know our place in the legal and social order before a new welfare program is instituted or an old one expanded. Each of us can roughly calculate the net distribution of gains and losses, and we know that the balance is far from even. A gaming analogy might help. If two players agree to start a chess game without queens, the benefits and burdens will be roughly comparable (unless one player has made a secret study of the queenless game). However, if one player can unilaterally remove both queens at any time during the game, he is likely to do it when his opponent's is poised to mate while his own stands helpless in a corner. The benefits and burdens will not balance out, either in chess or in life. Welfare remains a transfer system whose tiny insurance component does not furnish adequate compensation to those who are taxed to support it.

The possible escape hatches for government takings allowed under the taking clause point to the possibility of some minor system of transfer payments, but they go no further. The fundamental problem in a system of welfare is that it conflicts with the theory of private rights that lies behind any system of representative government. There is quite simply no private cause of action for want of benevolence that remotely resembles those causes allowable under the dominant actions of tort, contract, and restitution. In all cases liability depends upon the conduct of the parties to the dispute. In none does liability turn upon comparing the needs of the plaintiff with the wealth of the defendant. The standard tort obligations between strangers are always negative—do not trespass, do not attack. The legal system never has to ask the question of what level of resources individuals must spend in order to help their neighbors. It does not have to compare the benefits of the payers with those of the receivers. It does not have to make its obligations a function of changing levels of social wealth, in order to respond to worries over relative deprivation. Ideally, if the tort system could enjoin all losses, it would not have to measure damages at all. Yet as it cannot do that, it must set its tariffs equal to the harm inflicted upon the innocent party. One corollary of the tort system is the good-Samaritan rule, for there is

21. See Chapter 16.

no duty to rescue a stranger and no need to determine "how much" care is required before the hypothetical duty is satisfied. Similarly, the law of contracts does not make complex obligations for private parties. It only enforces the obligations already made or supplies a standard package of off-the-rack terms to govern in the event of contractual silence. It does not have to concern itself with interpersonal comparisons of utility or claims of benevolence. The same is true with all restitution claims which, mirroring the constitutional requirement, impose duties of payment only for benefits conferred upon the defendant. It does not demand that good deeds be done for third parties.

To move from these self-limiting obligations to an open-ended obligation of support is to transform the legal universe. No one has a theory of how much benevolence should be shown in the private area. All the law can do is to protect donors from forcible interference by third parties. The problem of setting levels of benevolence, which is intractable for the individual donor, is not overcome in the collective arena. The legal theory that recognizes no obligation to rescue a stranger in imminent peril cannot generate, let alone nourish, a system of transfer payments and welfare obligations.

All of this does not imply that because individuals are free to give or not give, there is no moral case for helping those who are in need. Nor does it imply that so long as an action is legal, everyone should be indifferent to its content. To the contrary, the traditional understanding captures the difference between charitable giving and ordinary consumption by recognizing a class of "imperfect obligations," which is the office of conscience and religion and not of public coercion.[22] Nor is

22. See, e.g., Joseph Story, "Natural Law," unsigned article in *Encyclopedia Americana* (1836), reprinted as an appendix to James McClellan, *Joseph Story and the American Constitution* (1971). The key passage reads: "We call those rights perfect, which are determinate, and which may be asserted by force, or in a civil society by the operation of law; and imperfect, those which are indeterminate and vague, and which may not be asserted by force or by law, but are obligatory only on the conscience of parties. Thus a man has a perfect right to life, to his personal liberty, and to his property; and he may by force assert and vindicate those rights against every aggressor. But he has but an imperfect right to gratitude for favors bestowed upon others, or to charity, if he is in want, or to the affection of others, even if he is truly deserving it . . . In regard to imperfect rights, although the sanction is wholly upon the conscience of the party under a sense of religious responsibility, the obligation to perform the duties corresponding to them is, nevertheless, to be deemed as imperative, as if they also possessed the strongest earthly sanctions; since they arise from the commands of God, and are to be done in obedience to His will." Id. at 315.

there any reason to doubt that this uneasy third class of obligations exerts a powerful influence upon the behavior of large numbers of persons.

To understand why charitable obligations are regarded as imperfect, it is useful to consider the problems of system design that confront anyone who wishes to organize a system of support payments. At some level any welfare system is designed to offer a kind of free insurance, against some hazard of birth, bad rearing, or misfortune. Yet it is hard to give away money or benefits in kind. Since welfare creates an insurance package of sorts, it must confront and overcome the standard insurance risk of moral hazard:[23] giving protection against poverty increases the likelihood of its occurrence. To simply set a level of welfare benefits open to all creates the risk that individuals will alter their primary behavior for the worse in order to capture those benefits. Anyone whose own efforts earn him less than the system pays has an incentive (or at least a temptation) to use his talents to obtain transfer payments and to forgo productive activity. If a person can obtain public housing only if he is homeless, the best strategy may be to not pay the rent or the mortgage, or in an extreme case (such as the South Bronx) to burn down the house. That everyone will not do this is quite beside the point. It is enough in any large-number situation to change the behavior of those individuals at the margin. To combat the problem, any welfare system must monitor individual behavior. How?

Private charitable organizations have always been sensitive to this problem. They impose means tests, waiting periods, and work requirements to ensure that the wrong people do not collect the benefits. They can demand visible signs of need—blindness or specific illness—to control the moral hazard problem. They can rely upon informal social pressures to prevent abuse, which probably accounts for many charities being organized along religious, neighborhood, or fraternal lines. These groups can use in-kind benefits to prevent the diversion of their resources to purposes that are against their own view of proper behavior, and they can impose nonpecuniary costs upon their recipients. It is no accident that the Salvation Army feeds the hungry instead of giving restaurant

23. Moral hazard refers to the increased likelihood that an untoward event will occur once insurance is provided in the event of its occurrence. In many contexts adverse selection, which refers to the tendency of individual insureds to acquire insurance when they know they have a greater than average chance of obtaining compensation for the covered event, is important. In this context adverse selection is less important because the insurance is not sold. On the two concepts, see, generally, William Bishop, "The Contract-Tort Boundary and the Economics of Insurance," 12 *J. Legal Stud.* 241 (1983).

vouchers, or that it has prayers before and cleanup after meals. If they gave cash, the money might be spent on liquor rather than food; if they gave the food to anyone who asked for it, no strings attached, they could not ration their limited resources to feed the hungry. Prayers and work and wait are nonprice forms of rationing that are most effective when money cannot (almost by definition) be paid.

The problems of making gifts are not confined to hunger and privation. Many a private foundation has found that its grant money has supported faculty leisure, so enormous sums are invested in finding individuals whose track records make them worthy of funding, to diminish the risk of diversion. Grant proposals, peer recommendations, progress reports, and short renewal periods replace prayer and cleanup, but the monitoring problems are the same. The elaborate institutional structures in universities (separate trustees, administration, academic departments) are likewise designed for the protection of the donors: who would give money to a university if they knew it could be diverted to nonacademic purposes?

There is also the question of how to set benefit levels. The private charity must set a level that protects those who are in need without encouraging productive people to become needy. No level of benefits is ideal. Set the benefits too low and they are of no assistance; set them too high and they will bring forth levels of demand that cannot be met, by people who are not "in need." In general, one can confidently predict that some principle of coinsurance will govern, as in other markets, so benefits must be set low, perhaps uncomfortably low, in order to discourage perverse behavior undertaken solely to become eligible for benefits.[24] There is no reason to believe that the political process understands where benefit levels should be set.

The common argument today notes that thousands of persons now receive welfare benefits, which is taken as a sign of the necessity that the present system must answer. But it is better understood as evidence of the system's manifest failure to constrain the demands for its services. By the law of supply and demand, the number of interested recipients varies directly with the level of benefits. The higher the benefits, the more people who will seek them out: if the costs of obtaining these benefits are kept constant, then the demand will rise in response to the greater expected return. This result is not dependent on evil or greed;

---

24. For the analogous discussion of low benefits in workers' compensation cases, see Richard A. Epstein, "The Historical Origins and Economic Structure of Workers' Compensation Law," 16 *Ga. L. Rev.* 775 (1982).

the normal rules of self-interest in human behavior work in the aggregate with welfare payments just as they do in other areas of human endeavor. Is the amount of medical payments consumed a function only of the need for health services? Or is it a relevant factor that third-party payment mechanisms both support high prices for services rendered and generate increased demands for those services? Does the increase in individuals on the welfare rolls bear no relationship to the increased levels of benefits? Does aid to dependent children have no effect upon the increase in illegitimate births and the breakup of the family?

None of the above argues that the ideal level of (voluntary) welfare support should be zero, but it does show the fundamental misconception in acting as if the demand for welfare payments is exogenously fixed at the present level, so that all the social system can do is respond to a problem it has not created. The short truth is that if the state had never undertaken welfare programs, the demand for them would be a tiny fraction of what it is today. At every level and in every way, it is difficult even for private charities to make intelligent gifts, in light of the narrow self-interest of the intended beneficiaries.

It may be asked what this has to do with the takings clause. Quite simply this. The basic rules of private property are inconsistent with any form of welfare benefits. One way to avoid failure is to throw the baby out with the bath water, to get out of the welfare business entirely. That judgment is not based simply upon some narrow sense of egoism or a belief that private greed is the highest form of social virtue. Nor does it rest on the hidden pleasure of watching small children starve or derelicts freeze on the street. To the contrary, it rests on the belief that once the state runs a transfer system, it can never extricate itself from the intolerable complications that follow. The higher the level of benefits, the greater the demand, until the political dynamic—rent seeking again—produces an aggregate demand that the system itself can meet only with great cost to its productive capacities. Rather than become mired in the quicksand, do not start down that path at all. If it is said that no system of private support could handle the current level of demands, the proper answer is that no system of private support would ever have spawned the current levels of demand. Need would be reduced by better policing, and the means to satisfy it would be larger, because the overall levels of wealth would be greater. A private welfare system becomes conceivable in principle once it is realized that the system would be much more modest than it is today. Charitable activities were common in the nineteenth century before the income tax, not only for the support of great universities and hospitals, but also for the relief of victims of tragedies.[25] Many programs for the poor were in place before the New Deal, but they were replaced by government programs that exhausted the public willingness to make welfare payments.[26] Reduce government involvement and private benevolence will again increase.

The position thus far is as hard as it is consistent. Is it possible to find some other way to meet the situation, some way to allow public benevolence into the Constitution which conceptions of private property seem to effectively forbid? Consider tax deductions (not possible under a flat tax) for charitable contributions. In the view I take here, such deductions are generally prohibited unless it can be shown that the net benefits are generated for those who do not take advantage of charitable deductions and who therefore bear a somewhat larger portion of the aggregate public expenditures. With ordinary transfer payments funded by government-initiated programs, it is very hard to find those net benefits to unwilling payers. With private programs supported by tax deductions, the answer might possibly be different. In the first place, a charitable deduction would be triggered only if some individual were prepared to make the financial sacrifice necessary to start the program. With private charity, it is difficult to envision the capture of the legislature by faction, for only persons who spend a good chunk of their own money can trigger the matching public expenditures. This need to bear heavy private costs in order to impose some public costs offers some protection against naked redistribution, protection that is wholly absent when benefit programs are financed entirely by public funds. In addition, the programs would be administered by private bodies that, while far from perfect, are better able to control the moral hazard problems. The benefits distributed and the external benefits provided by the programs will be greater in magnitude than if comparable programs are publicly administered.

These differences are not merely matters of the economics of charity; they have direct relevance to the takings analysis. The reduction in external costs means that less property is taken from noncontributors who, because of the greater efficiency of the system, probably receive more

25. See A. W. B. Simpson, "Bursting Reservoirs: The Historical Context of *Rylands v. Fletcher*," 13 *J. Legal Stud.* 209, 223–225 (1984), describing the public aid for those rendered hurt and homeless by a bursting dam. The Red Cross functions in the same way.

26. See Russell D. Roberts, "A Positive Model of Private Charity and Public Transfers," 92 *J. Pol. Econ.* 136 (1984).

substantial indirect benefits from its operation. These differences may just be enough to tip the balance in favor of the program, making the deductions constitutionally permissible. This small and uneasy concession should not be allowed to blunt the central proposition. If an individual does not have any obligation to rescue those in imminent peril when he can do so at little or no cost, then it is not possible to create a welfare obligation with the emergence of the state, given the representative theory of government. It is not possible to design a stable set of institutional arrangements for transfer payments to satisfy the just-compensation requirement of the eminent domain clause.

But the Slate Is Not Blank

With the possible exception of charitable deductions, the eminent domain clause in principle forecloses virtually all public transfer and welfare programs, however devised and executed, except in very narrow and limited circumstances captured by the police power and implicit in-kind compensation. If the challenges to these programs had been sustained at their inception, the only proper remedy would have been their invalidation, because the just-compensation requirement cannot be satisfied by either explicit or implicit payments. That easy remedial option is effectively foreclosed today because of two social facts. First, a whole host of taxes and regulations, which necessarily offend the eminent domain clause, have long been in operation. Second, virtually all recipients have acted, often over a period of years, if not decades, in reliance on the present legal order.

These are powerful considerations that can be ignored only through intellectual and moral blindness. The previous analysis must be modified. Yet is any constitutional effort to return to limited government only a quixotic effort to turn back the clock, to repeal the twentieth century? Or is it possible to undo some, if not all, of the mistakes? As ever, I cannot even ask these questions if I have misunderstood the intimate relationship among taxation, regulation, and confiscation. By the same token, I canot avoid them if that analysis is sound in principle, as some intervention is not precluded solely by the passage of time, any more than with government segregation in *Brown v. Board of Education.*[27]

27. 347 U.S. 483 (1954). Note too that the invalidation of racial segregation is far easier under the approach taken here than in the opinion in *Brown.* There is no reason to rest upon any concern with racial stigma. Instead, a detailed explanation of the way in which one faction seized power within the state to divert resources to its own use could easily make clear the disproportionate

In trying to sort out the influence of the past on the present, it is appropriate to begin with a private law analogy. Suppose A owns a certain piece of marble, which is then stolen by B, who sells it to C, who carves it in good faith. A now discovers that C is in possession of his marble and demands its return. What can be done? There is no easy solution. In a world that absolutely respects the claims of property, the owner should be entitled to restitution in kind. But even the threshold question, whether A can recover from C, has never received a uniform private law answer in the frequent cases where one of two innocent parties must bear the loss attributable to the theft, fraud, or indifference of a third.[28]

Suppose the claims of property (the general answer) are not defeated by the wrong of the intermediate party B. What then is the remedy? The egg has broken and, as we learned from Humpty Dumpty, the process cannot be reversed. Instead, the private law from the earliest times moves toward forced exchanges.[29] A is not simply given the sculpted marble, because he would then expropriate C's labor. Yet C is not allowed to keep the marble free and clear just because he has worked it. Generally C must provide a hunk of marble of like kind and quality, or a cash equivalent. Adjustments are made to handle the cases that might arise if the marble is destroyed, embedded in a larger structure, or resold to D. In each case the law tries to respect the force of the original claim while confronting the problems of valuation, tracing, and insolvency that prevent the return to the status quo ante. But at no point does anyone say that the reliance interest of C is so powerful that A's original claim must be wholly unvindicated.

The remedial situation with implicit transfers and welfare rights (including those discussed in earlier chapters) is doubtless a thousandfold more complex, but it exhibits the same basic analytical pattern. The proper response to complexity is to be sensitive in selecting and sequencing remedies; it is not to abandon the enterprise of undoing past

---

impact of the entire system of segregation. The reference in *Brown* to the "inherently unequal" nature of segregated public schools could have been a prelude to a sustained denunciation of the abuses of excessive state power. Against these wrongs the reliance interest isn't worth anything at all.

28. For a discussion of the point, see Douglas G. Baird and Thomas H. Jackson, "Possession and Ownership, an Examination of the Scope of Article 9," 35 *Stan. L. Rev.* 175 (1983).

29. See, e.g., Gaius, *Institutes* II §§73–80, discussing cases in which there is a merger of the property of A with the property or labor of B. For lucid discussion, see J. K. B. M. Nicholas, *An Introduction to Roman Law*, 133–140 (1962), noting that the modern law has not reached any consensus on the question either.

error. Where the reliance interest is powerful and pervasive, it must be repected, so caution, but not total inaction, is the order of the day. Where the reliance interest is weak, there is a strict constitutional duty to chip away more forcefully at the present structure.

As ever, there are better and worse ways to approach the situation. Suppose we entertained a proposal which abolished welfare payments while keeping the minimum wage in place. We would then deprive individuals of welfare payments at the same time they are blocked from gainful employment. It should not be done. Similarly, many persons have made substantial forced contributions to Social Security that have already been spent on transfer payments to others. To abolish Social Security *in medias res* is worse than foolish; it is evil. Too many individual accounts would have to be balanced. Too many individuals have forgone the opportunity to accumulate private savings in reliance upon the programs that are now in place. There is no way to refund the moneys paid into the program, with or without interest; nor can retired people save in a week enough money to make up thirty or more years of consumption. No frontal attack upon the system could ever disentangle the present financial nightmare.

The hard question is whether anything can be done, given the power of the reliance interest. One possibility is to try to prevent the expansion of the program upon its existing levels, but that is more easily said than done. Normal adjustments in benefit levels must take into account changes in the cost of living or changes in the market basket of services provided. The general prohibition against expansion therefore runs into a substantial difficulty on the definitional level. In addition the (faint) reliance claim that future benefit increases were part of the original program cannot be wholly dismissed, given that present patterns of investment and consumption are influenced by the prospects of future payments. Given the massive nature of the program, episodic of judicial intervention may well create more difficulties than it is worth.

If this modest form of intervention lies at the edge of possible judicial responses, more dramatic forms of constitutional intervention are, at this late date, highly implausible. One possibility might be to reduce benefit levels or to raise the minimum age for Social Security payments. But the intrinsic arbitrariness in setting the new limits makes intervention unwise, again because occupational choices before retirement are heavily influenced by the package of benefits available after retirement. Discretion is again the better part of valor. A court might try to take an intermediate position which, while not reducing benefit levels, would make it permissible to restore benefits to their previous levels once they have been cut. But that temptation should be avoided, because judicial intervention will lessen the possibility of any reduction in benefit levels, either through explicit program changes or through the effects of inflation. In the end, the problem admits only of a political solution, which may be saying that it admits of no solution at all.

The same observations can be made of medicare and virtually every other welfare program that has worked itself into the fabric of American life. The current patterns are so deeply rooted that they cannot be undone by constitutional means, even if there is some faint chance of containing them. The rhetoric of the living Constitution now has a somber twist, with the mistakes of the past determining the law of the present. *Error communis facit legem:* the error of the community hath the force of law.

But not quite, for in many places the reliance interest is not nearly so powerful. The basic tax rate structure is surely a fine place to begin the overhaul. In the 1950s the highest marginal tax bracket was over 90 percent. In the Kennedy years the level was reduced to 70 percent. The more recent reforms have lowered that to 50 percent, although inflation has brought many more people into this top range. Politics apart, no reliance interest prevents a responsible court from demanding that Congress not increase the levels of progressivity in future years. Indeed, only the persistence of transfer payments makes it difficult to strike down a progressive tax. With the frequent changes in brackets, there is surely no powerful reliance interest in the current tax structure as it relates to the tax rates for future income, even that arising out of past transactions. It is quite possible to invalidate the whole pattern of special exactions, like the windfall profits tax, that have luxuriated in the absence of any judicial supervision.

Nor is there any reason to stop with taxation. Direct regulation is surely not frozen in place to the point of no return. Is there any reliance interest that prevents the immediate invalidation of the minimum wage? To be sure, some would gain and others would lose, but those gains and losses are generally benevolent, and the overall effect would be clearly positive. Certainly, no one has ever said that the claims of private property are so powerful that a minimum wage cannot be introduced or increased even when it drives certain firms out of business. It seems very odd, then, to argue that the reliance interest now blocks changes in the opposite direction, especially since the current system is unconstitutional to boot. I am not arguing that all transactions done under the old rule should be undone once the new ones are instituted. I am only insisting upon the future ban, requiring prospective, not retro-active, invalidation.

Moreover, no constitutional ratchet allows us to introduce unsound programs but not to end them. If the new abolition undoes legal rights, so did the original statutes. Why then stop with the minimum wage? The National Labor Relations Act could be struck down. Future union-ization would have to take place within the framework of market rules, without the benefit of mandatory collective bargaining. The reliance in-terest need not be ignored, as current collective agreements could be al-lowed to run their course and some provision made (as is always needed when unions are decertified under current law) to protect contributions to pension plans and the like. Price controls on oil and gas? No reason (if present contracts were respected) why they could not be lifted tomorrow by judicial decision. Indeed, the disruption would be far less than it is with gradual decontrol, which creates perverse incentives for deferred development of energy sources.

Zoning? Here there could be no total abolition because some zoning properly passes constitutional muster. But should zoning be total im-mune from revision? Again, distinctions have to be made in order to re-spect the reliance interest. With developed land, excessive zoning is hard to change, for it has doubtless displaced the complex private covenants that might otherwise have regulated land use. The restriction on the state power to zone is a return not to the status quo ante but to a world with systematic underregulation of present land uses. As a first approxi-mation, the simplest solution is to let all existing zoning restrictions stand, without trying to find complex formulas to cut it down at the edges. But even this is too generous to the status quo. The strength of the reliance interest, for example, is negligible where zoning restrictions are sought over land that was previously uncontrolled or that was subject to common ownership. Nor does the reliance interest have any force when more restrictive zoning is suggested for lands that are already subject to zoning regulation. Again the institutional rollback can continue apace, with deregulation—the movement back to private ownership and pri-vate contract—taking place at both the constitutional and political levels.

Can we ever reach the ultimate citadel of welfare programs? I have al-ready argued that at most there is a principled case to hold the line with Social Security payments. Can any more be said about a road that lies so dimly in the future? Happily the problem may not be so acute. The other reforms I have outlined above will surely influence the political process and the economic structure. Production will rise; taxes will, in general, fall; the tradeoff between welfare and productive labor will shift in a favorable direction so that even if benefit levels remain the same, fewer people will demand them. That result in turn will reduce the taxes needed to fund them, which implies greater levels of productivity. If one has the courage to follow a course of action to its conclusion, then the process can be expedited to provide overall gains so large that they will swamp any distributional losses.

The question then arises whether there is a political will to carry out these reforms, either by the courts or the legislature. The short answer is that there is not. And there may never be. The long answer is perhaps more instructive. One reason why the will is wanting is because the dominant intellectual trend has been heavily against the positions taken here. Private property is thought to be a conclusory label; ad hoc considerations are thought to dominate the analysis of takings problems. Political deals are thought to be the essence of democracy. Undermining the conventional respectability of intellectual skepticism may in the long run help to rehabilitate the political will, even if it does not revive the constitutional doctrine. Although the vast network of social and economic programs cannot be wholly dismantled, the present structure of constitutional law does admit a high degree of play at the joints. A correct theory at the very least can lead to incremental changes in the proper direction, even though it cannot transform the world. When the stakes are high, any shift in course has important consequences.

CONCLUSION

Philosophical Implications

A Summing Up

The explication of the eminent domain clause in the previous nineteen chapters has covered cases that range from outright acquisition of land to the manifold modes of regulation and taxation so characteristic of the modern state. My central concern in this concluding chapter is not with the legal status of the takings clause, but with the larger questions of normative political theory: what are the intrinsic merits of the eminent domain provision when it is stripped of its present constitutional authority? If we were now in a position to organize a government from scratch, would its constitution include an eminent domain clause as interpreted here? My thesis is that the eminent domain approach, as applied both to personal liberty and private property, offers a principled account of both the functions of the state and the limitations upon its powers.

Representative government begins with the premise that the state's rights against its citizens are no greater than the sum of the rights of the individuals whom it benefits in any given transaction. The state qua state has no independent set of entitlements, any more than a corporation has rights qua corporation against any of its shareholders.[1] All questions of public right are complex amalgams of questions of individual entitlements, so the principles of property, contract, and tort law can

---

1. It is precisely on this view that limited liability has been often attacked as an anomaly. Within the framework of a liberty-based analysis, there is no particular difficulty with the position of contract claimants, for the agreement

be used to explain the proper extent of government power. These rules determine the proper relationships among private individuals, which are preserved when the state intervenes as an agent on one side of the transaction. These entitlement principles obey very simple rules of summation and hence apply with undiminished vigor to large-number situations involving modifications of liability rules, regulation, and taxation. A system of private rights provides an exhaustive and internally consistent normative baseline of entitlements against which all the complex schemes of governance can be tested. As there are no gaps in rights when ownership is first established, no gaps emerge when private ownership is transformed by state intervention, whatever its form.

The state, however, cannot simply arise (even conceptually) out of a series of voluntary transactions from an original distribution of rights. Free riders, holdouts, and radical uncertainty thwart any omnibus agreement before its inception. The question then arises, what minimum of additional power that must be added for the state to become more than a voluntary protective association and to acquire the exclusive use of force within its territory? The eminent domain analysis provides the answer: the only additional power needed is the state's right to force exchanges of property rights that leave individuals with rights more valuable than those they have been deprived of. The specter of the unlimited Hobbesian sovereign is averted by two critical limitations upon the nature of the exchanges that the state can force. First, the eminent domain logic allows forced exchanges only for the public use, which excludes naked transfers from one person to another. Second, it requires compensation, so everyone receives something of greater value in exchange for the *rights* surrendered.

In the final analysis the two conditions blend into one, because the power to coerce is limited to cases in which positive-sum games may go

---

to reach only corporate assets in satisfaction of a claim is no more problematic than a nonrecourse mortgage which limits the mortgagee's rights of collection only to the subject property. Tort claims are a very different matter. Here the legitimation of the corporate form is best understood as a set of complex forced exchanges. As a quid pro quo for limited liability, a corporation can be properly compelled to have liability insurance to meet its anticipated risks. And more generally, without limited liability no one could venture into any pooled investment, given the general rules of agency that hold all investors responsible for the actions of their employees. Limited liability thus channels suits for and against responsible parties, reducing transaction costs. Given its general nature and the positive welfare effects, it is very easy to conclude that limited liability meets the standards for implicit in-kind compensation.

forward with a pro rata division of the surplus they generate. It is always easy to construct examples whereby some individuals with distinctive personal tastes will be worse off in fact, because they will lose the power to rape, kill, pillage, and plunder. Yet the baseline for forced exchanges is individual entitlements to personal autonomy, not individual preferences regardless of their content. Aggrieved parties cannot complain if they lose under the state something they were not entitled to against other individuals as a matter of right. No requirement of unanimous consent prevents the move to a system of governance.[2] The single pervert cannot block the state. Once organized, the state has the power to govern because within its own territory it has the monopoly of force sufficient to protect all persons against aggression in all its forms. Finally, by a system of unbiased judges (long recognized as part of the tradition of natural justice) the state insures that all disputes can be resolved. The gains of final adjudication are the substantial gains of social order, while the errors tend to be randomly distributed, so all persons share pro rata in the surplus created.[3]

This eminent domain framework does not depend upon a hidden assumption that before the formation of a government all individuals, real or hypothetical, reside in a "state of nature." Quite the contrary, political theory is quite unintelligible if it assumes that prior to the establishment of a government, individuals have no common language, no conception of right and wrong, no common culture or tradition, and no means of socialization outside the state. The question of the state is narrower than is sometimes supposed. The state is not the source of individual rights or of social community. It presupposes that these exist and are

2. The insistence upon subjective preferences is developed in Frank I. Michelman, "Ethics, Economics and the Law of Property," in *Ethics, Economics, and the Law* 3 (J. Roland Pennock and John W. Chapman eds.) (NOMOS Monograph No. 24, 1982), but is forcefully criticized by Harold Demsetz, "Professor Michelman's Unnecessary and Futile Search for the Philosopher's Touchstone," id. at 41.

3. In principle one could argue that judges do not need absolute immunity, but that they should be liable when they act beyond their jurisdiction or with malice. Yet the dangers of that are great, because any disappointed litigant could seize on some exception. For this reason absolute immunity has remained inviolate even under statutes, such as Section 1983 of the Civil Rights Act, which on their face seem to subject judges to suit for decisions that wrongly award the property of A to B. See Pierson v. Ray, 386 U.S. 547 (1967). For my views on the relationship between official immunity to private suit and other forms of control of judicial abuse, see Richard A. Epstein, "Private-Law Models for Official Immunity," 1978 *Law and Contemp. Probs.* 53.

worth protecting, and that individuals reciprocally benefit from their interactions with one another. A unique sovereign emerges solely in response to the demands to preserve order. The state becomes a moral imperative precisely because there is something of value that is worth protecting from the unbridled use of force by those who foresake tradition, family, and friends. A set of forced exchanges from existing rights does not create the original rights so exchanged; like the constitutional vision of private property, forced exchanges presuppose them. A forced exchange does not create culture and sense of community, it protects them by removing the need for compelling or allowing everyone to act as a policeman in his own cause. The state arises because the rates of error and abuse in pure self-help regimes become intolerable. The strength of a natural law theory is in its insistence that individual rights (and their correlative obligations) exist independent of agreement and prior to the formation of the state.

Rival Theories

To get some sense of the power of the eminent domain approach, it is instructive to compare this view with two rival theories that have been very influential in recent times, theories with which it has both important similarities and important differences. These theories are the one associated with the work of Robert Nozick in *Anarchy, State, and Utopia* and that of John Rawls in *A Theory of Justice*. After reviewing them, I shall consider whether the theory of eminent domain is consistent with a vision of civic virtue in public life or is nullified by past acts that violate the theory itself.

NOZICK

Nozick's theory incorporates the first part of the eminent domain approach in its respect for the principles of individual rights. Nozick relies heavily upon "historical" principles of justice to account for the institution of private property and the inequalities in wealth it engenders. At one time those principles were widely accepted in both common and constitutional discourse.[4] Nozick's rules of acquisition have close affinity to the first-possession rules of property. His principles of rectification cover the terrain of the law of tort, and those of transfer cover the law of contract.[5] One great attraction of his normative theory is its power-

---

4. See Coppage v. Kansas, 236 U.S. 1 (1915).
5. See Robert Nozick, *Anarchy, State, and Utopia* ch. 7 (1974).

ful congruence with basic social institutions and human practices which provides a convenient data base on which to examine its implications. Another strong point is that by striking a responsive chord, the theory requires no great cost to be legitimated, because people do not need to be persuaded to abandon their customary moral views, as they would to embrace a highly abstract theory (like Rawls's) that cuts against the grain and commits them to outcomes they cannot understand by procedures they sorely distrust.

But there are difficulties with Nozick's theory. The first concerns its origin and the status of individual rights. Nozick follows closely in the Lockean and common law tradition, for his historical theory of justice begins with the proposition that ownership is acquired by taking posession of an unowned thing. Nonetheless, the proposition that possession is the root of title is not a necessary truth.[6] The linkage between possession and title can be denied without self-contradiction. Arguably, all things in an initial position are subject to some form of collective ownership. Some nondeductive procedure must be available to let us choose between competing visions of the correct original position. Nozick's view depends upon an intuitive appreciation of the need for autonomy and self-determination. In one sense his position looks like a bare assertion: private property and personal liberty are important because they are important or because they are inherent in human nature. Such efforts at self-justification are always uneasy, but they are not for that reason wrong. One way to look at Nozick's simple theory is to ask what the world would look like if the popular conception of autonomy was abandoned. On what grounds could one categorically condemn murder, rape, mayhem, theft, and pillage? Our instincts of revulsion are so powerful that one is loathe to adopt a theory of individual rights that rests solely upon the shifting sands of utilitarian calculation. Slavery by conquest is regarded as a categorical evil.[7] Do we want even to consider the

6. For a deeper exploration of the theme, see Richard A. Epstein, "Possession as the Root of Title," 13 *Ga. L. Rev.* 1221 (1979).

7. The question of slavery by contract is far more difficult, but two points do stand out. First, the illustrations of it in practice are so infrequent that one can doubt whether it ever comes about except by force or fraud. Even indentured servant contracts were of limited duration and imposed special duties upon the master. Second, and less often noticed, slaves also bargain away the rights of their offspring and thus are in breach of their natural obligations. Third, slavery has a corrosive effect on individual participation in public governance. None of these points is decisive, and each has counterexamples, but their combined weight supports the view that everyone is better off, ex ante, if slavery is banned altogether, as the theory of forced exchanges and implicit in-kind compensation allows.

argument that slavery is justified if the agency costs of control and supervision are small in comparison with the resource gains from subjecting an incompetent slave to the will of a competent master? Or is the incompetence of one person only an argument for guardianship by another? Is it really an open question whether the parent-child relationship is one of guardianship or ownership? Simple faith may not serve as the ideal foundation of an ethical theory, but it may be much better than the next best alternative.

Nozick writes in an antiutilitarian vein that places his historical theory in sharp opposition to a consequentialist one. Yet in one sense the intuitive base for much libertarian doctrine might be strengthened by a direct appeal to considerations of utility. Utilitarianism does not purport to rest upon mere assertion or past practice but seeks to show how these rules can be harmonized in the service of an end that is itself justified. If everyone is better off in World One than they are in World Two, who would want to interpose an argument about rights that, if respected, consigned everyone to the inferior world? A utilitarian argument is always filled with gigantic pitfalls because it makes all small decisions turn upon some vast social construct. Still, we shall not be too quick to attack a theory for mistakes in its application, especially if these can be corrected without abandoning the major premise.

Indeed, a sensible utilitarian theory does provide powerful support for Nozick's substantive commitment to individual liberty and private property. The simplicity of Nozick's system is surely commendable, for it cuts down the number of negative-sum games by setting boundary lines that other persons cannot cross without the owner's consent. The theory also tends to foster many separate sources of power, whether in personal talents or external things. It thereby tends to create competitive structures and to prevent the concentration of wealth and power in a few hands. Thus the first-possession rule itself makes it highly unlikely that any one person will reduce all things to ownership, especially when others enjoy the same privilege of original acquisition. Unifying the possession, use, and disposition of a determinate thing in the hands of individuals makes it far easier to organize subsequent transactions to correct original errors of allocation. Similarly, leaving things with their initial possessor creates a system of ownership that does not begin with state entanglements and that removes the dead-weight costs of shifting property from its present possessor to it rightful owner under the new system.[8] A

8. Donald Wittman, "Liability for Harm or Restitution for Benefit?" 13 *J. Legal Stud.* 57 (1984).

utilitarian theory, especially of the indirect sort, thus looks quite consistent with the simple rules of thumb to which common practice conforms and to which libertarians gave great respect.[9]

Utilitarian theory is often criticized because it is said to ignore differences between persons and to make rights turn on consequences, not origins. But quite the opposite is true. A good utilitarian should be driven to respect differences among persons, if only to avoid the common pool problems that the principle of autonomy is able in large measure to overcome. Similarly, future happiness depends upon a system of stable and well-defined rights. These can be had only if entitlements are made to turn upon individual past actions which, once their consequences are understood, can offer the signposts for intelligent planning. The contrast between ontological and consequentialist theories in ethics is much overdrawn.

The defense of liberty and property can be made in either libertarian or utilitarian terms, yet it does not follow that distributional issues are ignored. Even before the advent of the welfare state, many social institutions developed to share and pool risk. Certainly the family has this function, and the same role can be ascribed to the large clans of primitive society. Friendly societies and fraternal organizations have had a similar role, and voluntary support for charitable activities has worked to preserve the social fabric against all sorts of external shocks. There is a certain amount of luck as to who is born smart and who is not, who has a congenital defect and who has great talent. No libertarian could consistently oppose voluntary aid to the poor and needy, or the complex private arrangements used to secure it. This obligation can be recognized as an "imperfect" one that is not simply a matter of ordinary consumption, even if the dangers of state coercion in principle make transfer payments an improper function of the state.[10]

The original position taken first by Locke and adopted by Nozick has enormous appeal. Everyone does own himself, and no one owns any external things, and there are natural status obligations of support within the family. Nonetheless, Nozick's libertarian theory fails in its central mission because it cannot justify the existence of the state. Its chief weakness is that it views all entitlements as absolute, so all forced exchanges are ruled out of bounds, regardless of their terms. Yet without forced exchanges, social order cannot be achieved, given the holdout

---

9. See John Gray, "Indirect Utility and Fundmental Rights," 1 Soc. Phil. and Pol. 73 (1984).
10. See Chapter 19.

and free-rider problems. Nozick presents a wonderful discussion of the invisible-hand mechanisms that lead to the creation of multiple collective protection associations.[11] But no invisible-hand mechanism explains the emergence of an exclusive sovereign within any given territory. The need for forced exchanges makes this last leap from many associations to a single state, and the eminent domain argument supplies this step. Individual entitlements are respected always as claims for compensation and frequently, but not uniformly, as absolutes.

There are still limits on what the eminent domain theory can do. It cannot explain *which* protective association should become the exclusive one; for example, the place of honor might be awarded to the association with the most members. (Even here the specification of the territory can be decisive in choosing between rival claims.) The critical point is that any association which assumes power is hemmed in by a nondiscrimination provision: it owes the same obligations toward outsiders that it owes to its own members. Exploitation is made more difficult, if not precluded, when those who are bound without their consent must on average be left better off in their entitlement than before. The libertarian theory augmented by a willingness to tolerate some forced exchanges is vastly richer than a libertarian theory that wholly shuns them.

RAWLS

The theory of governance implicit in the eminent domain clause also has strong elements of similarity to, and distinction from, the contractarian theory of justice most prominently associated with John Rawls. Rawls has two central principles: liberty and the difference principle.[12] According to the first, the proper purpose of social organization is to expand the liberties of all individuals to act, without interfering with others' liberties. By the second principle, any adjustment in the position of the original liberties must work to the advantage of the most disadvantaged in society. These substantive principles are justified by an appeal to the idea of reflective equilibrium, which itself depends upon a set of procedures to determine the proper substantive rules. Rawls's recurrent question is, what practices would all members in society adopt if they made their fundamental choices about the social structure behind a veil of ignorance? So located, their only knowledge is of human nature in general and of the laws of physical and social interaction, such as that most individuals are risk averse and are motivated by an uneasy mix of

11. Nozick, supra note 5, at 12–25.
12. John Rawls, *A Theory of Justice* (1971).

self-interest, family affections, and a sense of obligation. They are systematically denied knowledge of their own personal preferences and social niche.

Rawls's contractarian theory permits a richness of discussion that cannot be generated by simple libertarian premises, but it is open to powerful and familiar criticisms of a different sort, which I need not recount at length. First, it is quite impossible to understand Rawls's use of contract as it relates to abstractions.[13] Contract within the private law is an effort to vindicate the unique tastes of discrete persons who are far more concerned with their particular places and preferences than with the general social good. The Hobbesian cry, "The value of all things contracted for, is measured by the Appetite of the Contractors; and therefore the just value, is that which they be contented to give,"[14] is as succinct a statement and justification of freedom of contract as one can hope to give. Voluntary exchanges presuppose that in general every person has reliable information as to what he values and how much he values it or, at least, that he has better information about those things than those who would limit his choices. Trades are a positive-sum game because each person attaches greater value to what he receives than to what he surrenders. To argue for contracts by disinterested, indeed disembodied, persons is simply to strain a metaphor beyond its breaking point. By removing all traces of psychological struggle and individual self-interest, the theory departs radically from any plausible view of the private agreements based upon personal knowledge that lie at its analogical root. The metaphor of contract is best dropped altogether from Rawls's conception, because a single composite individual could do everything that is required of a contracting group. Indeed it is only the residual allure of the contract idea of consensus that drives Rawls to consider the preferences of hypothetical groups. By the terms of his theory, the choice of the single mean (or median?) person should suffice as well.

A second line of criticism is that Rawls's method of inquiry suffers from radical, indeed fatal, uncertainty. What results does the procedure generate, and how do these tie in with any common intuitions of individual rights and duties that are supposed to be generated? Rawls admitted that he could not be certain whether his view of the system tolerated the private ownership of productive property,[15] a startling indeterminacy in itself and a troublesome admission for anyone commit-

13. See Ronald Dworkin, "The Original Position," 40 *U. Chi. L. Rev* 500 (1973).
14. Thomas Hobbes, *Leviathan*, ch. 15 (1651).
15. Rawls, supra note 12, at 270–274.

ted either to human freedom or to the power of normative discourse. Will the most ordinary of transactions—getting married to the spouse of one's own choice, having children, buying a home—be permissible under his theory? Nozick rightly points out that the theory offers no clear and powerful linkages between the micro level and the macro level.[16]

By degrees, the difference principle becomes the spider's web that traps the individual. Every individual's action will influence the utility others derive from their own holdings, whatever they may be. The irony should become apparent. The original objection to utilitarian thought was that it failed to respect the differences between persons. Yet that same objection can be leveled against Rawls's position, as the philosophical doctrine of internal relations is thus pressed into service to make the independence of human action, and with it individual liberty, a logical impossibility. If those left worse off are viewed as being harmed, then every human action contains a built-in justification for government intervention, even under the restrictive Millian principle that governments may intervene only to prevent harm to others. The libertarian position on rights does not suffer from this embarrassment. It contains a strong threshold condition—against the taking of private property, against the use of force or fraud—which must be crossed before one can regard the loss in welfare sustained by others as an actionable wrong. The proposition that all decisions must be collective because every action creates external harm can be rejected on principled grounds.[17]

The eminent domain approach to the question of political obligation meets these two central objections to Rawls's theory. The eminent domain theory does not have to deal with the entitlements of lifeless abstractions. Instead of relying upon a set of complex procedures to generate the needed substantive rights, it starts with a substantive account of individual rights, beginning with first possession and covering every aspect of the use and disposition of property.[18] The radical uncertainty of Rawlsian procedures is thereby averted.

The eminent domain approach also eliminates the need to resort to hypothetical persons with incomplete personal knowledge. All persons are treated as their own masters, who are entitled to the full benefits of

16. Nozick, supra note 5, at 204–213.

17. For development, see Richard A. Epstein, "Intentional Harms," 4 *J. Legal Stud.* 391, 421–422 (1975), which deals with the question of *damnum absque iniuria*—harm without legal injury—which was the common law technique of restricting compensable harms so that all purposive human conduct does not become actionable.

18. See Chapters 7 and 8.

their natural talents and abilities. When a person takes possession of that which was previously unowned, he does not do so both as an agent for himself *and* as trustee for all other persons with claims upon him. He does so only for himself. In contrast, the Rawlsian approach regards the distribution of original talents (and hence the gains derived from their application) as morally arbitrary, the product of luck, and thus worthy of no protection. The opposition to Locke's view that each person owns his own labor cannot be more vivid.

Rawls's position has none of the operational simplicity of Locke's, but instead gives each person a lien upon the product of every other person, so that the personal destinies of all persons, present and future, are forever intertwined. His position forces upon every individual obligations that run contrary to biological instincts of egoism, whereby some special genetic linkage, such as parent to child, helps explain why one person takes into account another's gain or loss. The strong opposition between obligations within the family and within society at large is largely suppressed in Rawls's picture of human obligation. It is as if every person enjoyed the fruits of his own labor by leave of some central authority, so taxation becomes no longer a charge on individual wealth for supplying public goods but an efficient means for the state to reclaim the product of human talents that it already owns as trustee for the public at large. This conception strikes at the very heart of personal self-definition and individual self-expression. It presupposes the kind of detachment from, and impartiality toward, self that no human being emerging from his evolutionary past of remorseless self-interest can hope to achieve.[19] Each person becomes so enmeshed in the affairs of others that even heroic efforts will never get them out. The theory is advanced in the cause of freedom, but the totalitarian abuse that it risks should be evident, for what happens if the wrong people gain control of the central machinery of social control?

The problems are also economic. The Rawlsian view is that personal talents are arbitrarily distributed in nature. That observation is used to justify social efforts to correct for the original imbalance, thereby expanding the occasions for social intervention. At common law the class

---

19. See, generally, Jack Hirschleifer, "Economics from a Biological Viewpoint," 20 *J. Law & Econ.* 1 (1977). For my views, see Richard A. Epstein, "A Taste for Privacy? Evolution and the Emergence of a Naturalistic Ethic," 9 *J. Legal Stud.* 665 (1980). "One central contribution of sociobiology to economics lies in demonstrating that tastes themselves are governed by discernible principles, and that self-interest, far from being merely an economic premise, is in the guise of inclusive fitness a biological conclusion." Id. at 679.

of individual wrongs only reaches harms inflicted by one person against another. Acts of God and of the injured person himself are outside the domain of legal rectification, either by courts or by legislatures. But once the distribution of native talents becomes a matter of social concern, then coercion is necessary to neutralize natural differences attributable to the luck of the draw. In principle, social intervention will now be routinely justified to correct for acts of God, that is, for all harms caused by natural events, running the gamut from birth defects to injury by lightning, and even some forms of self-inflicted harm, at least if not deliberately caused. On either view, the scope of legitimate government actions is expanded enormously, without any clear indication of their form or content. It is quite impossible to say that rectification of acts of God requires the return to some status quo ante, because there is no benchmark to return to. Before the levels of overall compensation are set, there must be some assurance that the resources are there to allow the transfers to take place, for it is no longer enough to say that where the defendant wrongdoer is insolvent the matter comes to an end. There need not be any wrongdoer in the sense that the private law uses that term; all assets are held in social solution, even if in possession of those who claim to be their natural owners.

This collectivization of risk in turn leads to the very types of managerial problems that well-functioning markets seek to avoid. If an individual does not own himself, then there is a classic agency-cost question, because he must bear all the costs of his own labor while retaining only some portion of the gain. When everyone perceives the conflict between production and yield, the problems become additive. If individual misfortune is socialized, then some common pool must be formed to determine what fraction of each risk each person must bear. This pooling is designed to remove arbitrary individual differences that are distasteful to risk-averse parties. But the diversification of this risk comes at a very high cost. Transactional freedom is reduced because no one has clear title to anything that he wishes to purchase or sell, so property rights remain ill defined over time. The system downplays the natural, if imperfect, form of risk pooling provided by family and religious units.

The system also tends to cut against the formation of voluntary insurance markets. In the effort to control the problems of adverse selection (that is, only a small number of self-selected people being part of the insurance pool) the system increases the risks of moral hazard—the tendency of individuals to take steps to reduce their share of the total burden while keeping their full share of the benefits. The lesson derived from the development of natural resources is that pooling should be undertaken only when that solution is dictated by the nature of the resource. Where individual property rights can be well defined, pooling should be avoided—hence the difference between land and oil. The Rawlsian instinct runs the opposite way. Every thing is thrown into a common pool, even though the natural limits of the human body make it an ideal candidate for individual ownership, which the classical liberal theories provide.

The dangers of totalitarian excess become greater because of the built-in justifications for extensive social control. The creation of collective enterprises where none existed before does not eliminate self-interest; it only finds new and destructive avenues of expression. Individuals blessed with natural talents will seek to conceal them to escape the taxation or external controls that are the concrete expressions of the social lien. Their conduct offers an ironclad justification for other persons to monitor their "personal" affairs, which can never be wholly personal because they always involve the use and deployment of collective goods, to wit, unearned individual talents. The Rawlsian system is designed to yield fairer distributions, but if it takes people as they are, then the price is paid in the enormous shrinkage of the pie, which goes along with the implicit truncation of any sense of individual responsibility and self-worth, the indispensable glue of any social order. Why opt for a system of cross-ownership of persons? The Lockean creed of individual ownership of individual labor is a far simpler and more profound starting point. When meshed with a system of forced exchanges, it gives a far more consistent and well-ordered vision of both government and society.

All of this is not to say that the eminent domain approach does not incorporate elements of Rawlsian theory. Determining implicit in-kind compensation often turns on whether parties lie behind a veil of ignorance. With Rawls the veil is a construct, but under the eminent domain clause it is a simple fact of life, and the doubts about hypothetical constructs disappear. Concrete individuals are free to seek their own self-interest with whatever vigor they possess. But there are certain general rules (as with tort liability), which in the future are as apt to help as to hurt them, in the same proportions that they help or hurt others in society. Acting out of self-interest, the individual will maximize the wealth of the whole because that is the best way to maximize his own slice of the pie.

Second, the difference principle bears a close kinship to the disproportionate impact test, sometimes called the equal protection dimension of the eminent domain clause. Within Rawls's system the difference principle is a way of judging the soundness of institutional arrangements by improving the position of the worst off in society. Yet the difference principle works far better when it is moored to a system of Lockean entitlements, where it sorts out permissible from impermissible forced exchanges. The object of the rule is to move everyone to a more valuable set of fixed rights. Where the increase in wealth is accompanied by a radical shift in shares, compensation is required to ensure that all participate evenly in the social gains, so that wealth orderings are left unaffected by collective action. In contrast, Rawls's difference principle tends to compress the distribution of wealth and other benefits, compromising the position of the well-off for the benefit of the less fortunate. The redistributive element in the difference principle is plain. Yet one can invoke (as Rawls indeed does) ideas of insurance and risk aversion to suggest that, ex ante, all will accept that arrangement because when everyone is behind the veil of ignorance the gains of extreme success are smaller than the losses of great privation. But the benefits of the bedrock foundation of personal autonomy and private property remain secure, as it is far easier to work transformations with an existing baseline than without one. Risk aversion still remains relevant because it requires a downward evaluation of compensation packages that contain contingent benefits and a more favorable attitude to government actions that substitute fixed payouts for uncertain ones. Nonetheless, risk aversion is still only one element in the package, not the package itself.

CIVIC VIRTUE

A final critique of the eminent domain theory comes from a very different quarter. It is often said that a theory that stresses the importance of private property and the fragility of government institutions ignores the role of civic virtue—devotion to public service, protection of the weak, advancement of the arts, participation in public life—which is central to understanding the highest aspirations of political life.[20] To be sure, there is something wrong with a view of the world that treats the renunciation of force and fraud as the noblest of human endeavors. Music, art, literature, science, and humanitarian endeavors speak eloquently against such a view. But civic virtue in public affairs is akin to happiness in private affairs. To make it the direct end of human conduct is to guarantee that it will not be obtained. Discreet indirection becomes the order of

20. See, e.g., Frank I. Michelman, "Politics and Values or What's Really Wrong with Rationality Review?" 13 *Creighton L. Rev.* 487 (1979). Frank I. Michelman, "Property as a Constitutional Right," 38 *Washington & Lee Law Rev.* 1097 (1981); Carol Rose, "*Mahon* Reconstructed: Or Why the Takings Issue Is Still a Muddle" 57 *So. Cal. L. Rev.* 561 (1984).

the day. As personal happiness is the by-product of a rich and productive life, so civic virtue is the by-product of sound institutional arrangements. The eminent domain approach works toward civic virtue, not by trumpeting its evident goodness, but by creating a sound institutional environment where it can flourish.

Consider the point that virtue and poverty do not go well together. Persons who are pressed to the edge of subsistence cannot render aid to others. Hunger breeds fear; fear breeds aggression; aggression, conflict; and conflict, civil disorder and decay. Civic virtue, then, depends upon sufficient personal liberty, security, and wealth to keep most people far from the thin edge. What set of institutions will tend to guarantee these political conditions? The first is the facilitation of voluntary transactions, which are generally positive-sum games, because people deal only with their own property. The second is control of legislatures, which have a propensity for negative-sum games because they allow people to deal in the property of others. To speak of the protection of markets is not to speak of unlicensed liberty to act as one pleases. At the very least, the ordinary law of contract rules out all forms of force, duress, misrepresentation, and sharp practice. Contract law forbids many things, and its commands are not easy to comply with, judging from the frequency of their violation. Nor is it necessary to license every voluntary transaction: the antitrust laws find their most powerful voice in preventing voluntary transactions with negative social yields, such as monopoly. Similarly, to speak of the dangers of legislation is not to condemn all legislative practices, for there are public goods that private markets cannot provide, such as police, highways, and regulation of common pool resources.

Civic virtue will be under constant siege if factions have free rein in the public arena. Those who possess civic virtue must constantly fend off initiatives, such as endless farm subsidies or import protection, that should be ruled out of bounds at the start. When the virtuous people fail, they are bound to feel cynical: why shouldn't I get mine too? Degenerative noncooperative games emerge in which everyone is a net loser. It is a subdued version of the war of all against all, transformed into a more genteel, but still destructive, game in a different arena. In such a world everyone can plausibly claim that he should get his because everyone else has, or will, get his too. How can civic virtue survive persistent temptation? The bad will drive out the good in a Gresham's law of political life.

The only way to foster virtue is to reduce the opportunities for illicit gains from legislative intrigue. Civic virtue can emerge in private charitable behavior. It can emerge in responsible participation in the provision of public goods—deciding how much should be spent on defense, highways, and courts or when war should be declared or peace negotiated—matters which cannot, by any stretch of the imagination, be regulated by the eminent domain clause. Civic virtue does not prosper in a world in which courts refuse to protect either personal autonomy or property rights. The eminent domain clause thus improves the soil from which civic virtue can grow. It controls abuse by demanding that losers in the legislative process retain rights that leave them as well off as they were before.

PAST INJUSTICES

Thus far the theory has talked about the principle of eminent domain against rival conceptions of political order. But it may be said that the theory is incomplete because it does not account for prior injustices in the distribution of rights. These prior errors undermine all present entitlements, even if sound normative theory protects private property while allowing forced exchanges. Much of the current stores of wealth were acquired by improper means, and these imperfections necessarily infect the system as it now stands. To insist that the game now be played straight (which assumes, rightly, that we know how to play it straight) is to entrench for all time the present imperfections. Since the preconditions of the normative theory are not met, the theory must be rejected no matter what strength it has on the blank slate, the state of nature.

This argument stands in opposition to the parallel problem considered in Chapter 19 on welfare rights, where the question was whether the power of embedded expectations was so great that one could not undo, especially by constitutional means, the social legislation of the New Deal and beyond, no matter how infirm its constitutional foundations. Nonetheless, there is a curious reversal, as the present argument places the claims of original justice above those of subsequent reliance on the current order. Yet the question has no conclusive answer.

One way to approach the argument, is to consider its principled analogy within the framework of the private law: the problem of *ius tertii*.[21] In the simplest case A owns property, which is then taken by B. C then takes the property from B. The question is whether the infirmity in B's title is sufficient to defeat his action to recover possession of the thing from C. The common law answer is no. Note what happens if the rule is otherwise. If B cannot recover from C, there is no way to prevent C tak-

21. See, e.g., F. Pollock and R. Wright, *Possession in the Common Law* 91–93 (1888); The Winkfield [1902] p. 42.

ing the thing from B in the first place. Yet C secures no title hence he cannot prevent D from taking the thing from him. Denying B's action has the unhappy consequence that once the possession of property deviates from the proper chain of title, it must forever remain beyond the pale of private ownership. The common pool problem that the law tries to avoid is now created with a vengeance. The consequences for economic development and social peace are easy to envision, given that it is impossible to make productive use of an ever-increasing fraction of resources.

The doctrine of *relative title,* then, is the common law response to the problem. B by his wrong has title superior to all the world save A and those persons who claim through A. Let C, a stranger, take B's property, and B may recover it or its proceeds. Yet both of these actions may be trumped by A, either by a suit against B or a direct action against the party in possession. Nor does the story end here. B may die and leave his cause of action to D. C may die and leave his property to E. To the extent of assets descended, D has a cause of action against E, as the relative title extends across persons and across generations.

Still, A or his successors cannot always have the right of action. With property titles as with contract claims, some statute of limitations is needed to wipe ancient titles off the books. As the classical article on adverse possession notes,[22] barring old valid claims is the price worth paying to protect valid titles against ceaseless attack. The social gains from forcing quick resolution of disputes are so enormous that everyone is better off with the limitation than without it. The abrogation of property rights by these statutes is fully and easily justified by the theories of implicit in-kind compensation already discussed.[23] The private law can specify the consequences of wrongful conduct, chiefly by drawing a radical distinction between the claims of the original owner and those of the rest of the world: flawed possession counts for naught against the owner but is dispositive against the world. Once the flawed title is cleared by a statute of limitations, the normal process of mutually beneficial transac-

---

22. Henry Ballantine, "Title by Adverse Possession," 32 *Harv. L. Rev.* 135 (1918). "The statute [of limitations in adverse possession cases] has not for its object to reward the diligent trespasser for his wrong nor yet to penalize the negligent and dormant owner for sleeping upon his rights; the great purpose is automatically to quiet all titles which are openly and consistently asserted, to provide proof of meritorious titles, and correct errors in conveyancing." In other words, good titles can be protected against false claims of prior ownership only if bad claims are so protected as well.

23. See Chapter 14.

tions can improve everyone's lot, notwithstanding the initial deviation from the ideal position.

As befits the subject, this theory can be carried into the public domain. Statutes of limitation may cut off (by our principle of summation) all claims for compensation demanded by one group for the property that was taken from another group. The fact that property was taken from the Indians, for example, affords no principled reason why the property should be redistributed from the present owners to the non-Indian poor. But the question is usually not so simple, for it must be asked whether each individual claimant is in the position of A, the original owner, or of C, the stranger to the title. The factual question may often prove intractable, as some of the claimants will be descendants of original owners, and others will be strangers, and still others a bit of both. Sorting out the claims introduces both administrative and error costs that come quickly to dominate the analysis. The doctrines of adverse possession and *ius tertii* depend upon being able to trace benefits and burdens across generations. There have been, in fact, so many false steps between the original error and the current position that it is quite impossible to go back and do things right, just as it is impossible to undo a system of Social Security after it has been in effect for fifty years. Any such efforts could well generate more errors than they eliminate. Can everyone claim to be the victim and not the perpetrator of improper government action? Efforts to sort out individual claims are wholly unpersuasive. Categorical efforts, those to assist blacks because of slavery and Indians because of dispossession, are likewise met with very powerful obstacles. Should other claimants be admitted to the list, given the vast amount of unjust regulation that falls short of total confiscation? Is it worth reducing total wealth, including that held by innocent parties, in an effort to run a compensation scheme that is sure to go awry if it is ever implemented?

Consider the practical obstacles to trying the large claims on their merits. It is not easy to figure out where the injured parties would have been if they had not been harmed in the first place. Is life in America for the descendants of slaves worse than life in Africa? Would migration have taken place on other and better terms? Would the Indian tribes subdued by the United States have been slaughtered by rivals, as happened in many tribal wars? If a cause of action can be established, what is the remedy? Is it possible to restore the property taken when it cannot be identified and when it has been improved by good-faith purchasers who reasonably believed that their claims were incontestable? Do we limit recoveries to damages? From whom and in what amount? Should some setoff be given for payments under government welfare programs, which were perhaps designed to offset these past injustices? How much have blacks, disadvantaged by slavery, received by block grants or welfare payments or private charitable actions? What about the efforts of the federal government on behalf of, or against, Indians? No one could ever get the information to answer these questions if they were litigated under the set of applicable private law rules, aggregated over all individuals.

Not only is the baseline of rights insecure, but the source of the compensation is likewise problematic. One can say that the burdens of compensation all fall on the state, but this only conceals the persistent problem that the state must tax (and hence take) from individuals who have no direct responsibility for past wrongs. Many Americans reached this country after the abolition of slavery, in the great migrations from Eastern Europe between 1880 and 1920, for example. Many who were here earlier fought and gave their lives to abolish slavery. The costs of undoing the past are greater than the cost of trying to reshape the future. It may be possible to take limited steps at feasible cost to rectify the greatest abuse. Doing this would be more easily justified in a country that has been plagued with recent caste discrimination or apartheid than in our own. My own judgment is that any effort to use massive social transfers to right past wrongs will create far more tensions than it is worth, so treating all errors as a giant wash is the best of a bad lot. In contrast to my stand on welfare rights, I would give zero weight to the reliance claims of those who want to maintain a system of caste or segregation. But it is best to recognize the limits of any principle of rectification and to set about building from the base we have instead of trying to reconstruct its foundations anew.

We have thus come a complete circle. It is possible, both as a matter of constitutional law and political theory, to articulate common conceptions of right and wrong to resolve disputes that individuals have with each other and with the state. These principles do not rest upon any single value but seek to merge the three dominant strands of thought—libertarian, utilitarian, and even redistributive—into a coherent theory of individual rights and political obligations. The difficulties that remain are factual, given the complexity of our history and the legal institutions we have organized. As constructed, this argument about the eminent domain clause provides a decisive linkage between private property and public law. The received judicial wisdom about the linkage recognizes all the important parts of the picture but combines them in ways that are indefensible to anyone who is seriously concerned with either private property or limited government. The extensive discussion of the decided cases is designed to show how to reconstruct the link between individual rights and political institutions in order to demonstrate the intellectual and cultural unity of private and public law.

Index of Cases

General Index

Index of Cases

General Index

adverse possession, 347–348
agency costs, 205n21
air rights, 64
Ames, James Barr, 241–242
amortization statutes, 193–194
annuities, 312–314
antitrust laws, 202–203
arbitral/entrepreneurial distinction, 197
assumption of risk, 151–158; notice and, 153–157
automobile no-fault systems, 252
autonomy, 333, 335

benefits and losses, 36–37, 52–53
bias, judicial, 196n2, 333n33
bilateral monopoly, 164–165, 229–231, 236
billboards, 139–140, 266–267
black lung disease programs, 257–259
Blackstone, William: on just compensation, 52n55; on property, 22–23
bonus values, 184–185
Brilmayer, Lea, 313n15

Carolene Products, footnote, 4, 215n37
causation: competition and, 311; directness and foresight, 241; nui-

sance, 115–121; wetlands, 121–123. *See also* proximate cause
charitable obligations, 319–322, 345–346
civic virtue, 334–336
class conflict, 251–252
Coase, Ronald, 116–117
collective bargaining, 280–281, 328
commerce clause, 218n6
common carrier, 168–169
common employment, 246–247
common pools, 202–203, 216–228; bankruptcy and insolvency acts, 224–228; DES, 260–262; oil and gas, 219–223; public waters, 223–224; zoning, 265
comparative negligence, 241
compensation, explicit, 182–194; amortization statutes, 193–194; bonus values, 184–185; cost, 182–186; dispensing with, 195–199; interim takings, 191–192; investment-backed expectations, 185–186; landmark preservation, 185–186, 189–190; market value, 182–186
compensation, implicit, 195–215; administrative costs and, 196; common pools, 202–203; judicial bias and, 196n2; Michelman on,